D0871283

Darius Milhaud

Darius Milhaud. Portrait by Imogene Cunningham.

Darius Milhaud

Paul Collaer

Translated and edited by

Jane Hohfeld Galante

With a definitive catalogue of works
compiled from the composer's own notebooks by
Madeleine Milhaud
and revised by
Jane Hohfeld Galante

Box 6800, San Francisco, CA 94101-6800

First published 1988 by
San Francisco Press, Inc.
Box 6800, San Francisco, CA 94101-6800, USA
and in the United Kingdom and British Commonwealth (except Canada) by
The Macmillan Press Ltd
London and Basingstoke
Companies and representatives throughout the world

Printed in the USA

ISBN 0-911302-62-X (San Francisco Press)
ISBN 0 333 485440 (Macmillan Press)

Library of Congress Catalogue Card No. 84-050720

Table of Contents

Translator's Note

In 1947 Milhaud's lifetime friend and advocate Paul Collaer published the first comprehensive book on the composer. It was neither a biography, strictly speaking, nor a technical musical analysis, but rather a sensitive appreciation of the personality and music of a man who, through letters, conversations, and shared experiences, had revealed himself to Collaer more than to almost any other friend of his mature years. Twenty-five years later, after Milhaud's death, the author once again took up his pen in order to finish the story. It was his intent to add comments regarding the compositions of those later years and to give an overview of certain characteristic patterns in Milhaud's musical intent and accomplishment.

The book must be read and enjoyed in this context. Because it was written in two parts, separated by many years, I found some redundancies and out-of-context interpolations of material which I have rearranged and in some cases eliminated. However, my intent has been to remain true to the letter as well as the spirit of the original, always keeping in mind the admonition, "Qui ne récrée pas, assasine."

As for the catalogue of compositions included in this edition, it has been edited in such a way as to make it serve the needs of performing musicians as well as music historians. Information supplied by the composer's widow has been rechecked, augmented, and amended where necessary so that this is doubtless the most complete and accurate list of Milhaud's works published to date.

Collaer never visited the United States and so was unable to sense fully the impact of Milhaud's presence in this country, particularly in that corner of California where he took up residence. I have therefore added a Preface concerning his American years. Every student, friend, or casual acquaintance who knew him during that period could add a string of personal reminiscences to my account, for Milhaud related to people in a very specially directed way. Perhaps some day the story will be told more fully. For readers who seek a more detailed analysis of the music, I would suggest perusal of the Bibliography. The 443 opus numbers have invited the attention of a considerable number of Ph.D. candidates and other scholars and will doubtless continue to do so; for, as Claude Rostand has remarked, "Darius Milhaud's stature becomes increasingly impressive as his music becomes better and better known."

*   *   *

Darius Milhaud was born at Aix-en-Provence on 4 September 1892. He entered the Paris Conservatory in 1909, but his studies were interrupted by the outbreak of the first world war. Wishing to serve his country but unable to join the military for reasons of health, he became secretary to the writer Paul Claudel, who had been appointed French minister to Brazil. When he returned from Rio de Janeiro to Paris in the autumn of 1918, he quickly became a leading member of the musical avant-garde and soon gained world renown. The fall of France during the second world war forced him to settle in the United States, where he became associated with Mills College in Oakland, California. After 1947 he spent alternate years in California and France, where he was appointed professor of composition at the Paris Conservatory. During the summertime he taught at the Aspen Festival in Colorado. The crippling effects of his precarious health never diminished his energies as a composer, and he continued to add to his prolific list of works up to the time of his death on 22 June 1974 in Geneva.

Jane H. Galante

vii

Preface to the English-language Edition

It is an interesting attribute of collective human mentality that, no matter how much we are shaken and bewildered by history in the making, once events have become part of the past, we tend to view them as inevitable. No one can forget the terrors of the years 1939–1945, but we have come to take for granted the influence that the artists and intellectuals fleeing European upheaval had on America. Rarely do we stop and ask: What if there had been no war and persecution? What if, for example, Darius Milhaud had not sought refuge in the United States? Now that over a third of a century has elapsed, it is timely to pose this question, in two parts: what special meaning did Milhaud's presence have for America? and what did the thirty or so years he spent here contribute to this unalterably French composer?

A perusal of Paul Collaer's admirable study partially answers the second of these questions. As Collaer has shown, Milhaud had been fully shaped as both man and musician long before he came to these shores. That being so, one wonders why it was that he continued to make California his home long past the time when he could have returned to France. The reason must stem from the very same qualities of mind and spirit that had formed him at an early age and that guided his inner destiny throughout a lifetime.

Loyalty was doubtless one sentiment that bound him to the country that had welcomed him so open-heartedly, for Milhaud was a man of selective but strong loyalties. His parents, his wife and child, a very few friends, his religion, his native country, the town where he was born, and the whole region of Provence—these were profound lifetime attachments and, along with his music, the only real essentials in his life. For all his love of people and of artistic stimulation, his joy at being with friends and colleagues, and his enthusiasm for the musical productivity of the great cities of Europe, above all Paris, it was to the quiet natural surroundings of Aix that he had retired almost every summer before the war to do his most felicitous creative work.

Aix as a heritage and a remembered haven never ceded its importance in Milhaud's affections, but when he returned there in 1947 after his years of forced exile, it had become a sad and alien place. As in so many other parts of the Continent, war had taken a heavy toll. Perhaps it was only then that he realized how much the little cottage on a California hillside had come to mean to him. Here were the same plants, the same bird songs, and the calm and detachment that he had found at Aix in earlier years. Here also was the opportunity to associate with kind and discreet colleagues, to be surrounded by youth, and to benefit from the stimulus of a lively city only a few miles away.

In numerous letters, interviews, and magazine articles, Milhaud referred to his enjoyment of the Mills College campus in Oakland, California. "I am very happy here," he repeatedly asserted. "I work well in this calm atmosphere." Visitors from abroad called the campus a terrestrial paradise. Truly, it was a place of trees—giant eucalyptus, pines, and acacias—of quiet walkways, ponds, and flowing streams. Time would have seemed suspended had it not been for the quarter-hourly reminder of bells from the campanile. Milhaud often described the verdure of his "enchanted oasis," the wild animals that visited it fearlessly, and most of all the birds. In spite of many attractive offers to leave this small, private women's college and join other institutions of higher learning, he always resisted. "How can I," he once explained to a Mills audience, "tell these kind people who invite me that I cannot leave Mills because of the birds?"

The simplicity and regularity of his life without a doubt also contributed to his happiness at Mills. Never a politician and unimpressed by pomp and pretense, Milhaud found that it suited his human and artistic needs to live in semi-seclusion, receiving into his home those who enriched his life without complicating it. His house became not only a workplace and a refuge, but also a classroom and a salon. Mornings would be regularly devoted to teaching and afternoons to composition, but there was always time for guests. A visitor from Aix remarked with some amazement that while he was paying a call, people of all sorts came and went without ceremony. At lunchtime, or on any given afternoon around teatime, it would be perfectly normal to find a professor of history, a French gardener, and a pianist who had been featured soloist with the San Francisco Symphony the night before chatting together in the main room, which housed a startling assortment of couches, wicker chairs, tables, vases of flowers, the piano, and a general clutter of paintings, scores, books, and papers. Some visitors followed the dwindling roadway to the end of Faculty Row and climbed the steep steps to the front door of the unpretentious little white stucco duplex, with its "California Spanish" tile roof; others entered from the patio at the rear of the house through the kitchen. It was this level access that made it convenient for Milhaud, even during periods of recurring arthritis, to maneuver from house to car and then to the rest of the campus and the whole San Francisco Bay Area.

For Milhaud was very much a part of both campus and community life. He had arrived in America fully conscious of his role as spokesman for French culture, which he sought to promote wherever possible, but he had equal enthusiasm for the cultural life that he found here. The two attitudes never conflicted; on the contrary, one perspective enhanced the other.

Mills in 1940 was already a culturally sophisticated center. For some years the college had sponsored a distinguished summer session that attracted, among others, members of the Pro Arte Quartet of Belgium, who, during 1933–1935, had introduced the second, eighth, and ninth of Milhaud's string quartets to Bay Area audiences. As Visiting Professor, he was greeted by an excellent music department and a strong French department. Across the bay in San Francisco he found an active Gallic community that counted among its members the conductor Pierre Monteux, a longtime friend of Milhaud's and like him a Jew from Provence.

As Olin Downes perceptively observed, "Some European musicians are incapable of blending with the American scene. M. Milhaud meets it without the batting of an eye, on its own terms, finds stimulus in its dynamism and many challenges." Both in the United States and later when he returned to France, he spoke and wrote repeatedly of the open-mindedness of American audiences. "All forms of contemporary musical thought are appreciated," he contended. "Americans come to hear music and to enjoy it. They feel it is a privilege to attend the première performance of any musical composition. In Paris every new composition is received as an unnecessary intruder, and the musical audience eagerly anticipates tearing it to pieces."

That said, friends and students will best remember the little nucleus of Gallicism created by the Milhaud household. Equally active on campus as her husband, Madeleine Milhaud taught French classes, directed plays in French, and, when invited to lecture, spoke in the community about her role as a European wife and mother. It was largely she who contacted the succession of Frenchmen invited by Mills to give conferences or classes on campus, a distinguished array that included André Maurois, Fernand Léger, Jules Romains, Henri Troyat, Georges Duhammel, and Vercors. It was she, too, who cooked and served lunches to every French musician, as well as many writers and artists, who passed through the San Francisco Bay Area. It was not unusual for a group of students, halfway through their lesson, to be joined by Robert Casadesus, Lily Pons, or Philippe Entremont. Youth and maturity, old and new, blended together gracefully under the shelter of Milhaud hospitality. And when the Milhauds left Oakland for visits to Dallas, Boston, and St. Louis or for summer sessions at Tanglewood, Santa Barbara, and Aspen, they transported French ambiance with them.

The beauty of his surroundings, a necessary calm, and the ability to preserve a portion of France even in America were all elements that conditioned Milhaud's decision to make America one of his homes. But there were some more practical reasons, too. America was a big country, and it had adopted Milhaud as its very own French composer. The musical centers of the United States rewarded him with an outpouring of appreciation. At least seventy compositions were commissioned by American musicians and musical institutions, and over a hundred received first performances in the United States. Also, it was in America that Milhaud first turned to teaching. Even though he referred to teaching as "my hobby," that was not a way of minimizing its importance. On the contrary, a hobby is something that is done with pure joy; and it is this joy, derived from contact with youthful creativity, that is perhaps the greatest gift that his sojourn in the New World bestowed on him.

By the same token, unquestionably Milhaud's greatest influence in this country has been conveyed through his students. On the occasion of his farewell concert in 1971, invitations went out to some 420 of them! Today, many occupy leading positions in several dozen music departments and schools throughout the United States and pass on to their students the attitudes and disciplines learned from their teacher. Note well that they have not attempted to impose any particular style of composition, for Milhaud himself was totally opposed to that. When *Time* magazine interviewed him, he made the unforgettable remark: "I only demand that my students work regularly and well. I don't interfere with the form they wish to pursue, but I remind them that if they wish to build a tall house, for example, they must not forget to put in a staircase."

The second group of people who directly benefitted from Milhaud's influence were those who knew him through performances of his music. Recognition was warmly accorded to the composer, even when audiences had difficulty with the unaccustomed sounds of the compositions. One of his treasured possessions was the telegram he received after the University of Saskatchewan gave a concert honoring his seventieth birthday. It read: "With our admiration and hoping that you will continue to write for many years to come and that you will enrich our lives with many more masterpieces," and it was signed by every member of the audience, as well as by the performers. He wrote *Music for Boston, Music for Indiana, Kentuckiana,* and *Opus Americanum,* and even though it all sounded quite French, audiences felt he was writing for them. He identified with the citizens of his host country by writing a piece in memory of John F. Kennedy, and he was recognized by people in high places as having made a commitment to American musical life. President Eisenhower wrote: "It is my hope that you will continue to enrich the cultural life of our nation." The National Institute of Arts and Letters elected him an Honorary Associate; he was made a Fellow of the American Academy of Arts and Sciences and was named to the Advisory Committee on Music of the National Arts Foundation of New York. Brandeis University, the University of California at Berkeley, and Mills College bestowed honorary degrees on him. In the music building on the Mills campus there is a plaque designating the place where he taught as "A Landmark of American Music." (The site is one of two hundred selected by the National Music Council as part of a bicentennial project sponsored by Exxon to celebrate the nation's musical culture.)

The facts of Milhaud's sojourn in America are evident, yet the true meaning of his presence remains elusive. To evaluate it, one must again attempt to reconstruct the moment at which he arrived. At that time the American musical experience, in both classroom and concert hall, was essentially conservative and predominantly Germanic. Not only were ears attuned to the "classics" and to nineteenth-century harmonic vocabulary, but *Sturm und Drang* emotionalism weighed heavily on attitudes concerning the creative process. True, a generation of post–First World War Americans had brought back from their studies with Nadia Boulanger in Paris a taste for Gallic lucidity, but not much of that influence had spread to the West Coast. Moreover, the leading influences coming from contemporary Europe tended to be those of Schoenberg's dodecaphony, which was also Teutonically oriented.

Suddenly, here was Milhaud in our midst, with his Latin composure, his equilibrium both in life and in art, and his attitude of a journeyman who plies his trade. A fresh breeze blew across the musical landscape of academia. An incident that epitomizes this dichotomy will be remembered by those who participated in a Composers' Forum Workshop held on the campus of a San Francisco Bay Area university. A student composition had just been performed, and it was time for the discussion period. The poor student was barely fending off questions from a particularly vocal fellow-composer who kept asking why he had done this or that, when there was a sudden commotion in one corner of the room, and Milhaud slowly raised himself out of a deep armchair. Silence fell as the students waited to hear a pronouncement from the master. "Why not?" Milhaud said, and sat down.

Music for him was not a tortured revelation of the innermost depths of the soul. It was a significant, but natural, emanation from a creative mind. It was not intended for making pronouncements; it was a means of reflecting and illuminating human emotion—universal human emotion, not individual suffering or ecstasy. It was an art, but it was also a *métier*. For him it was an all-consuming passion, but this did not blind him to the fact that all human endeavor, excellently and honestly accomplished, has enormous worth; only the shoddy and pretentious are without value.

It was this perspective, a combination of the reasonableness of the French mind and the humility of a truly great personality, that Milhaud brought to America. Most of us, knowingly or not, were touched by it. Some were profoundly changed. All of us remember.

Jane H. Galante

San Francisco, 1988

Foreword

The year 1909, more or less, marks the beginning of an exceptionally animated period in the history of music. By breaking away from the concept of harmonic resolution, Debussy had opened up new horizons and had proved that music need not be bound by the conventions of the Romantic period. Thus liberated, composers began to explore to the limit every component of musical language. Rhythm, melody, harmony, sonority—all these elements were placed in a crucible, to be examined and tested by a generation of composers in pursuit of an intensely personal kind of artistic expression.

The early period lasted until approximately 1930, but gradually there emerged composers whose sensitivity, intelligence, profound musicianship, consistent talent, and occasionally genius gave significant direction to the experimental trends and made the period that started with Debussy and ended around 1950 one of the richest and most vital in all of music history. This was not so much a period of schools of thought, but rather one of strong, individualistic statements that ranged in harmonic vocabulary all the way from the conventionally tonal to the most radically atonal.

The first half of the twentieth century owes its luster and its renown to this diversity of personalities, to their independence and their convictions. Witness Debussy, Ravel, Koechlin, Roussel, Satie, Milhaud, Poulenc, Sauguet, Honegger, Stravinsky, Prokofiev, Schoenberg, Berg, Webern, Bartók, Kodály, Hindemith, De Falla, and Malipiero, to mention only a few of those who contributed to this tremendous movement. At first, novelty and audacity attracted the most attention, but as the ears of the listening public became increasingly attuned to innovation, the expressive gifts of each individual composer began to make more and more of an impact.

This book is devoted to the examination and illumination of the works of one of the most important composers of the twentieth century. A first version, written in 1939, was published in 1947 by Nederlandsche Boekhandel in Antwerp for the Belgian Musicological Society. It included an analysis of Milhaud's compositions numbered opus 1 through 191—that is, those dating from 1910 through 1938. The Second World War cut off all contact between Milhaud, who had sought refuge in the United States, and his friends and relatives in Europe, so it was only at the end of that period that a study of his compositions could be resumed. The present volume thus includes the analysis of his works numbered opus 192 through opus 443—that is, up to 1974, the year of his death.

Milhaud belonged to that race of composers, which includes especially those of the eighteenth century like Bach, Mozart, and Haydn, for whom the daily discipline of composition was a habit and a necessity. Such composers have produced an enormous output, not all of which is qualitatively on the same plane. Much is masterful, some is routine, but all is endowed with an enormous craft and fecundity that is beyond mere facility.

It is the intent of this study, therefore, to offer a kind of guided tour through the composer's works, stopping before the masterpieces that have the greatest significance and pointing out their most salient characteristics. This book does not pretend to be a detailed biography; for all the requisite information along those lines, the reader need only turn to Milhaud's autobiography, *Ma vie heureuse.*

Paul Collaer

Antwerp, 1980

I

Aix-en-Provence

It is true that things must exist in a state of order, and that when order ceases, confusion takes over; likewise, that all people who are orderly in their lives and habits are to be greatly praised and their example imitated; but it is also true that too strict a regimentation is unbearable, especially in unimportant matters: for both sacred and profane books teach us that it is sometimes permitted, and even necessary, to disregard the rules, for rules were made for men, and not men for rules.

Jean Rousseau, *Traité de la Viole,* 1687

On the eve of my departure for Florence to study the art of the quattrocento, a painter friend who had spent considerable time in Tuscany gave me some good advice. He had approached the city by first acquainting himself with the surrounding region. As he sojourned on the banks of the Arno, in the Apennines and in Fiesole, he absorbed the light and spirit of this countryside in which the inhabitants, the vegetation, the earth, and the sky are in such complete harmony. Then he narrowed the circle. He strolled through the streets of Florence, settled down to work there, and gradually became more and more attuned to the mentality and inner vision that had inspired Florentine architecture. Still he did not venture inside churches or museums, until he had completely assimilated the mood and grasped the significance of all the forces that had concurred in the creation of the many paintings and sculptures contained within. Only thus prepared did he approach Giotto, Uccello, and Angelico, ready to receive their message in all its sensuous opulence.

One cannot generalize: many artists have only the vaguest relationship to their surroundings. On the other hand, there are those whose inspiration emanates from the landscape of their childhood; their sensitivities have been developed through contact with familiar persons and things; they are attached by powerful ties to their environment. Thus, Veronese, Gabrieli, and Monteverdi have become spokesmen of Venice's greatest epoch. Thus, too, Purcell's songs paint a vivid portrait of the English Downs.

How pleasant is that flow'ry Plain and Grove,
What perfect scenes of Innocence and Love,
As if the Gods, when all things here below
Were curs'd, reserv'd this place, to let us know
How beautiful the world at first was made,
Ere mankind by Ambition was betray'd.

It matters little that the glory of Venice has perished, since Monteverdi and Veronese have captured for all time its most noble quality; or that the pomp of Versailles is long gone, since Lully's music remains. The artist has the power to multiply life's miracles a hundredfold by transferring them to the world of imagination.

For most of us, the greatest art is that which transcends the fluctuations and fleeting quality of life and expresses the totality of universal, essential truths. When Herodotus recounts the Retreat of the Ten Thousand across Asia Minor, especially their arduous river crossings, his description is valid for all time. We recognize scenes from the *Odyssey* in the *calanques,* the little bays and inlets of the Moorish littoral and Corsica. Aeschylus reigns over the Mediterranean world as much today as yesterday.

On the simple virginal, Byrd, Bull, Gibbons, and Farnaby were able to give voice to the whole depth and stability of English life. Ockeghem, Binchois, Machaut, and Lassus translated into music that pervasive mysticism that permeated northern Europe from the islands of Zeeland to the hills of Champagne; and the angel on the Rheims cathedral, now as always, can fully understand the concert of angels painted by Memling. Each of these artists has drunk deeply from the life-giving source in his own land and has given it back to us, in all its richness and fullness, in song, painting, and sculpture.

Milhaud belongs to this same race. Like the others, he is attached to his part of the earth with all the fibers of his heart. As the hare takes on the color of the fields and the lion that of the desert and dried grass, so the great artist is colored by the countryside that has nurtured and molded him.

*   *   *

Before we approach the music of Milhaud, before we can absorb its expressiveness and appreciate its genius and skill, we must first imagine ourselves in Provence. There we shall surely encounter the composer of *Les malheurs d'Orphée*, either in Aix, his native town, or in one of the nearby villages. Descending the road from Avignon and leaving behind the imposing peak of Ventoux and the long line of Mount Luberon, a horizon so dear to Jean Giono, we see ahead a vast unfolding landscape. It is both wild and orderly, like the landscape of Tuscany but more glowing; for, along with grapevines and almond trees, the red charred soil is overlaid with the wind-shifted gray or sil-

2

ver haze of olive orchards. Above the lesser hills, which descend in a series of gentle undulations like the backs of woolly sheep, the proud lines of Mount Sainte-Victoire rise up in one energetic thrust, a call to arms. Its presence dominates every valley, imposes itself vigorously on all its surroundings, and gives meaning to the entire countryside. Cézanne's paintings have made its shape familiar.

Around a bend in the road, all of a sudden, in a hollow, is "yellow" Aix, or rather, "russet" Aix, basking in the sunlight. The sun here is truly "the great sun of the Durance" that inspired Bizet to write his brilliant song. It seems as though its rays penetrate the very heart of the stones, baking them thoroughly, and as if the octagonal tower of Saint-Sauveur is being roasted on some enormous spit. The abrasive sunlight, more than the mistral, has eaten away the trimming on balconies and cornices. What an ode to summer the spectacle of this town is, glowing in the sun and dust, framed by yellowing vegetation and ruddy earth: what an affirmation! The crack of a whip, the ringing of hammer on anvil, and the gay tinkling of bells sound out as clearly here as anywhere else on earth.

In fantasy, we may approach Aix in other ways. Ernst Křenek has suggested this one:

Once our car leaves behind the last gigantic and yet somehow unconfining Marseilles tenements, through which we catch a final glimpse of the Mediterranean glittering in the blinding afternoon light, we climb along the rapidly rising highway that leads to Aix-en-Provence and enter as through a gate between two steep hills into the Provençal countryside. It is in a certain obvious way classic—or even heroic, as in the paintings of Poussin, whose imaginary world seems to live on here. One feels that it can't have been too long ago that the Greek colonizers arrived, bringing bag and baggage, from which their major and minor gods somehow escaped and spread throughout field and forest, making themselves at home in their new surroundings. Over there is a little yellowed sanctuary among three cypresses where a friendly satyr might well make his appearance; we shall recognize him at once, even though now he prefers to go about disguised as a telegraphist or a glazier, like the angel Heurtebise in Cocteau's *Orpheus*. This explains also why the many gaudy gasoline pumps along the highway scarcely perturb the scenery, whereas in the categoric, unequivocal, clear air of our Alps, nature is so easily ruined by the hand of man. This is a dreamland of short circuits. Everything is charged with significance, and yet it all makes sense: the enormous figure of the famous Corsican who threateningly points to the "Brandy of Napoleon" every half mile, the dusty agave plant by the side of the road, the eternally blue sky, and the dusty little Ford that scolds its way through endless flocks of sheep. Soon we enter the good town of Aix, with its deep canyon-like streets incised between wonderful, Empire-style rock walls, where occasionally a black cat creeps among the shadows. There is the inevitable "Cours"—I believe it is the Cours Mirabeau—planted with four rows of plane trees, where the life of the town takes place, where the antediluvian cars of the provincial French (still untouched by the snobbery of progress) joyfully bark like little dogs and jump to and fro between the greengrocers' shops and the café terraces, while

3

the statue of the good, legendary Roi René surveys the scene with a benevolent eye. He lived around the 12th or maybe 14th century, yet people speak of him as if he had only just gone to his reward. In essence, nothing much has changed, and in these parts the thing we call progress is still servant to man, whereas elsewhere this concept has long been forgotten. (*Anbruch* 12: 135, 1930.)

These, then, are the elements that impress the visitor and urge him to return: the incandescent earth that generates an intense, incessant everyday life of seeming changelessness and the simple overall design that controls chaos without destroying impetus and mobility.

Many other delights await the person who searches further into the byways of the city and discovers the secrets of life that emanate from them. Above all, he will be aware of contrasts. Though Aix may be a symphony composed to the glory of the sun, there is also, beneath its plane trees, the deepest possible shade. It is so dense that it seems to have substance, like a pool of cool water. One has the feeling of swimming through it rather than walking. Coming from the side streets, blinded by light, one plunges into the Cours Mirabeau as if diving into an aquarium, where forms are distinguished only as moving shadows—carefree, happy shadows. In these Elysian fields the splashing water from mossy fountains, located at every street corner, murmurs unceasingly. As shadow complements the brilliance of sunlight, so water satisfies this thirsty earth. Where can this special equilibrium, this balance of contrasting passions, be better observed?

The unity of the city is evident at first glance. There is a sisterhood of dwellings, all with beautiful doorways and delicate Louis XIV ironwork, facades of yellow stone, and pink and russet roofs; they are silent abodes, amply constructed. It is good to lean against these walls that retain, long into the night, the warmth accumulated during the day and to feel their roughness. They are almost like living creatures. At one place, framing a porte-cochère and supporting a huge, protruding balcony, two giants have installed themselves—Atlases, flexing their muscles and astonishing passers-by and even the stones with their contortions, while the lions of the Madeleine sneer at this useless effort, and the four charming dolphins of Cardinal Street regard them with amazement.

What does all that matter, since the magnificent stones, the ridiculous Atlases, and the mocking lions are the same color? Of what importance are accidental details? They cannot stop the great ball of fire from returning each day to the sky, or the shepherds from guiding their sheep along the road that leads toward the Alps, or the almond trees from flowering at their appointed season. Nothing seems to belong to the present. Objects and beings appear immutable. Everything is stamped with permanence.

Out of this changelessness is born a collaboration between man and nature. A city usually gives the impression of being a molehill in the middle of a prairie, an anthill in a garden. It makes a blot on the landscape and is a foreign element. In the Provençal countryside a town appears to be inseparable from its surroundings. Man has lived there so long that Nature no longer remembers when he arrived. She need not adjust to him. Man has penetrated the land and has received from the earth its law and wisdom. It is the wisdom of the Latin, or even more so of the Greek way of life that gives special charm to the conversation of the Sardinian shepherd or the Aixois gardener, whether he is speaking about a game of bocce ball, a rabbit hunt, or the shearing of sheep. Giono spoke truly when he said: "The *Odyssey* is always alive; it is still a reality in the countries bordering on the Mediterranean." Man and his works are not placed around the countryside like furniture in a room; they form an integral part of it.

Aix is the city of Mount Sainte-Victoire, of olive trees, of the Méjanes library, of Mistral and Cézanne. If at Montefalco in Umbria our recollections of Gozzoli's frescoes are intermingled with our impressions of sunset over Mount Subasio, if we can no longer quite distinguish between what has been painted by man and what has been accomplished by earth and sky, if the Canticle of Saint Francis seems to blaze and the sun to sing, so in Provence one cannot tell whether Giono's observations of the yearly migration of flocks to the uplands inspired his marvellous books, or whether they existed from time immemorial. No more can we separate the music of Milhaud from this setting, for it is a manifestation of this bountiful earth and an inextricable part of it.

Nothing is merely picturesque or accessory in Provence. Everything is fundamental, and the Provençal song that Aude, the curator of the Méjanes library, sings for us is as much a part of the landscape as are a typical country dwelling, an olive tree, a dusty road; or, across the Rhône, "in the kingdom," a Camargue cowboy on his white horse. Again we are caught up in that ancient, pervasive lyricism of the land; the song of Provence is by necessity either a hymn or a psalm.

Now let our gaze scan the horizon. All the notable features, diverse though they may be, are like modulated tones of one great palette composed of fire, dust, and shaggy, pungent undergrowth. In the north the crags of Les Baux, like an empty skull, raise a bleached barrier. The wine of that region has a flinty taste. Beyond, we can dimly see the Comtat, the domain of the popes; we will go there later. Today, however, we turn toward Pourrières, Trets, and Saint-Maximin, strident names, resoundingly warlike. Saint-Maximin is where we eat scarlet crayfish and, especially at Tholonet, drink mulled wine. We can imagine that this wine has come from grapes that, unprotected against the arrows of Phoebus, have been warmed while still on the trellis. A short distance away, at Sainte-Baume, in the midst of interminable valleys hung with the gray tones of heat-haze that rises from the earth into the parched air, our thoughts roam toward Les Saintes-Maries-de-la-Mer. It was here that Marie-Magdalen died, and that, at the same spot facing Mount Sainte-Victoire, the barbarians were defeated. Did all that happen yesterday morning or centuries ago? Everything seems to have taken place simultaneously. On the horizon we see the trailing smoke of a forest fire, while the wind brings us the crackling sound of burning brush. But we cannot help wondering whether it is really the forest that is burning, or whether the terrible incinerators of Marius have brought us this whiff of death and this muted, desperate outcry.

The sea is not far off. Let us look for it at Toulon. As soon as we have passed the business section with its huge buildings, we come to the town itself, where the narrow alleys, bordered by several-storied houses, block out the sunlight. There is a musty odor. All sounds echo as though in an inner courtyard. One can hear on the fifth floor what is being said on the street. Voices are edgy, rapid. The blinds clatter too loudly. These streets have something sinister about them, as do similar neighborhoods in Genoa, Marseilles, and Barcelona.

At the corner where the arsenal meets the wharf, the view changes. Here, beneath a solitary palm tree that stands mournfully under the compassionate eye of a lone street lamp, we find three sailors. They lounge on the sidewalk, smoking silently; through the darkness the gas streetlights shine blandly, outlining the ripples on the water, which is as thick and black as oil. One could be at Bahia or at Pointe-à-Pître. Let us stroll along the waterfront, now silent, along this narrow quay where the houses push forward like spectators scanning the protected harbor. What is our longitude? This could be Vera Cruz, Malaga, or Piraeus. Shadowy forms pad slowly by on espadrilles. Then suddenly we pass the open door of a bar, from which a shaft of combined light and sound streams forth as if from a projector. The bar inside glistens gold and silver. The twisted columns of the counter are reflected in the mirrors. The nickelodeon bellows and roars a heavy beat. Its bells and brasses pierce the night, while on the red couches fat, perspiring girls lounge with their tousled sailors. Illusion is the luxury of the poor. Do not confound the words *marin* and *matelot*. A *marin* is a seaman, a sailor with a purpose, and someone to be reckoned with, but a *matelot* is a person who belongs to the changing ocean, who drifts with its waves and wanders across the seven seas without aim. He veers from left to right, blown by fortune's caprice, and ends up sooner or later on the sofas of the Admiralty Bar to kill time and banish care.

Marseilles is a bigger and more cosmopolitan Toulon. It is a city of haphazard encounters and re-encounters, a perpetual marketplace, always busy. Take a look behind the city hall, where the sailors' girl friends waddle complacently, an Arab picks at his beads, and the Annamites, baring their teeth in wide grimaces, contemplate the swarm of passing men being preyed on by the girls. At the end of the street a steamer rocks back and forth; it seems the ship is swaying, but perhaps it is the street.

And, to complete our Aixois journey, beyond the Etang de Berre is the rustling ribbon of the Rhône, which winds its way from Arles to the Camargue. Arles is golden as a pancake. If Orange is the site of the most beautiful theater in the world, where the sun is used for lighting and the native vegetation for décor, Arles is the guardian of the ancient Mediterranean games. The sacrifice of bulls in the *corridas de muerte* perpetuates the cult of Minos, and even today competitions are held to place cockades on bulls whose horns have been tipped with balls to protect the contestants. Three-thousand-year-old Cretan medallions portray the same contests. Where else does this spirit of ancient times remain so alive? Here one finds a marketplace in which human beings, confined like animals, wait to be hired in gangs to mow the fields of the Camargue. Out in Les Alyscamps on Saturdays, in the golden light of the setting sun, through the aura of mist and dust that spreads out under the immense canopy of plane trees, we can witness the most noble procession of all, as the bulls, surrounded by attendants, are taken to the arena. They come from the region of swamps where sky and water are inseparable. It is a region protected from intruders by curtains of mosquitoes that rise and fall, undulating like smoke at the will of the breeze. This is wild, primitive earth, a land of sun, sea, and salt. It is harsh and tenacious, permeated by nostalgia and bitter sorrow. All its paths converge on that impregnable church, that prayerful fortress, Les Saintes-Maries-de-la-Mer, whose bells, hung in the open air, seem to ring out to summon the waves, the dunes, the slender tamarisks with their deformed, twisted branches, and the blue statice that is able to grow along with and withstand the bitterness of salicornia.

This is the terminus of our trip; here, Van Gogh's hulls are pulled up on the shore, and the empty, thrashing sea tells us that it is useless to go farther. We have reached the depths of despair: terminus and sanctuary. That typically Provençal ceremony, the *ferrade,* in which young girls brand the bulls, takes on a significance equal to that of a Mass. Mireille died here, and it is here that the gypsies gather to worship Saint Sarah, companion of Marie-Magdalen and Marie-Salomé.

On first contact with Les Saintes-Maries-de-la-Mer, we feel strangled by its harshness and underlying violence. It is too strong, too concentrated; we must escape! But we shall come back, and our second encounter will be less brutal, once we have understood and accepted the message of this place: that time is unimportant and that only man is significant, his passions, joys, and sorrows unchanging throughout the centuries and bound inseparably to the plants, animals, water, and earth that surround him. We shall learn, too, that the men who pass this way, bearers of ancient knowledge and heirs to pastoral laws that are in force from Pont-Euxin to Palestine by way of Hellas, are profoundly wise, that they are members of a true nobility.

Today the Camargue drives us away, because we feel overcome by something so immense that it defies time and space, but someday, when the harshness of this vision has dissipated somewhat and we have absorbed the meaning of the customs and the way of thinking of this region, then everything stylish, artificial, and trivial that goes under the name of progress will appear ridiculously small and insignificant. We shall have passed through a trial by fire. On our souls will be inscribed in burning letters a law that is far from mundane; we shall have been initiated into the mysteries of Provence.

Up to now our rambles through Provence have dwelt on its most serious aspects. Many other perspectives are possible; however, the one we have chosen is the essential one, if not absolutely so, at least as far as the subject at hand is concerned. It is also important to point out the clarity with which this countryside is delineated, its forceful visual impact, which is more drawn than painted. The color of Provence is not the bright iridescence conceived by northern painters; it is not a riot of strong tones blended in vivid combinations. There are evenings when the countryside displays the nuanced tones of Umbrian paintings, and even in midsummer, when everything is overflowing with vividness, the colors are those of a cameo; warm, glowing shades of brown, black, and red. These are the tones one finds in the great Ribera paintings and in the restrained palette of Cézanne. On the other hand, there is a special Provençal kind of gaiety, a charming, gracious delight that is far removed from the coarse, rough humor generally attributed to inhabitants of the southlands. For, if ancient wisdom has conferred on the people of this region a certain restraint in their expression of sorrow, it has also tempered their expression of joy, adorning it with elegant irony, but never with sarcasm.

In summary, the majority of representative Provençal artists have brought together in their works all the characteristic features just described. From this synthesis is born a timeless lyricism, a canticle equally of earth and of man that celebrates man's brotherhood with all things, plant and animal, and shows him to be intrinsically bound up with a natural world that serves him. None of it is contrived, self-consciously picturesque, or artificial in any way. Rather, these artists feel a deep inner necessity to be cast in the same mold of wisdom that has shaped the Mediterranean mind from time immemorial; shaped it and given it its deep religious conviction. Mediterranean man celebrates a communion with natural forces with all the love and fervor that characterize religious belief. Cynicism is completely foreign to him. One can also speak of a Mediterranean spirit. It consists of a lyric quality based on eternal truths and commonly shared by all the inhabitants of the littoral. This is the spirit of the *Odyssey,* of Greek tragedies, the Hebrew scriptures, the Bible, and of Horace and Virgil.

New themes? The Provençal artist need not look for them, for he knows that there is nothing new under the sun. Picasso paints bathers; Fauré sings of Prometheus and Penelope. Think of the paintings of Cézanne: not one of his works is restricted to a particular moment in time. Recall, too, the poems of Francis Jammes (Jammes is from Languedoc, but no matter, the country is the same all the way to Catalonia). Of what importance are facts and events in his poems compared with their permanent elements?

Modernism is a transitory notion that loses all validity in this classic land. Ernst Křenek, whose penetrating study of Milhaud has already been cited, also notes this quality of timelessness.

. . . For the French, the past is not a self-contained entity, strange and even inimical, as it is for us. They do not conceive of it as a confrontation between new and old, nor do they pretend historic exactitude when referring to it. They summarize to an extent and continuously carry along with them that which has gone before. No conscious distinction is made between something that is a hundred years old or a thousand. The fact that it exists makes it an asset to be preserved and to be absorbed into contemporary life exactly as if it had just been created.

To have thought this way for centuries, to have distilled from man and nature such constant values—all this has given the meridional mind an element of security that certainly plays a large part in its legendary optimism. This attitude contrasts strikingly with the unrest and pessimism of more recent civilizations. The outcome is a measured, equitable approach to contemporaneous events, which is gained only through a wise belief in civilization as a whole. The distillation of ideas that results gives little comfort to the notion of progress; yes, one should certainly avail oneself of the advantages of modern life, but worship them—emphatically no!

It cannot be repeated too often: the Mediterranean temperament is above all lyrical. In color, sound, and substance, it proclaims eternal themes. It is also tragic, for it measures the world in terms of humanity. Through the ages, the transitory has been separated from the permanent, and lasting values, tough and immutable, have continued to grow. The result is that the Mediterranean mind endows every subject with beauty and grandeur and spiritually magnifies and purifies it. Of what importance are man's trivial errors compared with the things that

9

are permanent in him and that continually link him to the long chain of tradition? This ancient blue sea has long joined together everything that dwells on its shores and has given men and objects a certain homogeneity. All the steep little harbors, whether on the rocky coasts of Provence, Asia Minor, or the Adriatic, resemble one another, and everywhere one finds the same kind of boats beached in the same sandy inlets. Everywhere, too, be it in Corsica, Greece, or the Moorish countries, the ground is covered by the same growth of cystus, myrtles, and mastic trees, dominated by the pines of Aleppo and locusts. Residents of Marseilles, Athens, Jaffa, and Barcelona are all initiates in a single society based on lyricism and ancient wisdom; and if the *sabir,* that special dialect spoken in the Mediterranean region, unifies all who make their living on the sea's periphery, so, too, it joins those who subsist from the earth, since the shepherds who yearly move their flocks from the Camargue to the Alps are members of a clan in which it is impossible to separate out the Catalan, Sardinian, Corsican, and Languedoc elements.

This close relationship, which has tied together all the Mediterranean people since time immemorial, makes it easy to understand why the Jewish communities of Provence are much more integrated into the total population than is the case in northern countries. The Jews, merchants in Marseilles since the time of the Phoenicians, have met with a less severe fate here than in the rest of Europe. In the delightful preface that Armand Lunel wrote for his *Esther de Carpentras,* entitled "Purim in the literature of the Comtat," we learn about the relationship that existed between Jewish and Catholic populations of the four holy cities of the Comtat: Avignon, Carpentras, Cavaillon, and l'Isle-sur-Sorgue. After the French Revolution the Jews of the Comtat spread throughout Provence; they always felt at home in a region that not only offered them full rights of citizenship and a congenial Mediterranean atmosphere, but where they were given freedom to share the attitudes and customs of their Christian neighbors. As a result, there is no racial discrimination, and the difference in religion, the distinction between Old and New Testaments, neither provokes a violent confrontation nor raises an insurmountable barrier. In the refined Aegean world, religion on its highest level consists purely of spirit. This spirituality, which is the common bond between Jews and Christians of the Midi, underlies the respect between a Jewish composer like Milhaud and Catholic poets like Paul Claudel and Francis Jammes, and has made their collaboration possible.

*   *   *

By now we have become familiar with most of the general characteristics that support the total expressiveness of Milhaud's music. Since so many of his works spring from that distant, ancient heritage he shares with all his Provençal countrymen, let us, to complete the sketch, re-emphasize a few points. Of primary importance is the pervasive lyrical quality of the Mediterranean temperament and its characteristic way, transcending time and space, of dwelling only on the durable aspects of human sensibility. The artistry that results is an amalgamation of the individual revelations of poets, musicians, and painters who have lived in this region. Their collective soul projects out into the world and illuminates it in its own special way.

In pure lyricism, everything proceeds outward from deep inner sources. The world thus becomes a mirror for the soul of the creator. Such an approach may lead to a very subjective kind of romanticism, but in a person from the Midi, sensitivity becomes generalized. This is especially true of a Jewish artist, to the extent that his voice rises above everything that is narrowly individual and celebrates that most profound of all human experiences, the struggle of conscience. Moreover, Jewish sensibility is so lively, mobile, and intense that the struggle that impels and channels it makes it into a glowing flame. We feel it in the lamentations of Jeremiah and in the violence and intensity of the prophets, just as we have recognized it in the imprecations of Greek tragedy.

Milhaud's lyricism is filled with this passionate quality. It exists in the *Poèmes juifs,* in *Alissa,* in the *Brebis égarée,* and in *L'Orestie* and *Christophe Colomb* as well. Not only is there passion, but also piercing sorrow—that quality of anguish which is so typically Jewish. In writing about music of Black origin, Milhaud described this emotion. "These expressive melodies," he noted, are "filled with a quality of lyricism that can only spring from the experience of an oppressed people."

II

The Man

If I could name your color, oh my tenderness,
It would be neither green nor mauve
Nor gray,
But blue
Like the morning sky,
Like the sea,
Like the notebooks of Eugénie de Guérin,
Like those shadows which linger above you,
Vast ocean,
And which, at dusk, withdraw;
You are an exhalation,
An unceasing, eternal
Evaporation.

Léo Latil, Boulouris, 12 August 1912

How to describe a man like Milhaud? Every one of his friends and acquaintances could paint a slightly different portrait. All I can do, therefore, is to sketch some of my own experiences and enthusiasms.

Let us start with the years preceding the events of 1939. It is sometime between November and May. We have bought a ticket for Paris, but even at that time we cannot be entirely sure of finding someone at home in the Boulevard Clichy apartment. Most of the time, muffled in a great cape and padded with blankets, a soft hat pulled down to his ears, leaving only a glimpse of two roguishly twinkling eyes, the composer of *Le boeuf sur le toit,* accompanied by his wife—or rather accompanying her, for she will be at the wheel—is apt to be on the road, traveling hither and yon to concerts at Rouen, Strasbourg, Brussels, or Amsterdam. He may be in London conducting a ballet at the Savoy, or in Berlin for a performance of *Christophe Colomb,* possibly in Madrid, or even in the middle of the Atlantic en route to the United States. For, strangely enough, this French composer, so little appreciated in France, has long been regarded by the rest of the musical world as one of the most representative and significant artists of our time.

But let us pretend that we have the good fortune to find Milhaud at home. Enter with me, and then let me leave you chatting with the master of the house while I, exercising the prerogative of an old friend, wander through the apartment to see what additions have been made since my last visit. It is truly a strange abode. The entrance hall is more like a baggage checkroom, in which suitcases, trunks, coats, and long, cane-handled umbrellas issue a perpetual invitation to travel.

The work table—ah, yes, the work table—well, it is a little bit all over the place. On the piano, between piles of records and the latest scores of Stravinsky, Schoenberg, Sauguet, and other friends and colleagues, all of which have been perused with the same generous eye and secret desire to admire, there is a score that has just been orchestrated. Nearby, between the two windows through which the carnival noises of the boulevard penetrate, is a little table; here, if one is indiscreet enough to dig through the pile of correspondence, one finds a rough draft of some new work in progress. Atop the pile are two delightful drawings by Jean-Victor Hugo, as well as a sketch of a man's head crowned with a cap made from an ace of diamonds that Jean Cocteau has sent to his good friend Darius. Can it be that *L'Orestie* was composed on this table in the midst of such a monumental accumulation of scribblings? Let us look further. We pass a superb Picasso and a watercolor in which Dufy has captured the spirit of the dress rehearsal for *Maximilien* at the Paris Opera, and arrive at the study. This is no American-style study: what a joke! Through a barely passable doorway we enter a room four meters square, lined with bookcases, except where the wall space is crowded with photos of friends, and stacked with more books and scores that cover almost the entire floor. What next: the dining room? Here, order reigns; not a piece of paper is to be seen. So where is the music written? The last pages of his scores give us the answer: L'Enclos. It is during the summers at Aix-en-Provence, or perhaps even while he is away traveling, that his work is done, never in Paris; for in this city, what with concerts, plays, friends, and obligations of every sort, there is hardly time to do even a little orchestration.

Throughout the apartment one is surrounded by presences. Dufy, Braque, Léger, and Picasso look down from yellow walls on the beautiful Empire furniture. They seem uncomfortable in their crowded surroundings. On tables, in cabinets attached to the wall between great blue butterflies, multicolored calabashes, and primitive watercolors, all brought from Brazil, is a mishmash: gin bottles shaped like a hand, a heart, a horse, a woman, the Eiffel tower, boxes in blue opaline—the same blue that brightens the carpets, armchairs, and even young Daniel's clothes—shell-covered boxes and music boxes with chirping canaries and nodding gypsies.

Pity the poor visitor who arrives unprepared; his head will soon be spinning. Picasso and Empire furniture—well, that is permissible; but how to reconcile all these garish souvenirs from Brazil, this bizarre collection of trivia? Quite simply, there is one amalgamating quality, that of tenderness, which permeates Milhaud's entire existence. His tenderness extends to the craftsman who views an opaline box as a work of great value, and to all the unsophisticated people who, in their primitive ways, seek to bring beauty into their lives. The musician stoops to caress all humble things and the possessors of these things. Fashion, social usage, and the transitory formality of daily existence are unimportant, for beneath all these externals, life goes on, filled with joys and sorrows, most poignantly expressed by simple, humble folk whose sentiment is unpretentious and unadorned.

Now my tour of the apartment is finished, and I return to find you still chatting with Milhaud. Your encounter with him will have depended a lot on who you are. If you are a young musician or a writer, your conversation will have interested him, and he will have responded attentively. If you submitted a sample of even your most tentative attempts at composition, he will have extracted from your manuscript the few notes or phrases that show signs of talent. From then on he will be unstinting in his help and interest; he will certainly counsel you to study a great deal of counterpoint and most probably to work with his much admired colleague Charles Koechlin. Then, when you have managed to write a really respectable piece of music, his efforts on your behalf will be prodigal; he will promote your music whenever he is asked to submit his own. Neither suspicion nor envy will ever come between you, for he is kindness and loyalty personified. Like Satie, he follows the maxim, "Acknowledge the young."

However, if he senses that music is not a driving force and a profound necessity in your life, he will sink deeper into his armchair with an air of great fatigue; his gaze will become fixed, his eyes expressionless, and his whole physiognomy will sag downward into a double chin; to those who know him, this posture signifies a deep discontent that only politeness keeps him from voicing.

At other times you might see him emerge from the shadows near the stage where he has been sitting during an orchestra rehearsal, his hands in his pockets and his head tilted to one side, to suggest, most diplomatically, a few changes in the conductor's interpretation. Milhaud as a composer is always simple and direct. Likewise, in all his human relationships, he is open and uncalculating. In dealing with other musicians, his skill and subtlety are exceptional, even in the most difficult situations. Only a sparkle in his eye indicates when, by some ingenious verbal maneuver, he has managed to get the best of an embarrassing situation or has succeeded in turning a bittersweet encounter into a charming one.

These are only a few glimpses of Milhaud's personality. Ask other friends to elaborate, and they will add ten meters of film to these few snapshots. One sequence might be of Darius laughing until the tears come over a funny story or a comic adventure. He reacts intensely and unstintingly, for nothing is ever partial in the makeup of this man who, both in receiving impressions and in reacting to them, is as spontaneous and wholehearted as a child.

Now let us go to Aix. Only there, in the heart of the summer, can we fully appreciate the true depth and breadth of this remarkable temperament. L'Enclos is situated outside the town on the Route des Alpes. Dappled by the sunlight filtering through the leaves, the big square yellow house lies almost hidden in the shade of the plane trees that surround it. Two or three fountains murmur the same repetitious stories into their mossy beards. I have always suspected that Léon, the gardener, understands and participates in their conversations while he bends over his artichokes. Léon is a sage. He comes from the burned, bleached region of Pourrières. He is full of stories of hunting escapades, and there, among the dead leaves of the plane trees that strew the pathways and accent them with bright yellow splotches, he teaches me the secrets of *la pétanque*. I cannot conceive of L'Enclos without Léon, master of ceremonies at the perpetual spectacle of changing light and shade, beneficent deity who provides us with the perfume of ripe cantaloupes and the bright gloss of zucchinis, and who never fails, even on the hottest days, to surround the big pond with a whole symphony of floral color.

Then there is old Rose; she must have been there since the beginning of time. Like the fountains and like Léon, she repeats her stories over and over again, all the time rinsing out the laundry in the big tubs under the grape arbor. Her nephew was mixed up in some sort of political scuffle. He had lost an arm during the war and had had it replaced with an iron one. "Well, he really gave it to them . . . maybe a little too hard . . . but just think what a bad time he's had! After all, he didn't use a firearm; it was just the arm the government gave him!" That's the French sense of justice for you. She might as well be Thémis, sword in one hand, scales in the other.

But neither Rose nor Léon nor even the fountains disturb the man who writes music in his "study," an earthen-floored enclosure surrounded by four huge plane trees. There, near the soil, the flowers, the murmuring waters, and the violent contrast of sun and shade, the scenes of *Christophe Colomb* take shape. There, under the eyes of Thémis-arm-of-the-government, originates the inspiration for the scene of the tribunal that absolves Orestes. Summer passes with its vitality and its tranquility, but the composer remains at his rickety table as motionless as the yellow stone statues that look down on him as he works. Nearby, in the graciously intimate salon, with its venerable drapes all decorated with roses and figurines, nestles the piano around

15

which we shall gather in the evening to read through the pages of music completed that very day. At the entrance sits the delightful mother of the family with her needlework, from time to time glancing over the rims of her glasses to survey her little universe contentedly and silently—silently, that is, until the arrival of her good husband, at which moment, from behind a pile of music paper, trumpets forth the greeting "Bonsoir, Gabriel."

After he has finished a quartet or one act of an opera, Milhaud may take time to show us some of his favorite haunts. In one place he has discovered a rose-colored house, framed by the arch of an aqueduct and blending with the yellow of a freshly harvested field. It is silhouetted against a pale blue sky, and to the right of it we perceive the dark, energetic thrust of a cypress tree. From the village of Eguilles he points out the softly undulating valleys filled with the silvery, flickering leaves of olive trees. In another place a vast landscape stretches before us, a wild, vibrant panorama, yet somehow contained: lyrical outpouring on the one hand, order and clarity on the other. This is the very balance so intrinsic to the music and spirit of Milhaud. For him there must always be harmony between nature and man. He responds to landscapes that bear the mark of human endeavor; high alpine summits, devoid of humanity, have no charm for him, but he can be moved by a field of wheat. He loves the sheep and cattle herdsmen and the gypsies, not for their picturesque or exotic characteristics, but for their warmth and spontaneity. Wherever he finds natural, intense, unselfconscious manifestations of humanity, Milhaud feels at home. For him the Mediterranean stretches from Jerusalem to Rio de Janeiro, for everywhere he feels the same vibrant quality of human life. It is this great wellspring of love and faith that inspires his musical message to the world. How well we can understand his sympathy for the young Aixois poet Léo Latil, killed in 1915, who wrote: "My sorrow is universal."

This sense of obligation to transmit through music the song and sorrow of all humanity is a far cry from romanticism, for the romantic artist turns inward and relies on his own small store of sentiments as the source for his creative expression. It is even further removed from Henri de Régnier's shallow definition of composition as "the pleasant novelty of a useless occupation," a definition that completely divorces man from creativity.

Imagination and the ability to universalize are the qualities of mind that characterize the extrovert in contrast to the introvert. Intuitively, such people are able to add details to every experience and make it more meaningful. A passage in Milhaud's published *Etudes* illustrates this turn of mind: "I remember a spring evening in Naples when my friend Francis P. and I had hired a strange vehicle driven by half a coachman (a man with only one eye, one arm, and one leg who never-

A decisive encounter: Darius hears two musicians. Cartoon by Géa Augsburg, reproduced in 1947 edition of present volume.

With his parents at L'Enclos, their home in the outskirts of Aix-en-Provence.

A horseback ride in Brazil, with Paul Claudel and Henri Hoppenot.

Les Six with Jean Cocteau. Standing, left to right, Francis Poulenc, Germaine Tailleferre, Georges Auric, Louis Durey; seated, Arthur Honegger, Cocteau, Milhaud.

In Boulevard de Clichy apartment in Paris. Background: sketches for *Les malheurs
d'Orphèe* by Jean-Victor Hugo.

The Milhauds' first Mills College summer session, 1941. Milhaud, last row, fourth from right; on step below is Daniel Milhaud; Madeleine Milhaud is seated in front of him, next to Fernand Léger; center of front row, André Maurois.

Sixtieth birthday party at Mills College, 1952; left to right, standing, Leland Smith, Jerry Rosen, Nathan Rubin, a woman student, Dave Brubeck, Donald Weeks.

With son Daniel.

With Madeleine Milhaud in tent auditorium at Aspen, Colo. (Photo by Robert Gottlieb.)

Conducting rehearsal of *Le cantate de l'enfant et de la mère* at Mills College, 1957. Madeleine Milhaud, narrator; Budapest String Quartet; Jane Galante (editor and translator of present volume), piano.

Displaying telegram from Saskatoon.

Meeting with Pope Paul VI, after the first Ecumenical Concert held in Rome (1965).

At dedication of his home in Aix-en-Provence as national landmark.

In native garb at Dallas, Tex.

Composer's worktable.

theless succeeded in bounding into the driver's seat)." Another example occurs in a letter Milhaud wrote to me from Les Saintes-Maries in 1922.

I am thinking of you because I am sure you would love this countryside. I am so attached to it that, although I came for only three days, I have stayed on for two weeks. I borrowed a horse, which provides the only possible means of transportation in the Camargue, and I leave every morning and am out until nightfall. No place, with the possible exception of the great forest region near the equator, is as compelling to me as this one, especially if one immerses oneself in the way of life, so deeply intertwined with religion, of the local "cowboy."

The observance of religious rites here is made all the more impressive by the presence of an enormous number of gypsies. All night long they chant their litanies in the underground crypt dedicated to their patron saint, Saint Sarah. Unfortunately the assemblage of pilgrims is invaded by hordes of tourists coming from Marseilles with their Citroëns and motorcycles. The Provençal festivities are charming, but a little theatrical—sort of a poor man's Buffalo Bill.

The best part comes after everybody else has left and I am alone in this little heat-bathed village between the vast Camargue and the vast Mediterranean. I ride my horse to the other side of the Little Rhône and find a wild, deserted region dotted with swamps and rimmed on the horizon by parasol-shaped pine trees, or so it seems, for often the lakes and pines turn out to be only mirages, which are especially common at this time of year.

I had a chance to hear *Renard,* which I adore, but I'll have to skip *Mavra.* [The two Stravinsky works were being presented in Paris in June 1922.] I prefer my horse and my evening visits with the local people—cattlemen and fishermen—in front of the little café above which I am staying.

Time after time we find Milhaud reacting with joy to everything human and with indifference and even hostility to what he considers narrow individualism. In art he is opposed to any intellectual system that fetters the impulses of the heart and impedes the direct flow of creative energy between nature and man. He reproaches Wagner for his "abstract musical thoughts based on a purely formal dialectic" (*Etudes,* p. 12). Likewise, Schumann bores and annoys him with his interminable personal confessions, bombastic sonorities, and amorphous ramblings. Actually, "many young musicians had become anti-Wagnerians, but it was Milhaud who raised the cry: Down with Wagner!" (Boris de Schloezer, *Révue musicale,* 1 March 1925.) A good part of the animosity that Milhaud encountered at the beginning of his career was directed more at the frankness with which he voiced his musical likes and dislikes than at his compositions. People are more apt to react to words than to deeds.

By now it should be obvious that there is no opportunism in Milhaud's attitudes. Beginning with his earliest work, one can trace a steady evolution, devoid of such startling contradictions as may be found, for example, in Stravinsky's musical output. Milhaud's ideas, based on age-old foundations of race and religion, are simple, sensible, and unsensational, and despite his attachment to tradition he always looks to the future. He has been interested since childhood in the concept of an unfolding universe; and it is this spirit of unending discovery that he seeks to express in music. He is a born composer. Many other talented persons might equally have turned into painters, writers, architects, or physicians. But one feels that Milhaud was uniquely destined to become a composer. "I don't give a hoot for success," he once wrote to me. "I'm not impressed by the ability to do acrobatic stunts in front of an audience. All I want to do is write music."

His musical preferences are, first of all, for works of art that have a human quality; and second, for those that show inventive and imaginative qualities and a certain nobility of construction far removed from textbook rules and regulations. He loves Debussy for his originality, subtlety, and perfect formal equilibrium. Of Roussel he writes: "In *Padmavâti* the sentiment is always noble, the concept profoundly human, the orchestration serious; the vocal writing is full and rich and the dances are varied and never conventional. In this work the tradition of Berlioz remains intact." (*Etudes*, p. 48.)

His admiration for Satie's nobility and integrity is limitless. In the section of his *Etudes* devoted to Satie, Milhaud extols that composer's genuine melody, simple expressiveness, and clear, luminous form. Furthermore, he says again and again that he regards himself as one channel of a great stream of French composers that flows from Couperin and Rameau through Berlioz, Bizet, and Chabrier. If Berlioz seems at first glance to be out of place in this group, consider the similarity of temperament that unites Berlioz and Milhaud, despite the differences between nineteenth- and twentieth-century musical vocabulary. There is the same fecundity, the same almost volcanic outpouring of music, and a similar need to control this prolific inspiration. Isn't Berlioz's admiration for Spontini's *La vestale* and for Gluck's operas based on many of the same premises as Milhaud's affinity for Satie? Although Berlioz is a romanticist, his innate French sense of proportion and his repugnance for bombast save him from the heavy-handedness of nineteenth-century German composers. His works may be long, but they are never tedious; and all have a marvellous lucidity.

This authentic tradition of French music contrasts with the Franck school: "Franck, the great Belgian composer who nearly ruined the health of French music." Why? Because it was of course the Schola Cantorum that opened the door to Wagnerian influence, to formalistic development, and to an artificial sort of expansiveness with which the innate French desire for conciseness finds itself ill at ease.

The rather uneven compositions of Albéric Magnard, whose untimely death prevented the realization of his full talents, played a very special role in Milhaud's early development. His enthusiasm for melody also attracted him to the torrential melodic outpourings of Lekeu, another composer who died too young to fulfill his potential. He must have appreciated the strong beat of Magnard's music, which gives it its rhythmic organization, and in Lekeu's melody he found the same spirit of "universal sadness" that flowed from Léo Latil's heart and pen. As for Charles Koechlin, it is to him that Milhaud is indebted harmonically, and his admiration for the composer of *La course de printemps* is easily explained by their shared views on sensitivity and musical vocabulary.

All these friendships and enthusiasms date from before the war of 1914. In this period Milhaud must have been deeply impressed by *Le sacre du printemps,* with its cosmic sense, both human and religious. At the same time he was strongly attracted to Cézanne's paintings, those timeless syntheses of the land and people of Provence. The restrained color and intense but controlled passion of canvasses such as the *Mont Sainte-Victoire,* the *Vue sur Gardanne,* and *Les baigneuses* must have exercised a powerful influence on his intellectual development. I can never see the father in *Le pauvre matelot* without recalling one of Cézanne's classic visages, such as the wine drinker or the pipe smoker.

At Aix there were the friends Armand Lunel, about whom more later, and Léo Latil, who introduced Milhaud to Francis Jammes. Like Claudel, Jammes greatly influenced Milhaud's esthetic orientation, to be discussed in a later chapter. Finally, we should mention André Gide, who loomed large on the composer's horizon in those years prior to 1914. This was the Gide of *La porte étroite,* the writer who described with such delicate beauty the sensual pleasure of self-sacrifice and the restlessness of a soul that seeks to attain perfect joy through suffering and renunciation. Inspired by this noble sentiment, Milhaud composed some of his most intimate pages, in which the deep recesses of his soul are revealed more than in almost any other work.

A number of important compositions were completed prior to 1914: *La brebis égarée,* the first two string quartets, the sonata for two violins and piano, *Alissa,* some settings of poems by Francis Jammes and Armand Lunel, four by Léo Latil, *La connaissance de l'est,* and the chorus of *Agamemnon.* Then came the war. Rejected for military service and wishing to contribute in some way to France's war effort, Milhaud set sail with Paul Claudel, who had just been appointed French ambassador to Brazil. What did he encounter on the other side of the Atlantic? Much that reminded him of his Mediterranean world. Bahia resembled the Sardinian town of Sassari. Here, too, was the familiar sight of little white villages, bleached with loneliness and despair, dotting the landscape. But many new sights greeted him as well: the virgin tropical forest, an infinity of banana palms, tangles of clinging vines, monkeys and parrots, fantastic glowing insects. All these impressions filtered into many works of that period, most notably *L'homme et son désir.* Moreover, the recollection of those sentiments of longing and sadness, so typical of South Americans, that seem to find expression in a great primeval dirge lamenting the loss of Eden and the impossibility of a Paradise regained, continued to pervade his consciousness for many years.

In 1919 his life in the tropics came to an end, and a much matured Milhaud returned to Paris. He had added to his list of significant compositions *Les Choéphores,* the third and fourth string quartets, the second violin sonata, the sonata for piano and winds, *Printemps,* the *Poèmes juifs,* and *L'homme et son désir.* He returned in full possession of his creative faculties, his mind filled with magnificent new visions, but with his heart still retaining that incorruptible gentleness that continued to inspire his finest musical output throughout his life. In Paris, along with others of the postwar generation, he pulled loose ends together and settled down joyfully to work. It was then that a group of composers, widely diverse in their musical outlook but all inspired by a similar faith in the rebirth of the civilized world, began to meet on Saturday evenings. A music critic who erroneously regarded this association of colleagues as the beginning of a "new school" called them the *Groupe des six.* The phrase caught on, as phrases do among people who need to put labels on everything. However, a "group" as such never existed: the tastes and temperaments of the six members were too different. Only a feeling of friendly camaraderie unified them. Looking back, now that the story of *Les Six* is past history, we can see that Jean Cocteau's booklet *Le coq et l'arlequin,* although generally full of good ideas about music, was in no way a profession of faith by these composers. Some ideas came from Satie, others from Stravinsky; those about "musique à l'emporte-pièce" (literally, "punched-out music") applied solely to Georges Auric. This philosophy cannot have interested Milhaud very much. True, his *Boeuf sur le toit* derived from it, but that was a brilliant, off-the-cuff, one-of-a-kind piece. His creative personality had been too long formed for it to have been fundamentally altered by any chance influences.

He was always attracted to Satie and loved the melodic inventiveness and gentle humanity of his music. Milhaud admired the works of Poulenc, so full of charming spontaneity and overflowing with youthful vigor. Auric's whole approach to music was entirely different from Milhaud's own; still, he appreciated *Les fâcheux* and especially *Les matelots.* He was also sympathetic to the grandeur of certain of Honegger's works, notably *Horace victorieux* and *Antigone,* in which he found a certain compelling human emotion, but the "mechanism" of

Pacific 231 left him unimpressed.

Around 1921 he began to study the works of Fauré. "Fauré needs only to open his heart and the most tender, sincere music flows forth; in none of his compositions is anything in any way contrived," he wrote. "His discreet use of musical vocabulary and restrained lyricism prevent his music from ever being outmoded, and every time one hears his compositions, one is struck by the "newness" of his thematic material, by his harmonic inventiveness, and by the incredible diversity of his modulations." Here again it was a composer's melodic gift that drew Milhaud's praise.

His taste for broad expressive lines was never satisfied by the type of thematic shorthand in which one or two emphasized notes take the place of a melody. However, this preference did not keep him from appreciating Schoenberg's *Pierrot lunaire* and *Moses and Aaron,* as well as Alban Berg's *Lulu.* It was also invariably the melodic sense and sensitivity that drew him to the works of Stravinsky such as *Mavra* and the octet for wind instruments, as well as to the rhapsodic music of Manuel de Falla, the light elegant style of Henri Sauguet, and some of Prokofiev's music. At a time when it was fashionable to downgrade nineteenth-century composers in general, he even defended the works of Mendelssohn, for he found that same quality of "controlled lyricism" in them that was the common denominator of everything he appreciated.

With Paul Hindemith, Milhaud formed a solid friendship that was enriched by the interchange of musical ideas. It is not inconceivable that some of the felicitous melody in such compositions as Hindemith's concerto for piano, brass, and harps stemmed from this association, not to mention certain details of the musical vocabulary adopted by Milhaud, notably in *Maximilien.*

Among the younger generation of composers, several interested Milhaud: Nicholas Nabokov, a composer to whom he counselled restraint, but whose ebullient musicality he nevertheless appreciated; Igor Markevich, with his powerful dynamism; Olivier Messiaen, whose importance he recognized as early as 1936; Luciano Berio and Gilbert Amy.

Picasso was his favorite painter, and Léger, Derain, Braque, Dufy, and Pruna his collaborators in works for the theater. In literature, although all sensitive expression appealed to him, his great loves, apart from Jammes and Claudel, were the Provençal authors Jean Giono and his longtime friend Armand Lunel.

How many times we discussed the "artistic wealth" of our day as we sat under the plane trees at l'Enclos! But then, at the end, we would turn to the stars, the olive trees, the sun-baked stones, the bulls of the Camargue, and finally to the sea, with its heavy, rhythmic waves, its changing tones of blue, and its memory-laden breezes that had brought Marie-Magdalen, Marie-Jacob, and Sarah to Les Saintes and had cradled the destiny of men for thousands of years. It is the same sea that sings its dirge in *Le pauvre matelot,* howls in *Christophe Colomb,* and flings its foam at the sun and fashions rainbows in *Protée.*

*   *   *

Then came the war of 1939. Milhaud left his country after the armistice of 1940. With his wife and son he established himself in the United States, where he taught at Mills College in Oakland, California. All contact with Europe was broken until the liberation of 1944. During those years of exile and separation he continued to compose, and always, in spite of loneliness and estrangement, in spite of events and circumstances, his music remained in style and meaning the music of Provence.

III

The Art

There are really neither great painters nor great poets; there are only great men. I call great that work or human being which speaks to my heart, nourishes it, and enriches me with some new insight.

André Suarès, Vers Venise

It is better to talk about Milhaud's *art* than about his *esthetics*. Esthetics is a science that ties the means to the ends, implies that there is overall consistency, and for better or worse makes an artistic output conform to this consistency. It would be easy to give an esthetic evaluation of Stravinsky's *Pulcinella,* for example, since it is constructed according to an easily perceptible plan. Likewise, Schoenberg's esthetic point of departure is clearly stated by his use of the twelve-tone technique, and his works illustrate this organizing principle. But Milhaud's art cannot be systematized. His music is devoid of both calculation and speculation. It is neither the result of minute, carefully balanced elements nor a totaling up of effects. A composition springs forth from his imagination in one urgent thrust, completely amalgamating emotion, idea, and technique. In trying to describe it, one is reminded of Jacques Rivière's remarks concerning Claudel: "To do him justice, one has to describe his entire work in one breath, conveying its richness and complexity of detail and its absolute completeness at the same time. Of course this is impossible, and since analysis is required, let us simply admit that we are taking apart what genius has created whole." (*Etudes,* p. 63.)

Each of Milhaud's works, be it a sonata, a symphony, a piece for the stage, or a collection of melodies, is an entity in itself. At the same time, his vast output, apart from a few works written tongue-in-cheek, constitutes the chapters of one great book. Each composition is the extension of all the others. A vocal line from *La brebis égarée* is significant in relation to one of the string quartets, and this same string quartet becomes a prelude to *Les malheurs d'Orphée.*

There are no contradictions in Milhaud's prolific output. Rather than turning capriciously from one direction to another, this art proceeds in a single line, flowing sometimes like a sparkling stream, but more often like a torrent of burning lava that consumes everything in its path. It is an outspoken kind of art, which makes no concessions and asks for none, the kind that one either accepts or rejects. Those who reject it do so out of fear of its probing revelations; those who accept it are subjugated by its power, seared by its passion.

This kind of art is the expression of a sure, profound philosophy of life. The music is far more than attractive sound or pleasant entertainment. It is the means of communicating an idea that is beyond being aural, visual, or literary and is the manifestation of a spiritual, even religious, belief that relates all things through the common denominator of the human spirit. Inanimate objects, plants, animals, and even individual people are all spectators at the great, eternal drama of mankind related by Milhaud's music. Not only is one of his works called *L'homme et son désir,* his entire opus could be thus titled, singing as it does of the impossibility of happiness on earth, of man's unfulfilled desire and his longing for perfection, consolation, and the ultimate resolution of life's turmoil, which can be found only in God. It is this underlying philosophy that led Milhaud from dramatic music to a more flexible form of expression inspired by the dance, then to what can be termed "pure music" and, toward the end of his life, to such professions of faith as the *Service sacré, Pacem in terris,* and the cantata *Ani Maamin.*

Obviously, in this kind of music the particular must give way to the general. Claudel, in his *Traité de la connaissance,* describes "perceptual knowledge" as one that is possessed by all animals. Only humans have "rational knowledge," which allows them to distinguish timeless values from transient ones. This knowledge, which has already been identified as characteristic of old Mediterranean cultures, is Milhaud's guiding passion, and the expression of it through music his consuming preoccupation. Music like his is as far from being narrowly objective, "l'art pour l'art," as it is from being subjective. Man is neither an end in himself nor an individual separated from humanity. No narcissism here, or egocentricity. Everything turns outward.

Milhaud is a lyric poet whose language is music. He is one of those creative geniuses from whom men learn about the depths of their own souls and the common depth of the human soul. "You do not explain, oh poet, but by you all things are explainable," says Paul Claudel in *La ville.* According to this philosophy, all entities that surround us participate in our life and become witnesses to, and actors in, the human drama. We depend on the least grain of sand, but this grain will not have the same meaning tomorrow as it had yesterday. Other people will view it; another light will strike it; it will be warmed by a different temperature. The particular circumstances that combined to create yesterday will never exactly occur again. The chair on which Pierre sits in *La brebis égarée* is not a chair in quite the same sense as the one the father uses in *Le pauvre matelot.* What does the ocean in which Proteus frolics with his seals have in common with the one that Christopher Columbus struggles to subdue? Only its eternity and its omnipresence. The farm machines may be a part of the serene landscape of Beaune, but they torment Paul's mind in *La brebis égarée* as a gadfly stings a horse.

Milhaud's art does not attach itself to special subjects or themes; it is comprehensive rather than specific. The chair can be of wood or leather; as an object, it has no special identity; it becomes significant only in relation to whatever emotional situation surrounds it. In the first, admirable scene of *La brebis égarée* the chair, the cup, and the flowers, as well as the people, become absorbed into our consciousness in a way that transcends a merely sensuous reaction to the poet's and the musician's art. Sensation serves only as the point of departure for the completely felt and understood kind of universal experience that is communicated to us.

I never cease to be astonished at the attitude of critics who see an ocean as worthy of song, but not a cup or a table. It may be argued that all material things are inferior to art, but those who hold this opinion forget a simple phenomenon: the spiritualization of matter, its transformation by the mind of the observer. They will admire the same blue cup when they see it in a painting, for they have been told a hundred times that it is the play of light on the cup that has given it substance, not the material of which it was made (if the painting is impressionist) or its volume and mass in space (if painted by a cubist). But when a poet and a musician communicate a feeling of overwhelming sadness by describing a pair of shoes, no one understands the emotion with which such objects can be impregnated.

In his *Etudes* (p. 27) Milhaud has described how he was attracted to Jammes and later to Claudel:

When I first started to compose, I sensed immediately the dangers inherent in following the path of musical impressionism. Too many perfumed breezes, bursts of fireworks, glittering baubles, mists, and languors marked the end of an era, the affectations of which revolted me. In 1908 (I was sixteen) the verses of Francis Jammes emerged from the haze of symbolist poetry and revealed to me a whole new world, far easier to grasp, for one had only to open one's eyes. Finally, it seemed, poetry had turned back toward everyday life, to the beauty of the countryside, and the charm of simple people and familiar objects. What a splash of fresh water on my face! I found myself on the threshold of a vital, healthy kind of artistic expression, ready to submit to the influence of a force that could shake the human spirit, twist it, lift it up, soothe it, and transport it like an elemental impulse, alternately violent, harsh, gentle, and poetic: the art of Paul Claudel.

I heard of Claudel for the first time from Francis Jammes, whom I visited at Orthez. He described him as a combination of saint and monster, a person who hated the smell of vanilla, dressed in a Chinese robe, and wore the hat of a consul general. On the day of my departure, Jammes took me to the station and put into my hands a copy of *La connaissance de l'est,* which I was to read on the train. It was this that triggered my collaboration with Claudel. I was immediately tempted to set to music several of his poems, each of which is a concentrated little drama, powerful and lofty in concept, sustained by a rhythmic prosody that holds the reader in a viselike grip.

Milhaud's art is expressionist, but this is not the kind of Central European expressionism exemplified by Schoenberg. That composer, when he wrote *Pierrot lunaire,* seemed to contract, like a snail withdrawing into its shell at the slightest touch of its antennae, and in that state of hypersensitivity he expressed the convulsions of his own soul. By contrast, Milhaud's expressionism is concerned with the universality of life independent of the individual, who is merely an accidental apparition on earth. There is no trace of that kind of romanticism in which man becomes an end in himself; rather, he exalts the vital force of humanity in its combat with the despair that is man's constant companion, this force that can elevate a human being to a state of grace in which he is able to praise the Creator and all His creatures. We shall see how he does it when we read through a few of his scores. In all of them we shall note certain contrasting elements which are typical: for example, the tormented torrents of notes, the rough crackle of rhythms, and the dissonances that suddenly untangle, smoothing out rhythmically and harmonically, broadening melodically, bringing a feeling of peace and clarity without changing the musical material, as though this were the most natural conclusion in the world and one predestined by all the turbulence that has gone before. This process is easily observed in the second movement of his second violin and piano sonata and at the end of his second string quartet.

Then there is another constant: in no theatrical work do we find any psychological development. From the first notes of the first scene, the dramatic situation is present in its totality; likewise, the musical material introduced at the beginning is the same in the middle and at the end: the same harmonies, melodies, rhythms, and general style. This is as evident in *Maximilien* as in *Le pauvre matelot,* in *Les Euménides* as in *La brebis.* There is no dramatic development, as in romantic theater, but rather the establishment of a lyrical mood that permeates the entire work. Furthermore, notice that Milhaud avoids showy, noisy finales in dramas such as *La brebis, Le pauvre matelot, Les malheurs d'Orphée, L'homme et son désir,* and *La création du monde.* The music appears to become reabsorbed, removed, stripped bare as it moves toward silence, for the action of each particular work is only a moment in the total drama that continues from one dramatic composition to another. The only exceptions are in works that terminate in great scenes of thanksgiving, such as *L'Orestie* and *Christophe Colomb.*

Finally, we should point out another constant element: Milhaud's musical style never varied, from the day he first put pen to paper. True, he developed a technical fluency free of the fetters that must be always shed during the learning process; naturally his power to express ideas became more complete and homogeneous. But his basic melodic inspiration, his handling of counterpoint, and the whole mood that his mu-

26

sic communicates never changed after 1910, to the point that, when listening for a scene from *Maximilien,* for example, one is suddenly struck by a passage that seems to come straight out of *La brebis;* to the point, also, that in 1933 Milhaud was able, without difficulty, to rewrite and perfect the score of *Alissa* that he had composed in 1913.

As bases for his dramas, Milhaud chose texts by several authors. Aeschylus, Francis Jammes, Paul Claudel, Jean Cocteau, Blaise Cendrars, and Armand Lunel were his principal choices. Along with them we occasionally encounter Franz Werfel, A. Flament, Henri Hoppenot, Madeleine Milhaud, and Jules Supervielle. The differing temperaments of these writers call for a wide variety of musical settings, but knowing Milhaud's consistency, we can be sure that if he chose these authors from among all others, it is because he found some common denominator among them. Then he kneaded and pounded each text into his mind before finding just the right musical means for expressing its special significance.

Cocteau bears witness to this process in remarks that I must unfortunately translate from a German translation of the original:

Collaboration with Darius Milhaud is quite a different thing (compared to collaboration with Satie). Tricks and precautions are unnecessary. Everything is good-humored, open, vigorous, in broad daylight. It's highway robbery! He takes a miserable little creature, born on a rainy day in the country, carries her on his shoulders across the stream, and comes back married and the father of a large family! I have to admit that in some of these marvellous enterprises I have difficulty recognizing my material, creased and torn from one end to the other, which Darius has used as the basis of one of his latest triumphs. To chew vigorously, grasp powerfully, look things straight in the eye, take one mighty leap toward a goal: these expressions must have been invented to describe the music of Darius and the experience of collaborating with Darius. (*Anbruch,* April–May 1936.)

Milhaud's hallmark is his ability to take a combination of equivalent human and material units, involve them in a special situation and project through that interaction a sense of life's intrinsic drama. Neither deeds nor words will influence the outcome of the drama, for its course is dictated by inherent necessity, by the "fatum" of the ancients. The forces of the universe—fire, water, wind, the forest, animals, known and unknown objects—will preside over the fulfillment of this destiny, which is fixed, in contrast to daily existence, which is like moving water. All will converge on the human being, who stands uncertain in the midst of his anguish. Even in travail, he will observe these elements, experience them, and long for them; he will strike them with the fire of his own inner life, and the brilliance and energy that radiate from that encounter will, in return, unforgettably illuminate his own soul. It is this quality of dramatic encounter, in which all elements participate as either protagonists or spectators, that characterizes all the great masterpieces from the Bible and the *Odyssey* to *Don Quixote,* Shakespeare's plays, and *Pantagruel.*

Now let us consider the most ancient arena: Here is the slow gestation of mankind, first a larva, then a chrysalis that barely emerges from the primeval night, creeping, already dimly conscious of a primitive longing to find its meaning, its place in the sun as yet unknown. Destiny envelops it with spiderwebs before it has even emerged into the light; this is *L'homme et son désir.* Next we see man developing along with the plants and animals of the forest, unraveling the mysteries, and receiving his complement and companion, woman. This is the moment at which life emerges from its state of semiparalysis, when the tadpole, with a final thrust, leaves the egg and swims into the coolness of the stream. It is springtime, the dawning of *La création du monde.* From now on, the more he struggles, the more man will become enmeshed in the web that surrounds him: supple, elastic threads, sometimes invisible, sometimes, when they are silvered with dew, seemingly harmless, stretching with the movements of the prisoner, but never giving way. Man and woman, who are made for each other and whose mission it is to complete each other, yearn to join and rejoin. But in spite of their love and their instincts, it is their fate never to be truly mated. They pass each other like ships on the sea, bound for different ports. The great rift is there, and its presence leaves its mark, deeply engraved, on the human countenance. The lament of *Le pauvre matelot* murmurs it; *Les malheurs d'Orphée* cry it out.

Branded now by a red-hot iron, man has become aware of his own destiny. Knowledge of an impossible goal, an unattainable end, has taught him the inescapable role he must play in life's drama. Sometimes he tries to tear asunder the imposed order, believing with pathetic foolishness that he can attain the completeness for which he yearns. This is the theme of *Médée.* But he finds a certain degree of peace only when he restores the order that he has tried to disrupt: *La brebis égarée* is witness to that. If he has nobility of spirit he will accept, fully consciously, the destiny that he recognizes as his own. Tossed about by tempests of error, he nevertheless manages to steer his course; he ties himself to the mast so as not to succumb to the temptation of cowardice. Surrounded by misery, want, and crime, he never loses sight of the goal that his conscience has chosen, which is like a beacon guiding him to the harbor, where he will at last be able to lay down his load and redeem his spirit. This is the message of the composer's greatest dramas: *Maximilien, L'Orestie, Colomb, Bolivar, Saint-Louis,* and *David.* Thus, in his theatrical works Milhaud has sung the story of man from his chrysalis state to the fullest development of human conscience. This artistic edifice is crowned by *La sagesse.*

Concluding the summary of Milhaud's dramatic works, we turn to his satires, the pure satire of *Protée* and *Le boeuf sur le toit,* intended as a scenario for a Charlie Chaplin film, and the semicomic *Opéras-minute,* as well as *Esther de Carpentras,* that bantering opera which ends on a thoughtful note and portrays two cultures that meet but never join. Of all his dramatic production, only *Salade, Le train bleu,* and *Les songes* are moments of pure détente, like passing divertisse-ments on the highway of life!

Just as the eternal drama is presented in an infinite variety of forms, so are the verbal, visual, and tonal materials altered from one work to another. How could it be otherwise? The typical dramatic form of three acts and four scenes, such as is found in Wagner's lyric dramas, would be ill suited to Milhaud's thought. In his work, the music is the drama. Its length is the length of each individual situation. Therefore it moves quickly or slowly according to need. This suiting of musical length to dramatic necessity eliminates the need to add padding. In Milhaud's dramatic works, therefore, nothing is of secondary impor-tance; everything is there by necessity. An opera may last ten minutes, as does *L'enlèvement d'Europe,* or a whole evening, like *Maximilien.*

Furthermore, the word *opera* is not consistently applicable. It is doubtless used to avoid confusion with the term *lyric drama,* rather than in its traditional context. Still, these works are all dramatic, and the drama is set to music. But they are a far cry from the Wagnerian model, in which a system of conventions, symbols, and stereotyped de-velopment restricts the imagination. Out of Wagnerian lyric drama one can extract and treasure certain fragments: a funeral march, an overture, the love scene from the second act of *Tristan.* But everything that does, or should, constitute the onward flow of the drama is sub-merged in a mist of labored conventions; it loses the direct path to our hearts. Also, where we expect a struggle of conscience, we find only a discussion of abstractions; gold, power, and so forth are ideas in them-selves, but they are unrelated to the common human experience and therefore lyrical only to a limited extent. With Milhaud, everything is reality. It would be impossible to designate some parts of his operas as more significant than others. Likewise, there are no longer filler pas-sages such as abound in both the *Ring* and *Parsifal.* "The truly realistic artist never has to be afraid of being lyric," says Cocteau in *Le coq et l'arlequin.* "The practical world will always maintain its force, no mat-ter what metamorphoses are imposed on it by lyricism."

Milhaud also uses a wide variety of scenic devices, combined with musical devices, according to the demands of each drama. *La brebis* consists of a series of tableaux commented on by three women who describe the action. *L'homme et son désir* is a wordless plastic poem;

La création du monde is a ballet. In the short, concise operas *Les malheurs d'Orphée, Le pauvre matelot,* and *Fiesta,* attention is focused on the music as it is in Purcell's *Dido and Aeneas.* The *Opéras-minute* contain dramatic ingredients in a strikingly abridged form. In *L'Orestie* we experience the interpenetration of spoken text and music. *Christophe Colomb* is a mixture of opera, oratorio, and cinema, and *Le boeuf sur le toit* can accompany a performance by clowns, or equally successfully, a film by Charlie Chaplin.

The imaginative staging of each drama is conceived so as to highlight the effectiveness of the performers, and theaters that best understood the importance of the visual element entrusted the design of the décor to well-known artists rather than to routine stage designers. Thus, Dufy painted *Le boeuf sur le toit* and Cocteau directed it. Braque did *Salade;* Léger, *La création;* Derain, *Les songes,* and Jean-Victor Hugo, *Les malheurs d'Orphée.* Even the state-supported theaters relinquished their usual practices when confronted with a work by Milhaud: the Opéra-Comique commissioned Cocteau to do the décor for *Le matelot,* and the Opéra engaged Pedro Pruna for *Maximilien.* This form of homage cannot be underestimated, for it shows recognition of the exceptional nobility of Milhaud's art.

This art's rational aspect makes it profoundly French. The music says what it has to say with efficiency and economy. For along with his inexhaustible wellspring of inspiration, Milhaud also has a Cartesian turn of mind, which acts as a filter and which controls and channels the torrent that pours forth from his imagination. A work may be long and ample, but its expressiveness remains concise. As for the abundance of his music, in that he resembles older, pre-Romantic composers, for in the nineteenth century musical output became smaller and smaller as musicians increasingly turned their compositions into vehicles for personal confession. Moreover, Milhaud's fertile imagination and technical ease account for the individuality of his work. He has never needed to borrow from his predecessors, and one finds in his compositions neither the playful, skillful reconstructions of classical tunes, as in Stravinsky's *Pulcinella* and parts of *Oedipus Rex,* nor the witty and cynical use of ancient constructions, as in Poulenc's *Aubade* and the finale of *Les fâcheux.* Authenticity and faith are the hallmarks of Milhaud's art.

IV

The Music

Art which fails to evoke, whether by verse, phrase, melody, or brush stroke, a complete moment of life may be an elegant jewel, but it is not art.

Rémy de Gourmont

In the preceding chapter we examined the importance of Milhaud's humanistic philosophy of life, which makes him much more than a mere coordinator of notes and sonorities. Now it is time to turn to the music itself, to see what it is like and what makes it the way it is. First and foremost, it is melodic. Its absolute, fundamental premise is melody—true melody—which is a very special thing. A fragment like the following (Ex. 4–1) is not a melody.

Ex. 4–1.

This pattern, in and of itself, does not convey any particular expressive message. It symbolizes Fafner and impresses the listener who is familiar with Wagner's *Ring* because, the minute he hears it, he can poke his neighbor in the ribs and whisper, "Here's Fafner." It conjures up a nonmusical image and, because the image is impressive, we assume that the musical idea itself is also great. But this is an illusion. Likewise, the symbol of the sword, separated from the object it alludes to, could just as well be a bugle tune played in an army barracks to summon the soldiers to pick up mail or to report for sick call.

The two motives at the beginning of *Tristan and Isolde* (Ex. 4–2), formulas that are rhythmically and tonally ambiguous, do not, in and of themselves, have musical meaning. They acquire significance by virtue of the harmony that results when they are superimposed. These two thematic kernels of four notes each combine to make a motive that, by its very insignificance, lends itself to a multitude of adaptations. A true, autonomous melody is rare in Wagner's music; the beginning of the overture to *Die Meistersinger* is one exception.

Ex. 4–2.

In general, modern music has shown a tendency to replace a "melody" by a "theme." In Schoenberg's music this tendency reached the point where an interplay of accents and a series of only two or three widely and awkwardly spaced notes sufficed to express tension.

Another approach has been to use folk melodies. The Franck–D'Indy school took a popular type of melody, distorted it rhythmically, and altered the intervals until the original character and expressiveness of the line were completely lost. Stravinsky often incorporated folk melodies in his works without modifying them, as in *Petrouchka* and *Les noces*, thereby retaining their full, original impact. Meanwhile, Fauré quietly went about inventing his characteristic melodic lines, for example in *La bonne chanson* (Ex. 4–3).

-sé - e Qui m'apris l'â- me l'autre é - té; _____ espressivo

Ex. 4–3.

This is a true melody, a statement. The simple, unadorned line contains within itself tonality, rhythm, and inflection. It is complete and wholly intelligible; it can stand alone, without either harmonic or contrapuntal support; in short, it is a musical entity. No matter what other embellishments, in the form of countermelodies or harmonic elaborations, may be added to it, it will retain its identity.

Milhaud could never sufficiently praise his teacher, André Gédalge, for having impressed upon him the need to make melody the essence of musical composition. Before he let his pupils begin to compose or even to do technical exercises, Gédalge would urge them to write unaccompanied musical lines. Only after they had succeeded in fashioning a truly expressive melody, and so had discovered how to make a single line convey a total musical thought, would he allow them to start studying the technique of composition.

In 1921 an English musical review published some examples of fanfares written by a group of up-and-coming composers. Along with a copy of this review, I received a letter from Milhaud (Ex. 4–4): "Berlioz wrote a sublime melody for horn. Isn't it bold and original? All these people do is write taratata."

A true melody is always original. It defies time and guarantees music's perpetual youth. Mere themes or groups of accents can never replace melody, since they are only parts of a system and are condemned to become obsolete, because sooner or later systems go out of fashion. Harmonic novelty also wears thin. As soon as the ear has become accustomed to it, it loses its attractiveness. The same applies to rhythm. But one never tires of a true melody. The great musician is the one who invents great melodies. Defying time, melody is the expression of eternal wisdom. That is why folk song throughout the ages has been an expression of the collective experience of simple people. It follows, then, that a composer who understands basic human needs and who wishes to communicate with the hearts as well as the minds of his listeners, will do so through the use of melody. Melody has been the point of departure for all the finest composers: Monteverdi, Bach, Mo-

Ex. 4–4.

zart, Beethoven, and Berlioz all have this characteristic in common, no matter how different their styles.

So it is with Milhaud. The entire significance of his music depends on the indispensable presence of melodic line. With the first measure of *Les choéphores,* it imposes itself indisputably and completely, permeating the meaning of the text that it interprets. His is a simple, natural, tonal language. It rings so true that it seems almost to rise from the voices of those ancient Mediterranean singers (Ex. 4–5).

Ex. 4–5.

Turning to other excerpts, from *Orphée* and *Alissa,* for instance, we gain the same impression of universality. One could quote examples ad infinitum, but let us consider the supple tenderness of just one more melody, the song of Créuse in *Médée* (Ex. 4–6).

Ex. 4–6.

In this long, broad line, with its simplicity and sincerity, there is neither academicism nor banality. In sum, all Milhaud's melodies are straightforward and unambiguous.

Often he incorporates popular tunes, but rarely does he use them in their traditional form. With a slight twist of the wrist, he puts them into new focus. Melody for him is also a springboard from which to leap into expressive possibilities not available to those who ignore this fundamental source of energy. Composers may admit that melody is their greatest treasure, but often they don't know how to make use of it. If they did, we would be less inundated by trivial music. Likewise, painters agree that, before attempting to paint, one should learn to draw. Drawing and melody: think of the time and concentration needed to learn fully the importance of these comparable elements, and it will not seem surprising that in fact only a few creative artists have the real gift of invention.

Misunderstanding with regard to melody is more widespread than one might think. A famous composer asked me one day to play him some music by Fauré, hoping that I could persuade him to like it, for he couldn't discover any melody in it—or anything attractive at all, for that matter. To show what he considered melody, he played me one of his own little dance tunes. It was charming, but characterless. No, a melody is much more than that; it must be an expressive sum total of inflections, accents, and cadences if it is to form the kernel of a musical composition.

I have witnessed many expressions of surprise and doubt when people first hear that a certain Milhaud score was composed in a ten-day or two-week period. Such rapidity would be indeed disconcerting if it were strictly true; but appearances are deceiving. There is a story about Dumas, who had promised a play to the Théâtre Français. The evening before the reading rehearsal was scheduled, one of the actors asked him if the play were finished. "Yes," answered Dumas, "I only have to write it down."

A work of art is born in the mind of an artist; there the creative idea becomes thoroughly assimilated and synthesized. Then its meaning and energy must be channeled. With a composer, the first act is to invent a melody. After that, composition proceeds rapidly. Invention is the slow part of the process. For a composer like Milhaud, who developed his themes logically, the actual writing down of the whole work was a sort of game. How many times have I read in his letters: "I am starting to think about my sixth symphony (for vocal quartet, oboe, and cello). It is difficult"; or, "I am thinking about *La création . . .* it is difficult." He would write this way several times over a period of weeks, and then suddenly the manuscript would be finished: *La création du monde,* May–June 1923; *Les malheurs d'Orphée,* L'Enclos, 22 September–2 November 1924. But he had been talking about *Orphée* for years!

When an alloy cools to its lowest melting point, it suddenly becomes a homogeneous, crystalline mass. So it was with Milhaud's music; as soon as the elements of a drama had fallen into place in his mind, melody would ensue immediately, and it would define the entire work to be. That accounts for the feeling of rightness and completeness that all his compositions project. Putting the music down on paper was then hardly more than a formality, a task that could be accomplished while he was on board a ship, in port, or in any other place in which he happened to find himself. Nevertheless, all his great intellectual masterpieces, those that dominate his total production, took much more time. The composition of *La brebis égarée* took five years; *L'Orestie* took twelve; and *Alissa,* written in 1913, was revised three or four times and did not reach its final form until 1933.

Deceived by the rapidity with which Milhaud wrote down his compositions and mistaking speed for hasty conception, critics at first assumed that his music was "bungled" and "unkempt." But later they spoke of his "unusual virtuosity" and paid homage to the equilibrium found in his works.

One summer in Provence, on an evening laden with the sound of bells and the odor of freshly picked fruit, we were walking in one of the quiet side streets of Aix. It was at the beginning of our friendship. In front of the beautiful entrance to Saint-Sauveur, two steps from the "Burning Bush," we stopped a moment and I asked: "Darius, what made you turn to polytonality; how are you able to hear music in that special way before you write it down?"

"It is difficult to explain," he answered. "I don't know if you can understand. But when I am in the country at night, plunged in silence, and I look at the sky, it seems to me that from every point in the firmament and even from the center of the earth, rays and impulses come toward me; each of these impulses carries a different thread of music, and all the infinity of musical lines cross and intersect each other without ever losing their individual clarity and distinctness. It is an incredible feeling. I have always tried to express this emotion, this sensation of a thousand simultaneous lines of music launched toward me."

So that is the origin of his polytonality, about which so much has been written and which many have described as a calculated system. It is the direct expression of a perception, of one of those mysterious messages that the universe transmits to us when we are completely alone and our minds are uncluttered and free to receive such revelations. For a composer who had chosen melody as the inevitable means of portraying human drama, what more felicitous solution could there be than this combination of simultaneous, rather than successive, melodic lines, each one conserving its own individuality and freedom while joining with the others? Just as all objects and all creatures may at any moment confront each other, so can equally important melodic lines continuously meet in one encounter after another as they move independently through the musical fabric. By the use of this poly-

37

melody heightened by polytonality, the whole of nature seems to insinuate itself into the orchestra.

It is wonderful to observe how the shock of genius can blast open new avenues through which art enters to explore the human soul more deeply. All the rest—harmony, counterpoint, orchestration—can be learned. But even in these matters, Milhaud, like other great composers, demands a great deal of himself. Melody is beautiful only if it has inner compulsion; technique, too, must be the result of artistic necessity. Whatever merely follows a formula is sterile. Real technique begins where learned technique leaves off. It must be, like melody, an act of the imagination.

Once, when Milhaud was speaking about a gifted young musician who continually hesitated to put notes on paper, fearing to make a mistake, he said: "He has far too many scruples to be a composer." Such a remark could only come from the lips of a powerfully creative person whose music transcends academicism.

V

The Language

Tell me why it is that when I hear of young artists, painters, or sculptors, I am told all about their thoughts, opinions, and goals, but never about their technique except in cases of absolute necessity? Whereas when I am with musicians I never hear an exciting idea discussed: it's like being in school; all they know is technique and shop talk. Is the art of music so primitive that it must be studied in such a puerile fashion?

Letter from Mussorgsky to Stassov, 13 July 1872

The technique of an untalented composer is completely uninteresting, for such a person learns technique as a trade in the same way that a mechanic learns to fit a nut to a bolt. Many composers share the illusion that this acquisition of a trade is all they need in order to produce fresh, imaginative music. They forget that the formal rules of harmony and counterpoint are good only as exercises to develop ease and proficiency, but that as soon as they begin to compose, they must choose technical means that match the nature of their inspiration. Even technical terms, used so precisely in academic manuals, become debatable and open to a variety of interpretations as soon as one ventures onto the sea of the unknown.

When a chord becomes even slightly complex, it can be interpreted in various ways. Much ink has been spilled in attempts to describe the opening harmony of *Tristan and Isolde;* the complexities of *Le sacre du printemps* have been analyzed in countless ways; and nowadays, many unusual combinations of notes must be understood in their coexistent vertical and horizontal contexts.

The harmonic nomenclature used in textbooks results from the diatonic language of the eighteenth century. Consonances, dissonances, resolutions, and cadences form an entity in which the relationships are simple and relatively limited. Consider, for example, the figured bass, in which the harmonies are so predictable that it was not even necessary for the composer to write them out. However, there were exceptions even during that period, for example the brilliant harmonic texture of Philipp Emanuel Bach's extraordinary fantasies *Für Kenner und Liebhaber* (in full, K. P. E. Bach, *Klavier Sonaten und freie Fantasien nebst einigen Rondos für Pianoforte, für Kenner und Liebhaber,* Fifth Collection, 2nd Fantasy, Leipzig, 1785). With a daring that has been insufficiently acknowledged by modern musicologists, he went far beyond the scholastic formulas of his contemporaries and evolved a kind of harmonic vocabulary that anticipates the chromaticism of Liszt and Wagner.

The more chromaticism developed, and passing notes, appoggiaturas, anticipations, and suspensions became important, the more their original purpose became disguised. During the nineteenth century, conventional terminology tried to reconcile all these extraneous notes within the basic context of the consonant–dissonant system. From exception to exception, the rules of musical syntax became less and less applicable, until they finally reached the point of becoming completely obsolete. From the simple system of order that it was at first, harmony became a distinguishing tool of musical expression. With Schoenberg it turned toward atonality, the logical outcome of chromaticism; and with some French composers a form of diatonicism developed in which the use of several simultaneous tonalities affirmed, rather than negated, the feeling of tonality. Those who heard the first performances of some of Milhaud's works, in which polytonality was carried to a maximum of effectiveness and expressiveness, generally believed that this method of composition had suddenly sprung into existence. On the contrary, it was born slowly, represented a sort of progressive emancipation, and resulted in either melodic or harmonic polytonality.

It is impossible to emphasize sufficiently the importance of a composer like Charles Koechlin, whose perceptiveness led to the discovery of many polytonal resources. Used in a very personal way, they give unique charm to his delightful *Paysages et marines* and his *Sonatines françaises,* which are among the most significant pieces of music of the early twentieth century. His magnificent *Traité d'harmonie,* with its broad, balanced method of basing harmonic analysis on musical good sense, abounds in information concerning polytonality and in instruction how to use it. Any musician or music historian interested in the subject will find much food for thought in this book. Milhaud owes a great deal to Koechlin. He was well aware of this debt and acknowledged it at every opportunity. Koechlin played a considerable role in molding his perceptions and directing his technical development. The mark of this influence is visible up to the time of the composition of *Les Choéphores.* In fact, Koechlin and Debussy are the only composers who really influenced Milhaud at the beginning of his career. Other styles that occasionally seem to be reflected in his music are included only superficially. For example, he may give a passing nod to the styles of Chabrier, Stravinsky, or Satie, or may even tip his hat to his younger friend Sauguet, but that is only a way of contrasting their styles with his own. Like props in a play, which have nothing to do with the drama itself but highlight various aspects of it, Milhaud uses extraneous musical allusions to accentuate his own style without in any way altering it.

There is no point in embarking on a study of polytonality in all its historical and musical significance. A brief definition that Milhaud wrote for the *Revue Musicale* of 1 February 1923 will suffice:

If one accepts the system of twelve definite tonalities, each based on a different degree of the scale, and the possibility of passing from one tonality to another by means of modulation, then it is quite logical to go further and explore ways in which these tonalities can be superimposed and heard simultaneously. Contrapuntal writing should also lead to this conclusion. The day that canons, other than those at the octave, were conceived of, the principle of polytonality was proclaimed.

Milhaud then demonstrates the way in which Bach treated each of his superimposed melodies with complete freedom. When he turns to the subject of harmony, he asserts that as soon as "foreign notes"—that is, notes other than those belonging to the basic triads—were added to chords as integral parts of the chordal texture, they could no longer be regarded as passing notes or appoggiaturas: "Furthermore, the analysis of a chord is a purely conventional and arbitrary matter, and there is no reason not to consider a major ninth chord on C as a superimposition of a g minor and a C major triad, all of which leads to the next step, which is to superimpose two melodies, one in C major, the other in g minor." Milhaud next points out the different harmonic combinations that will result from this treatment, and their musical points of contact. He refers to instances of polytonality in Stravinsky's *Petrouchka,* Roussel's *Pour une fête du printemps,* and other examples in works by Ravel, Bartók, and Satie.

Then he examines the superimposition of three tonalities, a combination rich in possibilities. Thus, the chord that includes triads built on C, D flat, and D (Ex. 5–1) can be written in eight different ways.

Ex. 5–1.

41

The inversion of just one position of this chord, restated on the various degrees of the chromatic scale, opens up a great many coloristic possibilities (Ex. 5–2).

Ex. 5–2.

Furthermore, the nine notes of the three chords include the notes of a total of seven triads. Finally, if one uses each note of the scale as the basis for a triad, one has a complete chromatic vocabulary at hand, which sometimes gives the impression of an atonal texture. "In this way one can command a greatly expanded range of expressive resources; and, in the realm of dynamics, the use of polytonality adds the greatest subtlety and tenderness to pianissimo, and gives special force and focus to fortissimo. Chordal counterpoint has infinite possibilities."

According to Hindemith, there is no such thing as polytonality or atonality, for every chord has a fundamental that determines the tonality. This concept has as much validity as any other since there really is no absolute law. In all cases of complicated harmonic structures the ear is the final judge. Also, a chord's function depends on the way in which it is connected to what precedes and follows. A chord can appear to be tonal or polytonal according to the way it is used.

Linear polytonality is less ambiguous. It consists of the superimposition of melodies, each in a different tonality. The more diatonic the melodies used, the more apparent the polytonal character of the music. Note, for example, Milhaud's *Troisième symphonie,* op. 71, for chamber orchestra (Ex. 5–3).

The ear cannot easily distinguish too many separate tonalities at a time. The above example contains five simultaneous tonalities. They are perceivable only because of the very diversified instrumentation used: flute, clarinet, bassoon, violin, viola, and cello. Polytonality must be written with distinctly articulated parts for an ensemble of soloists in order to be clear. It is much less adaptable to a large orchestra.

In his works of the mid-thirties to mid-forties, Milhaud mostly kept to bitonality, which he had mastered to such an extent that he had made it into an exceptionally subtle means of expression. Polytonality using three or more voices appears mainly in works written between 1916 and 1922, and again during his last years, notably in the *Aspen Serenade* (1957), *Concert de chambre* (1961), *Septuor à cordes* (1964),

Ex. 5–3.

Musique pour Graz (1968), and the *Quintette pour instruments à vent* (1973).

Boris de Schloezer wrote perceptively in the *Revue Musicale* of 1 March 1925: "Milhaud's use of polyphony may originate in the sentiments and emotional needs of the composer and may serve to express a certain inner tension; nevertheless, it is always controlled and according to rule and follows a purely aesthetic logic. I would say that Milhaud's counterpoint, like Bach's, appears to be an expressive means or an organizational process depending on one's attitude toward it."

According to rule? Many contrapuntal sections are completely unanalyzable strictly according to the rules. It would be more correct to say that Milhaud writes according to the *spirit* of the rules, and that his counterpoint extends the existing regulations. Application of the rules of polyphony to polytonality, or to what is often erroneously called atonality, breaks down the old consonant–dissonant conventions. For all practical purposes, any note can be superimposed, which means that classic harmonic concepts are discarded in favor of greater developmental freedom. One result is "chance music" (controlled chance, of course) in which each player performs a melodic line as written, but chooses his own tempo. The result is a kind of kaleidoscopic sound, which can be fascinating if the composer has strictly anticipated the number of possible vertical combinations and has made sure that none of them lasts too long. Milhaud wrote chance music long before it became stylish to do so. His first experiment, in 1921, was the *Cocktail aux clarinettes.* Later, the genre was re-explored in *La Suite de quatrains* (1962) of Francis Jammes, the *Septuor à cordes* (1964), and *Neige sur la fleuve* (1961).

To see what is meant by "according to the spirit of the rules," let us examine one of Milhaud's favorite contrapuntal forms, the fugue. A textbook fugue has its subject in the tonic, its answer in the dominant, and its episodes and modulations according to convention. Milhaud uses this formula sometimes in passages that are entirely in one key. The amusing ballet *Le train bleu,* a kind of danced operetta, contains a "fugue de l'engueulade" (a scolding fugue) in C major that is perfectly orthodox. In *Esther de Carpentras* the four-voice Fugue of Purim, also in C major, has a classic exposition section (Ex. 5–4).

Ex. 5–4.

The contralto voice states the subject in C major, the tenor answers in G; the bass reiterates the subject in C, followed by the soprano in G. Then follows an episode based on the subject, which leads neatly and concisely to a minor and e minor. There is a new modulation to F major, which changes to d minor, a pedal point, cadence, stretto, and conclusion (pianissimo) in C major. The fugue in *Le train bleu* expresses movement and vitality; the one in *Esther,* which opens the second act of the opera, creates a tranquil atmosphere at first, but ends by becoming roguish.

In works where the tonality is complex, either because of a major–minor duality or on account of the use of bitonality or polytonality, the tonal rules that govern a classic fugue become obsolete. Even so, the structure can remain strict—that is, the fugal construction can perfectly acceptably be adapted to contain other harmonic interrelationships. In his *Etudes sur l'écriture de la fugue libre,* Koechlin writes about sixteenth-century fugues that start with three entrances of the subject, with the second on the dominant of the first and the third on the dominant of the second. This same sort of pattern can be found in Milhaud's polytonal fugues. Many of them consist only of an exposition, sometimes a stretto, and a conclusion. It would be wrong to refer to this abbreviated form as "fugato." In reality, the passages have their antecedents in the suites of short fugues written by earlier composers. (See, for example, F. X. A. Murschhausen, *Denkmäler der Tonkunst in Bayern,* vol. 18; J. K. F. Fischer's "Blumenstrauss," in *Sämtliche Werke für Orgel und Klavier,* Breitkopf und Härtel.)

In *La création du monde,* a theme with angular rhythms and wavering tonality is introduced as the basis of a strongly accented three-voice fugue. The other voices hammer out their entrances, and the series of shocks portray the sprouting and hatching of a new world, explosive yet organized. The subject in D ends on the subdominant. The answer is in E, a break with tonal convention. The second exposition is in A, the subdominant of E, and the answer is in D, which re-establishes equilibrium. Next comes an episode based on the countersubject, in d minor, over an ostinato in D major and C major. Modulation to F, C, G, and D, led by a bass figure taken from the subject, is followed by another episode based on the countersubject in D, again accompanied by an ostinato. Then comes an extremely compact stretto in which the voices are successively in D, A, and D. That leads to a new passage. The ostinato figure of the second episode continues to the end of the stretto and is crowned by still another ostinato figure, this one played by the trumpet. These ostinati seem to serve in place of a pedal point and add a kind of tonal ambiguity to this polytonal structure, just as the single pedal note does to the classic fugue. If this analysis is valid, we are witnessing the superimposition of the stretto and the pedal-point sections, a device that certainly extends the rules. However, this free treatment never violates the spirit of fugal construction; the novelty thus introduced is simply a consequence of expanded harmonic resources.

A further departure from the classic fugue can be seen in the third act of *Les Euménides,* a tremendously impressive passage in which the orchestration makes the music surge forward with the impact of a marching crowd. Starting as if from the shadows, it bursts into that state of frenzied joy which characterizes mass demonstrations. At first there is a series of heavy, thick chords, and then, little by little, the song of triumph emerges, reaching a climax with Athena's pronouncement: "Cry, crier, with bursting lungs, and call my cohorts hither."

Throughout this overture, leading it forward, supporting it, assuring its unity, organizing it into a great procession, and dominating it with its persistent rhythm, is a three-voice fugue, the subject of which lasts twenty-three measures. As it proceeds the texture is sometimes polytonal and sometimes atonal. It is impossible to assign a fixed tonality to the subject, which is strictly restated five times, along with a countersubject and without interruption by episodes or interludes. With the last entrance comes the addition of Athena's song, which leads to a climax. At that point the thematic material is presented in a triple canon at the octave, which serves as a kind of stretto—and at the same time, through augmentation of note-values, as a great conclusion and affirmation.

Without becoming too involved in minute analysis, we should nevertheless take note of a few of Milhaud's other fugal passages, which bear witness to his inventive genius. *Christophe Colomb* contains no fewer than four fugues. The form is used for the scene (the seventeenth tableau) in which the Indian gods in America foresee the coming of the Europeans and bemoan the loss of their primitive freedom, calling on all the other pagan gods for sympathy. They throw a cable across the ocean to be grasped by their African counterparts, and together they whip the waves into a tempest to block the progress of Columbus's ships. We see the gods, costumed in bizarre, idolatrous attire, grinning with evil indolence, and we hear music that portrays their motley garb and raucous clamor. It does not do it with simplistic means, but by generating a huge, five-voice chromatic fugue over an ostinato figure that encompasses and unifies all the modulations like a great pendulum marking time (Ex. 5–5).

Above, the fugue subject weaves in and out like a snake, passing without pause from F to E, E-flat, D, and C-sharp. After thirty measures (at measure 1370) it returns and is treated crab fashion. The ostinato figure is then repeated like a stretto by all five voices, simultaneously with the subject in counterpoint with its countersubject, also in retrograde motion. The result is a network of lines all based on the same melodic material, which admirably suits the dramatic situation.

Another fugue appears in the scene of Isabella's funeral (measure 923 of the second part). Here again we find an ostinato bass figure, so

Ex.5–5.

typical of Milhaud's polyphonic constructions, used to provide, on the
one hand, a solid tonal foundation; and on the other, a spatial effect
that evokes the grandeur and continuity of the drama, the immutabil-
ity of time, and the implacability of destiny. Over this bass line the orchestra introduces a long melody in e-flat minor. Passing to b-flat minor, it becomes the basis for a fugal subject, which is answered after
three measures in e-flat minor. The subject returns in E-flat, with its
answer in B-flat. After modulating through C and f minor, the stretto
begins, along with reappearances of the subject in augmented note-
values; and then the whole fugue ends in the clear, uncomplicated tonality of C major.

But that is not all: on top of the fugue is a chorale that starts in E flat major and ends in C major (a wordless chorus). Meanwhile another four-voice choir sings a psalm in c minor, concluding in C major, and two solo voices superpose their "divisions" on the whole orchestral and choral fabric.

It is a splendidly organized tonal spectacle, with musical ideas seeming to shoot forth from all points of the horizon: an immense edifice that comprises several simultaneous constructions. Out of the polytonal mass comes suddenly, in the space of two measures, the most natural resolution into one key. This example superbly illustrates the way in which polytonality, used to distinguish several coexistent musical structures, can add to the expressive possibilities of the music, reconciling different sentiments and bringing them to one homogeneous conclusion. To confirm this observation, one should also examine the polytonal fugue in *Protée*, with its successive expositions at the fifth degree; or the three different fugues and one canon in the *Etudes* for piano and orchestra, not to mention the fugue in *Le retour de l'enfant prodigue*. Only then will one fully appreciate the composer's rich inventiveness and the profoundly expressive power of his contrapuntal language.

Milhaud's work also contains contrapuntal constructions that are not based on the principle of imitation (as are canons, ricercari, and fugues), but stem from an imaginative concept that superimposes constantly evolving melodic ideas. The form results from a joining of compatible, simultaneously conceived ideas, rather than from any special plan of procedure, and it defies systematization and analysis.

With such complex constructions, it might prove difficult to maintain clarity, for the resulting texture could easily become cluttered and opaque. But this is not the case. Milhaud's music remains transparent, even in the most ponderous passages; he never confronts either the performer or the listener with an accumulation of difficulties. This clarity is due to the basic rhythmic simplicity of the music. If the melodic lines, like Stravinsky's, for example, were all of different shapes and irregularly accented, it would be hard to follow them in a contrapuntal texture. But Milhaud's melodies are quite uncomplicated rhythmically and fall into simple metric units, mostly $\frac{4}{4}$, $\frac{3}{4}$, and $\frac{6}{8}$. Only in accompanied monody does he use more complicated patterns. For example, a supple $\frac{5}{8}$ rhythm accompanies such exquisite melodies as those found in the "Bacchanale nocturne" from *Protée* and in the overture to *Esther de Carpentras*.

The Pastorale from *Protée*, which also consists of a single accompanied melodic line, has a $\frac{3}{8}$ plus $\frac{3}{8}$ plus $\frac{2}{8}$ rhythm; and the same pattern, with quite different expressive results, is found in the opening chorus of *Les malheurs d'Orphée*. Sometimes, too, when there is no harmonic or melodic polyphony, several rhythms are combined in a polyrhythmic passage, for example in the chorus of animals in *Orphée* (Ex. 5–6).

Ex. 5–6.

At other times it is the persistent use of one meter that underscores a dramatic mood. The first act of *Le pauvre matelot* is entirely in $\frac{6}{8}$, the second in $\frac{4}{4}$.

All in all, complex rhythms are found far more often in Milhaud's melodies for solo voice accompanied by piano than in his ensemble music or dramatic works. In the larger vocal compositions, even lyrical declamation has had to adapt to the demand for clarity and simplicity. Composers have always accepted the principle that a musical line must follow the accentuations of the spoken word in order to make the text intelligible. Wagner went one step further in making a musical symbol actually take the place of a word; "das Gold" or "der heilige Speer" are unmistakable musical entities. In Debussy's *Pelléas et Mélisande* the psychology of the drama is underlined by the subtle adjustment of the musical phrases to each inflection of Maeterlinck's sensitive text. The music is, so to speak, a submissive handmaiden of the words.

Milhaud's dramatic concept does not rest on the importance of individual words. The general feeling of the drama as a whole makes the significance of the actual text ephemeral. The parts of a libretto that interest him are those in which words have a powerful rhythm in and of themselves and which the music can confront with its own strong beat. He makes the text fit the music. Whenever he introduces a dramatic vocal line, in either a solo song or a staged work, it is never independent of the total polyphonic texture, and it ranks equally with the other voices of the orchestral score.

An example in which individual words yield to larger concepts is in *Le pauvre matelot* (Ex. 5–7).

Ex. 5–7.

As in traditional sea-chanties, it is far more important to keep the pulse and swing of the music going than to make it fit every accent of the text. The value of the syllables is reduced to the point at which they become equal in all respects to note-values. It is their general impact that is important. Why should the introduction of the voice part do anything but enhance the expressiveness of purely musical thought?

Then there are the sections where words are omitted entirely and the human voice is used like another instrument. In the voting scene of the last act of *Les Euménides,* where the drama portrays one of the great moral reversals of history, the entire chorus sings without words, leaving the conversation with Apollo to a single solo voice.

Sometimes the texts Milhaud uses are completely incompatible with a musical setting. In his own words, the two scenes of exhortation in *Les Choéphores,* "on account of their cannibalistic character, presented one of the most difficult problems. The sentiment is not musical. How could this outburst be represented in artistic terms? I therefore decided to have the text rhythmically declaimed and arranged in measures as though sung. I wrote spoken choruses accompanied by an orchestra made up solely of percussion instruments."

By retaining the musical rhythm, he preserved the unity of the work. To introduce natural speech against a background of piano or orchestra, as is sometimes done in romantic melodrama, is to mix fire with water; the rhythmic patterns of words and music are in conflict. Schoenberg tried to resolve this problem with his *Sprechstimme,* by using a singing timbre on notes of indefinite pitch. That compromise has the disadvantage that the composer, in leaving the choice of pitches largely to the interpreter, tends to lose control over the results. In contrast, adapting musical rhythms to spoken words and placing them against a background of percussion instruments leads to a homogeneous musical ensemble of indeterminate tones. This technique is not only admirably adaptable to particular scenes, but with rhythm and percussion used as connective tissue, the composer can easily pass on to subsequent scenes in which speech resumes its normal role. The recitatives of *Salade* are treated this way. It is as though, from extraordinarily elastic springboards, the music flies off in new directions. Obviously, such a device introduces enormous possibilities for diversity within large-scale works such as *Christophe Colomb.* It is only exceptionally that Milhaud tolerates spoken declamation that is not written out in musical rhythmic values. That kind of free recitative is found only in the *Cantate de l'enfant et de la mère* (1938), *Caïn et Abel* (1944), and the *Suite de quatrains* (1962).

One further word on the subject of orchestration: polytonality is not well adapted to the piano. The impossibility of differentiating sound makes it very hard to project independent lines and harmonies. What is so well marked by various timbres and intensities in an orchestral setting becomes one great blur in keyboard works. The orchestration also obviously affects the expressive results of different pieces. Some, like *Protée, Maximilien, La brebis égrée, L'Orestie,* and *Christophe Colomb,* require a large orchestra, with three or four players to every woodwind part. The *Sérénade* is written for an orchestra with two players to a part, minus trombones. Other works, including *Les malheurs d'Orphée, L'homme et son désir,* the *Etudes* for piano and orchestra, the chamber symphonies, and *La création du monde,* are conceived for an orchestra consisting of soloists—that is, one instrument to a part. This is the kind of instrumentation that permits the most complete differentiation of sonorities. It is in radically polyphonic works such as these that Milhaud probably communicates most effectively his own sensation of receiving simultaneous musical impulses from all parts of the universe.

After a period from the mid-eighteenth through the nineteenth century, when the orchestra became not only bigger but more standardized, many twentieth-century composers, including Schoenberg, Stravinsky, and Milhaud, seem to have re-established contact with the traditions of the seventeenth century. (For a full appreciation of the rational and varied orchestration in the compositions of Heinrich Schütz, consult the Spitta edition of his works. J. S. Bach also made use of prodigious orchestral resources, often obscured in modernized versions of his work; on this subject, see Charles Sanford Terry, *Bach's Orchestra,* Oxford University Press, 1932.) However, in so doing, these modern composers have combined technical means and expressive content to a degree never before achieved. The music of our greatest contemporaries conveys a quality of inspiration and inner compulsion unmatched in previous periods of musical history.

In summary, let us note that there are few sonata, minuet, scherzo, or lieder forms in post-Debussy twentieth-century music. Instead, the thematic idea and melodic inventiveness, orchestration and sonority, and the emphasis on either harmony or counterpoint have become points of departure for an infinite number of musical shapes designed to communicate certain specific impressions. In each of Milhaud's compositions it is easy to grasp the interdependence of the expressive intent and the chosen form. When one views his total output in this light, one comes readily to understand the diversity of his musical language. *Les Euménides* is constructed with contrapuntally combined harmonic blocks suited to the monumentality of Greek tragedy. The quartets and the work *Printemps,* for piano, are examples of purely melodic counterpoint, resulting in a supple style in which the combinations of tonalities and modulations have been freed from classic conventions. Sometimes a kind of rhythmic unrest conditions a piece, as in the *Hymne de glorification* or *Fiesta;* and in compositions such as *La muse ménagère* a feeling of intimacy is communicated by the utter simplicity of melodic ideas and rhythmic motion.

VI

The Dramatic Works

Always direct your thinking toward the perfection of your thoughts.
                                              Aeschylus, *Agamemnon*

La brebis égarée

Apart from some early childhood efforts, including the opera *Les Saintes Maries de la mer, La brebis égarée* is really Milhaud's first dramatic work. It was begun in 1910 and finished in 1915. During that period he also produced some important chamber music, several song cycles, and the first version of his incidental music for *Protée*.

The first sonata for violin and piano appeared in 1911, the first and second string quartets in 1913–15, and the sonata for two violins and piano in 1914. Simultaneously he was working on the *Sept poèmes de la connaissance de l'est* (Claudel), *Alissa* (Gide), and settings of poems by Léo Latil, Francis Jammes, and Armand Lunel. Finally there was his *Poème sur un cantique de Camargue* for piano and orchestra, completed in 1913.

Milhaud's stylistic course was set by the time he was eighteen. Without hesitation he unerringly chose the expressive tools that were to serve him throughout a lifetime. Even his choice of poetic texts and the range of authors selected indicate a turn of mind that remained constant from his earliest to his latest years. Of course, much time was needed for the development and perfection of his craft and especially for achieving mastery of his very specially conceived polyphony, but a surprising number of compositions from that early period retain their significance after more than half a century of turbulent artistic history which has seen the rise and fall of many musical experiments. *Alissa,* the Latil songs, the sonata for two violins and piano, and the second string quartet have all withstood the test of time and after seventy years are appreciated as works of great beauty and distinction.

*   *   *

In 1910 Francis Jammes's *La brebis égarée* was already known in France as a stage play. The characters include Paul and Pierre, friends

53

since childhood, and Paul's wife Françoise. Paul is kind and loyal. His sole ambition is to lead a quiet, industrious life, rather drab perhaps, but illuminated by the joy of seeing his two children grow and develop. He loves his wife and admires her as a devoted mother and an honest, intelligent woman. But Françoise's sensitive nature yearns for something more than a mundane life, and her long pent-up desire for beauty and creativity explodes into uncontrollable passion for Pierre, a composer. He is swept up by her emotion, almost in spite of himself.

The two ill-fated lovers flee their village in the Pyrenees and hide in the city of Burgos. Barely able to survive on the small salary Pierre earns from an insurance company, they are tortured with remorse as they think of Paul and the children. Their love and mutual compassion bind them closer and closer together as they stoically accept the consequences of their action. Then Françoise becomes gravely ill and undergoes surgery. As Pierre prays for her recovery, Paul sends a letter pardoning her transgressions. He has learned of his wife's and friend's agony, and pity has tempered his anger. He welcomes back his "lost lamb" with tenderness.

The action of Jammes's play is entirely internal and lends itself to a musical setting that is totally lyrical. The twentieth century has witnessed something of a rebellion against lyricism, specifically against the specters of Puccini and Leoncavallo. But why, really, are those composers classified as "lyrical"? The hallmark of the verismo school, whatever its virtues, is a superficial kind of emotionalism, not intended to penetrate profoundly either mind or heart. True lyricism is quite different. It probes deeply into the innermost souls of people and things. When Jammes mentions a cup, an agricultural machine, or a timetable, it is not the things themselves that have importance. Rather, it is the drama of life surrounding them that impregnates them with significance. The blue cup is an embodiment of Pierre's deep feelings; the throbbing of the reaper in the field and the dog-eared pages of the timetable are extensions of the intensity of his emotion.

As for the music of *La brebis*, is it not truly remarkable that an eighteen-year-old could have grasped the emotional essence of the play, to say nothing of the fact that he was able to transcribe it into sound? The expressiveness of the music is maintained throughout the entire two-and-a-half-hour score; sometimes it rises to a degree of exceptional intensity, for example at the moment of Pierre's prayer or in the scene in which Françoise reads her husband's letter. It is also important to place this music in its historical setting. In the period 1910–1914, what contemporaries would have influenced a young composer like Milhaud? Mainly Debussy and Stravinsky. Yet in none of Milhaud's works are there more than a few minor traces of Stravinsky's influence, though Debussy's mark can be seen in his early compositions, mainly in certain songs and in *La brebis*. Even so, borrowings are limited to some vocal inflections and the occasional use of ninth chords; in no way could one characterize the style as "Debussyesque." The elder composer's influence is external to the same degree that the compelling example of *Boris Godunov* is accessory to the composition of *Pelléas et Mélisande*. *Pelléas* may have served as a sort of springboard for *La brebis,* but the messages conveyed by the two works differ as greatly as do those conveyed by *Boris* and *Pelléas*. Debussy plucks all possible diverse sentiments from human experience, illuminates every degree of feeling, and with the insight of a genius weaves these emotional strands into a total psychological fabric. Milhaud brands with a hot iron. He probes deeply. Tenaciously and unremittingly, he examines every sentiment. The entire score is permeated by one dominant emotion, that of sadness, and all the other attitudes of pity, resignation, kindness, and immense tenderness serve to illuminate the central theme.

In terms of basic style, too, the composer is as far removed from Debussy as he is from Wagner, and his musical language is as fresh and individual as is its emotional impact. A perusal of the score immediately reveals the main elements: numerous broad melodies interwoven with ease and clarity, each line maintaining a kind of grand, unadorned simplicity; full, rich, but unencumbered sonorities; openly spaced chords and harmonies based on superimposition of fourths; and finally, the very low, massive bass lines that are generally characteristic of this period in the composer's life and that can be noted especially in his *Poèmes de Claudel*. Also apparent is a typical rhythmic independence of the musical line from the syllabic organization of the words. The declamation is arranged in groups of eighth notes, triplets, and sixteenth notes, the regularity of which confers a sort of solemnity, a fatalistic grandeur, on even the most excited phrases.

The very first measures presage the entire expressive tone of the opera. It starts off with a broad, serene downward sweep of sound, like the descent of an immense, four-octave staircase, with the notes of the E scale as steps. It is impossible to determine which mode predominates, so mobile are the intervallic connections, which also intertwine with a subtly introduced melodic line against a background of harmonies that imply constant modulation. Thus, a simple scale, in which each note plays its own special role, acquires infinite expressiveness.

Against this orchestral background the narration, in three female voice parts, sets the stage for the first scene. Even the stage directions are blended into the music. These voices reappear in each interval between scenes and communicate the poet's and composer's feelings of sympathy for the personages of the drama. The brevity of these commentaries is more than compensated for by their harmonic subtlety; in fact, with their gentle discretion, even at moments of dramatic tension, they emerge as perhaps the most quintessentially expressive parts of the opera.

It is by studying the opening part of this first stage work that one realizes how surely and directly Milhaud embarked on his life's work. The drama begins with the sounding of the first note, and there is no let-up until the narration that precedes Pierre's entrance (Ex. 6–1).

Ex. 6–1.

This is music that follows no particular operatic convention but speaks simply and naturally to the specific dramatic situation. The opening melody permeates the entire scene; it encompasses the meditations of Pierre and the enthusiasm of Françoise; it is tenderly insinuated into the delightful scene in which the two exchange recollections of childhood, and it murmurs mysteriously while the narration tells us that the sound of a kiss has broken the silence. The flow of the music is like the passage of time, at once inexorable and flexible. Then, suddenly, there is an outburst like a thunderclap, and all Pierre's hesitations are over-come as the music leaps, gasps, and surges forward in one powerful, unequivocal thrust. The simple candor of the first scene is swept away.

The music of the Burgos scene is full of painful, obsessive emotion. In their miserable little upper-story room, Pierre sings (Ex. 6–2).

Ex. 6–2.

Objects and noises become so much part of the drama that even mem-ories of these things become inseparable from it. By association, the most commonplace street song, "Timelo Pamela," assumes a signifi-cance quite beyond its intrinsic worth. It becomes an actor. However, even as the drama becomes more intense and painful, the vocal line maintains its gentleness and intimacy. What unforgettable passages describe the Burgos cathedral, as well as Pierre's vigil at the hospital, "room number four, bed fifteen"! The music continues its quiet rock-ing back and forth, indifferent to the emotional turmoil, placing its trust in the intrinsic goodness of those who have been caught up in a web of human error, even smiling inwardly as it foresees the eventual peace of mind that these tortured souls will find.

Then comes the long, magnificent prayer, in which Pierre humbly begs for God's assistance, and the arrival of Paul's letter, which Françoise reads aloud. These two scenes are the culminating points of the opera. Both are utterly simple, but the tone of Pierre's pleas is impassioned, whereas the music that accompanies the letter already presages Françoise's return home and all the thousand tokens of affection that will comfort her after her sufferings and desolation. The scent of lavender is already in the air. How can one choose musical examples to illustrate the beauty of the score? One would have to cite whole pages.

The third act ends with a return to the fresh, calm, musical ambience of the opening scene. The children await their mother's return. A harsh little symphonic interlude seems to scan the horizon; then there is a glimpse of the deserted little train station to which Françoise returns, and the music ends on a final note of tenderness.

*　　*　　*

La brebis égarée was first performed at the Opéra-Comique in 1923. Albert Carré, who had created *Pelléas,* recognized the opera's importance and made sure that it received a first-rate interpretation. Not only did he choose excellent singers, who were completely caught up in the spirit of the work, but he staged it with great imagination. At Milhaud's suggestion, the costuming was contemporary, which made the story seem like a parable for all seasons. To the rear of the stage the women who sang the narration controlled a curtain that opened and closed on a second, miniature stage. Against this backdrop a series of miniature tableaux duplicated the main scenarios, giving postcard views, as it were, of the action. This was an extremely effective device.

In the loges the response was utterly rude, and the press joined in the attack with a barrage of stupidly violent critiques, taking the Opéra-Comique to task for presenting the work of a young upstart. Carré stood his ground, and Maestro Wolff, who conducted, shouted to the public: "Come back tomorrow and hear Mignon." Pandemonium reigned. But the next day, in *Ecrits sur la Musique,* Paul Dukas wrote with a certain perspicacity of the controversial first performance:

The basic material of this work is as simple, banal, and barren as it could possibly be, and most likely it is this way on purpose. Apparently the reason is to make vivid the utter contrast between the radiant souls of the protagonists and the miserable platitude of their lives.

Emphasizing the disparity between text and music, he concluded:

Nevertheless, the two elements are expressively unified at those moments where the poetry intensifies and the dramatic situation reaches a climax—for example, in the scene in which Pierre prays in church and in the one in which Françoise, in her hospital bed, reads the long, forgiving letter from Paul. These two scenes are the culminating points of the score as well as of the play.

They are the ones that also made the strongest and deepest impression on the public. They reveal that M. Darius Milhaud has that true sense of theater that can get from a public more or less what he wants, all theory aside; and it was these passages that won over to his cause an audience that started out by being antagonistic to the very same strange and unfamiliar sounds that they ended by applauding.

Another composer who reacted favorably to the opera was Ernst Křenek. His resounding praise appeared in the Viennese publication *Anbruch*. Milhaud himself wrote: "This music really came from my heart, so what does it matter if the harmonies and orchestration are far removed from what I write and like today and, with luck, will probably hate tomorrow!"

Protée

Milhaud described the genesis of *Protée* in his *Etudes* (p. 30).

About this time (1913) Claudel had just finished his satiric play *Protée,* a marvellous mixture of energy and poetry, romance and sheer buffoonery. I found this unique dramatic formula extremely tempting and immediately set out to compose some choruses and instrumental sections. Altogether I wrote three versions of the score. The 1913 version included choral and orchestral settings; the 1916 version was for chorus and small orchestra, with some extra fanfares to accompany "the seals' banquet" in case it would ever be performed in a circus, with the orchestra placed high up. Finally in 1919 I wrote the score in its definitive form, for chorus and full orchestra, including overtures, interludes, and music to accompany a film which Claudel conceived as an ending to the first act.

The scene opens on a large expanse of linoleum, representing the sea, out of which arises an island on which Proteus sits enthroned in his bathtub, surrounded by his retinue of seals, while being teased by the nymph Brindosier and her satyrs led by a satyr majordomo. It is on this island that Menelaus lands, bringing Helen with him. Gods and heroes are treated cavalierly in this satiric drama in which gaiety, dreams, imagination, and grace dance rings around the stupidity of Menelaus and lovely Helen's conceit. There is no action for the music to follow. Its mood transforms the linoleum into a vast ocean with all its watery characteristics. The little choruses of bleating satyrs rock back and forth on the waves like skiffs at anchor, while the seals' fanfare tosses frothy foam into the air. In the overture, the oboe starts a saucy tune in the Lydian mode against a choppy rhythmic figure that suggests the sound of wavelets constantly lapping against the shore of little inlets. The melody trips along merrily, buoyed up by that perpetual motion characteristic of even the calmest ocean waters (Ex. 6–3).

Ex. 6–3.

Now, from every point on the horizon come strands of music which crisscross, protrude, rise, and fall until three trumpets superimpose their ringing, bell-like notes. Then everything calms down. The polyphonic texture blurs, and the overture ends, as if with a tired sigh, on a harmonic cadence above which linger visions of the sparkling sunlight, water, and clouds that the music has evoked (Ex. 6–4).

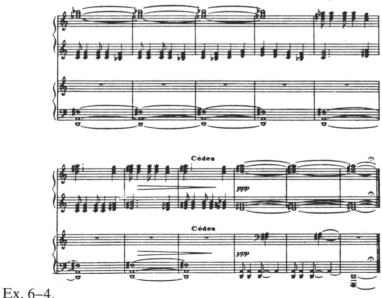

Ex. 6–4.

These beautiful last measures illustrate the suppleness and adaptability of the polyphony and the ease with which all the independent lines blend into a whole within the space of a few beats.

Note the next detail: the powerful, lively ocean is calmed by the conchshells blown by plump-cheeked Tritons. First we are caught up in a frenetic, triple-meter prelude, and then, when our ears are totally saturated with this rhythm, and without disturbing its continuity, the contrabasses begin a rumbling ostinato figure. As these two elements together develop elasticity of movement, they become a kind of trampoline from which spring nine consecutive entrances of a bouncing fugue, loudly proclaimed by trumpets and trombones. There are visions of dancing dolphins and flapping seals. The listener is also tossed aloft with the wind and the spray, as though a great tail had thumped the water. What a spectacle of youth, energy, and delight! The gods themselves are laughing.

Listen also to the Pastorale. Flowers strewn on the sea are being carried away from shore by a fast tide. Is it not a wonderful melody (Ex. 6–5) that balances between two waves as it slides over the smooth, glistening, pristine surface of the water?

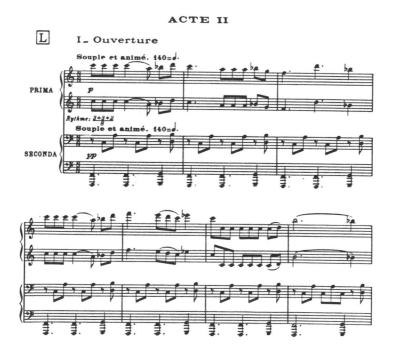

Ex. 6–5.

Eventually it tires of its course, spreads out, and, instead of struggling against the tide, allows the current to carry it toward an F-major goal, gradually overcoming the resistance of B-natural.

Next, the serene melody of the Bacchanale-Nocturne unfolds against a steady rocking motion in $\frac{5}{8}$ meter. On and on it goes, without stopping or repeating itself, dropping away finally on an E-major scale that, like a shooting star, falls into oblivion. This is all pure poetry, and the poetry becomes music.

The section entitled Cinéma is the only part unrelated to the scenic background. It depicts the metamorphoses of Proteus. Written in rondo form, it is full of grotesque motifs, good-humored in a noisy, unruly sort of way. Poseidon appears to be plunging his trident into the sea to provoke a merry disorder for his own divine amusement.

The play ends with two choruses. They accompany the departure of Menelaus, who has decided to take Brindosier with him and leave Helen with Proteus. As the sails are trimmed and the anchor is raised, the sailors' chorus sings: "Where are we going?" "To France!" "To Beaune, my friends . . ." The satyrs clap their hands and dance about like a bunch of young recruits going home on leave. They sing a rowdy kind of popular song, which blends grotesquely with the "heave hos" of the crew. The effect is incredibly droll, but all the while there is an undercurrent of noble sublimity in the music. At the end, the island rises up to the heavens with Helen still on it; the ship sails off and the sound of the chorus grows dimmer, leaving only the sound of the oars pulling against the waves. Proteus, left alone, prepares to dive down to his submarine palace.

In summary, the whole work is a synthesis, undisturbed by distracting details of story telling. It is a total portrait of the sea, and one's eyes, ears, mouth, and nostrils are filled with a salty memory as the sound dies away and one stands once again on terra firma.

*   *   *

The symphonic suite based on *Protée* was played at the Concerts Colonne in 1921 under the direction of Gabriel Pierné. By the time the overture was finished, the audience was already in a state of shock; after the fugue it was necessary to evacuate the loges and the balcony, so great was the furor. Pierné, who was unable to continue on account of the uproar, remonstrated with the public, explaining that if a work had been chosen to appear on one of his programs, it was because it deserved to be there. He responded to the demonstration by saying: "So be it; we'll start all over again on Sunday." To which the audience shouted suggestions relegating the performance to mental institutions: "Go to Charenton, go to Vincennes!"

L'homme et son désir

Is it Musset who wrote the words that persist in my memory: "The pulsation of blood in the arteries is a strange sort of clock that ticks loudly only at night. It is during those hours that man is truly alone with himself, abandoned by all external influences. Literally, he hears himself living." These words are a perfect counterpart to the music of *L'homme et son désir.* The gentle beating of the bass drum at the beginning and end of the work, coming out of nowhere and receding into silence, is exactly like the pulsation of the bloodstream that makes our physical life manifest.

First, let Milhaud tell his own story (*Etudes,* pp. 32–33).

In 1917 Claudel was appointed French ambassador to Brazil and took me along as his secretary. We passed two years in that marvellous country, surrounded by the experience of the tropical forest. It was during this period that we conceived our ballet *L'homme et son désir.* The Ballet Russes came to Rio for a performance, and Nijinsky, though nearing the end of his career, was still dancing with them. It was with him in mind that Claudel wrote his so-called "poème plastique." Working together toward the final realization of this work afforded us some of the happiest moments in all our years of collaboration. Isolated from most of the rest of the world, for even letters from Europe took a month to reach us, we had time to enjoy the gentle unfolding of the ballet as though it were a kind of beloved plaything. While I wrote my score, Claudel worked out the smallest details of the choreography with our friend Audrey Parr, who designed the décor according to his instructions. She had a delightful home at Petropolis, to which we journeyed on weekends to escape the tropical summer heat. There she constructed a table model of a theater, divided into three horizontal levels representing three levels of dramatic consciousness. On top were the Hours, the Moon, and the Clouds. The middle level presented the main drama, the interaction of Man and Forest, the elements of night and dreams, of memory and love. Below it was the reflection of Moon and Clouds. We cut out figures representing the participants from colored paper, each 15 centimeters high, and with them we worked out the staging. The work was performed in 1921 in Paris by the Ballets Suédois, then in Vienna and by the Ecole de Hellerau in Dresden, and many times since.

What a première that was! As the performance progressed, the audience drowned out the sound of the music with catcalls and guffaws reminiscent of those that greeted Stravinsky's *Sacre du printemps.* In fact, it was the same kind of reaction accorded to *La brebis égarée,* the *Sérénade,* and the *Protée* suite, when fighting actually broke out and the hall had to be evacuated. Actually, it became rather fashionable to create a scandal any time a new Milhaud work was performed.

It is hard to understand the strange antics of Paris audiences. They listen with one ear and look with one eye, while the other ear and eye are watching the reactions of their neighbors. They then leave the hall quite convinced that they have thoroughly understood the work just performed and are entirely competent to pass judgment on it. Even musicians and music critics are influenced by the public's reaction. There is nothing more misleading than to attend a dress rehearsal in Paris. All those who attend look as solemn as if they were at a funeral, and when they leave, their faces wear an expression of utter smugness. Then when the real première takes place and the public replaces the inner circle, the cards are stacked differently. On the occasion of that first performance of *L'homme et son désir* Milhaud's friends joined in offering condolences for what they considered a misguided effort at picturesque exoticism. But by the time the work was given for the third time, audiences began to listen a little more attentively and quietly, and eventually it won its way and was appreciatively received all over the world.

Do we know what a man is capable of when his inner life is dominated by a clear, sharp vision, when he alone can perceive the course to follow, and when no material or technical impediments stand in the way of fulfilling his dream? He stands isolated in the middle of the universe, and his art takes on a form that has never existed before and never will again. He is El Greco's *Dream of Philip II* or that long row of saints in Toledo Cathedral, works that are unique in their combination of perfectly equilibriated form, color, and light and in their spiritual revelation. Or he is Goya toward the end of his career, surrounding himself with those great brown canvasses that have continuously baffled historians and critics and that confront us with all the weightless, faceless spirits of terror and agony that hover in the atmosphere.

L'homme et son désir is another example of this kind of uniqueness. The composer has received a message that only his ears can hear and has unerringly translated it into his own special tonal language. The melodic lines seem to stream toward the listener simultaneously, like the purest rays of light coming from the far reaches of the universe. The music is a vast, mysterious shimmer, like the continuous twinkling of starlight, combined with sounds that rise upward from the earth toward the enormous dome of the firmament. These manifestations, these sounds, cross and recross continuously, forming an instrumental texture that is as much in a class by itself as are the visual compositions of El Greco. The texture is a combination of several solo instruments, including a piccolo, oboe, clarinet, trumpet, two string quartets, a bass, and a harp with a vocal quartet forming one group, and a percussion ensemble with drums of all shapes and sizes, cymbals, rattles, a triangle, a whistle, castanets, whips, and a hammer making up another.

Following the initial pulsating drumbeat, the sound becomes luminescent. Rising and falling scales are set against a background of soft arpeggios. Other lines of melody enter and fade away. Some become prominent for a moment and then subside. Here and there a motive seems to catch fire but is then extinguished by another exploding phrase. Finally, the voices move together in all registers, fusing the differentiated timbres of the various instruments and the voices (Ex. 6–6).

Ex. 6–6.

Now, a few melodies become disentangled from the mass, and some earth noises slide in and out among them. The wordless chorus sketches a gentle, plaintive theme. Then the Man appears, "sleeping while he stands, oscillating slightly as though he were waterborn, weightless." A few vibrant, nostalgic melodies, similar to so many of those that drift in the South American atmosphere, bring us the perfume of tropical forests. Then "the creatures of the forest come to look at the sleeping Man." The fixed-pitch instruments gradually fall silent and only one melodic line leads to a passage in the percussion section, which contrasts in every possible rhythmic and coloristic way with the preceding musical material. There is scraping, stamping, gnawing, and whistling, with an occasional reference to the gentle, nostalgic motive that represents the Man, but which is quickly swallowed up in the general clamor. As the soul of Man fills with passion, there is a "desperate, compelling, back-and-forth movement like that of a wild animal pacing in its cage."

All this emotion is finally gathered up into one immense pedal point on C-sharp, which persists through eighty measures, like the earth turning on its axis. This axis serves as a kind of musical gear to generate an ostinato figure, which, in turn, strikes against a mass of sonorities that emit showers of glittering sparks of sound (Ex. 6–7).

VI. Danse de la passion. Un mouvement de va-et-vient de plus en plus ardent et désespéré, comme l'animal qui rencontre la paroi et revient sans cesse à la même place. Peut être sans que les pieds changent de place. Toute espèce de modalités possibles. Par exemple au lieu d'un obstacle on peut imaginer parfois une odeur si délicieuse qu'elle lui ôte tout sentiment. Ou une main qui vient le chercher et qui le ramène en arrière. Puis l'idée fixe et le mouvement de désir désespéré recommence.

Ex. 6–7.

Finally the passion is consumed, the musical gyrations wind down and the C-sharp pedal point resolves to C-natural. At this moment the woman reappears and leads the Man away with her, always "at a distance marked by her outstretched arm." The music expressing intangible celestial radiance is reintroduced, and at the same time a melodic phrase mourning the impossibility of complete happiness is introduced above a new ostinato bass figure (Ex. 6–8).

Ex. 6–8.

Here is polytonality in its most unfettered form, clear, transparent, instrumentally articulated. The stage is empty. Far away in the forest a single voice arises above low, distant rumblings. It is a desperate call of farewell, but it bespeaks an age-old resignation.

VIII. La Lune I a disparu la première, la Lune II disparaît à son tour. Les heures noires se sont écoulées.

(Ex. 6–9).

Even that voice is stilled, and nothing is left but an echo, then silence.

Le boeuf sur le toit

There is a Brazilian popular song called "O boi no telhado." With tunes and rhythms similar to those of this song in mind, Milhaud composed a rondo originally intended to accompany a Charlie Chaplin film. It was to be a twenty-minute musical complement to the great Charlie with his bamboo cane, his baggy pants and oversized shoes, his strange little skips, and most of all his perpetual frenzy of motion that so poignantly portrays bewilderment and frustration. The score of *Le boeuf sur le toit* shows the same kind of frenzy that goes nowhere. The brash music-hall sonorities and the raw polyphony never relax. Fast tangos alternate with roughly strummed maxixes. The music keeps up a constant yapping as it strains vainly at the leash.

I do not know whether the score was ever actually used in conjunction with either of the films for which it was conceived. Milhaud gave it its definitive title when it was first presented at the Champs-Elysées theater in 1920, during that fascinating period when the musical antics of Les Six had put all Paris into a state of shock. Cocteau staged it as a pantomime for acrobats and clowns. The outrageous action was performed in slow motion, like a dream sequence, while the music, in complete contrast, rushed full speed ahead. Fauconnet designed marvellous masks; after his death, Raoul Dufy took over his job, finishing not only the design of the costumes, but the painting of the décor as well. The pantomime was entrusted to that wonderful family of clowns the Fratellini, whose childlike sense of wonder seemed to transform the whole world into one great, magical plaything.

I shall never forget one day when the three brothers, Paul, François, and Albert, had some time off from a performance they were doing at the Palais de Cristal in Marseilles. We met them at the station in Aix and then accompanied these incredible individuals as they wafted down the Cours Mirabeau. Suddenly, the attention of every denizen of the street was riveted on them, not due to any special effort on their part to get attention, but because they were so deeply immersed in their world of fantasy that they drew others into it. When they arrived at L'Enclos, they emptied their pockets of all sorts of toys and trinkets. Then they cavorted into the garden, squealing with delight as they discovered fruit that was not displayed in neat boxes under the glare of electric lights, and as they found that if one squeezed these beautiful pieces of fruit in a certain way, they would jump up like frogs.

For a long time, painters, writers, and composers made special trips to the circus to see these superb performers, who inspired many an artist. In turn, the Fratellini were influenced by some of the painters. Their interpretation of one of the scenes in *Le boeuf sur le toit* was in every way similar to the shadings, the pure line, and the rhythmic discipline of a Picasso work.

The performance at the Champs-Elysées theater proved to be an especially fortuitous collaboration. What remains from it today is the exuberant music, Cocteau's writing, Dufy's sketches, and also, in Milhaud's *Etudes,* a marvellous description of the Fratellini performing their outrageous skit *Miousic* at the Medrano Circus.

At first considered an amusing trifle, *Le boeuf sur le toit* has taken its place as one of Milhaud's most frequently performed and recorded orchestral works.

La création du monde

During a concert and lecture tour of the United States, Milhaud stopped off in New York and, while there, spent several evenings in Harlem. Jazz was not yet well known in Europe, and in New York it was looked down on as a form of entertainment suitable only for Blacks. But Milhaud immediately sensed that jazz expressed the deepest, truest emotion of the Black soul. He writes about his experiences with this art form in that chapter of his *Etudes* entitled "The evolution of the jazz band and Negro music in North America."

Eventually jazz took Europe by storm. Symphonic jazz proliferated based on so-called typical rhythms. But most of the music stemming from this influence was ephemeral. It died out quickly, because it was only superficially related to the real meaning of jazz. Only Stravinsky and Milhaud were able to use these new resources in such a way as to give rise to great works of art. Stravinsky concentrated on the rhythmic possibilities of the music, whereas Milhaud was attracted more to its "inner voice," especially the expressive potential of its instrumentation, in particular the eloquent use of percussion.

Excerpts from the above-mentioned chapter of his *Etudes* help us to follow the genesis of *La création du monde:*

Their primitive African heritage still remains deeply anchored in the souls of American Negroes, and therein lies the source of their formidable sense of rhythm as well as their profoundly moving gift for a kind of melody that only people who have been long oppressed know how to utter. The first examples of Negro music were spirituals, religious songs sung by slaves and based on popular tradition. These songs have the same sort of melodies as are found in, for example, W. C. Handy's "Saint-Louis Blues". . . . All have the same tenderness, sadness, and profession of faith as do songs like "Go Down Moses," in which the slaves compared their fate to that of the Jews in bondage in Egypt and cried out to Moses to save them.

Such reflections by Milhaud already indicate that his use of jazz elements in *La création du monde* was anything but superficial. But let us continue to read what he says about his choice of instruments:

In addition to their dance music, with its unique improvisational quality, the Blacks also adapt jazz to theatrical spectacle in a most felicitous manner. . . . In *Liza,* an operetta by Mr. Maceo Pinkard, the orchestra consists of a flute, a clarinet, two trumpets, a trombone, an assortment of percussion instruments all handled by one player, a piano, a string quartet in which the viola is replaced by a saxophone, and a double bass. . . . Moreover, Black jazz is far removed from the slick sophistication of so much contemporary American dance music. It never loses its primitive African character; the intensity and repetitiousness of the rhythms and melodies produce a tragic, desperate effect. And it is this capacity to arouse deep emotions in its listeners that puts it in the same category as the greatest works of art.

Once again, Milhaud's train of thought is consistent. Whether in Brazil, Africa, the France of Jammes or Claudel, or in the artistry of Charlie Chaplin, he always recognizes the same quality of expressiveness. He never wavers, and he is able to extract from all his experiences that single unifying element that binds them together. This is the true meaning of assimilation. He who truly assimilates is unable to be merely an imitator. To assimilate is to create; an experience must be so thoroughly absorbed that it can be transmuted into something that reflects the artist's own vision.

It was the Ballets Suédois of Rolf de Maré, the same company that produced *L'homme et son désir,* that added *La création du monde* to its repertory. The première took place on 25 October 1923. For the scenario, the writer Blaise Cendrars had chosen themes of the creation from African folklore. Fernand Léger designed scenery and costumes accordingly. The whole spectacle reflected a kind of typical primitive temperament, imaginative, guileless, confiding, and gentle, but robust. This concept of the creation of the world is peaceable rather than cataclysmic. First, the incantations of the gods evoke a harmonious assemblage of plants and animals. Then night turns into day, and a Man and a Woman appear. They become aware of each other for the first time and gradually begin their dance. Alone on this new earth, they perform a dance first of desire and then of fulfillment. Earth is aroused as this supreme moment arrives; then, assured of its future, all becomes peaceful again. The birds, still agitated, begin to try their wings. It is the beginning of spring.

With his generous nature and poetic sensibilities, Cendrars seemed particularly capable of probing the depths of the Black soul and incorporating its spirit into his script. Léger's décor and costumes stressed the themes of ardor and harmony without any trace of violence, and his staging consisted of simple planes and solids. Masterful lighting effects sharpened the rigid masques and costumes of the gods, emphasizing their absolute supremacy. By contrast, the Man and the Woman seemed small and vulnerable, almost lost in the awesomeness and solemnity of their immense, shadowy surroundings. The austerity of the scene was immensely effective.

As for the score, it is certainly among Milhaud's finest. It is charged with emotion from the first to the last note. Every page is full of ardor, yet the form is perfect. A feeling of gentle agitation, a sort of springtime ebullience, underlies the entire work. The syncopated style is directly inspired by African rhythms; but Milhaud, by a stroke of genius, has transported jazz to an entirely different level of expressiveness. Elements of ragtime and the blues become solemn and imposing. One can draw a parallel with the way in which Bach transformed the minuet from a simple dance to a distinguished musical form. Milhaud's music contains an entire range of emotion, from utter peacefulness to frenetic passion; yet nowhere is there any sense of human fear in response to nature's mysteries. For the African, nature is a luxurious, nurturing forest, not a desert.

The orchestration borrows heavily from jazz precedents, but the instruments are used quite differently. For example, instead of short, agitated notes, the most serene and beautiful melodies are given to the saxophone. They flow like great, slow rivers and are far more Handelian than African. The enormously colorful percussion section forms an integrally expressive part of the texture and provides a constantly pulsating support for the melodies, like an undercurrent of tender, suppressed desire. The combination of piano and percussion gives a kind of brassy, menacing timbre to the bass lines, which is further emphasized by the slide trombone. These are the characteristics of the overture, which, instead of introducing polytonality, begins with a kind of oscillation between major and minor (Ex. 6–10).

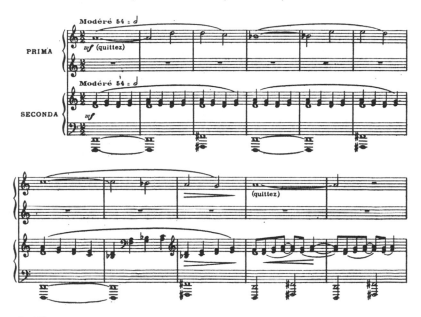

Ex. 6–10.

After the quiet ending of the overture comes the beginning of the fugue, already described in chapter V. Its choppy theme shakes up the orchestra and makes the entire texture appear to vibrate above the powerful beat of the piano and the characteristic jazz rhythms contributed by the percussion instruments. Someone has described the orchestral sound as a hailstorm. It is a good description (Ex. 6–11).

Ex. 6–11.

The fugue ends with a reference to the overture. It is followed by a simple, gentle blues melody, which welcomes the arrival of the plants and animals. Their very rhythmic dance is accompanied by a capriccio for two violins, punctuated by the sharp interjections of trumpets, the beating of a gong, and cascades of notes in the piano. Then the capriccio relaxes and is joined by the tender melody that preceded it, for now the Man and Woman appear (Ex. 6–12).

Ex. 6–12.

The dance of desire is a concertino for clarinet. Its sparkling melody is underscored by rhythmic figures in the piano and percussion parts that are derived from the countersubject of the fugue. It comes to rest at last on the theme of the overture. Then the dance of fulfillment engenders a prodigious burst of sound, with the concertino theme superimposed on the fugue, creating a veritable rhythmic tempest. This is another example of music that seems to come from all directions at once, though the spirit is completely different from comparable places in *L'homme et son désir*. It sounds as though all the bells in the world were ringing at Eastertime, yet not a single bell is used in the orchestration (Ex. 6–13).

Ex. 6–13.

Cendrar's script ends with the words:

The couple is joined.
The dance subsides, is slowed and restrained, everything grows calm.
Group by group, the dancers disperse, and the couple, locked in an embrace,
    drifts offstage as if borne by a wave.
It is spring.

The saxophone re-enters, recalling the calm mood of the overture, and then something marvellous happens: in a space of seven measures, the wind instruments sweep all the sound together in a tongued tremolo. It is an incredibly beautiful effect, as though the whole orchestra were taking flight like a flock of sparrows. The saxophone has the last word—not really, though, for it leaves one appoggiatura unresolved. The drama continues (Ex. 6–14).

Ex. 6–14.

Salade and *Le train bleu*

The year 1924 was a vintage year for French music. The "young composers" of 1919 had become a force to be reckoned with; Diaghilev's collaboration with some of the leading painters of the day added luster to the world of ballet; and some young musicians, notably the composer Sauguet and the conductor Desormière, both identified with the Ecole d'Arcueil, were beginning to play important roles. Of course, not all was smooth sailing. The immensely popular Olympic Games threatened to draw attention away from the world of art, and, regrettably, there were a number of troubling personality conflicts: Satie had a falling-out with Poulenc and Auric; Massine broke with Diaghilev.

But, as usual, Paris surmounted all obstacles. Diaghilev put on a magnificent season, which, with the exception of Stravinsky, presented exclusively French composers. Satie, Cocteau, and Picasso collaborated on *Parade,* Poulenc and Marie Laurencin on *Les biches,* and Georges Auric and Braque on *Les fâcheux; Le train bleu* was put together by Milhaud, Cocteau, and Laurens. Included also were revivals of Gounod's *Le médecin malgré lui* and Chabrier's *L'éducation manquée* with accompaniments for the old Opéra-Comique recitatives rewritten by Satie and Milhaud, respectively. Similarly, Poulenc made musical settings for the prose dialogues of Gounod's *La colombe.*

As was to be predicted, this showcase for young French talent incurred the wrath of the august musicians in the Institut de France. Indignation over the audacity of these upstarts who dared to tamper with the charm of Gounod and the truculence of Chabrier increased when Messager agreed to conduct the whole season. Satie's letter, written after he had read one of my articles on this subject, indicates the heat of the debate.

Dear, good friend: You did well to send me the two copies of *Arts et Lettres*. I gave one to Diaghilev, who read your article while I was present. Indeed, he took it with him to show to the Gounods, who are bellyaching and who want to stir up a lot of trouble (there's a lot of M . . . and R. H. . . . in all of this). Indeed, we'll give it to them, those two bums. Indeed, *Parade* went very well at the Opéra (Koussevitzky). The philistines digested it pretty well, except for Vuill . . . who is still "lost" when it comes to this good old work (seven years old already)! Your other article (the preceding one) is also superb. I beg you, continue. Rip the hide off those stubborn old mules.

Stormy times—but exciting ones! At the "Cigale" on Boulevard de Rochechouart, Count Etienne de Beaumont organized an equally brilliant series called Les Soirées de Paris. In borrowing this appellation from a journal recently founded by Guillaume Apollinaire, Count de Beaumont was appealing to a favorite Parisian theme: the catholicity of all the arts. In rapid succession he presented plays, ballets, music-hall revues, symposia, and poetry readings. The amazing array of creative talent included Cocteau, Shakespeare, Tristan Tzara, Paul Morand, Jean and Valentine Victor-Hugo, Picasso, Derain, Braque, Milhaud, Sauguet, Johann Strauss, Satie, and Marie Laurencin. Roger Desormière took a firm hand with the orchestra, which responded with almost military precision; Marcel Herrand, Andrée Pascal, and that universal man Jean Cocteau were among the performers. Loïe Fuller added the excitement of her beautiful lighting effects, and Massine, Idzikovsky, and Lopokova were key members of an enthusiastic group of dancers.

Beauty and talent blended in an overall atmosphere of elegant nonchalance that was half music-hall, half salon. The populace and the cultural aristocrats joined together in sharing a glass of wine and the enjoyment of this refreshingly spontaneous artistic banquet. Only in France could the two musicians that Picasso painted on the dimly lit curtain have surveyed so diverse but harmonious a gathering.

One work presented at Les Soirées de Paris was the beautiful ballet *Mercure* created by Satie and Picasso. On opening night it was greeted by boos from a group of young people who, at the instigation of the surrealists Aragon and Breton, had a great time shouting: "Long live Picasso; down with Satie!" The same season included the first performance of Stravinsky's piano concerto and some of Sauguet's earliest successes, including the opera buffa *Le plumet du colonel,* staged by Mme. Bériza.

It was also a vintage year for Milhaud. Two commissions fell into his lap simultaneously: *Le train bleu,* commissioned by Diaghilev, and *Salade,* a "ballet chanté" based on themes from the commedia dell'arte that the Count de Beaumont asked him to write. It was a big order, and to escape distraction, Milhaud left Paris and went to Valmont in Switzerland, where his mother happened to be visiting a health resort.

Occasional progress reports were forthcoming:

5 February 1924: I'm working like mad. The subject comes from sixteenth-century Italian comedy, so I use some melodies of that period, but not the way they were used in *Pulcinella,* at least I hope not. Some fast parlandos are accompanied by percussion. Lots of tricks. . . .

12 February: First act finished; hope to get it all done by the end of the month, and then I'll start on *Le train bleu.* That will be an operetta that is danced, rather than sung, and I'll be collaborating with Cocteau. I want to write a nonchalant, phlegmatic kind of music very much like a man-about-town who strolls along, hands in his pockets, whistling a tune and giving an occasional wink—in the style of Yvain.

16 February: The ballet for Diaghilev is going to be a riot. Music in the tradition of Offenbach, Maurice Yvain, and a real Verdi finale with nice bland harmonies and not a single syncopation. It's typically Parisian—naughty, sly, and sentimental, spiced with a little polka, galop, waltz, etc. . . . The whole thing is a little appalling, but fascinating.

Both ballets were finished by March 5. The première of *Salade* took place on May 17; *Le train bleu* was performed on June 20. Milhaud called them his "twins."

In no way could these works be called profound. Milhaud tossed them off quickly, without allowing a period of time for thoughtful preparation, as was his usual habit. *Salade* is a choreographic counterpoint in two acts with décor by Braque and choreography by Massine. The title is derived from a sixteenth-century Spanish collection (*Libro de Cifra,* by Luys Venegas de Henestrosa) that contained "ensaladas," described as clever artful mixtures of popular tunes. If Poulenc's *Les biches* can be said to mirror the spontaneous charm and grace of the Ile de France, then *Salade* is an appropriate portrait of the countries bordering the Mediterranean, where, from Genoa to Provence, all the women sing the same tunes, toss the same long, black tresses, and flash the same bright smiles. *Salade* is full of sun and good humor. Along with the original tunes are some snatches of Sardinian melodies and a song by Salvatore Rosa. One can practically hear the hooves of the herdsmen's little white horses as they trot along or leap chasms of tonality with almost maddening ease. French precision is combined with Italian nonchalance. Remember Milhaud's remark: "For me, Provence reaches all the way from Constantinople to Rio." The vivacity of this music is tinged with melancholy and often drifts off into a kind of lazy *dolce far niente* reminiscent of South America.

Salade is exuberant, but not superficial; it is typical Milhaud in the way in which it reflects the diversity of his musical gifts, joining delightful, inventive melodies with buoyant, folk-derived tunes. Four singers, seated in the orchestra, sing the dialogue, while the action is mimed by dancers onstage. The vocal lines are mostly in a high tessitura and stand out easily against the bright, glowing sound of the orchestra, so typical of the composer that it is unnecessary to read his signature at the end of the score. It's a delightful affair throughout. A special marvel is the immense parabola traced by a series of modulations that extend the conclusion of Cinzio's aria by twenty or thirty measures before finally coming to the point of repose that has been anticipated all along (Ex. 6–15).

Ex. 6–15.

Another remarkable passage, a kind of souvenir of Rio, is one that alternates between tango and maxixe dance rhythms. It is sung by the four voices to the accompaniment of a little drum, and, with its vacillating modality and swaying movement, it provides a languorous interlude before the flourish of the finale. Note also the delightful effect of the rhythmic declamation punctuated by percussion, which serves as a trampoline from which to launch the tunes into space.

Inspired by this music, Massine created a fabric of movement that was like embroidered tapestry, a sort of visual counterpoint. He himself danced the role of Punchinello with a marvellous mixture of authority, vivacity, and delicacy. In Braque's stage settings three grayish arches stood out against a faintly golden-brown backdrop.

Salade played to enthusiastic audiences throughout Central Europe. From the ballet, Milhaud extracted a few short parts and fashioned them into a suite for piano and orchestra, which he called *Le carnaval d'Aix*. *Salade* was restaged at the Paris Opéra in 1935, with choreography by Serge Lifar and wonderful stage settings by André Derain.

It was Cocteau's idea to concoct a danced operetta. However, *Le train bleu* is in no way as important a work as *Salade* and is, in fact, Milhaud's most superficial composition. Although never boring, and in some spots even amusing, it is also sometimes vulgar. It scandalized almost everybody, light-opera composers and serious musicians alike. Nonetheless, whereas most of their works are forgotten by now, Milhaud's is not!

Imagine a beach scene at one of those elegant English Channel resorts. It is a sunny day in August 1924; the sky is intensely blue, and the sand a burnt yellow. It is the time of day when the tarts and the gigolos come to swim, all beautifully tanned and decked out in fashionable swimsuits. It is a scene of utterly agreeable decadence! Games, flirtations, even minor passions, all are played out against a background of cool water and gently undulating waves. Everything is relaxed. The fellows are good-looking and the girls are cute. What more could one ask for? Let yourself go!

To project this kind of atmosphere requires great skill and impeccable good taste. Cocteau's notes read something like this:

The music has to keep moving and not get stuck on any particular detail. . . . The couple that enters the restaurant shouldn't follow the rhythm of the music exactly, but their actions should relate to it. When the curtain goes up, the performers must give the impression that they are satirizing an operetta chorus. (Don't be afraid to be a little pompous, which is quite appropriate.) There should be a beautiful sculptured relief to contrast with all the silliness. The stupidity of the story, the marble, the chic, and the fun-and-games are all part of the same package. The costumes should be really elegant and up-to-date, not just stage clothes. The date 1924 should be written on one of the fish that decorate the proscenium. *Le train bleu* is more than a frivolous work. It is a monument to frivolity!

Milhaud's music reflects this description quite aptly for the most part. A few places misfire. Emotions are skin-deep, to be sure, but suitable as far as they go. After a calm, sunny opening, reminiscent of Verdi, there is a series of French operetta numbers, typically shallow.

(Offenbach is an exception to this generalization.) Milhaud imitates the light-opera style, except that here and there he suddenly goes off in the direction of a perfectly delightful modulation, makes a little detour to include some silky tune, and ends up by creating quite a nice piece of music. Take, for example, the duet between Beau-Gosse and Per-louse: it starts in the chansonette style of Yvain and all of a sudden develops into a concerto grosso, the verses being performed by groups of solo instruments, while the refrains are taken up by the tutti. Each verse has a slightly different twist of tonality. There is also a waltz, first appearing unobtrusively in the winds, then played with full vigor by the strings. In the middle of it, the melody suddenly disappears, but the rhythmic accompaniment continues, first on the dominant, then on the tonic, and in a few moments the dance tune starts again as if it had never stopped. A door has been closed for a minute, then reopened. These are the ballet's redeeming details.

Les malheurs d'Orphée

In terms of chronology, Milhaud's next dramatic work is *L'Orestie,* completed in 1922, but we shall postpone discussion of large composi-tions like *L'Orestie* and *Christophe Colomb* that are major mileposts in his total output. Chronological order is not particularly important since, as has been noted, the tools of this composer's craft varied very little after about 1910. The second string quartet, composed between 1914 and 1919, relies on basically the same resources as does *Esther de Carpentras,* which was written after *L'Orestie.* By contrast, Stravinsky's style constantly evolved, and his *Rossignol* could not pos-sibly have been written prior to *Le sacre du printemps.*

Les malheurs d'Orphée was written at l'Enclos between 27 Septem-ber and 2 November 1924. The subject of Eurydice's death and Orpheus's utter desolation had long occupied Milhaud's thoughts. "One day," he wrote, "walking down a deserted street in Aigues-Mortes, I passed the window of a shop that was like a dark eye staring out into emptiness, and in that window I saw among the humble collec-tion of glass beads, celluloid combs, and exaggeratedly pink soaps an oval porcelain plaque. On it were pictured two clasped hands, promi-nent against a blue background. The inscription read: To meet again. . . . Which village fisherman would eventually buy this plaque to hang over his bed . . . for which village Orpheus might it be des-tined?"

The theme lay dormant in his mind for quite a while. He wanted to devote his optimum creative talent to the realization of the work. More than an obsession, it was a kind of deep, inner necessity that impelled him toward the story of Orpheus, an urge to release part of his own soul. He talked about it constantly, eager to start writing but not quite daring to do so, for fear that the music might not be sufficiently elevated and beautiful. By 1921 he already had the overall plan in mind. In one of his letters he wrote:

I am haunted by the idea of composing an Orpheus drama. It is such a magnificent subject, but I want to make it very human. Since life is always unfulfilled, it is important that Orpheus never be reunited with Euridice and that he go on without her, despite his breaking heart, living among his friends the animals until death finally brings the lovers together. I would like to present a series of tableaux that, through the dignity of the staging and the purity of the musical texture, project a total atmosphere of grandeur. Instead of a chorus, I plan to use a vocal quartet, and in place of an orchestra, a maximum of six or seven instruments.

Milhaud's approach to his subject reflects an attitude toward drama that is typical of Mediterranean countries, where the old myths are constantly relived in everyday life. His Orpheus is not a heroic figure, but a simple fellow of the region; the story is presented with neither classical pomp nor the bantering familiarity typical of much modern theater.

Around the beginning of 1924, the musical concept took final shape in his mind. Then the scenic disposition quickly fell into place. He discussed it with his friend Armand Lunel, who wrote the excellent, well-adapted text. Lunel, the delightful author of *Noire et grise* and *L'imagerie du cordier,* was also of Jewish background, and the Lunel and Milhaud families had been friends for eight hundred years. In this part of the world friendships, like stones, bear the patina of antiquity.

The opera is in three acts and lasts no longer than forty minutes. Why call it an opera? In order to avoid the term "music drama," which had acquired too narrow a connotation during the nineteenth century. The word *opera* should imply neither a certain length nor a particular arrangement of scenes. Rather, its use should denote an element of dignity.

Milhaud's Orpheus is a kind of folk doctor, a "rebouteux" (bone setter). He lives a solitary life on the edge of the village, beyond the workshops of the wheelwright, the farrier, and the basket-maker. These three join in singing a rhythmically vigorous opening trio which describes their own lives and expresses misgivings about their neighbor: "Oh, Orpheus, your mysterious and miraculous ways have concerned us for a long time. If you were only like the rest of us who go about tending our flocks and orchards! But no, you open your stable to all the wild beasts. You give healing potions to wolves, balm to wild boars. One day they will devour you!" But Orpheus is concerned with other things. He has just dismissed his animals and is waiting for a beautiful "bee" to fly to him. This bee, his betrothed, is Eurydice, the most beautiful of four sisters who passed by a few days before in a gypsy caravan. The chorus warns him: "Beware! Have nothing to do with this race of thieves and marauders! Misfortune will come to him who takes a wife from another region."

Both young people are breaking the laws of their societies, and when she flees from the "Bohemian" encampment at Les Saintes-Maries-de-la-Mer, the other gypsies follow her along the road, baked white by the hot, pitiless glare of the sun, in order to track her down and bring her back. Moved by the predicament of the lovers, the ensemble of tradespeople urges them to hurry and seek refuge among the wild beasts who will know how to defend them. They promise to try to put the brigands off the track, by showing them only Orpheus's abandoned house.

In the next scene the lovers are at a deserted hut in a hollow of the forest. The wolf, the fox, the bear, and the boar all stand around lamenting, for Eurydice is dying, and Orpheus is powerless to save her. The two exchange their last tender words of love, which are almost more felt than spoken. At this crowning moment Eurydice says farewell: "The shades of a night with no tomorrow darken my eyes." Then she kneels like a little girl and begs the animals to take care of her husband; and like an awkward group of children, they promise. Orpheus cannot control his sorrow and pours forth his grief in a brief lamentation, while Eurydice gently expires. The animals carry off her body and then join in a raucous dirge.

Orpheus returns to the village. We see him, his head in his hands, sitting at his table surrounded by the tools of his trade. He is alone with his sorrow; not even the animals have come to visit. Suddenly he is accosted by the three sisters of Eurydice, who sing with alternating rage and desire. They accuse Orpheus of causing their sister's death and swear vengeance. For him their ferocity is a solace, for he welcomes the death that will unite him with his beloved; and when these implacable Furies advance on him with scissors, whip, and cord, he offers no resistance and stretches out his arms to receive the embrace of death that he yearns for.

Few works elude analysis as much as *Orphée*. Each section is brief, concentrated, stripped to the bone, completely devoid of development. It is as though "mere music-making" is superfluous in the face of such sorrow. Measure after measure represents a cry, a sigh, or a shiver, as though the heart were being torn out piece by piece. Each note must sound true, necessary, beautiful. This is a work of quality, rather than quantity, a concentration rather than a diffusion of sentiment. Moreover, the music must be performed as a kind of offering, a ritual prayer to console and soothe the wounded spirit. The mood is set by the beauty of the melodic line, its subtle accentuation and expressive dignity. The ensembles of artisans, of animals, and of the three sisters are all made up of soloistic parts; singers of the finest quality must be chosen for the several roles. The instrumental ensemble is a chamber group, and each instrument has an expressive role equal in importance to that of each vocal part.

The first trio of artisans has a rough, rhythmic quality reminiscent of the Pastorale in *Protée*. It plunges us immediately into the drama. Fourths and fifths burst out of the orchestra, only to be moderated by sixths and thirds in the vocal ensemble (Ex. 6–16).

Ex. 6–16.

82

The individual lines of the three male voices blend strikingly. Then comes a solo sung by Orpheus. This is a quiet, intimate section, in which a long line of melody unfolds without development or repetition. The melodies of this opera are like various kinds of flowers, some as fresh as lilies of the valley, others somber like mauve tulips. Orpheus's melodic statement collides with the remonstrances of his three friends, and the music breaks up in a series of shocks and jolts. When Eurydice runs breathlessly onto the stage, the accompaniment thrashes about like an angry sea tossing into the air the melody of her passionate declaration of love (Ex. 6–17).

Ex. 6–17.

Only the last four measures seem to smile, and the music dissolves in a delightful modulation as Eurydice throws herself into Orpheus's arms (Ex. 6–18).

83

Ex. 6–18.

Orpheus and the chorus resolve their differences, and the artisans gently urge the couple to flee. A note of anxiety slips into the conciliatory key of C major as the three voices, lightly accompanied by two tympani, pronounce: "Fuyez."

The duet between Eurydice and Orpheus is full of restrained tenderness. It is hard to describe the effect. One must really immerse oneself in the music and let it speak directly. If one savors it by playing and singing it oneself, one will learn that each passage (for instance, Ex. 6–19) is found to communicate a full measure of tenderness and also of fear.

Ex. 6–19.

The act ends with a return to the initial chorus.

In the second act the animals gather around Eurydice, bemoaning her suffering, while an E-flat clarinet traces a complex rhythm that emphasizes the poignancy of the scene. Again, Orpheus and Eurydice sing of their love. The very simplicity of their duet, with its sobbing major-minor harmonies and the prolonged *échappée* that resolves only on the final chord, communicates tragedy. Gently, as if letting go of all the complexities of life, Eurydice speaks to the animals (Ex. 6–20).

Ex. 6–20.

The last Pastorale expresses sentiments that seem to stem from the beginning of time, cleansed of all superficiality by the wind and the rain. The animals respond with a promise that is brisk and almost jovial. They accept the charge to care for Orpheus, but they cannot comprehend its full implication. Eurydice's last lines are magnificent (Ex. 6–21).

Ex. 6–21.

In all of twentieth-century music there are few more starkly beautiful moments. As she dies, Eurydice releases her soul, and the music carries her spirit into the deepest recesses of the listener's subconscious, magically and mysteriously. Then the animals burst into sobs; their funeral dirge has the same breadth and depth as that which characterizes the Orestes trilogy. Note, also, in the third act the contrast between the utterances of the three sisters, which are alternately violent, verbose, and hypocritically restrained, and the calm response of Orpheus, who already dreams of his death. Then the music becomes raucous, brutal, and discordant; this could just as well be the death scene of Orpheus being destroyed by the Furies. The opera ends with a gradual decrescendo fading into oblivion.

Les malheurs d'Orphée was first performed at the Théâtre Royal de la Monnaie in Brussels in 1925 as part of a double bill with Mozart's The Abduction from the Seraglio. It received an excellent performance. Corneil de Thoran conducted an ensemble of outstanding vocal and instrumental soloists, who put heart and soul into the production of this masterpiece. Charles Thomas and Madame Bianchini were unforgettable, as was German Prévost of the Pro Arte Quartet, whose viola, like a trumpet call, marshaled the raucous tones of the funeral dirge.

In the Nouvelles Littéraires of 2 April 1927, Maurice Ravel wrote as follows about Les malheurs d'Orphée: "This is a magnificent, expressive work, one of its author's best to date and one of the finest that our group of young composers has produced in a long time. M. Lalo seems to have looked in vain for 'something alive and palpable.' He complains that 'the movement is almost always slow'; yet I found frequent examples of vivacity, which reveal an extraordinarily inventive talent for rhythm. Also, the orchestra is always extremely well balanced."

At a lecture given in Houston, Texas, in April 1928, Ravel continued to define Milhaud's musical attributes:

Darius Milhaud is without doubt the most important of our young French composers, and his compositions frequently assert the breadth of his musical concepts. This characteristic is far more singular than the fact that he uses several tonalities simultaneously, a device that we can find employed embryonically even in the chorales of J. S. Bach and in certain works of Beethoven, and definitively developed in Richard Strauss. If we consider one of his all-time greatest compositions, *Les Choéphores,* we see very quickly that not only was Milhaud able to support a succession of grandly tragic episodes by using all the possible resources of musical composition, including polytonality, but he was also able to probe the depths of artistic conscience in a scene in which he used nothing but scanned declamation accompanied solely by percussion instruments. In this passage there is no polytonality whatsoever, and yet it is the most profoundly typical of all his music. Also important is the fact that in one of his most recent works, *Les malheurs d'Orphée,* which was just given its American première at a Pro Musica concert, the occasional use of polytonality is so intermeshed with lyrical and poetic elements that it is difficult to separate one from the other, and it is the melodic inventiveness of this work that most strikingly reveals his artistic personality.

Le pauvre matelot

Le pauvre matelot is another drama of fate. In a little street of a seaport town, a woman and her father operate a bar frequented by sailors. Her husband, a sailor, left on a voyage fifteen years ago and has never been heard from since. Everyone else thinks him dead, but she is sure he will return one day, a rich man. In spite of everything, she still loves him and has remained true to him. Her father begs her to remarry, if only for business reasons, since their bar is barely making it. "Here's a joint that's in trouble up to its ears and you talk to me like Miss Prim and Proper."

Their next-door neighbor, a former friend of the absent sailor, arrives to borrow a hammer. Hardly has he left for home when the sailor himself appears on the scene. He starts toward the house, eager to see his wife and to lay before her feet the riches he has acquired. He has learned that she has remained faithful to him in his absence. But he hesitates, fearing that he will not be recognized, and decides to go first to visit his former friend and then later to the bar, incognito, so that he can witness "his good luck."

The following evening he does just that. His wife fails to recognize him, changed as he is by the scorching sun of the tropics. He tells her that he has encountered her husband who is on his way home, but who, unfortunately, will return poor and debt-ridden. His happiness is confirmed when he hears her profess her love for her husband. "What does it matter," she says, "if he is poor? I will do everything for him; I would even kill for him." Grateful to this bearer of good news, she offers to put him up for the night so that he can have a good rest before continuing on his journey. He goes to sleep, savoring his joy. The friend who borrowed the hammer uses the excuse of returning it in order to drop in on the household and witness the touching scene. Then he leaves, and everything is quiet.

But the wife does not sleep. She muses: "This man is a stranger. . . . Everyone will believe it if I say he left before dawn. . . . I can kill him and bury him in the basement." If he is out of the way, she reasons, I can take his riches to help my dear husband when he returns. She seizes the hammer and strikes him dead. In the final scene we see her joyfully awaiting her husband's return.

This is the kind of macabre melodrama that one reads from time to time in the daily paper. Yet in the hands of such skillful artists as Cocteau and Milhaud, nothing is lacking in taste. It becomes a kind of ballad, a sea-chantey. The subject lends itself to poetic narrative. Dreadful as it is, the crime nevertheless contains that required element of tragedy which is an essential ingredient of the melancholy, fatalistic songs sung by sailors. As staged, it appears to be more a parable than an actual happening. Ballads are still sung in some parts of Europe. Wandering minstrels travel from one community to another and, accompanied by an accordion, sing about the crimes committee in neighboring villages. They even paint scenes of such catastrophes on their wagons. The words vary, but the tunes are always similar. Listeners gather in a circle and join in singing a monotonous, vaguely sentimental kind of refrain to the verses that they have paid a few pennies to hear. This is the setting for *Le pauvre matelot.*

In spite of the story, the three acts of this opera are far from macabre. Both music and poetry have a gently rocking rhythm that expresses the persistent melancholy of humble people. Realism is transposed into imagery, and the artists' perception of events is communicated more directly than the happenings themselves. Obviously, such a potentially vulgar subject had to be treated with the utmost good taste, and so it has been. The final, fatal outcome is implied at the very outset of the drama, and it is made quite clear that the sailor is inextricably caught in a web of his own fabrication. The characters of the four protagonists are sensitively sketched; they are troubled, not brutal, people. Then, at the moment of the murder, when everything seems to be asleep, there is a sudden infernal outburst of sound from the orchestra, a dizzying hullabaloo, a mass of brilliant tonal colors so hallucinatory that they seem to hypnotize the wife into taking her deadly course of action. When it is all over, only the members of the audience know that she has killed her husband. As, trembling with anticipation, she opens her arms to the man she expects to welcome, neither the composer nor the onlookers dare betray the truth. Like the friend, who once again drops by, we must believe that the sailor is only sleeping, for "after traveling around the world, one needs a good sleep."

Milhaud searched at length for the exact musical means to capture the spirit of this humble tale. He talked constantly about it and looked and listened everywhere. Little by little, as he roamed the alleys of the Vieux-Port of Marseilles and the docks of Toulon, he distilled the essence of his musical thought. In those places, at evening, the sound of clinking gold and ice drifted from the bars, the mechanical pianos projected their harsh arpeggios into the balmy air; and a myriad of waltz tunes fused into one great hymn to Venus, goddess of love. A huge dome of noise, emotion, and red light sheltered the broad shoulders and blue collars of the sailors and the coral jewelry and furs of their girl friends. Under cover of the general hubbub, evil plots were whispered of; but even more deeply hidden was the tiny blue flower of humble sentiment, kindness, and selflessness. One morning, everything came into focus. Milhaud wrote his score in thirteen days, from 26 August to 5 September 1926.

The ballad begins in $\frac{6}{8}$ meter; later a waltz is grafted onto it, but the calm, rocking motion of the music remains undisturbed. Some passages in $\frac{4}{4}$ time are added for variety. These are the total rhythmic resources. An arabesque of sailors' songs is traced against this rhythmic background, mostly monotonous, but nevertheless containing all sorts of subtle variety. They are faintly disturbing, vaguely ominous; the song of death is a lullaby. Only the wife's account of her murderous deed disturbs the general homogeneity of style; she sings with all the detachment and indifference of a nightclub singer rendering a popular tune. The charm of the whole work, in fact, is its utter simplicity. Sailors and sirens sing quite differently from gods and heroes!

The orchestra makes no comment on the action. It is content to remain in the background, sensitive and sympathetic. Its subtle harmonies gently enhance the perfume of the melody. The music of *Le pauvre matelot* is a loving offering to simple people and humble circumstances. It is not illustrative of any new facet in Milhaud's personality. The candle of its inspiration had already been lit in *La brebis égarée*.

If we dare isolate just one passage from the firt act, it is only to illustrate the simplicity of the music, bare as a plaster wall, against which is laced an espalier of successive chromaticisms. Through the night, from the top of some lonely hill, comes the sound of a solitary trumpet. The music is redolent of sorrow and of the sea (Ex. 6–22).

Ex. 6–22.

A little farther on, there is a good example of the quiet harmonies that typify this score and of the sublime melodic line of the ballad (Ex. 6–23).

Ex. 6–23.

The second act ends in a strange way, with the solo contrabassoon fading into the night while the last A-natural in the vocal line creates a feeling of anxiety. Have you ever noticed, late in the evening, while walking along a deserted waterfront, the beam from a beacon sending its alternately red and green lights out into the darkness; have you listened at the same time to the little wavelets futilely chopping away at the shoreline? That is the image captured by this particular passage (Ex. 6–24).

Ex. 6–24.

Finally, an example from the very end. The intrusion of the dominant implies the dramatic conflict: the music knows that the woman's confidence, as represented by her final notes on the tonic, is false (Ex. 6–25).

Ex. 6–25.

It is details such as these that bear witness to the perfect suitability of this music to the dramatic situation.

La pauvre matelot was first performed in 1927 at the Opéra-Comique in Paris and at the Théâtre Royale de la Monnaie in Brussels. Between 1929 and 1931 it was performed in Berlin, Stettin, Gera, Dresden, Magdeburg, Vienna, Breslau, Barcelona, and later in Leningrad and some of the main cities of Italy. By 1970 it had received 269 performances, 125 of them in France and 144 elsewhere.

Esther de Carpentras

The four or five years of intense concentration that resulted in the creation of *Les malheurs d'Orphée* was followed by a period of quiescence in Milhaud's artistic life. It is hard for most people to imagine the marshaling of forces that is required to create a great work of art. First there is a period of time devoted to inward probing, and then many hours are spent in slowly fashioning the material and constantly testing it for complete artistic validity. Stravinsky has noted: "A great artist never makes a mistake." To do so would mean being untrue to one's artistic self. Mediocrity is not caused by lack of imagination so much as by lack of true concentration. It takes an enormous amount of discipline to probe the depth and breadth of a word, a melody, a line, or a thought. That is why there is so much insignificant art. Also, the greater the concentration, the greater the pain. Creativity is impossible without pain, but once an act of creation has been completed, there is no greater feeling of joy and release. Only then are the emotions of the creator liberated so that he can receive a new impulse.

The exuberance that characterizes the opera buffa *Esther de Carpentras* is the result of this kind of artistic rebound. Its vernal ebullience is a swing in the opposite direction from the passion of *Orphée* and the stringency of the *Euménides*. It was Armand Lunel who suggested the story. Whenever Lunel returned to Aix on holiday, he would soon be seen strolling around the town, hands behind his back, hat precariously perched on a head that was eagerly cocked in the direction of each shop displaying antiques and other assorted mementos. His connoisseur's eye would spot a pink silk umbrella, "Second Empire style," a few opals, some pieces of furniture, and those pewter cooking utensils that antiquarians are wont to bring back from their rambles in the countryside. He knew about all the idiosyncrasies of life in Aix, Carpentras, and Manosque, and he mixed this knowledge together with his pots and umbrellas and fashioned a delightful concoction of stories that were half truth, half fiction.

At Carpentras his imagination found a great deal to feed on. In this tiny capital of the Comtat Venaissin, the papal legates had established their ecclesiastical court. Sometimes, though, their financial planning got a little out of hand, so they found it expedient to encourage the clever Jews of the community to make a lot of money so that they could be taxed. As a result, the yellow-hatted Jews of the four sacred communities of Avignon, Carpentras, Cavaillon, and Isle-sur-Sorgue were treated relatively well. They maintained a polite relationship with the bishopric, and both sides benefitted. But each side kept a wary eye on the other. From time to time the Church tried to make a few converts, and then the whole community would begin to seethe. On the other hand, the followers of the Old and the New Testaments had a number of things in common—among other things, their language. The Jews had enriched the dialect of Provence with a number of expressions that were adopted by the Christians. Unfortunately, little remains today of this delightful patois. Also, it seems that, in spite of taxation and prejudice, the spirit of these Mediterranean Jews remained more cheerful than that of their co-religionists who lived in the dreary northern regions of Minsk and Vitebsk. In any event, they prospered in the Provençal towns, and as their populations grew, they erected taller and taller buildings within the confines of the ghettos to house their growing families. Prints from the eighteenth century make these rather incongruous structures look a little bit like American skyscrapers.

Each year one of the main Jewish festivals, known by the Persian word Purim, commemorates those terrible days when Haman decreed that all Jews should be exterminated, but which became instead a time of rejoicing, because of Queen Esther's courageous intervention. To this day observant Jewish families celebrate that time of deliverance by sharing delicacies especially prepared for the occasion: sugared almonds, fancy fruits, those lumpy, aniseed cookies called "oreillettes," which are supposed to represent Haman's long ears. In the old days, however, Purim was celebrated not only in the home and the synagogue, but also by a carnival complete with music and dancing, a parade of floats, and a masquerade. The poor received alms, and gifts were given to children. Most important of all was the staging of the story of Esther in front of the synagogue; for, like the miracle plays and mysteries of the Christian faith, the drama of Esther became a popularization of intensely experienced religious history originally reserved for the house of worship. How perplexing: there are so many similarities between Christians and Jews and yet, though their paths cross, they never meet. This is the underlying subject matter of the Lunel–Milhaud work, and this is the bittersweet result of the confrontation brought about by the carnival: the play may go on, but the tragedy remains.

To present their play *The Tragedy of Esther* in the public square of the ghetto of Carpentras, the Jews had to obtain permission from the cardinal-legate. This confrontation between representatives of the community and the church, as well as the idea of staging the age-old story of Esther under the sunny skies of Provence, provided a delightful double challenge to Lunel's ingenuity. His prologue and one-act scenario reflect all his historical knowledge and cultural sympathies. He affectionately portrays the idiosyncrasies of the Jews, but also the deep solidity of their faith, and he gently chides their antagonists. The prologue starts in the luxurious lodgings that the papal emissaries have superimposed on this far-off provincial landscape. The new cardinal is a boy of nineteen who has been sent to Carpentras by his uncle the Pope as punishment for his adolescent misdemeanors. His servant, Vaucluse, sits dozing in a deep armchair, dreaming of a little Christmas carol that he hopes will help convert some of the Jewish children. Timidly pushing open the door, Artaban enters, carrying his yellow cap in his hand. In the community he is a haughty financier, but here he treads cautiously. With him are Barbican, the shabby custodian of the synagogue, scared to death and ready to take flight at any moment, and Cacan, a self-styled impresario. The banker loses no time in estimating the worth of the silverware in the room; the custodian is muttering prayers to ward off evil Christian influences; but Cacan has only one idea in mind: he wants to put on a play. In order to do so, he needs official permission, and he urges on his two companions, whose hearts are in their boots. Vaucluse wakes up, humming his Christmas carol, to the consternation of the three visitors. When he turns around and sees them, all four bristle like cats and dogs confronting each other with bared claws. But in Carpentras, like everywhere else, a subtly exchanged purse serves to relax the atmosphere. After all, there is no harm in listening to what these people have to say.

The cardinal enters briskly, accompanied by the rustling of silk and lace, affectedly holding a lorgnette. The three petitioners assume attitudes of reverence. "Good day, my dear Vaucluse," says the cardinal; "Where did these three monkeys come from? They are more amusing than my pets." Finally, after a long discussion that bristles with thrusts and feints, the cardinal grants permission to perform *Esther*. After the three have withdrawn, with elaborate expressions of gratitude and verbose praise for His Highness, the cardinal unveils his plan. In order to earn forgiveness for his misdeeds and thus be able to return as soon as possible to Rome, he will use this occasion to convert all the Jews at once. This accomplishment will surely restore him to his uncle's good graces.

The curtain announcing "Queen Esther Improvised by the Jews of Carpentras" is raised, and we find ourselves in the square in front of the synagogue, where the whole community is gathered. The cardinal had remarked to Cacan, "Even with an improvisation, every actor has to learn his part;" but Cacan replies: "What you still haven't learned, Sire, is that this story is inscribed in our very bones. God has burned it into our flesh. Each one of the actors has chosen the role that best suits him, and he will make up the lines himself."

Cacan has chosen to play the guard of the seraglio; the stately Artaban will play the role of Ahasuerus; the whining Barbacan will strut as Mordecai. As for the role of the accursed Haman, that will be taken by the good-for-nothing astrologer Mémucan. The actress Hadassa has been invited to come from Avignon to play the part of Esther. As each actor appears, every detail of his costume is enthusiastically commented on and cheered by the crowd. The staging is enhanced by a brilliant collection of streamers and confetti.

Finally the play begins, and to give the impression that it is being improvised, Lunel has the actors declaim in a style that is half grandiloquent, half colloquial, all of which produces a very comic effect, though it is bursting with excitement and conviction at the same time. As soon as Hadassa arrives, she is readied for her entrance as Esther. The mood of the play changes. Haman unfolds his dark designs against the Jews because of Mordecai's transgressions. Just at this moment the cardinal and his entourage, including a boys' chorus, make a noisy entrance. After an initial moment of consternation, Cacan decides to take advantage of the situation:

"Make yourself at home, Sire."
"What! At home among Jews?"
"I mean, at home with the Old Testament."

96

He begins to introduce the actors:

"You know our Ahasuerus."
"Yes, of course, and I'll take his place."

Shock and alarm! And well may the people be frightened, for the cardinal immediately orders the Jews to confess Christ on pain of expulsion from the Comtat. Finding themselves trapped and refusing to be converted, the Jews cry out to Hadassa to save them from the cardinal and Vaucluse, who have assumed the roles of Ahasuerus and Haman. She must be for them "the Esther of Carpentras."

The comedy has turned tragic, and the audience flees, leaving the cardinal and his troop alone. But Esther enters as though she were unaware of the changed situation. Feigning surprise and shock when she discovers the cardinal in the role of Ahasuerus, she pretends to faint in his arms. Vancluse is scandalized, but the young prelate is absolutely dazzled. What can he do, with this beautiful young woman in his embrace? Obviously he must extricate himself as diplomatically as possible, and the best solution is to cancel his order for expulsion. Little by little, the spectators timidly reappear, and as the cardinal regretfully abandons both the lovely Esther and his plans for mass conversion, a gentle chant is heard in the distance. The anthem being sung by the departing Catholics blends with the joyous hymn of the Jews. The curtain falls on this final scene, while Cacan muses over the battle of beliefs: the masquerade has become a sermon.

The story has a lot of appeal, and Lunel, who had to change the ending several times to make it effective, has filled it with witticisms and gentle irony. It is well paced and, above all in spite of its clowning, it creates a very special atmosphere of joy combined with deep, authentic faith.

As early as 1922 Milhaud had become intrigued with the idea of setting to music a piece of literature that combined Provence and Judea. But his work on the *Euménides* demanded all his time and energy, and he also had *Orphée* in the back of his mind. "I attacked the third act of the *Euménides*," he wrote in July 1922. "I finished a big overture that gave me the devil of a time. It's hard to sustain the effort, but the thought of other works I want to get down to keeps me going, and it is my impatience to begin *Esther* that gives me the strength to finish the *Euménides*. It's driving me to distraction. I work all day long without stop."

The first act of *Esther* was composed at l'Enclos in August 1925, the second at Malines in November of the same year, right after he had finished orchestrating *Orphée*. The work was supposed to be given its première at the Monte Carlo opera house. After interminable discussions with the director, Raoul Gunsbourg, who wanted to make changes in every possible respect, the author and composer finally agreed to change the ending (which was for the best), but they stood their ground on everything else. *Esther* was therefore not heard until 1 February 1938, when it was given at the Opéra-Comique in Paris.

There is an abundance of melodies in this opera. They spring up spontaneously, and in the first act are characterized by an underlying modal quality which results from augmentation of the fourth degree of the scale. This same kind of Lydian effect was also used in the overture to *Protée*. (Ex. 6–26).

Ex. 6–26.

The fluidity of this mode underlies and unifies the entire score; the use of the Hypodorian also infuses the beginning of the overture and the very end of the opera with a luminous calm (Ex. 6–27).

Ex. 6–27.

The overture begins with an easy-going melody in $\frac{5}{8}$ meter. In the middle is a more animated section, still mostly pianissimo, and at the end the melody disappears, while the bass line lingers for a moment on an appoggiatura that is then resolved, like a sigh of regret for the departed tune.

A furtive little major-minor episode characterizes the first scene, which is the encounter between the Jews and Vaucluse. The situation is comic, but the music never lets us forget the underlying pathos. When Vaucluse awakens, the accompaniment broadens into a succession of ample chords (Ex. 6–28).

Ex. 6–28.

As the discussion between the Jews and Vaucluse intensifies, the music gets more and more excited, until it turns into a whirlwind with the entrance of the cardinal. It takes only two measures for the rhythmic pattern to etch his portrait (Ex. 6–29).

Ex. 6–29.

To indicate the cardinal's youth, Milhaud assigned the role to a high tenor. His dialogue with Vaucluse in scene 3 is excessively fidgety, which is also intended to portray the young prelate's volatile nature; but his closing prayer has more the tone of a repentant child. With this, the prologue comes to an end. The huge sign that serves as a curtain is rung down, and in preparation for the carnival, the orchestra strikes up a noisy "Java."

The second part of the Opera is a kind of jigsaw puzzle. The characters enter and exit and each has his own special musical delineation. Then comes the Fugue of Purim, which is followed by a sparkling display of sprightly tunes and arias. The one that accompanies Hadassa's entrance is reminiscent of Bizet; in fact, it is like a tribute to that composer, whose *Arlésienne* music so quintessentially captures the spirit of Provence. However, despite the kaleidoscopic effect of both staging and music, a perfect balance and control of all elements is maintained. Notable are the choral sections, which occur throughout and serve as a unifying factor.

Now the sky darkens; the drama of Esther is about to begin. As Mordecai begins to sing, the music becomes like an engulfing wave, pouring forth the impassioned melody that is so typical of the Jewish race. Haman's bullying entry casts a pall over the scene, and emotional tension continues to build as he twirls his wheel of fortune until it comes to rest on the thirteenth day of the month of Adar, which is then designated as the date on which the Jews will be exterminated. Mordecai ceases to be an actor, and the members of the audience are no longer mere spectators. They join in crying out the name of Mordecai and raise their voices in a powerful supplication to Esther (Ex. 6–30).

Ex. 6–30.

She responds with a passionate aria (Ex. 6–31).

Ex. 6–31.

In the midst of all the make-believe, there has been a brief vision of most profound faith, so that when the action continues, the emotion evoked by that moment of musical fervor continues to glow, like the eyes of a caged tiger biding his time. Ahasuerus resumes his elegant discourse up to the moment when the cardinal and his retinue arrive on the scene. Then the cardinal's menacing attitude and Esther's pretended fainting spell introduce a tragicomic situation, which is accompanied by music that is somewhat confused; in fact, it is a weak spot in the opera. But the music of the following scene resumes its accustomed eloquence. The opera ends with a procession of prelates, joined by the boys' chorus. The cardinal reaffirms his faith, but the Jews have the last word and join in singing a hymn of praise that firmly establishes the key of C major. Yet Cacan's final enigmatic statement is in a gentle e minor (Ex. 6–32).

Ex. 6–32.

The Opéras-minute

Les malheurs d'Orphée has already illustrated Milhaud's concept of a small opera—one, that is, in which the quantity of material is replaced by the quality of inventiveness and in which small groups of singers and instrumentalists are substituted for large ones. These works are not to be confounded with the short operas written by some of Milhaud's contemporaries in Germany—Ernst Toch's *The Princess and the Pea,* for example—which use the same theatrical techniques and types of musical construction as are found in full-length operas. They are small only in terms of length. An exception is Hindemith's *Hin und zurück.* That gifted composer, one of the half dozen or so of his generation whose music will survive for posterity, tried to shake his colleagues out of their dependence on a style halfway between Brahms and Richard Strauss. At yearly festivals held in Baden-Baden, he explored various new directions—for example, the synchronization of music and film, the writing of cantatas based on modern texts, the composition of chamber operas, and the formation of a body of musical works that would help initiate the nonmusical public. He devoted some of his best efforts to a collection of works entitled *Sing- und Spielmusik für Kenner und Liebhaber,* written in a tradition stemming from the seventeenth and eighteenth centuries. Among these compositions are some excellent canons for women's voices, and *Frau Musika,* a cantata based on a text by Martin Luther. In the same vein is a piece entitled *Lehrstück,* designed as a teaching aid, and a charming musical play for children, *Wir bauen eine Stadt,* intended to help form the taste of young people by giving them something simple enough in which to participate.

Hindemith invited Milhaud to take part in his festivals. The results of this collaboration included music for a newsreel *(Actualités),* for a film by Cavalcanti called *La p'tite Lilie,* and the first of the opéras-minute, *L'enlèvement d'Europe,* which appeared on the same program as *Hin und zurück.* The libretto was by Henri Hoppenot. The following fall Hoppenot and Milhaud completed the cycle by adding *L'abandon d'Ariane* and *La délivrance de Thésée.* Each of the works lasted from eight to ten minutes, and together they formed a short three-part drama. The triptych was first performed in its entirety at Wiesbaden in the spring of 1928.

The concept behind these works is the same as that which inspired *Les malheurs d'Orphée.* The difference is that the individual operas are shorter, and also that they are little showpieces, rather than intense emotional dramas. They are exquisite chamber music, with charming melodic lines, delicate sonorities, and a touch of irony. Using a masterful kind of musical shorthand, and with his usual sure touch, Milhaud places these dramas in their appropriate universal context. Their distinctiveness lies in the unaffected, jewel-like quality of the tonal language.

A fragment such as the following (the final measures of *L'enlèvement d'Europe*) has the elegant line and feeling of substance of a Greek bas-relief. Unfortunately, the piano score gives no idea of the sonority that results from the superimposition of the vocal lines (Ex. 6–33).

Ex. 6–33.

The ending of *Thésée* is also notable for its descending chromatic scale and the feeling of breadth given by well-spaced polytonality. Try not to let the blocks of sound produced by the piano keep you from imagining the separate sonorities of each solo instrument (Ex. 6–34).

Ex. 6–34.

I have not found the staging of these operas to be very successful. It is somehow incongruous to have the décor and acting follow the conventions of grand opera. Rather than watching actors, I should prefer to see silhouettes projected against a backdrop; or possibly painted figures could be used in a minimal sequence of postures. If that would make the production too stiff, then why not try miming the action while the singers join the instrumentalists in the pit? Facial expressions and the constant motion of the costumes is distracting. A more stylized production would enhance the cameo quality of the music.

L'Orestie

Up to this point, all the dramas analyzed have portrayed in one way or another the essential loneliness of the individual. The human being yearns to complete himself, to escape from his solitude through love, but his efforts are in vain. Paths cross but never meet. A sense of inexorable fate characterizes *La brebis égarée, Les malheurs d'Orphée,* and *Le pauvre matelot. L'homme et son désir* follows the same theme, but treats it wholly symbolically. Cosmic forces shape *La création du monde,* and human forces, those engendered by seemingly irreconcilable religious tenets, motivate the protagonists of *Esther de Carpentras.* But the group of works now to be examined have a different orientation. *L'Orestie, Christophe Colomb, La Sagesse,* and to a certain extent *Maximilien, Bolivar,* and *Médée,* are "totalities." They are syntheses of human belief, morality, and the kind of behavior that is conditioned by divine law.

The first, completely successful performance of *Les Choéphores,* along with the finale of *Les Euménides,* was given in 1927 by Louis de Vocht, his marvellous choral society Caecilia, and the orchestra of the Société des Nouveaux Concerts d' Anvers at Anvers and then in Brussels and Paris. It was an unforgettable experience. As the powerful *Euménides* finale moved toward its climax in the Procession of Liberation, the entire audience was swept up in a surge of emotion which matched that of the music itself. No one could remain unmoved in the presence of such unprecedented grandeur. For here was a composition thoroughly imbued with the passion of Aeschylus. This was no incidental music to a play; nor was it even an opera adapted from classical drama. It was an actual setting of the original text. Milhaud had dared to superimpose his creative insight on the work of one of the greatest poets of all time, and this performance proved that he had met the challenge. The inspiration of the music fully complemented the genius of the text, and it was this perfect unity that so impressed the audience.

Greek drama has inspired a number of operas. In works such as Richard Strauss's *Elektra* and Fauré's *Pénélope* the original stories have been adapted and modernized in a way that still utilizes the basic plots and some of the mythological symbolism. But a true realization of Greek drama calls for an entirely different approach. It has to communicate the whole ethical, moral, and conceptual fabric of Greek life as it was experienced during the epoch when the dramas were conceived; it should bring the auditor face to face with what may be called "the Homeric realities." It must provide a glimpse of a living world, not of archeological remains.

Claudel's translation of *L'Orestie* conveys this kind of immediacy. It goes beyond more philological accuracy and transmits both the spirit and the impact of the original. First and foremost, Claudel has preserved the rhythm of the text, which is an absolute essential. He has grasped the sense of each Greek word and has been able to find a French equivalent that carries the same weight and force. We feel as though we were hearing the original phrases, not just some academic copy of them.

If one loves the molded frieze of the Parthenon with all its light and shadows, if one pictures the Mediterranean filled with ships from Tyre, Egypt, and Crete, senses the hundred lurking dangers, hears the oars dipping in and out of the water as the boats head for sheltered coves at nightfall, if, in fact, one has a Homeric vision of the Hellenic world, then one can appreciate Milhaud's absolute fidelity to the spirit of Aeschylus. It is no wonder, for his world of parched hills, sparse vegetation, and gray olive trees was the same environment that the Greeks had known. When he traveled to Greece in 1925 after having finished the music for *L'Orestie,* he wrote: "Piraeus delighted me. Disorder, clamor, swarms of people: these were my Athenians, the very same fishmongers and fruit-sellers that I had imagined crying out for Orestes in *Les Euménides.*" Had he really imagined them, or were they the crowds he had seen all his life at the Vieux-Port in Marseilles and on the wharves at Genoa? Consider also that Greek thought at the time of Aeschylus synthesized many cultural influences from the entire Eastern Mediterranean. According to numerous writers, many similarities can be found between the Jews and the Greeks, and it is by virtue of this compound heritage that no great gulf of understanding separated the twentieth-century composer from the Greek dramatist who had lived two and a half millennia earlier. Moreover, Milhaud was one of those rare souls who could absorb human experience into his heart and then bring it forth again in musical terms.

Let us hear Milhaud's own account of his "Collaboration with Paul Claudel" (*Etudes,* 1927):

I met Claudel when he passed through Paris in 1911. From that time dates our long collaboration, which is the best thing that ever happened to me as a composer and which led also to a deep, rewarding friendship. Immediately Claudel envisioned the possibility of setting Aeschylus's Orestes trilogy to music. He had already, at Foutchéou, completed the translation of *Agamemnon* and was at work on the *Choéphores.* Aeschylus's language, at times, in certain choruses and dialogues, becomes so metrically accented, so full of emphasis, that it cries out for a musical setting. With that in mind, Claudel wanted the drama to be punctuated in various places by vivid outbursts of music, and he asked me if I could write such a score. I wanted to avoid the ordinary kind of background music, which is a musical genre that I thoroughly detest. There is nothing more out-of-place than the sudden intrusion of musical sound while actors are trying to make themselves heard; the spoken phrase and the melodic line are two completely incompatible media. If words are to be joined to music, they must be sung. In *Agamemnon* it is only after Clytemnestra has committed her crime, when she emerges from the palace brandishing her bloody knife, that she begins to sing. It is a scene of tremendous violence, this confrontation between Clytemnestra and the elders, and it ends with a chorus that proclaims Aegisthus king. Once this moment of turmoil has passed, the play resumes its normal course. The music ceases, and the actors continue to speak their parts up to the end of the work. It was in Hellerau, where I joined Claudel, who was attending rehearsals of *L'annonce faite à Marie,* that I wrote the score for *Agamemnon. . . .*

In 1915 I wrote *Les Choéphores,* adopting the same principles as in *Agamemnon,* only in the case of this play, it seemed appropriate that several passages should be sung: the Funeral Chant accompanying the entrance of the Choephoroi; Electra's Libation; the Incantation sung by the chorus at the tomb of Agamemnon with Electra and Orestes present; then two violent, cannibalistic scenes that posed the most complex problems of all. The expressive content of these scenes does not lend itself to musical treatment. How, then, to capture and intensify their meaning? Suddenly I got the idea of having the text spoken in a metrical way the same as if it were being sung. I then accompanied these lines with an orchestra made up solely of percussion instruments. And to conclude, after the murder of Clytemnestra, there is a ponderous Hymn to Justice, a setting for chorus and orchestra that reverts to the usual musical conventions.

. . . In 1916 Claudel sent me from Rome his just completed translation of *Les Euménides,* which I made into a three-act opera. In this work everything is sung. I can think of no more beautiful subject to set to music. After crimes and horror, after the two somber, savage first acts, Orestes is acquitted by vote of the people of Athens and the Furies are appeased; light and joy gradually reappear. There is a triple chorus composed of Athena's three voices, the placated Furies, and a crowd of Athenians. The latter are the same sort of Mediterranean people that today frequent the port of Piraeus: fishermen, grocers, merchants, traders, schemers, and good-for-nothings, all plying their trades beneath the great dome of the Latin sky.

My score was begun in Rio de Janeiro in 1917, and the first act was finished in Martinique in 1918. The second act was written in Paris in 1922, the third at Aix-en-Provence in 1923; the whole score was orchestrated in 1924. Altogether I worked on *L'Orestie* for twelve years.

The subject of the Oresteia is the conflict between divine law and the human destinies that it determines. It is also a story of strife between theocracies that results in the overthrow of old beliefs and in an upheaval in morality as well as religion. It is a drama of the human condition rather than of individual suffering. Understandably, therefore, this music will prove to be quite different from that written for the previous dramatic works. It must express universal, rather than individualized, sentiment. In *La brebis égarée* and *Les malheurs d'Orphée* sadness was given an eternal dimension. Both sing of human sorrow that is shared by all those who witness the events. A scene in *La brebis* develops from the interaction between Pierre's nervousness and the noise of the mowing machine that he thinks causes his unrest. Eurydice's last song is given relevance by the animals and the forest that surround her. In other words, the music is conditioned by the specific situation.

In *L'Orestie,* however, there is no morally supportive landscape. Emotion is completely generalized and the music is on a plane totally removed from surrounding contingencies, as it is, for example, in a Mass or some other religious piece. Even the "cannibalistic" scenes are ritual; and if the composer has portrayed the people of Piraeus in the last act of *Les Euménides,* he has done so in an objective, rather than subjective, manner; he has eliminated all empathy for individual human qualities. The finale of *Les Euménides* has the same kind of universal spirituality as the last movement of Beethoven's Ninth Symphony.

In the scene in *Agamemnon* in which Clytemnestra is joined by the chorus, everything has a timeless quality, including Clytemnestra's solo line, its accompaniment, and the choral declamation (Ex. 6–35).

Ex. 6–35.

The same accented eighth-note rhythm in $\frac{3}{4}$ meter underlies the entire section. The music is static, unified, undisturbed by any kind of psychological tension. The setting of the text is also devoid of normal inflection and is therefore emotionally monochromatic. The words are uttered in a rapid, clipped succession of eighth and sixteenth notes, relentlessly equal in value. Note the lack of any accent in the passage

"Ores que voici tué. . . ." Stress is permitted only on "Il a perdu par le fait d'une femme, la vie," and it occurs without any relation to the bar lines, thereby further underlining the feeling of strife. Try to declaim this passage in contemporary theatrical style or in conformity with the accents of spoken language; then sing it precisely in the rhythm and meter in which it is written. It will quickly become apparent that the composer has chosen the most appropriate and simplest possible means to convey a feeling of tragedy (Ex. 6–36).

Ex. 6–36.

It would have been so easy and "natural" to begin the above-quoted declamation with an anacrusis on the last beat of the first measure, so that the word *soin* would fall on the first beat. But that would have interrupted the inexorable flow of the whole section. In music such as this, incidentals are of little importance.

The choral section is made up of six strophes and six antistrophes. A musical phrase corresponds to each portion of the text, so that the melodic structure remains clearly outlined, while the orchestral accompaniment is a series of variations on an ostinato bass. Each section, choral or solo, modulates downward by one half-step, finally reaching the original tonality as the work closes with a raucous fanfare. The effect of this organized violence is shattering; the music itself, not only the story it depicts, has become an expression of outrage.

There is less music in *Agamemnon* than in the rest of the trilogy. It is also simpler. As the drama proceeds, the texture becomes more and more polytonal until, at the end, the number of contrapuntal lines seems limitless.

Les Choéphores starts with the funeral lament that has already been mentioned in Chapter IV. This choral section begins with open fifths in the orchestra, against which a rigid, unyielding melody, levered by powerful bass chords, climbs upward from C to D, E, F, and G. Having arrived at G, it bursts forth above a harmonically polytonal instrumental accompaniment that takes over from then on.

To the women's voices is added the clamor of the men's, while blocks of instrumental sound are piled on top of one another, like the construction of a Cyclopean wall, superimposing C-sharp major and B major. Relaxation in the strophes, alternating with increased tension in the antistrophes, builds toward a climax of great orchestral power (Ex. 6–37).

Ex. 6–37.

The entire resources of the orchestra are called into play. The huge chordal blocks extend from the lowest to the highest notes possible. Still, the texture remains transparent; there are no bunched-up sonorities. For a short while, sonic space is completely filled with this enormous sound, but immediately afterward the music dissolves into single contrapuntal lines that seem to flow into one's very bloodstream (Ex. 6–38).

Ex. 6–38.

The epode restores a feeling of calm, the polytonality dissolves, and the music simplifies (Ex. 6–39).

Ex. 6–39.

It broadens out gently in F-sharp major, and the strings end in a questioning vein (Ex. 6–40).

Ex. 6–40.

Electra's libation, "Go, my tears, drop by drop to the buried man, and disappear with him. . ." is sung by a solo soprano accompanied by a six-part a cappella chorus, which is wordless except for a final ritual repetition of the sound "Iou" uttered in unison.

The incantation of Electra, Orestes, and the chorus reaches a climax with the following words:

Orestes	Ares against Ares
	Justice against Justice
Electra	Justice, oh gods, for that which is just.
Chorus	I listen and am filled with terror,
	Reluctant destiny is finally fulfilled.

The music returns to center stage carried upward on a giant musical staircase that uses portions of the theme as it steps until there is a final outburst:

> Inveterate misery,
> Atreus's bleeding wound,
> Merciless race, heavy with sorrow,
> Interminable evil,
> Your salvation must be sought, not in others,
> Not outside yourselves, but within, with fire and blood.

In this passage, as, indeed, throughout the first two parts of the trilogy, the music is enormously affirmative.

The following two scenes are the ones that require the spoken declamation to follow precise musical meters. The effect of this "orchestra" of voices, with their different timbres, rhythms, and cadences, their complete range of volume and energy, supplemented by the brusque utterances of a sole choephore and an unbelievable agglomeration of percussive sounds, is indescribably powerful. These passages are like magical incantations, which literally force the listener out of himself and into the bowels of the tragedy. Reading the score, it is impossible to imagine the impact of such writing. It must be heard under perfect performance conditions, such as existed when Louis de Vocht directed it at Anvers. Fortunately, one of the scenes from that performance has been preserved on records.

After Orestes commits his crime, Justice is satisfied. The choephoroi proclaim his deed in a ponderous, compelling hymn (Ex. 6–41).

Ex. 6–41.

It is absolutely unique in its rhythm, melody, harmony, and orchestration: artistry of an incomparable sort. Then follows the preparation for the final part of the trilogy, *Les Euménides* (Ex. 6–42).

Ex. 6–42.

A short, rhythmically declaimed concluding section summarizes the crimes that have been committed and subsides into a kind of fitful repose.

The final part of the Hymn to Justice points up a curious fact. Our concept of consonance and dissonance has changed. In his book on harmony, Koechlin speaks of "the degree of dissonance." In this passage of Milhaud's music it is interesting to note that the superimposition of F- and C-major triads, in relation to the other harmonies that have been introduced, actually constitutes consonance. It gives us the same feeling of resolution as does the tonic triad in more conventional music.

The first scene of *Les Euménides* opens in front of the temple of Pythia in Delphi. Against the discreet, muted background of percussion instruments, the priestess intones a prayer of homage to the goddess Gaia and to the other deities from whom she derives her power. Then the full scope of this broadly conceived opera begins to unfold. The music wells up painfully from the obscurity of the lowest orchestral register and proceeds in a series of ostinatos, while Pythia recounts the dreadful scene she has witnessed in the house of Loxias. There, a hideous heap of sleeping Furies surrounds the prostrate form of Orestes.

This music no longer has the ironclad rigidity of *Agamemnon* and *Les Choéphores*; it is more plastic. Throughout the orchestral texture flows a broad theme, which connects the repeated segments so that the whole passage becomes one giant ostinato. The starting, stopping, and reappearing of these recurrent groups underline the declamation as inexorably as Time itself. Only when the priestess describes Orestes's gesture of supplication does the pace of the music intensify; then, a harmonic canon, which illuminates the sonorous texture like a light penetrating the universe, presages the arrival of Athena (Ex. 6–43).

Ex. 6–43.

The repetition of these three or four ostinato figures and the theme that weaves in and out among them introduces an unusually agonizing quality, ominous and mysterious, into the music.

The entrance of Apollo, after Pythia leaves the stage, is accompanied by a broad, peaceful phrase, persistently pianissimo, which flows over the underlying agitation of the scene like a healing salve. It is redolent of heavy sleep, of sepulchral shadows, and invisible presences; the music is at once mysterious and illuminating (Ex. 6–44).

Ex. 6–44.

The meeting of Orestes and Apollo continues in the same mood. Orestes has entered undemonstratively. His sorrow is beyond turbulence; it has a lucidity that transcends human emotion and is crystalline and transparent like a block of ice. The god's wisdom and the hero's profound suffering have placed them on a plane far removed from mere passion, and their encounter is marked by the noble, deliberate pace of the scarcely audible music. All this creates a sense of grandeur and totality.

Orestes withdraws, and the ghost of Clytemnestra appears, castigating the Furies to the accompaniment of violent, gnashing parallel chords: "You snarl, curs, but your victim is already far from your reach, for there are gods who have answered his supplications." Her voice is like a whip striking out at the pack, inciting it with enormous vocal leaps and plunges to continue the chase. The Furies stir in their sleep, already dreaming of the pursuit. Then they awaken with an outcry of vicious hatred for the new god who protects men against the old deities and who has destroyed the ancient order. There is a violent wave of sound. But Apollo abruptly interrupts their clamor and imposes silence by his very presence. He chases them from the temple. Reason triumphs over uncontrolled anger as the act ends with a kind of serene halo of sound brought about by a succession of four chordal groups, each moving in a different rhythm (Ex. 6–45).

Ex. 6–45.

The second act takes place in a little temple in which there is an old statue of Athena. Orestes has taken refuge there. Purified of his guilt, he is nevertheless still harassed by the Furies. They enter the temple and try to entice him into their sphere of influence through the power of their sorcery. Athena hears their diabolical hymn and Orestes's cry and comes to mediate the dispute. Refusing to pass a judgment that will leave the moral issue unresolved, she insists on bringing the matter before a panel of judges.

The music of the second act starts mysteriously. Beneath the black dome of the sky, which enfolds a murmuring universe, a simple, dignified theme of supplication emerges (Ex. 6–46).

Ex. 6–46.

The man whose destiny has reached beyond the limit of his own individuality and who has become the embodiment of all humanity speaks without pretense. The gods, with their timeless knowledge of human fate, also speak quietly. Orestes's declamation is utterly tranquil; but violence is the hallmark of the Furies. They re-enter with their thrashing music, a succession of great chordal masses flapping in the wind. Orestes's response reflects the wisdom that comes with accumulated sorrow. He is purged of passion, but the mark of suffering is still on his countenance. The violence born of outrage that characterized the beginning of the trilogy is now transformed into nobility. As he sings, the aggregations of notes representing elemental earth sounds continue uninterruptedly, along with the chords that provide rhythmic punctuation. These repeated-note patterns must obviously be performed more pianissimo than the other components of the total texture. Think of them like fast, compact C-major scales (Ex. 6–47).

Ex. 6–47.

He is answered by the Hymn of the Furies who, after a long preparation, spin out their magic on the notes of the B-mode.

Characteristic of the choruses of the two first acts of *Les Euménides,* as well as those of *Les Choéphores,* is the succession of complete melodies that pile up without any intervening development of the material in what amounts to a kind of unremitting assault. Then Athena makes her impressive appearance. Her pronouncements, issuing from within the statue, are given to a trio of female voices: the soprano declaims the text, the mezzo and contralto provide a wordless counterpoint. Athena's voice, therefore, becomes a self-fulfilling trinity of sound. Milhaud restrains the dynamic level so that the music is compelling by reason of its intensity, rather than its brilliance. The effect is one of benevolence and serenity, slightly tinged with melancholy. Such is the joy experienced by priests and ascetics, which eludes ordinary human definition.

The orchestral accompaniment to this section consists of a series of triads that arch over the musical landscape like the Milky Way spanning the revolving sphere of the earth. Such a vast firmament of sound is without precedent in all music history (Ex. 6–48).

Ex. 6–48.

Athena's beautiful response to Orestes develops into the long orchestral section that underscores her divine decree. After hearing the Furies' charge against Orestes, she turns to him, and the tone of her address overflows with compassion. The same gentle spirit permeates the orchestral accompaniment to her subsequent decrees. Even Orestes's defense of his past actions, though still filled with agony, is infused with a kind of harmonic luminosity. The act ends as the Furies, prostrate and immobile, murmur their apprehensions in a sort of breathless litany (Ex. 6–49).

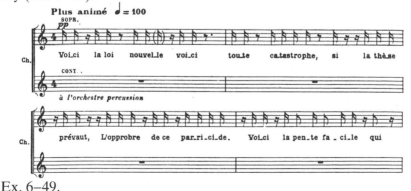

Ex. 6–49.

When Act III begins, Athena has called together the people of Athens. They are assembled just below a platform on which the statue of Athena stands. Orestes is on one side, with Apollo as his witness; the Furies are on the other, ready to plead their cause. Finally the matter is put to a vote. The count is evenly divided, but Athena tips the balance in favor of Orestes and he is acquitted. The new law is proclaimed, but the tragedy is not over yet, for though the people bow to the decision of the goddess, the Furies will not accept it and they vow to wreak vengeance on the city. However, Athena is as clever as she is wise, and she promises them that they can live not only in peace, but with honor. They will be made special collaborators in the future well-being of the city and no longer will be called Furies, but rather the Eumenides, or "gracious ones." A new era has dawned, and the citizens celebrate with a great, triumphal procession.

Up to this point we have followed a long, dark pathway but now, from the shadow of the mountain, the music will begin to ascend, rising from rock to rock, climbing melodically and harmonically toward the light and the pure joy that await at the summit. The overture is the point of departure. We have already described, in Chapter V, this formidable heaping up of blocks of sound through which winds an enormous fugue. Its subject will become the principal theme of the ensuing symphonic accompaniment. There is also another phrase that accentuates the marchlike character of the overture (Ex. 6–50).

Ex. 6–50.

After this comes Athena's three-part "voice," distributed over a two-octave span, presiding over the gathering of the people (Ex. 6–51).

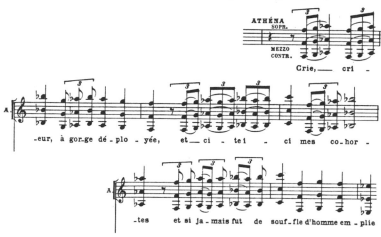

Ex. 6–51.

Like the populace surging toward the statue, the music of the overture has thrust forward toward this moment. Immediately the Furies start their harassment, but Apollo takes control, singing in firm, persuasive tones that bring about a change in quality in both the melody and the texture. In this passage the accompaniment consists of a theme and its inversion sounded simultaneously, which finally reaches a harmonic resolution, while in the background the rhythmic palpitation continues. The passage in which Orestes answers the Furies is marked by the contrast between guttural, aggressive choral utterances and the calm, firm solo line based on the original fugal subject, now in a more rapid, but less intense, form. The polyphonic texture becomes increasingly dense; imitations and canons on the one hand and chordal polyphony on the other form the warp and woof of a tonal fabric on which a new melody is embroidered.

Never absent is the feeling of an ongoing march, the movement of this river of humanity that surges toward a distant, ineluctable goal. The flood tide is constantly enriched by tributaries, each one bringing with it a new melody that refreshes the enormous flow. Sometimes these phrases well up to the surface for a moment and then are sucked back into the current, never to reappear. Thus, the music of this huge, rhythmic deluge, continuing for sixty-six pages of the score, appears as diverse and tumultuous as life itself.

Athena puts an end to this surge when, clearly and with quiet assurance, she proclaims the new law. After her edict, the orchestra descends to the depths of silence, its sound gradually extinguished as it sinks chromatically to the lowest bass tones. Then comes the heart of the drama, the voting scene. The wordless a cappella chorus is based on motives from the fugue of the overture and Athena's proclamation. The Furies interject their chatter and continue to harass Apollo, who defends his position. Above the other voices, the trio representing Athena sings in luminous two-octave intervals. The feeling of joy increases, but it has to struggle to get the upper hand. Altogether there are ten to fourteen vocal parts in the polyphonic texture. When Athena proclaims Orestes's acquittal, the orchestra re-enters in the low register to which it has so recently descended and rises upward in a series of chords that broaden until the beginning of a new section, marked by an ostinato that combines four rhythmically different patterns in the tonalities of F-sharp, E-flat, C-sharp, and D major. This passage is filled with the ecstatic anticipation of a new era to come (Ex. 6–52).

Ex. 6–52.

It is with this material that the music begins to build toward the final Processional. Already the rhythmic patterns begin to change places, moving from one tonality to another. There is a kaleidoscopic effect as keys and rhythms are juxtaposed in four different ways.

The defeated Furies have lost some of their bravado. They grumble, but on such marvellous harmonies (Ex. 6–53)!

Ex. 6–53.

Gradually they become calmer, as Athena placates them with a beautiful series of descending dominant sevenths and a texture of interwoven canons and subtle harmonic triads. Finally resigned, the Furies abdicate their violent role, and the Finale proceeds with an increasingly joyous spirit. To the tonality of d minor are added major tonalities of E, G, and B-flat, all sustained by the same rhythmic ostinato that accompanied Orestes's expression of gratitude for his redemption. Athena and the Eumenides join in singing a jubilant hymn in praise of the gods, mankind, and nature.

Now the stage begins to fill with a countless number of people, who flood in from every direction. After twenty-six measures, the patterns in the instrumental accompaniment interchange tonalities. E-flat minor is added. Fourteen measures later there is a new change of positions (coinciding with the strophes). The orchestral part now includes six patterns, three lower ones in G, A, and B-flat, converging logically on A, and three upper ones in D-flat, E-flat, and F, resolving to E-flat. Three by three the six voices change tonalities (on p. 347 of the piano score). The new groupings are: D-flat, E-flat, E with A-flat, A, B. Then comes E-flat, A-flat, A with A, B, D-flat (p. 352); A, B, D-flat, with E, D-flat, E-flat (p. 358). Intermediary voices effect the fusions between tonalities. Of the six tonal combinations, only these remain: B, D-flat, B, D-flat, D, A (p. 361); B-flat, B, B, D-flat, D-flat, B (p. 375). With Athena's words "Voici, que je prends les devants" and later, with the Eumenides' salutation "Salut, et de nouveau salut," there are so many intermingled melodies that it is impossible to sort them all out.

Inspired by these prophetic voices and by the brilliant rays of the sun shining down on them, the people reach a state of ecstasy. On p. 378 the dazzling texture includes Athena's part in C-sharp (D-flat), the Eumenides in B-flat, the people (a six-part chorus) in D-flat and C-flat (B natural), and the orchestra in B-flat, B, B, D-flat, D-flat, B, modulating to B, C-sharp (D-flat), B, C-sharp, B, C-sharp—in other words, the orchestral part is bitonal. The following example shows one of the polytonal modulations in progress (Ex. 6–54).

This section, in D-flat, C-sharp, and B, occurs just before the climax of the opera. The whole world is filled with rejoicing: let the sound ring forth! The orchestra holds back for a moment, and then the whole formidable conglomeration of sound makes a final modulation to a unanimous E major. The ringing of a bell (the only such effect in the entire score) adds to this moment of supreme grandeur.

The world has been reborn, and the Processional, which takes the soprano line up to D above high C, continues with its majestic text and sovereign music. The orchestra ends by affirming the entire C-major scale, an effect that, in its integrity and plenitude, is far more impressive than any full chord could possibly be.

To set Aeschylus's trilogy to music, Milhaud invented a type of melody and chose harmonic and contrapuntal textures that were thoroughly compatible with this most beautiful and complete of all dramas. With neither a tinge of sentimentality nor a hint of personal emotional involvement, he created a work of great artistic expressiveness, which moves from the first dialogue in *Agamemnon* to the final Processional of *Les Euménides* in one unabated lyric sweep.

During the entire period that he was working on the Orestes trilogy, Milhaud envisaged the possibility of one day presenting it in the Roman amphitheater at Orange. Obviously, such a setting would perfectly suit a musical work based on Aeschylus's drama. In addition to the visual impact, the composer had certain acoustical properties in mind. Because of the shape of the theater and its high surrounding walls, everything sung on stage projects with force and clarity, whereas the location of the orchestra below stage level prevents its sound from reverberating with the same intensity. That explains in part Milhaud's use of four saxophones and three saxhorns. They also give a somewhat "vocal" sound to the instrumental texture and reinforce the impression that the assembly of the Athenians is a real, live public gathering. Furthermore, he intended to have the music grow in volume, by adding voices, until it burst out in the final glowing Processional that concludes *Les Euménides*. The result is that the orchestral score of this last part of the trilogy is not well suited to performance in a conventional theater. The choral-orchestral sound easily covers the solo voices, and it is virtually impossible to differentiate the melodic material assigned

Ex. 6–54.

to the various participants. Only in a great open-air theater, such as the one at Orange or that at Epidaurus, would the placement of the several groups of singers permit their lines to stand out in relief, one against the other. Like the works composed for St. Mark's in Venice, or the Sacred Symphonies by Heinrich Schütz, this is spatial music. Of course nowadays the placement of microphones can help effect the intended contrast when such music is performed in concert halls.

The concert version of *Les Euménides* given in Brussels in 1949 was guided by these considerations. Additional voices reinforced the upper line of Athena's trio of singers and the same reinforcement was added to certain parts of the Furies' chorus. Orestes's and Apollo's solo parts were amplified so that the singers were not obliged to force their tone. In the Processional, where the tessitura stays in the high C and D register, the soprano part was doubled by an electronic sound that gave the music the kind of brilliance the composer had in mind, and which is literally beyond human capability. Similar techniques were employed for the Berlin Opera performance in 1964, when the composer had the pleasure of hearing and seeing for the first time in its entirety the work he had finished forty-five years before!

Christophe Colomb

While the Berlin Staatsoper was preparing its presentation of *Christophe Colomb,* the Viennese periodical *Anbruch* brought out an issue devoted to French music, which included an article by Paul Claudel regarding his play. In it he stated that it was not his intent to write a historical account of the discovery of America. Rather, he wished to interpret the multitude of philosophical and symbolic concepts that the story has engendered during the ensuing four centuries. He conceived a format in which the great Christopher, who had dared to prove for the first time that the earth was round, would be called before the people of the world to give an accounting of his deeds. The cast includes a reader who enumerates Columbus's prodigious adventures, and a chorus of auditors who react to the account, sometimes acclaiming, sometimes condemning the navigator and occasionally asking for clarification. Each time an event is described by the reader, a scene dramatizing that event is interpolated, so that there is an alternation of dramatic episodes with the more static tribunal scenes. These dramatizations are presented to an audience of which Columbus himself is a member. The role of the chorus can be compared to that of a church choir, which is a kind of intermediary between the celebrant and the congregation, rather than to that of a Greek chorus, which merely comments on the action. It is the author's protagonist and interprets his thoughts to the great, anonymous mass of humanity.

Columbus lies dying in an inn at Valladolid. His whole life passes before him and he reviews it both as spectator and as judge. He sees a dove, symbol of the Holy Spirit, that flies across the ocean and delivers a message to a child who is dreaming of great exploits. Then he is a sailor in the Azores; next, a person of renown surrounded by creditors, by courtesans, and by skeptics. Finally he sees himself as the captain of his ship, controlling his rebellious crew. And then comes the moment of his greatest travail: he, who has proved that the earth is a sphere, becomes a victim of envy and pettiness and is lashed to the mast of his own vessel, where he is whipped by the fury of men and of the elements. He learns the bitterness of having the whole world, with the exception of one woman, lose faith and turn on him. Now, at Valladolid, the end of his life approaches and a dove *(la colombe)* appears, bringing an olive branch of hope and peace.

None of this dramatic material is presented in a strictly anecdotal manner. Each use of a voice, word, or gesture elicits an echo, a response, or a reaction. The chorus acts almost like today's press corps, which is present whenever an important event is taking place. It conveys information and stimulates public opinion.

The stylistic diversity of the text is treated in the score by alternating spoken dialogue, rhythmically declaimed speech, and lyrical vocal passages, all of which combine to create an extraordinarily varied kind of musical and dramatic atmosphere.

Christophe Colomb is designated as an opera in two parts and twenty-seven scenes. In form and spirit, it relates to the tradition of musical theater as a fusion of opera and oratorio. The use of film projections is not intended for stage effect only, but is supposed to add a spiritual dimension by enabling the audience to view the flight of the dove, the vision of the Holy Cross, and so forth.

No French theater had the resources to produce a work requiring such complicated staging, but the two opera companies in Berlin vied with each other for the honor of staging the première of this important new work. The *Staatsoper* ("Unter den Linden") prevailed. Franz Ludwig Hörth was stage director; the scenery was provided by a Greek painter, Panos Aravantinos. The difficult chorus parts were prepared by Hugo Rüdel and Alexander Curth; Erich Kleiber conducted. The first performance took place on 5 May 1930. Actors and members of the chorus acted and sang to perfection. Kleiber's conducting was sensitive to the last detail, and Hörth carried out Claudel's every intention faithfully. The mood on stage and in the audience was electrifying; there were twenty curtain calls after every section. Milhaud sat with Hindemith in the main loge, but Claudel was unavoidably detained on business in America and had to see the performance a few days after its opening. The production was a triumph in other ways, too. The lavish care devoted by the *Staatsoper* to the production of a distinguished French work seemed tangible evidence of republican Germany's new-found friendliness. We know only too well that this mood was not destined to prevail until much later.

Claudel had shown his poem to Milhaud in August 1927, but it was not until the next February that Milhaud began work on the score, sometimes completing as much as one scene per day. The work almost seemed to compose itself. In March a few remarks indicated that things were going well: "The tremendous diversity of the scenes and the enormous rhythmic drive that animates the entire drama make it an absolutely fascinating challenge. I have a whole lot of ideas that will make it easy to produce (providing we can have a chorus as good as "Caecilia" to represent the mass of people on stage). It's amazing how each work makes one turn one's back on all previous ones and find the special vocabulary that the new one requires."

Claudel's *Christophe* is in many ways analogous to his drama *Le soulier de satin,* written just previously. In both, theatrical art has been pushed to its limits. It has become an extension of all the confusion and shock that a man can experience, and of the mass of errors and truths in constant flux that impel him eventually toward "knowledge" of the world. The play's message is that Christopher Columbus is a great man because, when all is said and done, he united the world and thereby made it possible for Christianity to triumph over paganism. Columbus is redeemed by the Holy Ghost. To convey this message, the individual, society, morality, and religion are all pitted against each other in what is really a drama of conscience. In a way, the combination of these different elements makes this work resemble the Orestes trilogy; but, whereas in the Oresteia, water, fire, earth, and plant life are viewed as parts of one encompassing natural phenomenon, in *Christophe Colomb* cosmic elements are assigned anthropomorphic dimensions. The natural events have such immediacy that we, the spectators, are swept up as participants in the orbits of celestial bodies and the fury of tempests. We even develop a special feeling for time, due to the arrangement of the material: actions start, are aborted, resume again; and, finally we end where we began, at the moment of Columbus's death. This involvement with material reality combined with temporal imbalance calls for a kind of musical writing entirely different from that employed in the Oresteia, which was dominated by an inexorable sense of forward motion. There are similar kinds of massive polytonal structures in the two works, but the Orestes trilogy is built like a pyramid, with block placed upon block. Its expressiveness is due to a gathering of resources, and its conclusion is a revelation of all that has gone before. In addition, the thematic material is broad and spare, and is often regulated by underlying ostinato figures. Polytonality grows out of tonality. The texture is harmonically simple to begin with and becomes more and more contrapuntal until all the elements are heaped up in a finale that uses horizontal and linear resources to their utmost limits.

Christophe Colomb, by contrast, has an irregular construction. Claudel puts his finger on "first one part, then another, emphasizes a page here, then points to another one over there that must not be overlooked." The music cannot grow consistently, building up a groundswell of emotion. It must move expressively from scene to scene, catching the appropriate mood of each. Also, since the sea is so prominent throughout the story, it is depicted musically in many guises, as it was in *Protée* and *Le pauvre matelot.* All these diverse musical elements must, of course, be amalgamated. In *L'Orestie* the music attacks the essence of the dramatic situation, assured that the action will follow a predestined course. In *Christophe Colomb* it is only at the end that a sense of destiny emerges; at least, that is when we, the spectators, add up all the debits and credits and recognize which parts of the hero's life have portended its outcome.

Throughout, the music must be ready to turn its beacon on the dramatic situation at hand. It cannot proceed by logically and unswervingly building up a complex polyphonic and instrumental texture. The musical character of *Christophe Colomb* is therefore much less complex than that of the earlier trilogy. It rarely ventures into the deepest forests of polytonality, and there are frequent moments of repose on consonant triads, which act as control points. Each scene starts simply and consonantly, then develops, and at the end unravels its accumulation of sonorities. Scenes do not generally lead from one to another; each starts afresh. Polytonal complexity and the use of an extended orchestral range are found only at certain key places, as for example in the scene between Isabella and Santiago and in the scene in which the African and Indian gods churn up the sea in order to prevent the Christ-bearer (Christopher) from crossing it, as well as in the typhoon scene and at the moment of Isabella's funeral. Even the final Hallelujah avoids the use of polytonality. This last section is, in fact, not the end of the drama, but rather, a reflection on the judgment that has been passed. It is apparent throughout this opera, as indeed in all his works, that Milhaud uses polytonality for very specific kinds of expressiveness and not just as a technique applied across the board.

In summary, there are three categories of musical writing in this opera. Many passages, including those in which the history book is read and some of those in which the chorus responds, expressing public opinion, use rhythmic speech. The second category is reserved for scenes of action, including The Man at the Window, Recruitment for the Ships, Columbus and his Creditors, and so forth. This music is structurally simple and is based on a folkloric type of melody (Ex. 6–55).

Ex. 6–55.

But when a scene is a moral commentary, the musical texture becomes more complex and polytonal.

The third category of compositional technique involves the same kind of radical polytonality that was used in *L'Orestie*. In *Christophe Colomb* it is reserved, as has been noted, for the scenes that illuminate Columbus's destiny. For example, the scene of The Dove over the Ocean is accompanied by an ensemble of solo instruments reminiscent of the chamber symphonies. The Fugue of the two Indian Gods has the same quality of intransigent cruelty heard in the Orestes score, but here it has a grandiose barbaric quality, which makes one think of a huge Aztec mural.

There is actually even a fourth category of writing, which accompanies ceremonial scenes such as the great Processional (Ex. 6–56).

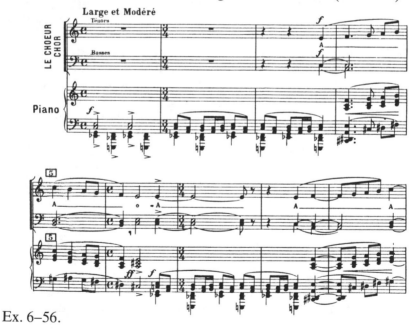

Ex. 6–56.

Solid chords cushion the beginning of these solemn proceedings. The strict, precise music of the eight-voice Te Deum is in the same vein. Derived from the opening Processional, this hymn brings to a close the first of the two main divisions of the opera.

These are some of the musical elements that, although they can be examined separately, will only be truly appreciated in relation to one another—that is, as a whole. It is impossible to gain an impression of the work by merely reading it through at the piano. It has to be studied and analyzed as one would a sonata or a cantata; otherwise the impression obtained will be purely superficial. Also, the variety of detail will appear overwhelming. All those images and expressive outpourings, the fearsome discussions of morality, combined with the movement of the ocean, which alternately seduces and rejects, the falling stars, and God on His heavenly throne—in short, everything that the combined imaginations of poet and composer have been able to conceive—is included in one huge structure. It bears out the Portuguese proverb with which Claudel ends his *Soulier de satin: Deus escrivo direito por linhas tortas* (God uses crooked lines to write straight).

Christophe Colomb is typically Milhaud. It is a synthesis of everything he had written before and is prophetic of his future dramas. There are reminders of *La brebis* and *Le matelot,* a hint of *Orphée* and *La création,* the powerful thrust of *Protée*, and even the liveliness of *Salade.* The opera is a musical sum total. Finally, there are a few more marvellous details to point out. Note, for example, the simplicity with which the calm surface of the ocean is depicted (Ex. 6–57).

Ex. 6–57.

Observe also the quasi major–minor tonality that accompanies the departure of the dove and imparts a feeling of indescribable regret (Ex. 6–58).

Ex. 6–58.

Listen to the swelling of the ocean in a full orchestral passage that provides a backdrop for the sneering sarcasms of Columbus's creditors (Ex. 6–59).

Ex. 6–59

The scene between Isabella and Santiago is one of exquisite fervor. A group of solo instruments embroider a delicate fugue, above which a men's chorus intones the meditation, while the women's voices sing "Isabelle" on the augmented notes of the theme. On this altar of sound, Isabella prays.

The scene of the sailors' mutiny is the dazzling culmination of a series of scenes that start with the carnival atmosphere surrounding the recruitment of seamen and continue with the episode in which the heathen gods, dressed like lyrebirds, birds of paradise, and parrots, whip the sea into a frenzy. First speaking, then singing, then speaking again, mixing musical and nonmusical sounds, the men's voices, obsessed with fear, increase in volume until they cry out "La mer, toujours la mer" so powerfully that the sound drowns out the waves. Columbus stands resolute against the howling crew. Then, all of a sudden, from the crow's nest, comes the cry "Land!" Everyone rushes forward to glimpse the shore, and the enormous outcry stops as suddenly as if an anchor had been dropped to the seafloor, leaving no sign of its impact except a quivering chain (Ex. 6–60).

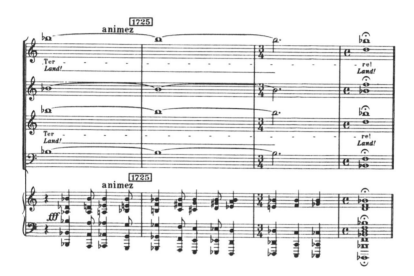

Ex. 6–60.

Notable in the second main part of the opera is another section in which a powerful force—in this case, Columbus's conscience—stills the howling of the tempest. Then follows the magnificent scene of Isabella's funeral, with its combined agony and faith.

There is only one page left to be read. The scene is again the inn at Valladolid. Columbus is dying; he has nothing left but his shackles. He has suffered so much, from injustice, the tortures of his own conscience, and the death of Isabella, that he is beyond feeling. But he must still face the ordeal of dying, the painful process of separating himself from life, thread by thread. And then, at the last moment, he finds peace (Ex. 6–61).

Ex. 6–61.

There are only a few moments as beautiful as that in all musical literature. The score of *Christophe Colomb* contains many such fine passages.

Few theaters have the resources to mount this opera with all the scenic apparatus that it requires. Another difficulty in presenting the work is that the first part is dramatic, whereas the second, which reflects Columbus's inner struggle, is static and seems more suited to a concert hall than a stage. In 1962 the editors suggested a revised version that would make some large cuts in addition to those decided on after the first performance. Both Claudel and Milhaud refused to consent to what they considered a mutilation of their work. Out of consideration for their editors' concerns, as well as for the difficulties involved in staging the work, they did agree to reverse the order of the two main parts. In this way the public's interest would tend to increase as the opera proceeded. This format became the definitive version and it was performed with great success at Graz and in several Rhineland cities.

Opinions differ as to the effectiveness of this inversion. The stage director Herbert Graf, asking the editors why they had reversed the order, said: "The original form is a masterpiece. The spiritual interpretation follows the action as the second part of *Faust* follows the first." In all honesty, however, it must be admitted that the second part of *Faust* is rarely performed, in spite of the magnificence of the text. Musically speaking, one has to agree with Graf, while admitting the validity of dramatic considerations.

Note added in translation. In October 1984 the Marseilles Opera performed *Christophe Colomb* in its original version except for the addition of a twenty-eighth scene showing Columbus as a colossus astride the ocean. The conductor, Jacques Karpo, based this addition on Claudel's original play, in an effort to complete satisfactorily the grand design of the opera. Jean Roy, reviewing the production in the November 1984 issue of *Diapason,* wrote: "Inverting the two acts, while superficially advantageous, alters the meaning of Milhaud's *Christophe Colomb.* The Marseilles production proved that the return to its original version by no means diminishes the impact of the work."

Maximilien

A remarkable new work is about to be presented by the Paris Opera; how will it be received? The answer came swiftly the day following the preview of *Maximilien.* From members of the press there was universal hostility; with unabashed delight, they pounced ferociously on the composer, bent on destroying him once and for all. There was virtually no discussion of the score, and no consensus on the few details they did admire. One writer praised the choruses, another found the libretto excellent, a third commended the orchestration. But they all agreed heartily that *Maximilien* was a generally worthless piece. How was it possible to be so mistaken?

The answer can lie only in the attitude of the auditor. It is quite apparent to German, English, Belgian, Dutch, or Russian audiences that music is written to be listened to. In those countries the public goes to a performance with the idea of participating in a meaningful experience. Not so in France. The Parisian goes to a theater or a concert hall to be entertained. On the evening of the *Maximilien* preview, people dawdled in the foyer and entered the hall after the music was already in progress. Even then, they continued to talk, discussing the economic situation and similar subjects throughout the entire performance. One lady even walked out in the middle of the second act, complaining that there hadn't been a single love scene or ballet. How can one expect such a public to understand new serious music? Even French musicians, with some notable exceptions, seem to expect music to please the ear without demanding too much of the mind. If a composer like Stravinsky or Milhaud—or Berlioz for that matter—shakes the audience out of its euphoric state, he is punished for overstepping the boundaries. In his day Berlioz first found acceptance from a German public, and only after his reputation was well established did the French begin to acknowledge his worth. History repeats itself. Milhaud's fate has been similar to that of Berlioz, and for the same reasons.

Maximilien is a very ambitious opera. It was composed in 1930 and staged for the first time in 1932. On a return trip from the United States in February 1927, Milhaud had read a book about the tragedy of Querétaro, written in 1880 by Count Corti. He was struck by Emperor Maximilian's tragic fate and intrigued by the countryside of Mexico's high central plateau, where the story had unfolded. The following May Milhaud began to plan an operatic setting of the drama. The first step was to find a libretto. His editor, Emil Hertzka, referred him to Franz Werfel's 1924 play *Juarez und Maximilian*. It was R. W. Hoffman who wrote a libretto from the Werfel's text and Armand Lunel who translated it into French.

This opera, based on historical fact, contains three acts and nine scenes. Milhaud proceeded slowly because it proved to be the most theatrical work, in the accepted sense of the word, that he had undertaken so far. The story is about the Hapsburg archduke Maximilian who, after many intrigues, became the emperor of Mexico. He was a person of many fine qualities, but he was a weak man and was completely dominated by his wife Charlotte, who pushed him to act in ways that satisfied her own pride and ambition.

The most forceful presence in the drama, though he is never seen on stage, is Juárez, president of the Mexican republic. He personifies destiny, and no one escapes the influence of his will and determination. Maximilian and Charlotte are surrounded by a few friends, including the Princess of Salm; the emperor's councillor, Herzfeld; and General Porfirio Diaz, with his cadre of young officers. They struggle in vain against the course of destiny. Quite different in character are Marshall Bazaine and Cardinal Labatista.

The succession of events between 1865 and 1867 is well known to history. The guerillas loyal to Juárez drained the resources of the insufficiently armed French expeditionary forces commanded by Bazaine; Charlotte tried to get help from Napoleon III and the Pope; the expeditionary forces retreated; Charlotte imprudently delayed her return from Europe. All these circumstances undermined Maximilian's leadership, though he remained faithfully at his post until the end, when he was shot by a firing squad at Querétaro.

This story is not so much an account of a dramatic event as the documentation of an inevitable tragedy, as Charlotte's despair deepens and Maximilian's inner forces become paralyzed. The play is well constructed; all the characters are believable. The plot centers around the struggle between Juarez and Maximilian. There is a good balance between lyrical passages and scenes of action. The libretto's only fault is that it has too much dialogue; and, unfortunately, Milhaud has been overzealous in setting all of it in detail. One might point to a similar flaw in the Isolde–Brangäne dialogue in Wagner's *Tristan*.

On the whole, and given its historical framework, Milhaud's approach to *Maximilien* is the same as in his other operas: that is, the form is made to adjust to artistic necessities as he perceives them. Here is a chorus of desperate people, exiled in an inhospitable desert relieved from time to time by an oasis, but otherwise unshielded from the brutal sun. Only the nights are deep and mysterious, and full of tragedy. These contrasts and the resulting mood of conflict predestine Maximilian's pitiful downfall. As in *La brebis égarée,* a person is shown to be inescapably the prisoner of his environment. Even the faithful followers of the emperor are unable to exorcise the curse of these diabolically destructive surroundings. If Maximilian had not been shot but had retreated to Vera Cruz, the message of the drama would have been the same, for the story unfolds far more as a result of his solitude and inability to act than from any actual events. It is his state of mind that inspires the agonized tone of the musical score from beginning to end.

Each scene is shaped for the most part by its symphonic construction. The first act, the end of the second, and the first two scenes of the third are lyrical; the other parts are devoted to action. There is an abundance of melodic inventiveness. A number of themes appear in several, varied forms. They are so delicate and uncomplicated that even a slightly modified accompaniment changes their import. One example is the soldiers' song, which is accompanied by an instrumental canon over an ostinato bass (Ex. 6–62).

Ex. 6–62.

The vocal lines, as in other works by Milhaud concerned with an individual's inner struggle, tend to be subservient to the orchestra and join with the lines of instrumental melody without dominating them. Instead of writing characteristic music for each of the protagonists, he provided little differentiation between them. Their parts contribute to a kind of generalized emotion. Operas like the *Opéras-minute, Le pauvre matelot,* und *Orphée* are different in this respect, for in those works the vocal line is kept quite distinct from the accompaniment.

Maximilien does not differ greatly in either tonal language or impact from the large dramatic works already analyzed, so there is not much point in reiterating the salient points of Milhaud's style. However, it is worthwhile to point out the symphonic construction of the scenes. The first scene is a moderato in $\frac{6}{8}$ meter which introduces two very expressive melodies. This is followed by a kind of scherzo in $\frac{2}{4}$ meter which accompanies the entrance of the generals. Short as it is, the scherzo is complete, with a trio section and a da capo. Then comes a calmer portion, similar in feeling to the original moderato, and finally a repeat of the first section. A violent, concentrated fugal section serves as an interlude.

The music of the second scene, in the palace gardens, is a rhapsody based on the following few notes (Ex. 6–63).

Ex. 6–63.

It acts as a delicate prelude to the romance of Lopez and the scenes that follow, which are also based on the same motive. Next there is a splendid duo between Maximilian and Charlotte, then a short, mysterious symphonic interlude, marked by the rumble of a bass clarinet, that in a marvellous way separates the duo from the roar of the canon fired by Juárez's army. The fright of the imperial entourage is depicted by a rapid, nervously energetic five-voice fugue. Bazaine's entrance is underscored by a strong cadence. A coda momentarily recalls the mood of the rhapsody.

The whole of the first act is superb, as is the end of the second, with its sad, calm orchestral interlude. Note also the funeral march in Act III, solemnly announced by a solo trombone, as well as the melancholy folk melody of the interlude that follows. Most impressive of all is the dungeon scene. Maximilian is attended by Salm and Herzfeld as he prepares for death. Milhaud's rare insight into the state of heart and mind of a human being faced with disgrace and defeat is reflected in this sober, restrainedly emotional adagio.

Perhaps one can admit that *Maximilien* is not a completely successful work. Its musical texture is probably too dense and complex for a theatrical piece. The effort required to follow its tightly woven polyphony and the effect of its generally severe emotional quality are exhausting. But when certain passages, especially the orchestral interludes, are heard alone, as they have been in numerous concert presentations, their brilliance and expressiveness are almost universally applauded.

La sagesse

Madame Ida Rubinstein's importance to contemporary music is well known. She was the creator of *Le martyre de San Sebastien,* by D'Annunzio and Debussy, and *La Pisanelle,* by D'Annunzio and Pizzetti. Ravel wrote his *Boléro* for her, and Stravinsky *Le baiser de la fée.* At her request Valéry and Honegger wrote *Amphion* and *Sémiramis,* and Gide joined Stravinsky in creating *Perséphone.* In 1935 her patronage extended to Claudel, who wrote two works: *Jeanne d'Arc au bûcher* and *La sagesse.* Honegger was chosen to write music for the former, and Milhaud undertook the setting of the latter. By the time the works were finished, the worsening political situation in Europe had made it impossible to contemplate any large stage productions. *Jeanne au bûcher* was heard in concert form in 1938, just before war once again plunged the European continent into a state of chaos; but the première of *La sagesse* was held over until peace had returned. On 7 November 1945 Manuel Rosenthal conducted a performance of the work under the auspices of the Radiodiffusion Française.

Claudel envisioned a staged cantata based on the parable of Wisdom's feast. The action would be choreographed, and the singing entirely choral. The first part is set against the background of a ruined temple. In the middle of the stage are two columns, and between them lies a woman enveloped in heavy veils. The chorus sings of the prodigal son who abandons his father, which is symbolic of the creature who abandons his Creator. The singers ask: "Who is this woman? Music, speak to her and ask who she is!" Wisdom answers that it is she who has been present since the beginning of time. The chorus admonishes her to search for all who have gone astray.

The second part shows Wisdom issuing invitations to her feast. While the chorus intones the Latin text of the parable, Wisdom vainly urges groups of people to attend, but all refuse.

In the third part, the chorus interrogates Wisdom and her servants. They have returned empty-handed from their quest and are now assembled at the foot of the Mountain of Human Endeavor. Wisdom climbs to the summit; around her she sees only desert. The chorus makes a last appeal:

> She who sells without price,
> Who buys without money,
> She offers herself to you.
> Take her unto yourselves,
> Come, eat, drink, live!

But when the righteous and the prudent still hold back, Wisdom turns to the sinners, the blind, and the insane. The chorus sings a dialogue:

> And what if, in spite of everything, they stay huddled in their dens,
>   then what shall I do?
> Force them to come out.
> How can I force them?
> Send your servants.
> And what shall I place in the hands of my servants?
> The whip!

The whip is illness, war, suffering, lust, and sin, and the following scene is a dance in which the servants harass mankind, beating the people and driving them apart in order to force them to attend the feast that Wisdom has prepared.

The stage setting of the fourth scene shows a half-completed building. Seven columns are already in place, and Wisdom is directing the work of construction. The people who have assembled are complaining. Wisdom has promised them a feast, and all they get is a lashing. But "there is something more powerful than the sting of the whip . . . and that is Music." Wisdom is building a house that rests on the seven columns, which represent the seven degrees of the scale. It is by drinking from the pure fountain of music that mankind will restore itself. For, as Alain says in *Les Dieux,* "The spirit enclosed in the body is bigger than all external worlds; spirit is only a word, but it is everything. It is most evident in music and poetry, for those are the two voices through which it speaks most eloquently."

This subject was certainly attractive to a man like Milhaud, whose whole life had been dedicated to celebrating through musical means the struggle of the individual conscience. He composed a strong, solemn score. The work has no dramatic action, so there was no need for the music to be dramatic. In many places it is entirely static, and the phrases unfold like garlands of sound draped over relatively immobile blocks of harmony and interlaced with rhythmically declaimed vocal lines (Ex. 6–64).

Ex. 6–64.

The more mobile passages are animated by iambic rhythms and by the orchestral introduction of certain melodic phrases that seem to emanate from the depths of Provençal folk tradition. This type of melodic configuration was typical of Milhaud's writing during this period. The culmination, in terms of concentrated rhythmic and melodic energy, is the dance of the third scene, in which truly "the movement of air from the winnow separates the wheat from the chaff."

The entire last section is a hymn of praise, eloquent in its simplicity. The coda is intoned rapidly, like a litany, and then comes to rest unexpectedly on a chord in its first inversion, which leaves the listener with a certain feeling of restlessness (Ex. 6–65).

Ex. 6–65.

La sagesse is one of the composer's most homogeneous works. Theatrically speaking, it derives from both opera and ballet; but in fact it creates a genre of its own, one in which singing, dancing, and staging are fused into a lyric whole.

Médée

Médée is another of those stories that had intrigued Milhaud for a long time before he actually set it to music. Fascinated by its tragic combination of utmost tenderness and horrifying cruelty, he had been thinking about it for at least fifteen years when, in 1959, the French government approached him with a proposal to compose an opera. This was part of a patronage program for painters and sculptors that had been newly extended to composers as well. At his request, Milhaud's wife Madeleine undertook the writing of the libretto for *Médée,* and since she knew to perfection the rhythms and verbal sonorities that best suited her husband's music, as well as his approach to drama, she produced a highly successful text. It follows the general outlines of Euripides' tragedy, conserving all the essential elements. In its treatment of the choruses, it is similar to Cocteau's adaptation of *Antigone.*

The story is as follows. Jason repudiates Medea and prepares to marry Creusa, daughter of Creon. Medea takes revenge in the most terrible way; she sends a dress saturated with poison as a gift to her rival. Creusa will die the minute she puts it on, and so will her father when he comes to her aid. But for Jason she conceives an even more terrible punishment: she murders the two children she has borne him.

The score of *Médée* is beautiful in every respect. Each character is finely drawn; the melody is conceived in sweeping phrases, often containing sections of vocalise; and the choral parts are eloquent. All in all, the various musical elements are in perfect balance. Creusa sings with charm and sensuousness (Ex. 6–66).

Ex. 6–66.

The haughty, cruel character of Medea is expressed by means of a rapid, angular vocal line, so terrifyingly unyielding that the singer can hardly take a breath (Ex. 6–67).

Ex. 6–67.

But when the children arrive, the music shows us the other side of Medea, her pitiful sorrow and tenderness (Ex. 6–68).

Ex. 6–68.

The score's center of gravity is Medea's beautiful prayer to Hecate, in which she begs the goddess to give her strength to accomplish her horrible act of sacrifice. This long invocation, built along simple, classic lines, sets the tone for the entire score, which is possibly the most architecturally perfect of all Milhaud's works for the stage.

In spite of the gathering war clouds, the Flemish Opera of Anvers premièred *Médée* on 7 October 1939, and the Paris Opera staged it with great success on 8 May 1940. The invasion of the Low Countries on 10 May prevented any subsequent performances.

Bolivar

In 1936 Milhaud wrote some incidental music for a Comédie Française production of Supervielle's *Bolivar*. The text especially appealed to him because of its combination of a revolutionary subject and a song- and dance-filled atmosphere typical of South America. Several years later, after coming to the United States and with happy memories of his previous sojourn in Brazil, he returned to this subject, viewing it doubtless also in the context of his own country's suffering and loss of freedom during the war years. Independence and the unfettered expression of indigenous culture were, indeed, the ideals for which the entire embattled world was struggling. In his autobiography Milhaud wrote:

The subject of *Bolivar* suited me perfectly because I wanted a story that was full of action and involved a male hero; in addition, this was a subject dominated by the spirit of liberation and liberty that so preoccupied me in 1943. I had already written incidental music for this play when it was produced at the Comédie Française, but in my opera, I used none of that material. As for the script, some changes were necessary in order to make it suitable for an operatic format. Supervielle, who was in Montevideo, sent me some "arias" to insert into the action, and Madeleine constructed a libretto that carefully preserved the poet's beautiful words; only at the end, when the dying Bolivar dreams of his young, dead wife, did she add a scene in which Bolivar writes his will, and for this part she used the exact text of the will itself.

Bolivar was the third drama based on American history that Milhaud set to music. The first was about Christopher Columbus, who opened the New World to European influence. The second, *Maximilien,* was about the struggle between the native peoples and the Europeans who had come to dominate them. *Bolivar,* finally, was a celebration of the successful fight for independence. Taken together, these three works can be considered as Milhaud's "American trilogy."

Christophe Colomb is an opera-oratorio and *Maximilien* a symphonic drama, but *Bolivar* is a grand opera in which singing predominates. Three acts and ten scenes outline the career of the hero as follows:

Act I, scene 1: 1803. Bolivar is a colonial landlord in San Mateo, Venezuela, living there with his devoted wife, Maria Teresa, and surrounded by his slaves and confidants. His wife becomes ill and dies, and Bolivar swears never to marry again.

Scene 2: Bolivar frees his slaves in memory of his wife who had begged him to do so. After a violent encounter with the visitador, the governor of the province, he decides to become the leader of the oppressed people in their struggle against Spanish authority.

Scene 3: 1812. Colonel Bolivar is the hero of the Caracas earthquake.

Scene 4: 1813. The mayor of Caracas is seen speculating on who will be the victor in the Battle of Taguanès. It turns out to be Bolivar, who enters the capital at the head of his army of independents after defeating the Spanish troops. He meets a young woman, Manuela Saenz, who becomes his mistress.

Act II, scene 1: 1814. Having been defeated at La Puerta, Bolivar leaves Manuela in haste to go and defend the capital. Bovès, the Spanish general, arrives.

Scene 2: Bovès devises an unorthodox strategy. He plans a ball in honor of Bolivar's mistress. She, her mother and sister, and the faithful Nicanor escape being shot only because Bovès suddenly becomes terrified at the sight of the widows and orphans of the Independent Army as they pray for help from their deceased husbands and fathers.

Scene 3: 1819. Bolivar crosses the Andes, and this daring expedition significantly contributes to his victory over the Spanish.

Act III, scene 1: 1826. Bolivar, at the height of his glory, is received at Lima in Peru. He refuses the king's crown, which is offered by the delegation from Colombia, but accepts the naming of a country, Bolivia, in his honor.

Scene 2: 1828. The negress Precipitacion warns Manuela of a plot against Bolivar. His faithful Nicanor dies. Manuela saves the Liberator.

Scene 3: 1830. Betrayed by his old friends, sick and impoverished, Bolivar dreams of his young wife, Maria Teresa, whom he has never forgotten. Dying, he envisions their reunion in a life of simple obscurity and devotion.

In this opera the historical subject is presented through narration and scenes of action. The Orestes trilogy had enveloped the main characters—Orestes, Apollo, and Athena—in a web of moral conflict and philosophical dialectic that molded their actions. *Christophe Colomb* also involved a generalized interplay of ideas, with the result that the individual protagonists became symbols of moral issues. But an opera of action treats its characters in an entirely different way. Each one has a characteristic profile, and the orchestral background, as well as the choral sections, must support and emphasize the various personalities.

The orchestra comes into its own in the interludes that separate the scenes and also in the dance in which Bovès forces the women to take part while their menfolk are being shot. This impressive scene includes an onstage orchestra, which plays over and over a kind of Mexican "bamba," while the music of the main orchestra in the pit comments on the horror of this repugnant event. The lyric high points of the work are the arias of Bolivar and Manuela.

Rhythmically, as well as melodically, the score is shot through with the South American motifs that so intrigued Milhaud. One dominant rhythm is that of the bamba, introduced in the very first measures and later used in the terrible second act dance scene, which is the focal point of the entire score.

Bolivar was given its first performance at the Paris Opera on 12 May 1950, under the most favorable circumstances. André Cluytens was the precise, sensitive conductor; Janine Micheau took the part of Manuela, and Roger Bourdin that of Bolivar. Fernand Léger's stage designs, perfectly realized by Maurice Moulène, were masterpieces. Léger had always appreciated Milhaud's music, and it was he who had designed the mobile, lively sets for *La création du monde*. He outdid himself with *Bolivar*. "His designs for the crossing of the Andes epitomized the whole unforgettable effect of the opera. Léger's combination of the Andes of legend with the Andes of reality was a tour de force." So wrote Hélène Parmelin in her study *Cinq peintres et le théâtre,* published in 1956. The first performance was a triumphant success. Of course the critics did everything possible to try to close it down, but the enthusiasm of the public kept the work in the repertory for two seasons.

David

Like *Bolivar, David* is an opera based on history. Whereas the American trilogy and the compositions celebrating Provence reflect Milhaud's sympathy for a Mediterranean culture that appeared to him to stretch from Palestine to the Gulf of Mexico, the subject of *David* returned him to the very roots of his spiritual heritage. He himself has described the circumstances that led to the composition of this opera.

Koussevitsky . . . proposed that I compose an important work for the Israel Festival that he was arranging in celebration of the three-thousand-year anniversary of King David and the founding of Jerusalem. Commissions always stimulate a composer's imagination; this is the kind of discipline to which only a well-developed technique can respond without constraint. In this case I was fortunate in being able to work with a musical format that I liked; in addition, the responsibility of composing for such an occasion filled me with pride, notwithstanding considerable anxiety. Koussevitsky left the choice of a collaborator up to me. I immediately suggested Armand Lunel; I had always enjoyed working with him, and we could discuss the problems of a libretto without having to worry about the kind of misunderstandings that sometimes arise.

Milhaud conceived his opera not only as a tribute to the grandeur and leadership of King David, revered by Christians as well as Jews, who consider him the embodiment of their law, faith, and comportment; he also saw in the founding of Jerusalem a parallel with the establishment of Israel by modern Jews, who had returned from all over the world to work with joy and energy at the rebuilding of their homeland. He clearly explains this view in *Ma vie heureuse,* when he describes traveling to Israel in order to submit Lunel's text to the religious authorities who, according to the laws of the country, had to approve it.

The Minister of Education and Culture had assigned two young men to show us around the country, an assignment that they executed with utmost fervor, pointing out the places made famous by Holy Scripture, as well as those where they themselves had fought four years earlier. The story of their stubborn, glorious struggle implied such a strong bond between their heroism and that of their ancestors that we were inspired to draw a similar parallel in the opera by using two choruses: one associated with the action taking place, and the other, composed of modern Israelis, to comment on the situation and make a comparison between ancient and modern times. For example, just as David had faced Goliath, so had their small state confronted the armies of five countries. I used neither popular nor liturgical melodies in the score, although I had heard many beautiful ones.
The writing of a libretto for *David* required great delicacy, given the diverse characteristics of the man. It had to show David as poet, patriarch, and lover . . . and it had to portray Bathsheba without offending any religious sensitivities. Lunel succeeded admirably. My score presents no performance problems.

It was Milhaud's intent that the Israelis should be the ones to sing about their own history. The score, published in Tel Aviv, gives detailed instructions as to the distribution of the work into successive dramatic episodes. The score is notable for its prominent use of successive parallel thirds and sixths, which firmly accentuate the tonalities of the bitonal texture. This tonal reinforcement, which was necessary for the choral participation of the people of Israel, is used consistently throughout and contributes to the opera's homogeneity of style (Ex. 6–69).

Ex. 6–69.

In certain passages reflecting a kind of mysterious anguish, the composer has joined two contrasting themes: one almost disappears in the highest orchestral registers, the other rumbles in the extreme bass. The middle registers are completely empty. Berlioz used an analogous but more rudimentary device in the Sanctus of his Requiem (Ex. 6–70).

Ex. 6–70.

The finale of the third act is built on a uniform metric pattern, a repeated rhythmic figure, as in a sonata movement. From a dynamic point of view, the energy of this finale culminates in the Dance before the Ark which opens the fourth act. The sequence is so obvious that one regrets the pause that separates the two acts. The Dance before the Ark starts with a brief prelude, as imperious as a Bach concerto, and then develops over an exceptionally spacious rhythmic ostinato (Ex. 6–71).

Ex. 6–71.

These pages contain some of the most convincing statements of the entire work.

The Dance before the Ark is followed after an interlude by a scene in which "David and Bathsheba, somberly dressed and seated side by side on a bench, carry on a dialogue that blends tenderness with despair." The duality of passion and guilt is a strangling emotion when deeply experienced; a person can neither weep nor rebel. Other great pieces of music have portrayed this same feeling of desperation: Dorabella's aria in *Così fan tutte* and the finale in *Aïda,* to mention only two examples. Both Mozart and Verdi employed, for expressive purposes rather than for brilliance, a vocal line characterized by great intervallic leaps. In Verdi's music, plunges of a tenth downward or unexpected upward major sevenths followed by augmented fourths, the *diabolus in musica,* disrupt the usual vocal progressions. The tonality becomes somewhat disoriented, and this effect contributes to the impression of doubt and distress. Moments such as these have a timeless expressive validity.

The scene between David and Bathsheba belongs in the same category. Devoid of special coloristic effects or emphases, it projects an aura of resignation, even of transfiguration. Their distress is expressed with utmost tenderness. Unlike Mozart's music, this vocal line stays simple, while the great intervallic leaps are heard in the orchestral accompaniment. Also, the slow tempo and the subtle dynamic nuances emphasize the underlying tension of the dramatic situation far better than would any vocal acrobatics. When Nathan enters toward the end of the scene and prophesies that David will be punished, one is also reminded of Mozart, specifically of the commandant's second appearance in *Don Giovanni.* The similarity of the two situations has induced Milhaud to make use of the same series of eight notes that were uttered by Mozart's avenger. These notes then become the basis for a tone row that is transposed and inverted in the accompaniment to Nathan's aria (Ex. 6–72).

Ex. 6–72.

David is certainly one of the most important and successful of Milhaud's works. It is a summation of his enormous technical mastery, gained throughout a lifetime of daily practice, as well as of his most profound musical insights.

Fiesta

In 1958 Hermann Scherchen asked Milhaud to write a one-act opera for the Modern Music Festival in Berlin. It was Francis Poulenc who suggested that he ask Boris Vian to provide a libretto. Vian (1920–59) was an engineer, jazz musician, and writer of popular lyrics. He was also, according to one of his admirers, "a romancer of paradox, fantasy, emotion, and of the absurd." In relation to the generation of St. Germain des Prés, he was thirty years ahead of his time. With his black humor, his combination of serenity and anxiety, of smile and grimace, Vian had come to be considered a prototype of his era. He was immediately sensitive to Milhaud's temperament, and the script he produced had certain similarities with that of *Le pauvre matelot*.

His story takes place on the bleached sand of a little fishing village somewhere in the American tropics. Salt-stained fish baskets and primitive tackle lie scattered about under the blinding rays of the sun. The sea is almost white, and the sky unrelentingly blue. As the curtain rises, two tattered figures, half hidden by their giant sombreros, are seen stretched out near a lamp post. Men and women circulate lethargically. Then a child spots a disabled ship nearing the shore. In it lies a half-drowned man. The people lift him out, warm him, give him something to eat and drink, and gradually coax him back to life. The man's spirit is so revived by all this attention that he gets a little too lively and begins to flirt with the ladies, especially with the girl friend of one of the two idlers. As calmly and with the same detachment with which he had fished the half-drowned stranger out of the sea, the idler strolls over and stabs the newcomer in the back. Now the people have to decide what to do with the body. The solution is simple; it is thrown back into the sea, and the torpor of midday once again envelops the port.

The score calls for a dozen singers and thirteen solo instruments. They are distributed in the high and low registers, engendering a certain acid quality that bites into the more prevalent atmosphere of nonchalance. The middle registers are reserved for the vocal lines, with the result that the singers never have to force their sound in order to be heard. This lack of loud outbursts and grand gestures contributes to the mood of quasi-indifference. The characters show no particular awareness of the irony of the situation; in fact, the whole sequence is dreamlike.

The uniformity of the musical material also adds to the impression of lethargy. It contains two seemingly contradictory elements, a passive rocking back and forth, like the waves of a tranquil ocean, and a rapid instrumental commentary, which indicates the nervousness that lies beneath the apparent indolence. The velvety sonorities of flute, clarinet, and bass clarinet, seasoned with the zesty sound of an alto saxophone, counterbalance the harsh harmonies (Ex. 6–73).

Ex. 6–73.

155

The work's center of gravity falls near the end, at the moment when the girl flirts with the shipwrecked sailor, who is then suddenly struck down. After that, the torpor resumes. However, from beginning to end, a certain underlying feeling of uneasiness is never absent. Is it the sound of the poet's humorless laughter?

La mère coupable

For some time Mr. Valcarenghi, the director of Ricordi, had been asking me to write an opera. The idea of doing *La mère coupable,* by Beaumarchais, occurred to me. This is the last drama in the cycle that includes *The Barber of Seville* and *The Marriage of Figaro.* It has the same characters as the previous two; only they have become older, wiser, and perhaps more human. The play is subtitled "The new Tartuffe," perhaps because Beaumarchais introduces a new element in the person of Begaers, a traitor who tries to enrich himself by ruining Count Almaviva; only Figaro is able to thwart him in his diabolical attempt. Valcarenghi asked Madeleine to make a synopsis of the play; and after reading it, he asked her to write the libretto. She reduced five long acts to three, speeding up the action and building the suspense, without ever departing from Beaumarchais' original text. [*Ma vie heureuse,* 1st ed., p. 281.]

The work was conscientiously produced at the Grand Théâtre in Geneva on 13 June 1966. It isn't a good play to begin with; that fact has been acknowledged for a long time. It never had the success of the other two, but Milhaud thought it would adapt well to operatic treatment. Madeleine Milhaud made an intelligent adaptation of the Beaumarchais original, bringing out the contrast between the more dramatic posture of Rosina and Begaers and the lively wit of Suzanna and Figaro. Count Almaviva's role, being less important, was more stylized. To enliven the plot further, there is a love affair between Léon, the son of Rosina and Cherubino, and Florestine, an illegitimate daughter of the Count.

But in spite of all attempts to tighten it up, the text remained little more than a succession of prosaic dialogues that offer meager opportunity for lyric treatment. All the complicated intrigues are difficult to follow. The only way the problem might have been solved would have been with a series of lightly accompanied secco recitatives; for it is absolutely essential to understand every word of the complex tangle of maneuvers and explications. That type of musical style was, of course, completely incompatible with Milhaud's musical temperament. He chose instead to give the dramatic puzzle to the orchestral voices. The score, as a result, is vivacious and compact, but lacks the contrast inherent in the plot. There is absolutely no opportunity for lyricism. The result is tiresomely monotonous, with only a possible moment of relief at the end of the second act.

Saint-Louis

This work was commissioned in 1970 by the French Minister for Cultural Affairs as a commemoration of the seven-hundredth anniversary of the birth of Saint Louis. Milhaud has written as follows:

Henri Doublier was given the task of coordinating this project, and he made an appropriate selection of thirteenth-century texts for the dramatic part of the opera. To provide more lyrical episodes, I chose excerpts from two poems that Claudel had written about Saint Louis. I composed an opera-oratorio involving four characters. It is an austere work without fantasy. The action is carried by the soloists and by a madrigal group of sixteen singers who have minor roles. They are accompanied by a thirteen-piece on-stage orchestra. The full orchestra and the chorus are in the pit, and they are heard only in the interludes between scenes and at the end of each act. . . . This opera has had a strange career. Though it was commissioned by the government, the French radio refused to perform it. It was first performed in Rome and first staged at the Opera House in Rio de Janeiro [*Ma vie heureuse,* 1st ed., pp. 287–289.]

The four characters are France personified, King Louis, Queen Marguerite, and the Seneschal Joinville. The plan of the work is as follows:

Introduction
Prologue: France
First part: I. The chronicler and the poet
                    II. Saint Louis and the poor
                 III. Saint Louis and France
                IV. The King's justice
                  V. God is Love
                VI. Announcement of Queen Blanche's death
               VII. King Louis's two wives
Second part: VIII. The king's council at Acre
                IX. The king is a prisoner of love
                 X. The personification of the lily
               XI. The king's death at Carthage

From the titles of the scenes, it is evident that there is very little action and that lyrical opportunities predominate. Like Schoenberg's *Moses and Aaron,* Milhaud's *Saint-Louis* creates an entirely new musico-dramatic form.

During the last years of his life, Milhaud became more and more introspective. From 1968 on, he turned almost entirely to the creation of abstract music, a medium that he had spent a lifetime perfecting in his extensive output of chamber music. His thorough mastery of free contrapuntal technique had developed to full fruition over a period of at least fifty years. Now, too, his deeply religious nature became more manifest. The works of his later years, such as the music for Claudel's

Tobie et Sara, the choral work *Promesse de Dieu,* and the cantata *Ani Maamin,* along with *Saint-Louis,* all reflect his preoccupation with the ultimate encounter of a man with his creator. This music proclaims, as it were, the moral outcome of such a dialogue.

His instrumental music of this period reflects the same, almost monastic single-mindedness. Works such as the Trio (op. 428), the *Musique pour Graz, Musique pour Ars Nova,* and his final opus, the *Quintette à vent,* consist almost entirely of a free-flowing kind of counterpoint in which a constant succession of ideas evolve one from another. Without parallel in our own age, this style of writing is reminiscent of the Ars Nova of Philippe de Vitry and Guillaume de Machaut.

The score of *Saint-Louis* represents a superb combination of religious conviction and musical distinction. Also, Doublier did a fine job of selecting the most beautiful texts by Joinville and Claudel. The sections that are spoken, by the poet and the chronicler, alternate effectively with those that are sung. The balance between the smaller and larger groups of singers and instrumentalists also appears to have been successful judging by the taped recording of the Rome performance. It is difficult to classify the genre. *Saint-Louis* does not belong on the opera stage; it has too little action. Yet, in a concert version it loses its full impact. For one thing, the words tend to be buried under the weight of orchestral sound, and that is serious because of the extreme importance of the poetry. Richard Strauss's *Capriccio,* which he subtitled "conversation piece" rather than opera, and Schoenberg's *Moses and Aaron* present similar problems. Neither is an opera in the true sense of the word, and yet both require some sort of staging in order to be fully effective. The adaptation of *Moses and Aaron* for the screen provided an entirely felicitous solution for that work. The form of the music is complemented by a rather architectural distribution of soloists and choral groups. This spacing of the singers makes it possible to hear every syllable, and at the same time the camera need not move in so close that facial expressions become disturbing. The visual presentation is in every way integrated into the music and helps it to be understood. Let us hope that a similarly successful solution will be found for *Saint-Louis,* for it is a work in which beauty of text is fully matched by music of superior quality.

In this score the vocal lines express inner spiritual conflict, rather than externalized sentiment. To achieve this effect the composer has used a pure, abstract chamber-music style, which by the way is not one familiar to most opera singers. For a good performance, the members of the onstage orchestra should be experienced chamber musicians, not just players who are accustomed only to being in a large orchestra. The singers likewise must consider themselves soloists performing in ensemble, and they must be especially careful to enunciate clearly.

Last Works

In spite of the general severity of Milhaud's musical vision during his later years, there were many moments at which his habitual charm, and even gaiety, prevailed. Note, for example, the music of his ballets. After *Moïse* (1940) came:

Les Cloches (after *The Bells,* by Edgar Allan Poe), 1945
'Adame miroir (Jean Genet), 1948
Vendanges (Philippe de Rothschild), 1952
La rose des vents (Roland Petit), 1957
La branche des oiseaux (André Chamson), 1958–59.

Add to these the dances of *La cueillette de citrons,* written for *Barba Garibo.* This is a sunny, charming work which Lunel and Milhaud adapted from Mentonaise folklore.

'Adame miroir is a work of exceptional verve. A young sailor and his mirror image flirt with death. It is the image, rather than the sailor, who vanquishes death. The ballet ends with a fugal danse macabre.

Vendanges is the title of a poem written by Philippe de Rothschild. It describes the cycle of nature. First the sap wells up into the plant; then come bud, flower, and fruit. The fruit is taken from the vine-covered hillsides to become wine. Beneath the earth are a Man and a Woman, symbols of fertility. They elude the watchful vigil of the Black Harvester. On earth, the harvest proceeds. The wine is left to ferment in a huge vat. While a wedding is in progress, the Man and Woman rise up from beneath the earth, excite the guests, and inspire the newly-weds with passion. The Great Red Fawn, king of the feast and eternal lover, appears. For a moment he seeks his prey. But his old adversary, the Black Harvester, is ready for him. The natural cycle continues. The Man and Woman return to their quiet vigil; everything is in suspense until the next year's awakening. "Thus," says Alain Bosquet, "the harvester becomes his own harvest." Obviously this subject had great appeal for the composer of *L'homme et son désir* and *La création du monde. Vendanges* was given an excellent première performance by the Nice Opera Company on 7 April 1972. Included on the same program were *Fiesta* and *Le pauvre matelot.* The occasion was planned as a tribute to Milhaud, who was made an honorary citizen of the city on that day.

It was Roland Petit who suggested the text of *La rose des vents,* a work that seemed to call for the insertion of several "café-chantant" tunes reminiscent of an old-time bistro.

The last ballet, *La branche des oiseaux,* appears to have been conceived by its author, André Chamson, as a kind of extension of Milhaud's own personality. It synthesizes impressions of places where the composer had lived and worked. Thus, at the end of his life, Milhaud once again found inspiration in the environment that had first nurtured his creative spirit: Les Saintes-Maries-de-la-Mer, the world of antiquity, and Provence.

*   *   *

This concludes our study of Milhaud's dramatic and choreographic oeuvre. His final theatrical piece was a choral comedy, *Les momies d'Egypte,* which used figures from the Italian commedia dell'arte combined with some French bourgeois characters. In the tradition of Orazio Vecchi *(L'amfiparnasso)* and Banchieri *(Il festino),* the individual roles are sung by a choral group. "Presented in concert," wrote the composer, "it would be quite possible to mime or dance the story." This little comedy by Regnard is one of those often given at the Foire St. Germain. The text is a delightful mixture of French and Italian. For example, Harlequin says: "Alessandro Magno quel gran filosofo aveva ragione di dire che la donna est une girouette d'inconsistance et un moulin à vent de légéreté." Then follows an uninterrupted exchange of bilingual repartee. The idea of writing an a cappella work of this sort had been at the back of Milhaud's mind for quite some time. *L'amfiparnasso* and *Il festino* were written for five voices: two sopranos, one contralto, a tenor, and a bass. This distribution facilitated considerable differentiation between male and female roles. For example, the two sopranos and the contralto (or a countertenor) would be used for the female parts, and a countertenor, tenor, and bass for the masculine ones.

Milhaud limited himself to only four voices, however. He juxtaposed the women's against the men's timbres with truly "Italian" dexterity. When a female role is being sung by the four voices, the soprano and alto chatter along in eighth notes, discreetly punctuated by the tenor and bass. The reverse obtains when the voices take a man's role: that is, the lower two voices sing the rapid notes. The resulting effect is a delightful burlesque. *Les momies d'Egypte* was written for the chamber chorus of the Graz Academy at the same time that the new version of *Christophe Colomb* was being prepared for performance in that city.

Incidental Music

Milhaud's stage works include a number of pieces of incidental music. In this category can be included the music to Claudel's *Protée,* already discussed. As a general rule, Milhaud used music in connection with plays in order to give moments of lyric relief, rather than to comment on the action. Almost all these interludes are short, completely

160

self-contained little pieces. In this, he follows the tradition set by Bizet's *L'Arlésienne* and Fauré's *Pelléas et Mélisande*. Accordingly, all these scores are easily adapted as concert suites, as was, for example, his music for *Protée,* which became the second symphonic suite.

Examples of the composer's best incidental music include the first version of *L'annonce faite à Marie* and *Le château des papes,* on a text by André de Richaud, from which excerpts were taken for *Adages,* a composition for vocal quartet with instrumental accompaniment, as well as for *La cheminée du roi René.* Aside from their charm, these pieces exhibit some interesting instrumentation. It is no secret that the Théâtre de l'Atelier had little room for an orchestra. But its director, Charles Dullin, was so fine an artist that composers went to great lengths to compose music of the highest quality for him, using the very modest resources available. *Le château des papes* was scored for two pianos, one trumpet, and ondes Martenot. This last instrument is capable of producing almost any kind of sound, as well as a complete range of dynamics. The tones are nonpercussive and have variable timbres. They can be made quite expressive and add a new dimension to musical texture. Milhaud made excellent use of the instrument on several occasions. In *L'annonce faite à Marie* Milhaud accompanied the scene of the miracle with a vocal quartet and wrote preludes before each tableau. This work also used the ondes Martenot, combined with vibraphone, organ, piano, winds, strings, and percussion.

The Théâtre Antique at Orange commissioned music to accompany the play *Bertran de Born,* by Valmy-Baisse. It was from this score that Milhaud extracted one of his most famous compositions, the *Suite provençale.* None of the themes are actually taken from folk music, but they conjure up a joyous world of troubadours and street players so typical of medieval Provence. The rhythms and sonorities all bear the stamp of total authenticity. This is the best kind of popular music.

In the same vein, the *Marche funèbre* for Romain Rolland's *Quatorze juillet* captures the same mood as that projected by Rude's sculptured *Marseillaise* on the Arc de Triomphe. There is also another fine *Cortège funèbre,* written as a conclusion to a film about the Spanish Civil War that Malraux produced in 1939. It, too, is very successful in concert version. From the incidental music to *Le médecin volant,* by Molière, comes the sparkling *Scaramouche* suite for two pianos, which has had such a big success.

In 1942 Jouvet asked Milhaud for a new musical setting of *L'annonce faite à Marie.* He wanted to produce the work in Rio de Janeiro, and the original score was in Paris and therefore unavailable during the war years. From that version came extracts known as the *Neuf préludes* for organ and the *Cinq prières* for voice and organ. Other scores include music for Berthold Brecht's *Mother Courage,* which, in fact, was never produced, and Luigi Sturzo's *Cycle de la création.* The austere music for Claudel's *Tobie et Sara* has already been mentioned.

The *son et lumière* spectacles, which are presented at various places of historical and architectural importance throughout France, are a kind of modern phenomenon. Milhaud's contribution to this genre is *Vézelay, la colline éternelle,* on which he collaborated with Maurice Druon. Also, in 1936, he and Claudel contributed to a spectacle combining light and water, entitled *Fête de la lumière.*

VII

Vocal Music

Intelligence is the passion of youth. But life is the passion of the mature man. One lives by heart alone.

André Suarès, *Vers Venise*

Songs

Lyricism is out of fashion nowadays. Form and construction are considered prime virtues, and to call an artist intelligent is to pay him the highest compliment. Certainly, creative intelligence is a necessary ingredient of art, but it is wrong to place it above emotion. Pure abstraction may have a certain validity, but it is only when inspiration is combined with intellect that art reaches its highest pinnacle. Especially in troubled times, it is understandable that an artist will thirst for order, but there is a risk that formalism may come to be worshipped for its own sake. Only the great artist incorporates feelings and sensations to the enhancement of design.

That explains why the paintings of a genius like Picasso continue to delight long after many of his "formally perfect" contemporaries have been forgotten. His work is beautiful, not because he is an intelligent painter—which he is—but because he communicates human emotion. When he attaches a strip of cloth, a shred of paper, or a faded rose to a board, it is as though he were speaking to us. We feel the intensity of his vision and hear his heart beating.

Intelligence divorced from its role of ordering inspiration can lead to a kind of self-consciousness that, in turn, becomes eccentricity. Certain of Cocteau's writings suffer in this respect, as does some of Stravinsky's music; and it is this lack of balance that occasionally spoils the work of even so gifted a musician as Francis Poulenc. Too much self-analysis can swiftly destroy the habit of imagination, and when that happens, taste replaces vision and the artistic horizon is narrowed.

Again turning to painting for illustration, we can readily recognize the charming, perfectly harmonized landscapes of an intelligent

163

painter; but as conceived by a great master, a well-equilibriated landscape becomes only one of many expressive elements. "In Goya's paintings," writes Eugenio d'Ors, "background is as important as the human figure. Cosmic emphasis replaces a purely anthropomorphic one (as in Rembrandt). It is what leads to intimations of the infinite."

This observation applies equally well to the complexities of a musical composition. Each well-thought-out and technically correct element is related to all the others by a higher formal concept that is shaped by the heart. True lyricism, which has nothing to do with sentimentality, is the result of this equilibrium between mind and spirit.

*   *   *

All Milhaud's songs for single voice are lyric in the above sense of the word, and some of them are extremely beautiful. They are not all alike. In France the word *mélodie* is applied to songs by Fauré, Debussy, and Duparc—that is, to vocal works that do not fall into a specific form such as the *Lied*. In other words, the term is applied to all freely constructed pieces for solo voice with piano accompaniment. It would seem more appropriate, however, to reserve the appellation for compositions that follow a symmetrically constructed poem, such as Duparc's *Invitation au voyage* and most of Fauré's songs. On the other hand, pieces like *La vie antérieure* or "La vague et la cloche" of Duparc and the *Poèmes de Baudelaire* and *Proses lyriques* of Debussy have nothing in common, either in form or in content, with Fauré's "Les berceaux" or "Nell." Debussy's "Colloque sentimental" is even further removed from the simple designation *mélodie*.

Perhaps it would be appropriate to call them lyric fragments. Although written with keyboard accompaniment, they are more a kind of vocal chamber music than concert pieces. During all of music history, free-form songs set to either dramatic or lyric texts have existed side by side with more symmetrically constructed ones. Think of Monteverdi's *Lettere amorose in genere rappresentativo* in a collection dating from 1623. Instead of writing a canzonetta, which would also have been appropriate for salon performance, Monteverdi chose to create a kind of dramatic interlude based on a long poetic fragment. It is this genre, quite different from that of the *chanson* or the *mélodie,* that created a precedent for works like those of Debussy and Duparc mentioned above, for *La bonne chanson* of Fauré, and for dramatic interludes like Milhaud's *Alissa* and *Poèmes de Claudel.*

In this kind of composition the writing is part pure melody, part recitative. The more lyrical of those by Milhaud are: *Trois poèmes de Lucile de Châteaubriand, Catalogue de fleurs, Machines agricoles, Chansons bas,* and *Deux petits airs de Stéphane Mallarmé.* In a dramatic vein are the *Sept poèmes de la connaissance de l'est, Quatre poèmes de*

Claudel, Quatre poemes de Léo Latil and a *Poème de Latil* taken from his journal, *D'un cahier inédit d'Eugénie de Guérin, Soirées de Petrograd,* and *Alissa,* based on André Gide's *La porte étroite.* Then there are some true *melodies:* the *Poésies de Catulle* for voice and violin, and the *Child Poems,* by Rabindranath Tagore. Finally, there is a series that reflects the religious lyricism of the Jews in southern France: *Poèmes juifs, Chants populaires hébraïques, Prières journalières à l'usage des juifs du Comtat Venaissin,* and *Liturgie Comtadine.*

It is impossible to discuss every one of the 265 songs (64 different opus numbers), which stand like mileposts in the composer's life and thought, but we shall mention a few general characteristics.

By 1908–09 Milhaud's poetic, as well as musical, preferences were already pronounced. At school he had formed two deep friendships, about which he writes at length in his autobiography *Ma vie heureuse.* These youthful companions were Léo Latil and Armand Lunel. Through Latil, Milhaud discovered the writings of contemporary poets, including Maurice de Guérin and Francis Jammes. He was affected by Latil's sensitive nature, his tenderness, profound religious sentiment, and tragic concept of life, which were combined with an elemental love of nature and also of music. Lunel, though not gregarious, was a far more energetic, even theatrical, personality. He too loved nature, but unlike Latil sought out the burning, passionate aspects of his surroundings. Both were writers: Latil was romantic, elegiac, and refined; Lunel exuberant and extravagant. Both were passionately supportive of their friend's early attempts at composition.

The divergent, outwardly opposed characteristics of his two friends actually corresponded to two complementary aspects of Milhaud's own personality, and he veered alternately toward one or the other before finally amalgamating the two tendencies. Writing in his autobiography, he recalls: "At night as I was falling asleep, I would close my eyes and imagine that I was hearing music of such extraordinary freedom that it was impossible to write it down. How could I express it? It was a great, mysterious experience in which I immersed myself, a kind of retreat to the deepest recesses of my subconscious, where my musical language could expand and develop."

To reconcile and give voice to all this complexity within him, Milhaud needed to develop a very personal kind of musical language. The means that he chose were based on simplicity and precision. By 1909 he had settled into a lyric climate provided by Jammes, Latil, Lunel, and Debussy. This period lasted until 1913, when Paul Claudel entered his life and mind, opening up vast new horizons.

Between 1910 and 1912 he composed, in order, the settings of sixteen poems by Jammes and three by Latil, a first sonata for violin and piano, the opera *La brebis égarée* by Jammes, a string quartet, and three more songs on texts by Jammes. His youthful desire to give form to intense emotion surged through all these works. Writing to Léo Latil, he exclaimed:

Oh, your poem! I understand it so well. You know, I want to take all the themes and developments of my andante and join them to your words. I sing them as I am playing through my andante. Later I'll do just that and I'll burn my sonata, for it will have no reason to exist except for the second part that came to me when my solitude met yours as I read the part of your diary written at Boulouris. That was the greatest emotion of my life, because I felt you so close to me and a part of me, only it was you who had expressed the closeness, as you always express it, and I felt that same sentiment so strongly in the diary that when I came home, I sat down and wrote my whole andante without stopping. So you are the one responsible for it. Now everything is condensed into your poem, and all I want is for my music to sing out its message even more strongly. But I want my music to support your words humbly, so that everyone will know I wrote it for you.

Also illustrated by these first six opuses is Milhaud's pattern of turning to chamber music after he had finished a vocal work. As a counterbalance to the freedom permitted in vocal writing, he seemed to need the contrapuntal restraints imposed by chamber music. There was no dichotomy between the two media. At the end of the first song in his opus 1, for example, he wrote: "Sketch for the quartet." The rhythmic motive of that song later became the theme of his first quartet. In this way he was able to fulfill his inner requirements for both imaginative freedom and technical discipline.

Opus 1 consists of two sets of songs on poems by Jammes. Even in these early works a distinctly personal style is discernible, as for example in the time values and accentuations given to certain syllables. In some of the phrases there are hints of the variety and flexibility that will characterize future melodies. However, the influence of *Pelléas* still lingers—for example in the repetition of the same note on consecutive syllables. The piano accompaniment is purely harmonic and homophonic and is marked by a predominance of parallel fifths, though some strange and unexpected modulations disrupt the conventional tonality. These modulations are obviously introduced for expressive purposes, and they seem to be harbingers of the composer's desire to free himself from tonal restraints. The best songs in the collection are the first one, "Avec ton parapluie," the theme of which was later used in the first string quartet, and "Prière pour être simple," in which the harmonic writing is clearer and more assured than in some of the others. The prevailing sentiment reflects Latil's somber melancholy superimposed on Jammes's bucolic charm.

The three songs of opus 2, on texts by Latil, continue in this vein. And then, in the fall of 1912, the composer's preoccupation with melancholy suddenly dissipates. Was the change due to Milhaud's trip to Orthez, where he visited Jammes and found him so full of enthusiasm and so joyously surrounded by the simple, good things that he loved? Or was it due to more frequent contact with Lunel, who, like Milhaud, had moved to Paris to continue his studies? In any event, his developing youthful spirit was becoming more and more fascinated with human beings, and his third group of songs on texts by Jammes was a collection of three portraits. In this opus 6 the musical style has become more subtle and flexible. In one portrait, "Clara d'Ellebeuse," note how some phrases end on the seventh degree or leading note of the scale. Is it a suspension, or the beginning of a modulation? The question is never answered except in one's subconscious.

The *Sept poèmes de la connaissance de l'est* date from 1913 and mark the beginning of Milhaud's collaboration with Paul Claudel. Each of these musical settings is a noble little drama, broadly and powerfully conceived to match the poetic inspiration. Without hesitation the composer has chosen just the right manner of supplementing the words. His music is incised into Claudel's poetry. Technically there are still flaws, but in spite of Debussy-like triplets and a Franckian excess of arpeggios, the fresh vision of an innovative musical mind is much in evidence. This apt, sharp style of writing is well illustrated by the song "Tristesse de l'eau" (Ex. 7–1).

Ex. 7–1.

There is a similar strident quality in the *Quatre poèmes pour baryton* (1915–1917), also by Claudel. These are weighty pronouncements, not lightweight entertainment. Note the stormy, frigid atmosphere, like a spring squall, of "Le sombre mai," the unrelieved sorrow of "Obsession," and the starkness of "Ténèbres." Great clusters of harmonies well up from the bass. The outbursts of sound anticipate the *Choéphores* and bring to mind visions of the emperor's burned countenance in Claudel's *Le repos du septième jour*.

The *Poèmes de Lucile de Châteaubriand,* written in 1913, are quite different in style. In this elegant, happy work, a stylistic characteristic begins to appear which later becomes typical. This is the expressive device of accenting the first syllable of a word, followed by relaxation on the second (Ex. 7–2).

Ex. 7–2.

Accenting of this kind, which highlights emotion by altering the natural cadence of the language, is even more pronounced in the settings of
Eugénie de Guérin's beautiful poems (1915: Ex. 7–3).

Ex. 7–3.

The music is deeply moving, without being the slightest bit sentimental.

The so-called romantic song cycles date from this period (opus 11
and 19). It seems strange that, after having been captivated by
Jammes's simplicity and Claudel's energy, Milhaud should have
turned again to texts by Romantic poets. Perhaps Latil's influence still
dominated a part of his soul. But there may have been other, purely
musical reasons as well. The setting of the long elegy by Lamartine, for

example, is actually a kind of exercise in giving a more thematically interesting role to the piano accompaniment. This virtuoso treatment of the instrumental part becomes an important element in the *Quatre poèmes de Léo Latil* (1914) which followed immediately and are truly masterful. In these, the half harmonic, half contrapuntal accompaniment, rising and falling in great swells of sound, is particularly sumptuous as it undulates beneath a rapidly declaimed vocal line. The poems invoke the deepest shadows of night, invisible clouds driven across the sky by moisture-laden breezes carrying the muffled sounds of barking dogs, bird cries, and the rumbling wheels of a cart. Altogether, they contain a feeling of voluptuous nostalgia. The third song, "Le rossignol," full of lights and shadows like a beautiful watercolor, is one of the finest pieces of twentieth-century vocal music. Accompanying Latil's moving description of awakening springtime, Milhaud's music rises as if beating its wings, falls back, and then, with a trill above a chromatic series of minor-thirteenth chords, mounts upward until it disappears in the luminous vapor that presages dawn.

Les soirées de Petrograd, composed in 1919 on short poems by René Chalupt, are quite remarkable. They are like a series of snapshots capturing scenes from the time of old Russia and the revolution. There is a disturbing quality to these songs, an underlying unrest. The poetic portraits of the shivering grandmother and the monk surrounded by his tolling bells ring only too true. In all these songs the vocal line has an appropriateness that is reminiscent of Mussorgsky or, for that matter, Monteverdi. The richly sonorous piano accompaniments are laden with meaning. Unfortunately, concert performances often relegate the instrumental part to second place. It is high time that the piano be recognized as an equal partner with the voice, and that a great singer be matched by a great pianist. Such a combination is, in any event, indispensable if the public is to savor fully the songs of composers such as Milhaud and Debussy.

Alissa, written in 1913, is a setting of long portions of André Gide's *La porte étroite.* In concept it can be compared with the *Lamento d'Ariana* by Monteverdi. The sorrowful monologue, which releases its tenderness so gently that one feels a treasure is being unveiled, is beautifully complemented by Milhaud's music. The melodies envelop the words with great poignancy. In its combined austerity and voluptuousness, this is probably one of the composer's most sensitive and eloquent works. He revised his 1913 version several times, trimming the length and rearranging certain harmonies, but the definitive 1931 version actually differs very little from the original except in these details.

Two song cycles have provoked considerable amusement: *Catalogue de fleurs* (1920) and *Machines agricoles* (1919). However, their raison d'être is quite logical. The first pictures a person sitting by the fire and listening to the spring rain fall outside. He leafs through a seed catalogue, and each entry gives rise to a vision of the flowers he will soon be planting in his garden, of warm summer days ahead, and of the colors that will complement the green foliage; his is that special joy known only to those who live in contact with the earth. *Catalogue de fleurs* is a first ray of sunlight piercing the white mists of winter.

The *Machines agricoles* are also pastorales. They conjure up visions of great fields of wheat in the middle of summer, and if the text says: "The combination plough-seeder-trencher has stanchions and certain reinforcements so it can bear the weight of the seed-box. It has as many distributors as there are blades to the plough . . .," it is not incumbent upon the singer to make each word clear. Rather, he should let the verse float above the accompanying instrumental texture, projecting an atmosphere of bucolic serenity and fecundity. In both these collections the instrumental accompaniment has abandoned the use of harmonic clusters and taken the direction of contrapuntal flexibility.

The *Poèmes juifs* (1916) are well known. This cycle of eight songs springs from the deep recesses of Milhaud's soul and is a true profession of faith. Intense yet tranquil, a secure, affirmative expression of inner joy without a trace of lamentation, this music imparts a feeling of passionate conviction and a vision of hope for all that gives life meaning: hope for better days ahead, for the Promised Land, and for abounding faith that will impart energy to all daily pursuits. There is such urgency and sincerity in these songs that they provide us with a key to understanding the composer's entire life and thought.

The first song, the "Chant de nourrice," is in a warm and intimate mood and projects visions of a child's happy future. The second is also a kind of lullaby, cradling the destiny of man. The cycle reaches a climax in the "Chant de laboureur," which gathers its forces into a paean of praise for the land of Israel, where the sower flings forth his seed and a mighty race of men springs into being. One has the impression that nothing can interrupt this growing tide of movement, this enormous outpouring of will, which becomes more and more menacing until it ends triumphantly in an outburst of shattering, incontrovertible sound. This song is like a call to revolution for all those who suffer or who descend into the streets to fight against injustice.

Nothing could be in greater contrast than the sixth song, the "Chant d'amour" with its pure melodic line above rippling arpeggios. Then come the broad sonorities of the "Chant de forgeron" and finally, to close the cycle, the "Lamentation," which proclaims the coming of the Messiah. An imitative, polytonal texture combines a whole cluster of melodic and rhythmic motives, which are gathered together finally in a march that stamps impatiently and ends up going nowhere . . . because "the Messiah's robe is not yet ready." The *Poèmes juifs* are strong, lean, and sure. In a few pages the whole of Hebrew religious sentiment finds expression.

The *Chants populaires hébraïques* were composed on melodies derived from Polish or Ukranian Jewish tradition, but completely reconstituted. Milhaud has distilled their latent strength and discarded all traces of rhythmic or harmonic banality. The sun of the Midi does not shine on these songs; rather they are the product of an emotional climate dominated by unending struggle and fear for an uncertain future:

What's to be done? Nothing helps.
Plenty of children
But no money
And hardly any bread to eat.
Good week, good week . . .

Always, though, there is faith that God will provide for His chosen people. The song "Gloire à Dieu" hurls defiance at the cruelty of life:

God is my strength and my defense;
I am poor
But my hope is in God;
I believe in Thee, Oh God,
Oh God Zebaoth! . . .

This affirmation is harshly proclaimed on quarter notes that give equal value to all the words, with accents on *my* strength and *my* defense. In the orchestral version, the trombone sustains the motion while the timpani reinforce the defiantly accentuated words.

The "Chant hassidique" somewhat playfully recites the seven points of the faith:

Seven's for the Sabbath and six for the parts of the Talmud,
Five goes to the parts of the Bible and four to the ancestors,
Three to the patriarchs and two for the tables of the law,
But it's God and God alone,
God without equal, who is one.

The six songs grouped together under the title *Rêves* were composed on anonymous texts that happened to come to the composer's attention. They have the same kind of confidentiality as the piano suite *La muse ménagère*, which was written only a short time later. They communicate a kind of inner vision, thereby lending themselves to performance in the intimacy of a home.

Two sets of songs were written on texts by Camille Paliard, a poet from Aix; her pastoral simplicity resembles that of Francis Jammes. The *Voyage d'été* dates from 1940. It is a delightful promenade through a sunny countryside among friendly people who are far removed from the artificialities of city life. In a way this summer excursion is the musical antithesis of Schubert's *Die Winterreise*. The same author's *Chants de misère* (1946) are an expression of the suffering that the French experienced during the German occupation, and in these musical settings Milhaud voices his own agony of separation from his parents, who died before he could see them a last time.

None of these compositions from the 1940s show the preoccupation with experimentation that characterized so much post–Second World War music. The *Petites légendes* (1952) on texts by Maurice Carême continue the same spontaneous, gentle style of the earlier *Cantate de l'enfant et de la mère* (1938) by the same author; and in 1956 Milhaud turned again to the poetry of Francis Jammes, setting two cycles: *Fontaines et sources* and *Tristesses*. This faithfulness to the spirit and art of Jammes is moving and at the same time revealing. If Claudel was the greatest influence on Milhaud in terms of lyric drama, Jammes's sensitivity and feeling of closeness to nature touch the deepest recesses of his own temperament. It is significant that his first opus had contained a setting of one poem from the *Tristesses* collection, and that now, much later in life, he should have returned to the same source of inspiration to make musical renditions of twenty-four more of these poetic sketches. This 1956 cycle, a work of great skill and maturity, is a suite for baritone and piano, magnificently constructed in every detail. What need is there to make a formal analysis, to point out the way in which the main theme is presented as a twelve-tone row, arranged so as to differentiate four separate tonalities, and to show how it provides the framework for the entire work? Why give example upon example of all the resulting contrapuntal possibilities? The importance of the music lies in its expressiveness, not its technical cleverness, and in the way it manifests the composer's unique genius.

To conclude this subject, it is necessary to mention that, among Milhaud's compositions for solo voice and orchestra, several bear the subtitle "cantata." In addition, there are two for speaking voice and instrumental accompaniment. These works will be considered in the following chapter in the section devoted to cantatas.

Vocal Ensemble

In addition to songs for solo voice with either piano or orchestral accompaniment, Milhaud wrote several duos and a quintet, all accompanied by orchestra, and many vocal quartets. The unaccompanied vocal quartets and at least one of the accompanied ones can also be performed by choruses using several voices to a part. There are a few pieces specifically written for vocal quartet with instrumental accompaniment and in addition a considerable number of works for either men's, women's, or mixed choruses, some accompanied and some *a cappella.* Add to these a group of compositions for soloists with chorus and instruments, and one has a good idea of the composer's output for vocal ensembles.

Milhaud's vocal quartet writing follows logically from that of Debussy and uses similar series of parallel fourths, so appropriate to vocal ensemble music, as well as some typical formulas for modulation. Worthy of note are the *Deux poèmes* (1916 and 1919). "Eloge," on a text by Saint Léger-Léger, floats languorously through luminous harmonies. The four voices are rarely used all at once. Two or three parts weave a background, out of which the melody emerges and is nonchalantly passed from voice to voice. "Le bric," by René Chalupt, is a seascape. A little breeze swells the white sail of the music, making it glide swiftly and easily.

In 1932 Milhaud set two poems from the *Anthologie nègre,* by Blaise Cendrars. The "Danse des animaux" is spontaneous and childlike; the "Chant de la mort" recalls certain parts of *Les malheurs d'Orphée* with its charming alternation of vertical and contrapuntal writing.

Two works for unaccompanied women's voices date from 1933: the elegant *Elégies romaines,* by Goethe, and *Devant sa main nue,* by M. Raval. In the same year the composer wrote a collection of twelve short pieces that he called *Adages.* These pieces are for mixed vocal quartet with the accompaniment of a small chamber orchestra (or piano). The charming *Amours de Ronsard* is for the same combination.

Brief mention should also be made of a strange composition based on Francis Jammes's *No. 34 de l'église habillée de feuilles* (1916) for mixed vocal quartet and piano six hands! The text reads:

I am the ewe that runs through the carnations.
She trembles and her voice sounds damp
When daylight follows night,
For dawn is cold until the ewe
Is warmed by the colors of the rainbow.
The sun returns
From the dark regions
Recreating its dazzling miracle
For the ewe that trembles among the carnations.

The soprano part is in C, the alto in A-flat, the tenor in E, and the bass in C. The upper piano part is in E, the middle part in A-flat, and the lowest in C. The modulations between these three tonalities pass them around from one register to another, and the shimmering sound-effect that results especially suits this poem. This curious piece, written around the time he was working on the *Choéphores,* is one of the composer's first experiments with polytonality. Up to now it has never

173

been published.

*   *   *

The designation *Cantate* cuts across several vocal categories and implies neither a specific musical form nor a particular poetic type. There is great diversity especially in the choice of texts, for whereas songs have a certain lyric similarity no matter in what language they are written, the texts of cantatas can be narrative or dramatic, mythological or historical, and may be invectives or accolades. In one respect, cantatas are all alike: none is intended to be staged. They are meant either for church use or for performance on special occasions.

Most composers have adopted a certain formula for all their cantatas. Rameau and Bach, for example, always used alternating recitatives and arias, and in his religious cantatas Bach added choral sections based on Lutheran chorales. However, Milhaud's cantatas assume several different formal arrangements, depending on the expressive characteristics of the particular text. About thirty of his works can be included in the cantata category, though not all have that explicit designation. Thirteen are for one or more soloists with instrumental accompaniment and sometimes a chorus; seven are for chorus and orchestra; seven for mixed chorus a cappella; and two for narrator with instrumental accompaniment. None of them is divided into arias and recitatives. By and large, the cantatas with soloists have a lyrical quality, those for chorus are primarily dramatic; and the ones on religious texts blend drama and lyricism. The circumstances that gave rise to each work, as well as the texts chosen, have led to a dazzling variety in expressive quality, in treatment of both voices and instruments, and in form. Milhaud's cantatas differ from his songs in both style and spirit. The songs are a reflection of his own sensibilities and moods; the cantatas speak in a general way about the concerns of humanity. Religious belief, moral conviction, and a sense of duty are all intertwined. The cantatas are about ideas; the songs are personal confidences.

Outstanding among the cantatas is the early *Retour de l'enfant prodigue* (1917). André Gide's text inspired Milhaud to write music of the greatest refinement. The Prodigal says: "I felt too strongly that the house was not the universe," to which the older brother answers: "From what chaos man has arisen; you will know it some day if you do not already. He is an imperfect creature, clumsy and ponderous, and would fall back if the Holy Spirit did not sustain him." The five parts of this cantata treat the impact of the Prodigal's return as reflected in his conversations with his father, older brother, mother, and with the younger brother who himself will soon flee the confines of the house.

The musical setting is exquisite. Twenty-one instruments, including a counterpoised double string quartet, accompany the voices. The polytonality is partly harmonic, partly contrapuntal. The overall ex-

174

pression of the work is restrained and gentle. The soloistically treated instruments interrelate their individual melodies in a way that makes one think of a shower of meteorites, and the aggregate harmonies of the strings produce an atmosphere of otherworldliness. It is as though one were standing beneath the great vault of heaven on a dry, warm, eastern Mediterranean evening.

The first part creates a very unusual effect. Ninth and seventh chords, with unresolved appoggiaturas, are stretched like double garlands between some tonally ambiguous anchoring notes in the bass. The key of C is implied, but up to the very end, a tissue of exquisitely subtle harmonies veils both the tonality and the modality of the harmonic texture. The dialogue of the prodigal with his mother is another remarkably effective part, beautifully illustrating the way in which the composer gives distinction and individuality to each instrumental line. The final part (the dialogue with the younger brother) is based on a fugal subject that starts out in D-flat major, goes to F major, and ends in G major, all tonalities that lend themselves to superimposition. The counterpoint is suspended over a three-beat harmonic motive (in $\frac{4}{4}$ meter), which acts as a kind of ostinato bass. Three triads (on F, G, and D-flat) are repeated over and over in quarter-notes and simultaneously in eighth notes, which affords a large range of polytonal possibilities.

La mort d'un Tyran (1932) is a powerful work composed to a text by the late Roman poet Lamprides. It is scored for a small mixed chorus which half sings, half speaks in musical meter. The accompaniment is given to percussion instruments except for a piccolo, a clarinet, and a tuba, which occasionally raise their clamorous voices; these particular instruments were chosen because together they cover the entire range of sound from highest to lowest register.

Pan et la Syrinx dates from 1934. Of this work, Claudel writes as follows:

"De Piis is a poet of the generally discredited First Empire and is barely more distinguished than the rest of his contemporaries, whose vaudevilles and diverse ditties have mercifully been swallowed up in oblivion. By what whim of Apollo did this poetic hack become the author of two masterpieces? One is a poem in four cantos called *Harmonie imitative,* which should be given to every schoolchild to read; the other is *Chanson de Pan,* a fresh, beguiling bit of verse which I read for the first time while visiting one of the most enchanting spots on earth. The natives would hardly recognize it if I whispered the slightly fantastic name of Pont d'Eyzieu. That is the place where the broad Rhône river, divided by pale willows and rosy spits of sand, emerges turbulently from a massive jumble of alpine ridges. On both sides of this fast-flowing, icy water stand rows of unequal poplars, like the reeds of gigantic, natural panpipes bound together by bands of dust particles turned into bright ribbons by the light of the setting sun. How can one be unmoved by this magical harmony; how can one fail to see the evasive nymph in her bowers of flick-

175

ering leaf and water patterns or to hear her answering the merry propositions of the goat god? The second part of the cantata shimmers like moonlight; the third is the "Danse de Pan," in which range upon range of hills join hands, as it were, and dance in a circle around Pan, the inventor of the musical scale. He stands in the middle, pawing the ground impatiently as he dreams of implanting a kiss on the lips of the protesting Syrinx.

To this text Milhaud has composed a little masterpiece. Each of the three titled sections is preceded by a short nocturne for vocal quartet with several accompanying instruments (flute, oboe, saxophone, bassoon, and piano). These calm, dreamy interludes frame the lively songs. Pan's air, for baritone, has an elastic, flexible, bounding rhythm, accompanied by little outbursts from the piccolo. Syrinx answers with a melody that sparkles like a diamond. In the "Danse de Pan" the vocal quartet joins the two soloists to sing a brief but quite stunning rondelay.

Mention should be made of the *Cantate nuptiale* based on the *Song of Songs*. It was composed in 1937 in honor of the golden wedding anniversary of Milhaud's parents. Like all his works from that period, it is characterized by stylistic simplicity and unaffected melodiousness. Note also the *Cantate de l'enfant et de la mère* (1938), in which the poems by Maurice Carême are narrated against an accompaniment of string quartet and piano. The disparate sonorities of strings and piano, so difficult to blend successfully, are perfectly fused in this work.

Several cantatas for a cappella chorus on poems by Claudel, including the *Cantate de la paix* (1937), *Cantate de la guerre* (1940), and *Les deux cités* (1937), are examples of Milhaud's best style. They are simple and precise, emotionally restrained, and melodically supple in conformity with the rhythm of the poetry.

Two other cantatas (from 1951) are worthy of note. The *Cantata from Proverbs* is sung by a three-part women's chorus (soprano, alto, and contralto) to the diaphanous accompaniment of oboe, cello, and harp. The biblical texts are presented in an almost bantering mood. Quite different is the setting of the texts, also taken from the Bible, in *Les miracles de la foi*. These texts are recited by a young boy or girl around thirteen years old and are then commented on by a solo tenor and a mixed chorus, with relatively uncomplicated orchestral accompaniment. The piece consists of four sections, an orchestral introduction and three vocal settings. A firm but flexible rhythm and a swift-flowing, cohesive style endow this almost childlike music with great joy and enthusiasm.

Le château de feu (1954), for mixed chorus and orchestra, has been described by Hélène Jourdan-Morhange as follows:

Among the diverse works by Darius Milhaud, a considerable number have been devoted to the expression of human compassion. Milhaud wrote *Le château de feu* at the request of the "Réseau du souvenir," which placed, in the words of Vercors, "a few dedicated men bow-tight against oblivion" and which honored those who had been deported to concentration camps or shot by Hitler's Gestapo. The work is in memory of the composer's nephew Jean Milhaud and of Éric and Hélène Allatini, who were murdered by the Germans.

Le château de feu has that unlimited grandeur characteristic of greatly inspired works. There is no need to analyze style and method; tonality and polytonality are adapted to the shades of expression desired by the composer, and the music springs from innermost emotion and is an outpouring of love and compassion for suffering humanity. This cantata is written for chorus and small orchestra, three instruments to a part, without horns or violins, to a text by Jean Cassou. After a long introduction in which the harsh harmonies already impart a feeling of horror, a vigorous theme wells up from the brasses and muted strings. The choral parts mostly interact canonically. We know how marvellously Milhaud manages great choral masses. The poem suggests the horrible march toward execution of the martyrs and the cold cruelty of the executioners who are represented by "la voix terrible." After the curious traveler has posed many questions to a "bonne femme," the chorus of the doomed sing a tremendous anthem: "We are entering the final kingdom. Open the door!" This plea is repeated over and over again like a leitmotif, stark and imperious. Finally "la voix terrible" orders: "Give me your hands. . . . give me your eyes" and then, with a mighty shout, "give me your children." The divided choruses answer: "Here is our milk, here is our blood, here is our supreme agony and our supreme outrage." "La voix terrible" replies: "Enter and burn!"

The final chorus, rough, noble and magnificent, is a hymn to the flames, a work of vast expressive scope. One senses that Milhaud is completely caught up in this tragic subject. His music faithfully follows the construction of the poem, which builds toward a tremendous crescendo of victory over persecution; but this victory has been won at the expense of too much horror and too much physical and mental suffering. After reaching a triumphant climax on the words "Dans les flammes, Dans la musique des flammes, La victoire chante Victoire," the music breaks into sobs and ends in desolation.

The refreshing cantata *Fontaines et sources* (1956), for solo voice and orchestra, was followed in 1959 and 1960 by the *Cantate de la croix de charité,* for soprano, tenor, bass, mixed chorus, and children's chorus with orchestra. Written for the centennial of the Red Cross, this work was broadcast throughout the world in homage to the charitable work of that organization.

A *Cantate sur des poèmes de Chaucer,* for mixed chorus and orchestra, commissioned by the University of Iowa in 1960, alternates orchestral sections with the three poems "Captivity," "Escape," and "Rejection." The vengeful account of unhappy love is underlined by an uneasy, discordant musical setting.

The *Cantate de l'initiation (Bar mitzvah Israël),* for mixed chorus with chamber orchestra or organ, also dates from 1960. After an introductory, instrumental hymn, there are five liturgical texts that must be declaimed very distinctly and precisely by the singers: the Aliyah, a

reading from the Torah, the benediction after the Torah, the benediction preceding the Haphtarah, and the reading of the Haphtarah.

The *Invocation à l'ange Raphaël* (1962), for two groups of women's
voices and orchestra, uses the text of the last act of *Tobie et Sara,* by
Claudel. This is a hymn of pure music, without any descriptive or at-
mospheric allusions.

Also in 1962, Milhaud turned once again to the poetry of Francis
Jammes, for the text of the *Suite de quatrains.* In this work the spoken
voice has as a backdrop an improvisational accompaniment provided
by seven instruments, each of which enters on certain prescribed syllables and then proceeds at will. This kind of controlled chance music
had fascinated the composer since he first experimented with it, in a
piece called *Cocktail* for voice and three clarinets written in 1920.

In 1958 Milhaud had composed *La tragédie humaine* on a sixteenth-
century poem by Agrippa d'Aubigné. He found "the verse of this period so free that many rhythmic settings of it are possible." He turned to
this century again for texts to his *Suite de sonnets* (1963), a work of considerable complexity and inventiveness.

A very interesting work dates from 1963. In *Caroles* the poet
Charles d'Orléans laments his sufferings while imprisoned in England.
His verse is characteristically restrained and elegant, and Milhaud has
captured this mood of discreetly expressed sadness. Three carols are
arranged for mixed chorus accompanied by nineteen instruments; the
performers are divided into five groups, which are arranged in a semi-
circle with the chorus in front.

Group II
Tympani, xylophone, celeste

Group I	Group III	Group V
Picolo, flute, oboe, English horn, clarinet, trumpet, violin	Tuba, contrabassoon, contra-bass, harp	Bassoon, trombone, contra-bass, clarinet, horn, cello

Group IV
Sopranos, tenors, basses,
contraltos

Conductor

Such distribution of instruments to achieve a certain kind of spatial sonority follows the same principle as that of the double chorus at St.
Mark's in Venice. It is also the basis of the music of Heinrich Schütz.
Actually, the exact distribution of the musicians must depend on the
acoustical properties of the particular hall in which the work is being
performed.

The *Adieu* cantata (1964), for voice, flute, viola, and harp, is based
on the closing poem of Arthur Rimbaud's *Une saison en enfer.* Since it
uses the same instrumentation as Debussy's *Second Sonata,* it makes a
delightful companion piece on a chamber-music program. According

to François Mauriac, both Rimbaud and Jammes were poets who lived apart from society; one can say that they were also detached from time. During his mature years, one might remark that Milhaud, too, was beginning to seek release from worldly concerns and physical suffering.

From 1966 comes *Hommage à Comenius,* for soprano, baritone, and orchestra, a sparkling musical setting of two texts, "Le soleil" and "L'instruction universelle," by the Czech philosopher.

The beautiful *Cantate de psaumes* (1967), for baritone and chamber orchestra, composed to celebrate the centenary of Claudel's birth, is a setting of that author's translations of Psalms 129, 145, 147, 136, 128, and 127. A work of great emotional intensity, amounting almost to violence at times, the style is reminiscent of *Le retour de l'enfant prodigue.* Once again Milhaud shows his predilection for treating each instrument of the chamber ensemble soloistically.

The last cantata, *Ani Maamin,* written in 1972, has the subtitle "Un chant perdu et retrouvé." It is a statement of absolute, uncompromising faith, impervious to criticism. Written for soprano, mixed chorus, four narrators, and full orchestra, on a text by Elie Wiesel, it is an austere, intransigent work that may well be regarded as the composer's final spiritual testament.

*   *   *

Apart from the cantatas, several other a cappella choral works should be mentioned. They include the *Cantique du Rhône* (1936), the *Quatrains valaisans* of Rainer Maria Rilke (1939), and *Trois psaumes de David* (1954), in which Gregorian chant alternates with sections of four-part polyphony. There are also the *Promesse de Dieu* (1972), on biblical texts, and the *Huit poèmes de Jorge Guillen* (1958), which are outstanding in quality but difficult to perform because of the very free tonality and the extremely high soprano register.

Finally, there is a delightfully witty, lively choral comedy, *Les momies d'Egypte,* based on an adaptation of a commedia dell'arte text by Régnard that mixes French and Italian dialogue. It is a worthy companion of such masterpieces as *L'amfiparnasso* by Orazio Vecchi and Banchieri's *Il festino.*

Religious Music

Two monumental works dominate the composer's choral compositions. Both are religiously inspired. The first is the *Service sacré* (1947), for baritone solo, narrator, mixed chorus, and orchestra or organ. The other is the choral symphony *Pacem in Terris* (1963). The distinguished composer Henri Barraud has kindly permitted the inclusion of some of his observations regarding the great Sacred Service:

179

Milhaud was of Jewish persuasion, but his religious sentiment was far more than mere compliance with tradition. He was a profoundly religious man and deeply immersed in his people's communal faith, which Edmond Fleg once characterized as "a long unified memory." This long memory, handed down through the centuries, keeps alive in each Jew an awareness of those ancient times when belief first became a compelling, inextricable part of human history. It is like yeast in dough, this constantly nurtured and revitalized sense of religious transcendence, supported by age-old traditions and resistant by necessity to outside persecution, which provides the cohesive force unifying far-flung members of a great spiritual family from which have come so many scholars, writers, and creative and enterprising people in all fields.

It is in this light that we must view Darius Milhaud if we are to understand the musical fecundity which was the raison d'être for his whole life: "Je suis là pour ça." And it is for this reason that the Sacred Service which he composed for Temple Emanu-El in San Francisco, where he conducted the first performance in 1947, has such magnetism.

The very idea of joining polyphony to the texts used in the Saturday morning service places this as a modern work. Traditional Hebraic music is purely homophonic, and up to the time of the French Revolution, this was the only kind sung in a synagogue. A single exception can be found in the work of Salomon Rossi, a contemporary of Monteverdi, who composed polyphonic settings of Jewish melodies in the then current madrigal style. But there is nothing to indicate that those works were ever performed as part of a temple service.

Jewish music is then, I repeat, purely monodic and has been handed down from ancient times transmitted by oral tradition until the third century A.D., when the Masoretic rabbis, who compiled the texts of the Hebrew Bible, invented a form of notation more or less integrated with the Hebrew alphabet. This alphabet consisted of consonant sounds only, however, and left the vowels, which are the more melodic part of any language, to the interpretation of the officiant or to the chorus that sang the so-called cantillation, or psalmody, to use a less technical term. Approximate as it was, this new way of notating the inflections of the voice led to a certain codification of traditional melismas and their preservation throughout the centuries, side by side with the burgeoning of medieval plainchant, which itself eventually became formulated in the Gregorian code. Traditional Jewish music, like that of the Catholic liturgy, therefore, remained modal up to the time of the disastrous innovations of recent years.

It was during the nineteenth century that this venerable tradition began to change under the influence of powerful trends in western romantic music. Polyphonic singing began to invade some, though by no means all, synagogues. Instrumental music also began to be introduced, and that accounts for the synagogue on the Rue de la Victoire in Paris, constructed in 1874, acquiring an organ in its loft which, nevertheless, remained significantly silent on the Sabbath as well as on Yom Kippur and which today is never used for any ceremony except marriage.

In the twentieth century there has been a certain amount of reaction to the innovations of the nineteenth, and a gesture has been made in the direction of a return to traditional purity. Only a gesture, however, as in the suppression of instrumental music. For, though solo cantillations may retain the characteristic melodic figures of the past, choral responses are still full of lush harmonic vocabulary and the dominant–tonic cadences that put a stamp of C major on the old modal phrases. Furthermore, even in the solo cantillations,

180

which evidence considerable discrepancies between the texts and the parts of the service to which they pertain, one finds long sequences constructed on the three tones of the major triad—a most telling sign of recent influences. It would be interesting to study these passages in relation to the age of the texts, but that is not the subject that concerns me at present. I have dwelt at some length on these various aspects of liturgical music as found in a synagogue like the one on the Rue de la Victoire because it is in this frame of reference that one can more effectively evaluate Milhaud's *Sacred Service.*

Commissioned to write a composition for voices and instruments, Milhaud found himself from the beginning outside the tradition I have just described. What he attempted, and superbly succeeded in accomplishing, was to uphold traditional stylistic purity, while using the broadly expanded resources of his own vocabulary, which is itself a composite of a long spiritual heritage and the dynamic, innovative influences of our present century. Only he could have met the challenge so well. I am struck by his imaginative use of ornaments and inflections, by his augmentation and diminution of motivic material, all serving to enhance a basically modal, rather than tonal, melodic line, and by his alternate use of syllabification and vocalise on the one hand, while, on the other, certain of the cantor's cantillations appear to be completely authentic and free of alien influences. That is why I sense in his harmonic writing not only a frequent tendency to avoid tonal references that might interfere with the direction of his melodies, but also a need for these textbook sonorities that have somehow come to stand for spirituality. Notable also is the way his linear writing superimposes various melodic designs, each one carrying with it and maintaining inviolate its own special aura.

The *Service sacré* emanated from the deepest reaches of Milhaud's heart and soul. It is all love and tenderness for God and for his creatures. The choral symphony *Pacem in Terris* takes a completely different point of departure. Rather than projecting emotion, it is addressed to mankind's moral nature. It is an exhortation, a stern warning that humanity must conform to superior law and to the precepts set down by the Fathers of the Church, and before them by the Prophets and by Scripture, that govern relationships between people, stipulating their rights and duties. During the troubled middle years of the twentieth century, when lack of discipline, lack of principle, egotism, and the self-serving interests of various social classes threatened the very existence of western culture, Pope John XXIII issued, on 2 April 1963, his famous encyclical "Peace on Earth," in which he reaffirmed the fundamentals of human society—that is, the behavior befitting human beings in their natural environment and in their interrelationships as members of a national and international community. He prescribed the ecumenism of the Christian Church, freedom of thought, abolition of racial discrimination, and the protection of the poor and oppressed. In brief, he set forth the professed virtues of Christianity, as well as those inherited from the Old Testament. The force and power of these fundamental ideas, if respected and adhered to by world leaders, could certainly assure the survival of humanity. The great moral lesson of

Pacem in Terris resounded throughout the world, because it was a solemn and vigorous assessment of the delinquency of civilization and its abrogation of responsibility.

Michael de Bry suggested to Milhaud that he write a choral work based on this encyclical, to be performed at the inauguration of the new auditorium of the Radiodiffusion and Télévision Française headquarters in Paris. Keeping in mind the text of Isaiah (2.4), "They shall beat their swords into plowshares and their spears into pruning hooks," the composer undertook to write this score while at Aspen, Colorado, in July 1963. The first performance was on December 20 of that same year in the new hall. It was repeated in the cathedral of Notre Dame in Paris for a seven-hundred-and-fiftieth anniversary celebration attended by all the leaders of Church and State. This occasion, in the spirit of ecumenism, honored the Catholic Pope John XXIII, author of the text, and the music of a French Jewish composer. The work was conducted by Charles Munch, a French Protestant.

The composition consists of seven parts:

I. Peace on earth, the fundamental aspiration of mankind throughout all the ages. Progress in science and technology bear witness to the greatness of God, the greatness of the universe, and the greatness of man.
II. The right of each person to worship God according to his own conscience and religious heritage. The right to move about and be accepted in the great family of man. Rights and duties of all members of society. Human endeavor should be guided by reason.
III. Recognition of the inherent dignity of man. All men should be treated with equal justice.
IV. Reciprocal rights and duties of political communities. Truth proscribes racism and pride, both individual and national. "Government without justice is simply large-scale crime" (Saint Augustine).
V. Stability of working conditions. The deplorable condition of refugees.
VI. A plea for cessation of the arms race. Avoidance at all cost of a Third World War. "Nothing is lost through peace" (Saint Augustine).
VII. Let men of good will establish an orderly basis for peace. "Peace shall be within you" (Saint Augustine). Let the Savior enlighten the leaders of men, and let men exist in peace as brothers.

The first part is an affirmation of the unity of the universe. The second confirms the rights of man, and the third demands the equality of man under the tenets of universal law. The fourth is a proscription of prejudice and arbitrary behavior by national, social, and religious groups. After these directives, the fifth section calls for stability, and the sixth is an exhortation to avoid conflict. The seventh, concluding section is a prayer for peace and an expression of hope.

The music starts off imperiously, but every affirmation is followed by a contemplative section, unemotional and serene. Vigorous accentuation and abrasive harmonies are reserved for the setting of stern decrees and for the orchestral portions preceding them. For the most part the melodies move freely, almost without accentuation. They are clearly tonal but join together to form a mildly polytonal texture that from time to time becomes canonic and at the end includes a somewhat disguised reference to a Bach chorale. The simple but richly inventive music utilizes a constantly evolving succession of melodies to create a form that is far removed from nineteenth-century concepts of thematic progression and dramatic juxtaposition. The choruses conscientiously project the message of the text, while the orchestra remains consistently lyrical, underlining subtly and without ostentation the declamation of the soloists and choir.

VIII

Instrumental Music

Piano

Although the twentieth century has generally been considered inimical to piano music, considerable evidence proves that many post-Romantic composers had a marked predilection for the instrument that was cherished by Schumann, Chopin, and Liszt. Fauré's preludes, nocturnes, and barcarolles, and works for the keyboard by Debussy and Ravel, as well as by Déodat de Séverac and Erik Satie, found their way sooner or later into the virtuoso repertory. Composers who succeeded the generation of the keyboard giants remained faithful to the piano, although, with the exception of those mentioned above and certain others (including Ferruccio Busoni and Béla Bartók), their compositions for that instrument may not have played a predominant role in their total output. But music for piano with orchestra never lost its popularity. Hindemith, Prokofiev, and Bartók wrote three concertos each; Stravinsky composed one and the *Capriccio*; Poulenc produced two; and Schoenberg one. Milhaud wrote five concertos, several compositions of various types for piano with orchestra, and two concertos for two pianos.

Though the concertos composed in the second third of the twentieth century continued the bravura tradition, works for solo piano tended in a different direction. Concentrating neither on virtuosity nor on the brilliant coloristic displays of so-called impressionistic style, composers of this period used the keyboard for some of their most characteristic statements. Stravinsky, in his *Piano Rag-music,* his *Sonata No. 2,* and his *Serenade,* treated the piano as a percussion instrument. Hindemith adapted eighteenth-century forms to his own harmonic vocabulary in *Ludus Tonalis,* as well as in his sonatas and etudes. Schoenberg used the instrument for his first hyperchromatic tone-row compositions, and Satie's characteristic irony was reflected in his ultra-simplified, harmonically refined style of keyboard writing. Bartók supplemented nineteenth-century Brahmsian formulas with rhythms and modes inspired by Hungarian folk music.

Rather than using the instrument for problem solving, Milhaud turned to it to express his most intimate sentiments. Coloristic effects are minimal: polyphony, whether polytonal or polymodal, does not lend itself to sonorous ambiguity. To communicate the sense and logic of his musical language, Milhaud's piano pieces must be played very clearly and precisely, with minimum use of pedals and without prolonging the duration of the notes beyond what is indicated in the score. There is nothing very remarkable about this approach. It is the same one that should be adopted in interpreting Fauré, or Mozart for that matter. The superposition of melodic lines requires that they be differentiated according to their relative importance. This is accomplished by phrasing and by careful dynamic control.

Except for a few pieces, mainly those included in collections, all Milhaud's piano compositions are works of considerable interest. Most of them are grouped not exactly into suites, but rather into cycles, each of which revolves around a different subject: the seasons, the hours of the day, family life, religious festivals.

Printemps, consisting of six little pieces composed between 1915 and 1920, is the fresh, unsophisticated work of a young musical personality. They are in the same spirit as Mendelssohn's *Songs Without Words* and have a similar spontaneity and guileless quality. The supple polyphonic lines intertwine to create a charmingly graceful texture. They must be interpreted delicately, with a light, precise touch that differentiates dynamically the various sonorities, without ever exceeding the dynamic range of *piano*. This subtle control of sound is essential; exaggerated dynamics, as well as other artificial effects such as rubato, would be completely out of character.

Saudades do Brazil (1920–21) is a collection of twelve tangos, each named after a different district of Rio de Janeiro. The unifying idea is the same as in Chopin's collections of dances, notably his mazurkas. The dance rhythms, reflecting their popular origins, are treated in a many-faceted way. By extracting and highlighting the most essential elements of each, the composer has succeeded in creating a group of distinctive musical portraits. There is elegance is "Sorocaba," tenderness in "Leme," and brilliance in "Ipanema"; and "Gavea" explodes in rhythm and shattering harmonies before settling into amiable nonchalance. "Tijuca" presents another combination of sentiments: restrained sadness tempered by charm. Passing through an array of emotional nuances from lightheartedness to vivacity to mystery, the collection ends with "Paysandu," a serene meditation. This is an inspired set of dances most felicitously written for the piano. It is a real joy for the performer to exploit the shades of instrumental color by differentiating detached and legato notes, projecting the interplay of contrapuntal lines, highlighting the modulations, and balancing the polytonal elements.

During his years in the United States, Milhaud wrote *La muse ménagère* (1944), a calm, intimate evocation of family life. This beautiful expression of appreciation has a confidential quality. Most of the fifteen pieces could even be described as "silent music," meaning the kind of silence that descends on a household toward evening, when thoughts turn inward, few words need to be exchanged, and all is at peace. This music of intimacy, tenderness, and affection requires very few notes. But for the performer who brings the music to life, each note has deep, emotional reverberations. Published in America under the title *The Household Muse,* this is not a work for the concert hall. It is the private diary of a tranquil, loving, protected home and needs to be performed in a similar atmosphere. In order to appreciate its evocative quality, one should play it as though for oneself. It is a moving experience on a quiet evening to read through the several sections entitled "Poetry," "Music together," "Evening quietude," and "Reading at night," to penetrate the veiled, vague murmurs of the "Fortuneteller," to conjure up the image of the beloved muse herself in those sections entitled "The kitchen" and "Doing the washing," and to discover with amusement the turbulence of "The son who paints."

This collection is continued by another, *Une journée* (1946), which traces a child's responses to the world around him from dawn to dusk. The sentiment in both these works may remind one of Schumann, but the style is uniquely Milhaud.

Contrasting with this intimate genre, two works bear witness to the composer's profound religious conviction. *Le candélabre à sept branches,* the menorah, is the symbol of the Jewish people. Milhaud has translated this symbolism into music with a cycle of pieces (1951) representing the principal festivals of the Hebrew calendar: "First day of the New Year" (Rosh Hashonah), "Day of repentance" (Yom Kippur), "Festival of the booths" (Succoth), "Resistance of the Maccabees" (Chanukkah), "The festival of Queen Esther" (Purim), "Passover" (Pesach), and "Pentecost" (Shevuoth). These are energetic, affirmative pieces, completely devoid of folkloristic or descriptive allusions. They express the spiritual essence of these festivals and their significance not only for the composer, but for the Jewish people and, by extension, for all humanity. The cycle conveys a feeling of power without ostentation and of genuine fervor.

Another religiously inspired work, the *Hymne de glorification* (1953–54), might well have served to crown the previous cycle. It is a glorification of the Almighty and reflects the vehement emotions of the psalm texts:

The Lord also thundered in the heavens, and the Highest gave His voice; hail stones and coals of fire.

Yea, He sent out his arrows and scattered them; and he shot forth bolts of lightning and discomfited them.

Then the channels of waters were seen and the foundations of the world were discovered at thy rebuke, O Lord, at the blast of thy nostrils.

[Psalm XVIII, 13–15]

Worthy of note is the straightforward, refreshing style of the *Sonatine* (1956) and the creative fecundity of the *Deuxième Sonate* (1949), in which the outpouring of inventive melodic patterns reminds one more of Mozart's style than of the nineteenth century's emphasis on thematic development.

*   *   *

Milhaud wrote some delightful works for two pianos, overflowing with gaiety. They may not be among his most important, musically speaking, but as the hands of the pianists leap over the keyboards from top to bottom, joining sounds together like strings of pearls, the effect is scintillating. It is as though a thousand bright lights were sending signals of pure joy to the listener, and to communicate joy in these somber times is no mean accomplishment! *Scaramouche* (1937), a three-part suite originally written to accompany a production of Molière's *Médecin volant,* with its devilishly lively first movement and Braziliera finale, has earned itself an incomparably popular place in twentieth-century two-piano literature.

The *Bal martiniquais* was written in a state of exultation over the liberation of Paris in 1944. *Paris,* a suite for four pianos, is in the same vein. Jean Roy has described it as follows:

Written in 1948, after the rediscovery of postwar Paris, this suite contains six movements, "Montmartre," "L'Ile Saint-Louis," "Montparnasse," "Bateaux-mouches," "Longchamps," and "La Tour Eiffel," which alternate between the animation of the city and the calm presence of the Seine. The music makes no pretense of being descriptive, but it succeeds in communicating a sense of place and a certain realism by purely musical means. A barcarolle rhythm propels the bateaux-mouches. Double, then quadruple, octaves in ascending motion are the tiers of the Eiffel Tower; the harmonies pile up, superimposing finally as many as twenty-five notes sounded together, to create a hymn to life, a triumphal march, or what might even be described as 'a piece in the shape of the Eiffel Tower.' It is happy, spontaneous music, which refuses to be limited to a single, constraining programmatic interpretation. That is its right and its privilege.

The concertos and diverse works for piano and orchestra are discussed in the part of this chapter devoted to symphonic music.

Chamber Music

Milhaud's chamber music includes duos and trios for various instruments, with and without piano, eighteen string quartets, quintets, several pieces for larger combinations of string and wind instruments, and six chamber symphonies.

In the second issue of *Le coq* (June 1920) Milhaud wrote: "I want to write eighteen quartets." During that postwar period of innovation and insouciance, this statement was taken as a kind of bravado and perhaps an impertinent challenge to Beethoven. But it was nothing of the kind. Milhaud, in 1920, was no young upstart. He had already produced the *Choéphores* and was working on the *Euménides,* as well as on his fifth string quartet. His declaration of purpose was perfectly serious and was merely a statement of a well-thought-out plan. And, in fact, he did compose eighteen string quartets, between 1912 and 1951.

Before becoming aware of his destiny as a composer, Milhaud trained as a violinist. During his youth in Aix, he participated with his teacher and other older friends in many chamber music sessions and became thoroughly familiar with the quartets of Haydn, Mozart, Beethoven, and Debussy. This early exposure to chamber music taught him all about the resources and possibilities of string instruments, and his theoretical studies, in harmony and counterpoint, introduced him to the intricacies of writing for an ensemble.

On many occasions Milhaud asserted that after composing operas, ballets, cantatas, and songs he felt the need to return to quartet writing; the more concise, stringent demands of that medium were apparently an antidote to the freedom permissible in lyric works. Right after finishing *La brebis égarée,* he started work on his first quartet, and following a characteristic urge for equilibrium and symmetry, he used in it the opening melody of his opus 1. This same theme reappears at the end of the eighteenth quartet, thus bringing the cycle full circle.

Consistency, sense of purpose, the translation of ideas into deeds— these are all hallmarks of a strong personality. This combination of attributes accounts for the impressive success of Milhaud's chamber music. Throughout the history of music, some ensemble music has been light and improvisational, but the main body of the genre has been deeply probing and has challenged the composer to explore all possible interrelationships between instruments. It was in this spirit that Milhaud approached not only his eighteen quartets, but all his other ensemble music, including the six *Symphonies de chambre.* This use of the term "symphonie," by the way, has the same connotation as in the Italian Baroque—that is, it refers to a short instrumental piece used as an introduction or a transition in a lyric drama.

Until recently most of Milhaud's fifty or more chamber music works were virtually unknown to the listening public, for they were presented only occasionally in various far-flung music centers of the old and new worlds. Fortunately, all the string quartets have been recorded now, so that the listener can begin to assess the full impact of this body of compositions. It is by studying the quartets that we can most clearly observe the development of Milhaud's musical language. In them one can trace the evolution of his polytonal counterpoint and his growing mastery of time-honored polyphonic conventions such as augmentation, diminution, inversion, cancrizans, and so forth. One is reminded of Philippe de Vitry and Guillaume de Machaut, but of course Milhaud's music bears no external resemblance to that of the Ars Nova. Still, it is true that in both periods freedom and imagination were expressed within the confines of formal conventions.

It is also interesting to observe a certain general trend. In his early chamber music works, all three movements have equal weight. Starting with the fourth string quartet, attention is focused on the slow central section, and the allegros before and after are shortened. By the time of the eighth and ninth quartets, the fast movements again increase in importance. We note also that Milhaud's treatment of the strings is according to classic convention. There are almost no special coloristic effects—col legnos or flautandos, for example—that might divert the listener's attention from the melodic flow. In this respect Milhaud differs from many of his contemporaries, although Hindemith and Schoenberg (especially in the latter's third and fourth quartets) are also, for the most part, protagonists of classic string writing.

*   *   *

The *Premier quatuor* (1912), written in memory of Paul Cézanne, originally consisted of four movements, but in later years Milhaud suppressed the third, leaving only the ones marked "Rythmique," "Intime, continu," and "Vif, très rythmé." As was his custom, he gave no metronome markings, but used instead a double adjective, which should provide sufficient guidance to the performer as to a suitable tempo. The first version of this quartet was notable for its thematic fecundity; however, it was excessively repetitive, and a later revision eliminated a number of superfluous passages.

The *Deuxième quatuor* (1914–15), dedicated to Léo Latil, is in five movements. It starts off as a wild riot in a surging $\frac{6}{8}$ meter, with the cello theme standing out boldly against the breathless sixteenth-note figuration of the second violin part. A feeling of strength and tension was characteristic of Milhaud's style during this period but is rare in his later works. The slow second movement is a dirge, which increases in rhythmic intensity in a fugal middle section (Ex. 8–1), before returning to a calmer treatment of the opening theme.

189

Ex. 8–1.

The lively scherzo is based on one of those typically Milhaud pastoral melodic lines, and it appears successively in the various voices while the other instruments hum along like a spinning wheel (Ex. 8–2).

Ex. 8–2.

The rhythm slackens off into a few measures of pizzicato, which lead to a trio section in which the viola introduces a joyful theme, later reiterated by the other instruments (Ex. 8–3).

Ex. 8–3.

The calm, rustic fourth movement basks in the sunlight of the Midi, and, while listening, one envisions a broad, fertile countryside, undulating fields of grain, and verdant pastures stretching to the horizon. The finale is once again tempestuous. An arresting opening theme is highlighted by the jagged chromaticism of the viola part, and altogether the texture is impressively rich and sonorous (Ex. 8–4).

Ex. 8–4.

In a slower middle section, the cello enunciates a deeply moving melody punctuated by a subtle progression of chords that complement and enhance the harmony implied by the melodic line. Then the tempo and rhythmic energy increase, and there is a brief animated section, which finally relaxes into a series of harmonic progressions leading to a concluding minor triad (Ex. 8–5).

Ex. 8–5.

This is a splendidly integrated work, thematically felicitous and technically brilliant.

The *Troisième quatuor* was written between March and August of 1916, as a memorial to Léo Latil, killed in action in 1915. At the end of the piece is this note: "In memory of the spring of 1914." The death of his closest friend was a devastating blow to Milhaud. They had shared a common view of the world and of art, and the same kind of sensibilities that the composer translated into musical phrases inspired the poet's verse. It was a unique and irreplaceable relationship.

In early 1916 Milhaud began to think of writing a string quartet that would consist of two slow movements. On 26 February he wrote to Francis Jammes:

Most of all, I want to thank you for offering to write a poem about Léo for me to set to music. For quite some time I have been thinking about writing a quartet in two movements dedicated to his memory, and I think it would be beautiful for a voice to be added near the end of the second movement, singing a quiet, simple melody on words which you would write. The title could be: "On the death of a friend," and the whole quartet would be a reflection of his deeply melancholy spirit. I would like to reveal the Léo of "Les cahiers bleus," which he willed to me, his feeling of close communication with nature, . . . his faith, and his great tenderness even when he was inwardly weeping bitter tears.

Tell me what you think of the idea of using a poem like this to terminate my quartet. The first movement will be melancholy. My inspiration is his poem about springtime, which I already set to music, written as he walked, sorrowful as always, through the countryside of Aix. This music will be heavy and slow, but the second movement will convey more a feeling of sorrow assuaged. It is in the context of this gentle, resigned mood that the human voice should sing forth its message of consolation. If you agree with this idea, please let me know; write the poem and send it to me. I will devote all the energy of my poor heart to working on it, and I thank you most deeply and affectionately.

Only a single melodic line moves through and above the unvaryingly somber accompanying texture of the first movement, reflecting the more melancholy parts of Léo Latil's private diary. The melody itself is an instrumental adaptation of the first part of the poet's "Rossignol," which Milhaud had set to music in spring of 1914. The project to include a poem by Jammes in the second movement was abandoned in favor of incorporating words by Latil. The poet questions:

But what name shall I pronounce,
And upon whom shall I call with the tears of my voice?

And now he yearns for spiritual fulfillment as he calls on God:

Therefore I invoked the name of God
Saying: Lord, Lord!
With a yearning for death
So that God could hear my voice.
What is this passion for death
And whose death will it be?

The music for this part of the text is developed from the closing theme of the second song in the cycle *D'un cahier inédit du journal d'Eugénie de Guérin,* which Milhaud had composed one year previously.

This profoundly moving though simple work brings to an end the series of compositions of Milhaud's earliest period, a time of romanticism and introspection, of preoccupation with nocturnal and bucolic themes resulting from the dual influences of Jammes and Latil.

The sojourn in Brazil with Paul Claudel was to open up a world of light and exuberant nature that would dissipate the heavy anxieties of his adolescence. It was in Rio that he wrote his *Quatrième quatuor* (1918). The first movement, a lively pastorale, introduces two themes, the first of which moves along with an air of confidence (Ex. 8–6), whereas the second, first heard in the viola, seems to be questioning anxiously (Ex. 8–7).

Ex. 8–6.

Ex. 8–7.

The contrapuntal writing is graceful, the harmony lighter than in previous works. There is no complicated development of thematic material, but rather a lightly strung-out succession of elegantly terse phrases. The middle movement is marked "Funèbre." Above an ostinato bass consisting of viola and cello lines that are placed at intervals of the minor seventh and ninth, a marchlike motive emerges which gives rhythmic cohesiveness to the entire movement (Ex. 8–8).

Ex. 8–8.

From time to time it is interrupted by a succession of translucent, ethereal chords, and more than halfway through, it accelerates until it turns into a kind of fanfare. Then the harmonies cascade downward, and the dynamics become more subdued in preparation for a solemn fugal entrance (Ex. 8–9).

Ex. 8–9.

Following this, the mood again intensifies, then returns to the quiet, rocking motion of the beginning. At the very end, the cello moves quietly toward an urgently anticipated but harmonically ambiguous conclusion (Ex. 8–10).

Ex. 8–10.

The finale, like the first movement, is brief and lively.

The *Cinquième quatuor* (1920) is quite another story. Having fully mastered the medium, Milhaud was now ready to use chamber music to express his vision of simultaneous streams of celestial light as he had done in *L'homme et son désir*. At this point and, in fact, throughout his lifetime, he considered the string quartet as a main protagonist of polytonality. Whatever else it may be, the fifth quartet is certainly an exploration of the outer limits of polytonal technique and, like the *Cinq études* for piano and orchestra, written at the same period, is highly experimental. It requires that the instruments exploit their entire pitch range and project each individual line with complete clarity, whether the texture formed by the superimposition of the parts is dense or sparse. Though entirely different in its premises, the experimental nature of this quartet partially reflects an exchange of ideas with Arnold Schoenberg, to whom this work is dedicated. The work seems austere and rigid. Nonetheless, the composer has written at the start of the first movement "Chantant, très expressif." At the end, it fades away into a rapid kind of whisper. The rich-textured second movement that follows is marked "Vif et léger."

An elemental four-note motive opens the slow third movement and is serenely developed throughout, weaving together richly varied garlands of melody. The finale is characterized by an energetic $\frac{5}{4}$ meter. A bizarre composition at first glance, difficult to listen to and even more difficult to perform, the fifth quartet deserves careful, patient examination. Who is to say whether it succeeds more as a study or as a communicative work of art? After all, are not the late quartets of Beethoven also combinations of intellectualism and expressiveness, to say nothing of his Piano Sonata, opus 106, or, for that matter, Bach's *Art of the Fugue?*

The *Sixième quatuor,* written in 1922, returns to a more accessible style. It is all smiles and charm. However, the expert handling of individual instrumental lines that was so evident in the fifth quartet is again manifest. A long, flexible g minor melody starts in the viola part and is soon joined by the second violin playing a bantering rhythmic motive in G major (Ex. 8–11).

Ex. 8–11.

Once again, it is the slow middle movement that is the heart of the work, a majestic adagio, expressive in its calm and noble reserve (Ex. 8–12).

Ex. 8–12.

The lively finale has a folklike quality as it swings along in alternating $\frac{3}{8}$, $\frac{4}{8}$, and $\frac{2}{8}$ meters.

In the *Septième quatuor* (1925), mention should be made of the second movement, with its quite tonal vocabulary and berceuse rhythm; also of the witty little finale, which is like an elegant serenade, the violin simulating a vocal part, while the other instruments provide a delicate accompaniment. This work was dedicated to the Pro Arte Quartet of Brussels. When that group transferred its base of operations to the United States, Mrs. Elizabeth Sprague Coolidge became the group's patroness. The members of the quartet suggested to Mrs. Coolidge that she commission Milhaud to write two new quartets, and they asked the composer to conceive these works in a somewhat more complex and substantial vein than that of the two preceding ones. Their request coincided with a change in Milhaud's own artistic outlook. He had ended a carefree period with the compositions of the two ballets *Le train bleu* and *Salade* and had become deeply absorbed in such epic projects as *Christophe Colomb* and *Maximilien*. It was seven years since he had written a string quartet, and in returning to this medium, he brought to his chamber music style something of the vigor and passion of his operas.

One of a composer's main resources is contrast, and the *Huitième quatuor* (1932) is an excellent case in point. The first movement, marked "Vif et souple," is based on the melodic and rhythmic contrast between the measures written in $\frac{12}{8}$ meter, which carry the steady flow of the music, and the asymmetrical $\frac{5}{8}$ measures, in which each note is accented. These two meters are also differentiated dynamically, pianissimo to mezzo forte in the $\frac{12}{8}$ measures and forte to fortissimo in the $\frac{5}{8}$. The "Lent et grave" movement derives its feeling of suppressed energy from the contrasting use of long and very short note-values. This pent-up emotion then erupts in the fast, energetic finale.

A similar feeling of decisiveness pervades the *Neuvième quatuor* (1935). After a brief, calm first movement, the second is an agitated "Animé," that is quite unlike a scherzo. It is more like an "Allegro," such as the one that concludes Bach's *Italian Concerto,* not, of course, in style, but in expressive content. The third movement is slow and meditative, whereas the fourth is full of rhythmic energy, which is quite in keeping with the general mood of this pair of quartets. A marchlike theme, which constitutes the middle section of this "Décidé," is combined with other thematic elements in the coda and brings the movement to a rousing end.

Nineteen thirty-nine marked the beginning of the war. Around that year Milhaud finished the opera *Médée* and composed some incidental music. He also wrote his first symphony. He had waited to compose a symphony until he felt sure that he had reached full artistic maturity. The work had been commissioned by the Chicago Symphony Orchestra in commemoration of its fiftieth anniversary. Milhaud was invited to attend the première, but when he and his wife and child set sail for the United States, they were also fleeing Europe for the duration of the war. Among other things, this meant that his access to most of his compositions, all in the hands of European publishers, would be cut off.

On board ship he immediately set to work on another quartet which, like the two previous ones, he dedicated to Mrs. Coolidge. This one, the *Dixième quatuor* (1940), was written as a birthday present. It is more brisk and uncomplicated than the two preceding ones. A particularly notable characteristic is the very high tessitura of the first violin in the finale. He uses this same technique in his symphonies, of which more will be said later. By placing one part so high, he extends the whole range of sonorities to a maximum and thus spreads out the melodic lines at considerable distances from each other. Also, the high notes give the impression of being natural harmonics (at the seventh and eleventh) of the lowest notes, with the result that the whole harmonic texture has a shimmering iridescence. Interesting as this harmonic effect is, it is not an essential ingredient of Milhaud's polyphonic style. One should always, first and foremost, listen to the voice-leading and consider the harmonies only as points at which the lines converge cadentially. In fact, instead of actually cadencing, these brief resting places act as springboards from which to launch the various melodic lines into orbit with new combinations of tonalities. These places are to polytonality what modulation is to harmony. And, after all, polytonality is only an extension of tonality.

The *Onzième quatuor* (1942) starts off in a moderately animated tempo. The four voices seem to be engaged in a quiet conversation, each one contributing to the general subject at hand. This discussion changes in the second, lively movement to a kind of mysterious whispering, not without a certain malice. Rapid, intermittent, and muted, the movement reminds one of the scherzo in Mendelssohn's *Midsummer Night's Dream* or Berlioz's *Romeo and Juliet*. After a pause, the third movement carries the conversation in still another direction, and finally the murmurings return in the rather boisterous last movement whose topic is quite different from the one that occupied the gossips earlier. The leaping figures with double stops, all very pianissimo, are punctuated from time to time by more static measures in a contrasting meter, and give the impression of simultaneously uttered exclamations. At last, everyone reaches an agreement, and the discussion ends on a happy note. I hope I will be forgiven this rather literary description of the eleventh quartet. I have never been able to listen to it without envisaging some sort of scenario, even though the musical material is completely nonprogrammatic.

Milhaud wrote his *Douzième quatuor* (1945) to commemorate the hundredth anniversary of the birth of Gabriel Fauré. It was not a commission, but rather a spontaneous tribute to the outstanding melodist whose serene music stands in distinct contrast both to the esthetic of Vincent D'Indy's Schola Cantorum and to Debussy's impressionism. Within the boundaries of classical form, Fauré developed a very personal harmonic language and a supple, graceful, contrapuntal style, rightly termed "Fauréenne." Milhaud admired Fauré as a perfect example of integrity and equilibrium. These qualities of mind and art were uppermost in his thoughts as, at the age of fifty-three and with the tragic war years behind him, he himself was beginning to enter a period of relative serenity and euphoria.

The first movement of the quartet starts with a brief, dreamy violin and viola duo, which is followed by a more animated but harmonically and dynamically uncomplicated main section. The quiet motives of the introduction return to end the movement. The second movement is the focal point of the work. Some composers excel in first-movement sonata form or in finales; Milhaud is an adagio specialist. The slow movement of this quartet combines two themes, the first of which is a deeply moving melody underscored by subtle harmonies. This theme enters into a dialogue with a second, more rhythmic, theme, which is fairly elaborately developed and then subsides as the first theme is reasserted toward the end of the movement. The third, lively movement makes a particularly effective contrast with the contemplative mood of the previous two. It is a joyous, dazzling display of thematic fecundity and instrumental éclat.

In 1946 the Milhauds embarked on a trip to Mexico at the invitation of Carlos Chávez, who had organized a concert devoted to Milhaud's compositions under the auspices of the Bellas Artes de México. It was his first return to an Iberian-Latin milieu, and the climate and vegetation, reminiscent of Mediterranean countries, made him feel tremendously at home. It was here that he wrote his *Treizième quatuor* (1946), dedicating it to his wife, because the number thirteen had always brought them good luck. The whole piece is sparkling and joyous. It begins with a movement marked "Très décidé," which in spirit seems to follow directly from the last movement of the twelfth quartet. The impression of rollicking, almost popular joviality is augmented by the use of pizzicato chords, like the plucking of guitars, that whirl into a final frenzy of motion. In the second movement one can imagine oneself floating through the delightful canals of the Gardens of Xochimilco. Nothing troubles the calm of these perfumed waterways. A diabolic "Mexicana," instrumentally brilliant and vivacious, terminates the quartet with an allusion at the end to the Mexican "Mariachis."

To celebrate the hundredth anniversary of the French Revolution of 1848, Milhaud composed his fourth symphony. After the performance of this work, a friend gave him a little green notebook decorated in the charmingly ornate style typical of the previous century. It contained eight musical staves on each page and was completely blank; there were no girlish sentiments translated into verse, no sentimental melodies accompanied by guitar! "I got the idea," Milhaud writes in his autobiography, "of using the eight staves to write two quartets which could be performed simultaneously as an octet, as well as separately." Naturally, a live performance of the *Octuor* would require two separate quartet groups. But when Columbia Records made a recording, the Budapest Quartet did the entire album. First they recorded each quartet separately. Then, wearing earphones so that they could follow their own playing of the fifteenth quartet, they re-recorded the fourteenth. Thus the octet was perfectly synchronized. This whole opus is dedicated "to Paul Collaer, in appreciation of thirty years of friendship." Together with the *Création du monde,* the Percussion Concerto, and the *Cantate de l'enfant et de la mère,* this constituted the most wonderful gift that I could possibly have received. Actually, our friendship started in 1914, when Milhaud came to La Libre Esthétique in Brussels to perform, with Georgette Guller, his first sonata for violin and piano. It lasted until his death. In all that time we never had even a passing moment of misunderstanding. For sixty years we maintained similar outlooks on life and art. Our mutual affection even extended to include our respective families. It was one of those rare phenomena that Goethe called "elective affinities" in his novel *Die Wahlverwandschaften*.

Obviously, it was necessary for Milhaud to have achieved complete mastery of contrapuntal technique, as well as a thorough understanding of the full potential of polytonality, to write a work for eight instruments, giving each equivalent importance and at the same time providing for subtle differentiation between them. This work is indeed a tour de force, albeit difficult to listen to, as well as to perform. The lyric theme of the first movement of the fourteenth quartet, soaring to the top range of the violin, contrasts with the skipping motion heard at the opening of the fifteenth (Ex. 8–13).

Ex. 8–13.

The second movement of the fourteenth begins with the rocking motion of a berceuse, which lends its motives to the melodic material that develops and intensifies up to measure 64, where the cello enters with a new theme, which initiates a fugal section. At measure 101 the berceuse rhythm returns briefly to end the movement. Meanwhile, the fifteenth quartet proceeds calmly up to measure 30, where a relatively thick polyphonic passage begins. Then in measure 73–101 there is a recapitulation of measures 1–28, only in reverse. The process is clearly observable, and its fascinating complexity reminds one of constructions by Machaut and Ockeghem. It is interesting to note that at this same period Stravinsky was working on his *Cantata on Old English Texts* (from the fifteenth and sixteenth centuries). The third movement gives equally brilliant material to both groups of players. When the work was given its first public hearing each quartet was played separately and then the two were replayed as an octet. Alfred Frankenstein wrote in the *San Francisco Chronicle:* "The two together produce an effect of immense depth, resonance, size, and far-reaching musical perspective. It also produces an effect of tonal and contrapuntal involvement compared to which the effect of the average symphony is childishly simple. Milhaud's quartet style is notable for its elegance and clarity, but his orchestral style is often thick, rough, and glowing, as the paint on a canvas by Rouault, and the octet suggests that orchestral manner without cracking the framework of chamber music." It is interesting that Francis Poulenc also compared Milhaud's symphonies to Rouault paintings. Does that indicate a similarity of temperaments, or merely a shared artistic epoch, or both? It is impossible to deny that there is excess complexity in the octet, as also in some of Milhaud's symphonies. Rouault has been accused of the same thing. But one can say of the music, as has been said of the painting, that it "bears the stamp of grandeur, of independence, and of joyous freedom" (Léon Lehmann in *Le Point* 26–27, 1943).

The *Seizième quatuor* (1950) is dedicated "to Madeleine, for our twenty-fifth wedding anniversary: 4 May 1925." Tenderness and joyous vivacity alternate within a simple framework. Once again the first movement places the first violin part in a high register, not for the sake of brilliance, but so that it can float dreamily. The themes of the third movement are quietly impelled by an asymmetric $\frac{5}{8}$ meter. Lyricism is the hallmark of this quartet, whereas the fourteenth and fifteenth were more intellectual.

The *Dix-septième quatuor* (1950), written "for Daniel's twenty-first birthday," combines influences from all three of the preceding quartets. It begins with a movement marked "Rude," in $\frac{12}{8}$ meter, in which an extended melody is passed around in varied guises among the different instruments and lends itself to canonic treatment (Ex. 8–14).

Ex. 8–14.

This melody is combined with another, introduced by the cello, which dominates the entire development section (Ex. 8–15).

Ex. 8–15.

Above this melody the violins embroider various melodic figures. The texture of the movement is thick and detailed. The restful simplicity of the second movement contrasts with the preceding turbulence. A third movement, marked "Léger et cinglant," follows. The capricious rhythm of this section, resulting from its constantly changing meters, all very pianissimo, makes one think of a young colt cavorting in a field (Ex. 8–16).

Ex. 8–16.

Into the general texture of the movement and growing out of previous thematic material, a four-part fugue is introduced and developed to a brilliant conclusion. The last movement recaptures the turbulence of the first, but at the end, after several attempts to find a resting point, it finally trails off ambiguously. Throughout this work, polytonality is exploited to the utmost.

Milhaud's last quartet, his *Dix-huitième quatuor (1950–51)*, is dedicated to the memory of his parents, who died during the war without a last glimpse of their son. The two outer movements are quiet and gentle, whereas the second and third, each entitled "Hymns," are more energetic. The first is brisk and somewhat imperious, the second more flowing. At the start of the first movement the violin introduces the main theme, which oscillates between major and minor (Ex. 8–17).

Ex. 8–17.

The chromaticism of the theme makes it easy to modulate to allied tonalities. The first hymn is probably derived from the Jewish religious tradition of the Comtat. The theme mostly revolves around E-flat major, although in certain episodes it moves through several divergent tonalities. The flow is strongly punctuated by full chords, played on three or four strings of each instrument. The second hymn is based on one melodic line, which is spun out into garlands of sound. The suppleness of these intertwined lines is due in part to the equating of $\frac{6}{8}$ and $\frac{3}{4}$ meters, a rhythmic resource inherited from the Italian Baroque. It creates an impression of strength combined with elegance. The last movement is subdued throughout and falls into a three-part form, with measures 77–97 repeating the opening twenty measures. A brief coda quietly restates the first theme of the first quartet. At the bottom of the page Milhaud has written:

FIN
Des Dix-huit
Quatuors à cordes
1912–1951

Of all his compositions, Milhaud probably had a secret preference for his cycle of string quartets. In addition to his previously stated need to fall back on purely abstract music as an antidote to more programmatic works, he appears to have found quartet writing a perfect medium through which to express his inmost thoughts. However, this cycle is no personal diary. Rather, the various works stand as markers along his path, and it is significant that all were dedicated either to members of his family or to people whom he especially admired. Considered as a whole, the cycle traces the profile of a man who liked neither to reveal his inmost thoughts nor to explain his music in words. His reticence was the natural reaction of a sensitive spirit, which shied away from the turbulent aspects of the time in which he lived. In fact, he was a man for all seasons.

In a series of interviews published under the title "Entretiens avec Claude Rostand" (Paris, 1952), Milhaud defined the string quartet art form: "It is at once an intellectual discipline and a crucible of the most intense emotion." For those who perform it, it is the object of lifelong preoccupation. As one grows to appreciate this most private of musical media, one sharpens one's perception of the truly essential ingredients of artistic expression and tends to discard all stylistic superficialities. For chamber music is something we play for our own delight in the intimacy of our homes. It loses a great deal when transferred to the concert hall. Actually, the practice of presenting small groups to large audiences has led to a certain blurring of the identity of chamber music. A number of modern composers have written in a virtuoso style that seems to contradict the traditional values of the medium. Emphasis is more on bedazzlement than finesse. A successful adaptation of this intimate genre for performance in a large concert hall can be illustrated by some of Bartók's works. They are rich in thematic content; their brilliant virtuosity and rhapsodic complexity project to a sizable audience, yet they retain the typical precepts of chamber music. The same can be said of Schoenberg's first two quartets.

Debussy, Ravel, and Fauré, however, continued the string quartet tradition in its more classical sense; even Schoenberg respected its exigencies. His second quartet, with voice, which is movingly dramatic, and his third, which is formalized but not too exclusively intellectual, bear up well under the scrutiny of both performers and listeners. But of all contemporary chamber music works, it is the quartets of Bartók and Milhaud that best carry on the tradition: Bartók in the Beethovian spirit and Milhaud in the Mozartian.

Milhaud is a musician for all seasons, yes, but that does not mean that he stood apart from his own era. Quite the contrary. His music is typical both of his epoch and of his milieu. However, he refused to follow mere fads and ephemeral artistic directions. Moreover, his art is timeless in the sense that his music does not follow any chronological path of development. Rather, from his adolescent years to the end of his life, he conceived his artistic creation as a total entity, the various elements of which could be drawn forth at any moment for whatever purpose.

An examination of his chamber music for strings yields evidence of his particular, individual relationship to time. The works in this category comprise a total exploration of the medium, but they were composed in no particular sequences. The chamber symphony for ten instruments, for example, dates from 1921, whereas the solo sonatas were mostly composed much later. The octet was conceived in 1948, whereas the quintets and sextet are all works of the fifties. In other words, there was no deliberate progression from duos to larger ensembles with a corresponding systematic development of technique. From the outset his artistic vision encompassed the entire range of possibilities and the methods for realizing them. Then he proceeded to fit in the different pieces as his inclination or the situation of the moment required. The general plan had been outlined from the start. Only the quartets were spaced at certain significant points along the route of his spiritual journey.

The same observation can be made regarding his use of monotonality, bitonality, and polytonality, whether harmonic or polyphonic. His use of various technical resources did not start with simple tonality and then grow constantly more complex. He used them all with equal ease at all periods of his life, beginning in 1915, and chose those elements that suited a particular expressive imperative. The fifth quartet from 1920, for example, is radically and exclusively polytonal, whereas *Les rêves de Jacob* of 1949 uses a tonal-modal vocabulary.

One can understand how such a free and universal concept of the world of sonority might be confusing to many listeners as well as to performers. In this respect he shares the stage with Stravinsky and Schoenberg. With the appearance of each new work, Stravinsky was thought to be veering off in a new direction. When *Moses and Aaron* appeared, Schoenberg was accused of being unfaithful to dodecaphonic serialism. The same was said of his *Ode to Napoleon Bonaparte*. Schoenberg answered his critics by pointing out that he introduced consonant chords into his music whenever he needed to for expressive purposes.

Creative artists are completely free agents. They can build on previous tradition or strike out in new directions. To try to confine them within the bounds of rules and dogmas is an error. Wagner knew this well, and there are always plenty of Beckmessers around, not only among conservatives, but also in the ranks of the so-called avant-garde. Alban Berg responded to the universal quality of Milhaud's art when he wrote to him on 23 April 1923 to acknowledge receipt of the score of the chamber symphonies.

My very dear M. Milhaud:
    I thank you sincerely for your five symphonies. After a first quick glance I was delighted with them and eager to study them further. My first impression is that I find your work extremely "sympathique" as well as fresh and original. And, thanks to you, I believe I have come to appreciate polytonality. Furthermore, even though these pieces were composed between 1917 and 1922 and at places as far distant as Rio de Janeiro and Vienna, they possess such unity that I am convinced of the high quality of this composition.
    I am sincerely delighted, and I thank you.

Berg later confirmed this opinion in a conversation I had with him in which he linked Milhaud, in this respect, with Debussy.

There is no point in postponing further a discussion of Milhaud's other ensemble works. "A pearl of chamber music:" this is an apt description of the sonata for two violins and piano that he wrote in 1914. It is difficult to blend the timbre of the piano with that of the strings, and except for its soloistic use in concertos, the piano rarely joins with other instruments without overpowering them. In chamber music, notable exceptions to this rule are Fauré's piano quartets and second piano quintet and both the violin and cello sonatas by Debussy. Milhaud's early composition for two violins and piano also succeeds in weaving sonorities into the most silvery, transparent texture. A sunny, placid work, it is among his finest for ensemble.

Dedicated to André Gide, the *Deuxième sonate* (1916) for violin and piano evokes, by coincidence, a mood corresponding to certain pages of that author's *Symphonie pastorale,* which, however, was not published until 1919, two years after the sonata.

Two sonatas and a suite entitled *Quatre visages,* for viola and piano, composed in 1943 and 1944, make an important contribution to the not very ample viola repertory. The second sonata, in particular, exploits the entire expressive resources of the instrument.

The group of compositions combining piano and strings is completed by a cello sonata, a trio, a piano quartet, and the first quintet, works that are solidly constructed and written with great attention to detail. The construction of the trio is particularly interesting. The first movement, marked "Modéré," begins with three introductory measures. The following A section proceeds by means of a short transition to a contrasting B section. A short piano cadenza serves as a hinge between the first and second parts; the latter starts with B in slightly altered form. Then the A section returns, followed by two variants of B, and the movement concludes with a reference to the introduction. As each thematic element reoccurs, it is transposed in range and is assigned to different instruments. The second movement, "Animé," has a similar type of arrangement:

209

aABCD
ABDCa

The third, marked "Calme," is an ABCBA, and the finale, "Violent,"
has six sections which are recapitulated in altered order:

aABCDEFG
EBDFAGCa

The abundance of melodic and thematic ideas is remarkable in this
trio. The piano quartet is conceived in much the same vein, whereas
the piano quintet is best grouped with the other (string) quintets.

Of these, the *Deuxième quintette* (1952), for string quartet and string
bass, presents no problems to the listener. Clear and good-humored, it
assigns a discreet, vivacious role to the bass, so that nothing disrupts
the homogeneity of sound. In the last movement, the interplay of the
instruments becomes less and less complex, until the final cadence
comes to rest in the tonality of F major, which is grounded by the bass
repeating and prolonging the lower F.

The contrapuntal style of the *Troisième quintette* (1953), for two violins, two violas, and cello, contrasts with the relative simplicity of the
second. But of all the group, the expressive quality is greatest in the
Quatrième quintette (1956) for two violins, viola, and two cellos, written in memory of Arthur Honegger. Its four movements have subtitles
in the manner of the seventeenth century:

> Lament for the death of a friend (Très modéré)
> Recollections of youth (Animé)
> The pleasure of a long friendship (Assez lent)
> Hymn of praise (Animé)

There is no excess or dramatic exaggeration in this very beautiful, tempered work.

Also excellent is the *Sextuor* (1958) for two violins, two violas, and
two cellos. This work makes use of a full range of contrapuntal devices.
The perfectly symmetrical theme of the first movement is a two-
measure canon, which the second violin starts half a measure after the
first violin. Then the violas have the same figure, and in measure 6 the
cellos have it in reverse order. The second movement is somber in
mood as is the case with so many of Milhaud's slow movements, and
the third is a contrast in nervous vitality. The piece comes to a forceful
end as the polyphonic tissue tightens into a sort of stretto.

Milhaud's general ensemble style has already been discussed in connection with the quartets. What may be termed "kaleidoscopic" constructions are typical. He usually starts with an exposition section in
which one or more melodies are introduced, along with embellishing

counterpoints. These thematic ideas, both the principal and the subordinate ones, are reiterated in somewhat varied form and with changes in range and texture. This constant redistribution of shapes and colors, like the patterns of a kaleidoscope, is always symmetrical, however. Every kind of polyphonic resource known since the Middle Ages is used, as well as some homophonic conventions—the Sonata form, for example, but without a development section. To these traditions the composer has added his own skill and imagination.

As an excellent example of the above, let us examine the *Septuor à cordes* (1964), for two violins, two violas, two cellos and string bass. It consists of four movements. The first starts with a main theme, stated by the first violin and embellished by the other instruments. The second theme, introduced by the second cello, forms the basis of a subsection. Then the first viola repeats this theme against a new contrapuntal background. Altogether this constitutes the first half of the movement. The second half brings back the first theme, now played by the second viola with the accompanying motives transferred to other registers. The second thematic idea reappears in the first viola, and near the end, the cello takes up this idea in slightly varied form. The string bass, which was used sparingly in the first half, becomes a more important part of the texture in the second half.

The second movement is called "Etude de hasard dirigé," or controlled chance music. Each measure is supposed to last one second, and the instruments take turns in maintaining the basic time frame throughout the movement, sometimes singly, sometimes in groups. While this basic metronomic beat continues, other faster phrases, all of different lengths, must be repeated several times for a certain prescribed number of seconds before the next section begins, even if the time limit expires in the middle of a phrase. The effect of this music is more like that of a whirling propeller than that of a kaleidoscope. Milhaud first tried his hand at chance music in his *Cocktail aux clarinettes* (1921) written forty-five years before proponents of new music in the nineteen-sixties hailed it as a great new discovery. He turned to it again in one of his much later compositions, the *Suite de quatrains* (1962).

In the third, meditative movement of the septet marked "Modéré et expressif," the entire range of string sonority from lowest to highest is called into play. Five sections present different, but related, ideas. These sections are separated by solo passages. The second half of the movement is a recapitulation without repetitions of the five sections, but in a different order. The "Alerte" has the same symmetrical construction as the first and third movements and, like most of Milhaud's finales, is typically energetic.

211

Turning to works that include wind instruments, we should make special mention of the brilliant, but graceful Sonatine (1922) for flute and piano. There is both subtlety and daring in the way the voices intertwine, and, although it appears to be carefree and capricious, the construction is actually tight-knit and logical. All three movements are full of life. The first moves along amiably; the second is an animated barcarolle; and the last is sparkling and vivacious. It is a thoroughly French work in the tradition of Rameau and Jannequin—French in spirit, that is, not in any particular stylistic sense.

The austere *Sonate* (1918) for flute, oboe, clarinette, and piano, is a different story entirely. The tension in this composition is allied to that of Milhaud's dramatic works. The four movements present four moods: quiet, joyous, passionate, and sad. The first two are pastorales; the second superimposes a torrent of woodwind sounds on heavily compressed harmonic blocks in the piano. The fourth movement is like a funeral march; above a chordal progression in the piano, the clarinet and then the oboe spin out long, expressive themes, interrupted from time to time by rebellious outbursts, before reaching a solemn conclusion. The first and fourth movements of this sonata are extremely beautiful, but the third is too preoccupied with rigid formulas to be altogether successful.

Among the wind quintets, the amusing *La cheminée du roi René* (1939) is especially worthy of note. Its folkish, Provençal character has made it almost as famous as *Le boeuf sur le toit* and *La création du monde.*

The light, pleasant style of the *Divertissement* (1958) for the same combination, in spite of its dramatic middle movement, harks back to the spirit of the genre as developed by Haydn and Mozart. By contrast, the *Quintette à vent* (1973), which is Milhaud's last composition, is extremely stark. In its severe austerity it can perhaps be taken as a final affirmation of the composer's idealism and of his uncompromising personality, which refused to make concessions.

In the author's opinion, the finest of all the wind ensembles is the dixtet, which is actually the composer's Fifth Chamber Symphony (1922). Written for piccolo, flute, oboe, English horn, clarinet, bass clarinet, two bassoons, and two horns, it is dramatically intense, but crystal clear in construction. The first movement, marked "Rude," brings the instruments together in lyric apposition. The slow movement gives a strange, shivering impression. It begins with veiled woodwind harmonies moving against a background of sustained trills. Against this, the bass clarinet unfurls its melody, supported by muted bassoons and horns. The music seems to be locked in deep, magical slumber. Then the last movement bursts forth with a prancing rhythm, spontaneous but controlled.

Like the fifth, the rest of the chamber symphonies written between 1917 and 1923, are definitely to be considered chamber music, since each instrument is treated soloistically. Starting with Schoenberg's *Kammersymphonie,* it became general practice to apply the term *symphonie* to small groups of soloists. Stravinsky used such an ensemble in his *Chants de la lyrique japonaise,* as did Schoenberg in *Pierrot lunaire.* The constant growth of the orchestra in the nineteenth and early part of the twentieth centuries had brought with it progressive abdication of musical quality in favor of quantity. How can one achieve subtle nuances in rhythm or articulation with twenty violins and with other parts doubled or tripled? The ear hears only a mass of undifferentiated sound. Expressiveness by quantity has its place, but there are many effects it cannot achieve. Already, among French composers, Debussy had started a revolt by giving greater prominence to solo instruments. As the twentieth century proceeded, there was a noticeable return to the smaller-scale tradition of the Baroque. And even if Berg wrote *Wozzeck* for a 100-piece orchestra, he rarely used all the instruments together; rather, the ensemble is broken up into sub-orchestras of soloists, alternating with each other. The large number of players is needed to supply a wide range of sonorities from which to draw.

Milhaud's chamber symphonies are very short. The three mini-movements in each merely present themes, without developing them. The first, subtitled "Le printemps," uses a string quartet and four winds, accompanied by harp. The second, "Pastorale," is ingeniuosly written for flute, English horn, bassoon, violin, viola, cello, and bass; the third, "Sérénade," substitutes a clarinet for the English horn, but is otherwise scored like the second. The fourth is for double string quintet. Milhaud has separated each pair of instruments in range and timbre, so that one has the impression of hearing ten very distinct parts. In particular, the double bass covers a range from low C up to the second E above the staff. At the bottom of the score is written: "This 'symphonie' can also be performed on the instruments that constitute the double-quintet of Léo Sir (that is, sur-soprano, soprano, mezzo-soprano, alto, contralto, ténor, baryton, basse, sous-basse, contre-basse)." One wishes that instruments like the tenor viol, halfway between viola and cello, and the violino piccolo were still in use! The fifth chamber symphony, a dixtet for wind instruments, has already been discussed. In the sixth, a wordless vocal quartet is accompanied by solo oboe and cello.

Toward the end of his career, Milhaud returned to his earlier practice of giving solo instruments privileged status in an orchestral ensemble, as witness his *Concerto de chambre* (1961) and the *Aspen Serenade* (1957). This latter work is an especially remarkable example of his mature polyphonic style, applied more in the spirit of intellectual inquiry than of communicative immediacy. Composed for performance at the Colorado music center where the Milhauds spent so many summers, the work is scored for nine instruments: four woodwinds and four strings, with the addition of a trumpet. In the first movement the strings gravitate toward the tonality of C major, while the tonal axis of the winds is E-flat major. The movement contains two symmetrical halves, and the trumpet is used to articulate this main division, as well as the subdivisions within each section. The second half is characterized by an exchange of tonalities and melodic material between the two instrumental blocks. The second movement, marked "Souple et printanier," is arranged according to a similar two-part plan. The texture is flexible and delicate, and the trumpet is important melodically. The third movement has a three-part ABA form, and the fourth starts off with a series of melodic ideas which are then reversed, crab fashion, halfway through. The last movement superimposes two four-voice fugues. The one played by the winds is in $\frac{6}{8}$ meter and returns to the E-flat tonality of the first movement, while the string fugue, in $\frac{2}{4}$ meter, also returns to its original key of C major. In the final stretto, there is a certain interchange of melodic material between winds and strings. Throughout the movement, the trumpet sings forth in augmentation the themes of the two fugues. The construction of this work, with its vivid instrumental coloring, is very clearly projected. One can compare it to a beautiful stained-glass window, when the sunlight makes each pane of different-colored glass glow intensely.

Symphonic Music

Up to 1938 Milhaud's efforts were mostly divided between the composition of dramatic works (operas, ballets, and incidental music) and chamber music. A few concertos and other pieces using a large orchestra diversified this pattern. He had without question thoroughly mastered the skills of orchestration and had developed his own very special concept of sonority, which was in distinct contrast to the use of instruments for highly coloristic effects that had characterized the impressionist period. However, with the exception of a sparkling *Serenade* (1920), the *Suite provençal* (1936), and the second *Suite symphonique* (1919),these last two adapted from some of his best incidental music (*Bertran de Born* and *Protée,* respectively), he had written virtually no independent symphonic music. Within the sum total of his musical output, he viewed symphonic writing as something he would do only when he had reached full maturity, and therefore he had decided to wait until he turned fifty. Like his decision to compose only eighteen string quartets, this attitude reflected the way he considered his music a totality and a conscientious, orderly statement. Technical ability had nothing to do with his decision to wait. Rather, he felt very strongly the responsibility of continuing the great symphonic tradition. He knew that he had to reshape it in a way that reflected his own musical values and at the same time transcended mere personal whim.

For the great nineteenth-century masters Beethoven, Schumann, and Brahms, and even for César Franck and for Mahler, a symphony was both dramatic and psychological. It was dramatic in the way that a literary work is dramatic—that is, it realizes the consequences of an action, or actions, taken. In the case of music, action is represented by themes, and dramatic development by the development section of sonata form, with its intertwining and juxtaposition of thematic material. In addition, the dramatic quality of the music was also a reflection of a composer's view of psychological struggle, as witness Mahler's symphonies and Richard Strauss's tone poems. The tradition was even prolonged in the twentieth century by Schoenberg and Berg, in whose music symphonic development dominated theatrical implications.

Milhaud venerated this great epoch of German symphonists, with the exception of Brahms and Bruckner. His favorites were Beethoven and Mahler, and also the tone poems and operas of Richard Strauss. He loved *Wozzeck* and *Lulu* and Schoenberg's Five Orchestral Pieces, but it was not his temperament to compose in the same manner. It must have taken him years of thought before he discovered just what means to use in continuing the symphonic tradition without emulating the Romantic period form which had so admirably served and dominated an entire century of musical creativity. Therefore, it was not until 1939, when an invitation came from Chicago to write a work in celebration of the orchestra's fiftieth anniversary, that he felt ready to embark on the series of twelve symphonies that were to occupy him between 1939 and 1961.

In both form and content, these works represent a distinct break with the nineteenth century. In their lack of dramatic intensity, they are closer in spirit, though in neither form nor style, to Haydn and Mozart. They also use the device, not untypical of Mozart, of grouping a succession of melodic ideas into one thematic block, and they reject the Romantic period concept of juxtaposing two themes in strong psychological and dramatic contrast. Beethoven's music acts; Mozart's flows. Using, of course, a strictly twentieth-century vocabulary, Milhaud found Mozart's model particularly compatible with his own temperament as well as with the age in which he lived.

One can observe a certain analogy in literature. In France the nineteenth century was the era of the novel, be it adventurous, sociological, or psychological. Whether written by Alexandre Dumas, Flaubert, Stendhal, Balzac, or Zola, the novel related a series of events involving various people. In the course of the story, these personalities would confront one another. First would come the initial meeting, then the development of a complex interrelationship, culminating finally at a point of greatest tension. After that there would be a conclusion, which usually embodied a certain feeling of relief. What was true for French literature applied equally to the writings of Thackeray, Goethe, and Dostoevski. In sum, the form of the novel was a kind of exposition, development, and coda.

Turning, by contrast, to the works of André Gide, such as *Le voyage d'Urien* (1892) and *Paludes* (1895), and to Guillaume Apollinaire's *Le poète assassiné,* one finds that these are no longer novels of action. Rather, their chapters reflect states of mind that remain static, rather than being points of departure for psychological evolution. Milhaud's symphonies are to their romantic counterparts what such works of Gide and Apollinaire are to the Romantic novel. Because Milhaud's art is primarily melodic, development of material was not congenial to him. Rather, he preferred to unfold a series of constantly new melodic ideas, either similar or contrasting. He used these in repetition, juxtaposition, superimposition, and retrograde motion, in animated, but nondramatic, interplay. Each symphonic movement portrays a different state of mind but makes no attempt to translate attitude into action. Moments of dramatic development are very rare.

Another characteristic of these symphonies is their use of a full range of instrumental sonority. Widely spaced distribution of melodic material is necessary so that the various thematic ideas can be clearly differentiated. Technically speaking, the instrumental parts are not particularly difficult, with the exception of the violin parts, which are often written in a very high register and are full of rapid passage work. Absolute clarity, particularly in the strings, is essential to the projection of this music. It is also extremely important, as well as quite difficult, to assign just the right degrees of intensity to the various instrumental groups, so that the thematic ideas come through in proper balance. Obviously, a conductor must understand all these basic concepts and an audience must be able to divorce itself from nineteenth-century expectations to appreciate these works fully; and one can pass judgment on them only if one has been privileged to hear a truly well-conceived and well-executed performance. The difficulty in regulating balance, as well as the novelty of approach and vocabulary, have made conductors shy away from programming Milhaud's symphonies. One is tempted to wonder whether electronically controlled performance might not be the answer.

*   *   *

For a detailed analysis of the twelve symphonies, one should turn to Ralph James Swickard's study (R. J. Swickard, *The Symphonies of Darius Milhaud: An Historical Perspective and Critical Study of Their*

Music Content, Style, and Form, Ph.D. diss., University of California at Los Angeles, 1973). A conductor who wishes to perform these pieces will find Swickard's thesis indispensable, but for the purpose of the present book, a brief summary is sufficient.

Basically, the organization of the symphonies is much like that of the string quartets. The first movements generally consist of an exposition of several successive ideas; these ideas are then reworked according to various contrapuntal formulas and are finally restated as in the opening section, only in a different sequence and often with an exchange of tonalities. The slow movements are frequently in three-part "song form;" the scherzo is replaced by an interplay of contrasting material, either capricious or mysterious in mood; the final movement tends to be a fugato or free fugue. The movements rarely receive classic tempo designations, but are instead suggestive of moods: Pastorale, Mystérieux, Avec sérénité, Tumultueux. Sometimes mood and tempo designations are combined: Vif et cinglant, Lent et doux, Joyeux et robuste. A brief review of the twelve symphonies will show how they fit into the composer's total output.

Milhaud anticipated by three years the date he had planned to begin work on a symphony. But that is of no importance, for when he received the commission from the Chicago Symphony Orchestra, his philosophy, as well as his technique, had come to full fruition. He had thoroughly mastered the problem of maintaining tonal clarity within the framework of polytonality, and to this end he had definitely decided that his melodies must be diatonic rather than chromatic.

The first performance of his *Première symphonie* took place on 17 October 1940 and was attended by the composer, who was able to come to the United States during wartime largely on the basis of the invitation from Chicago. American musicians immediately grasped the distinctive characteristics of the music. Swickard points out the surprisingly broad range of emotions that are translated into music in this piece, and Aaron Copland described some of its expressive components as follows: "A violent dramatic and almost brutal mood, a relaxed mood of almost childish gaiety and brightness, and a tender and nostalgic sensuousness." The lively contrapuntal style and simultaneous presentation of contrasting ideas was remarked on. Stravinsky said later to Robert Craft that, when he heard Milhaud's music, he was reminded of two bands playing on opposite sides of the Piazza San Marco in Venice. Leland Smith has noted "the appearance of various musical fragments or modules during the reprise sections and has found that these fragments are often arranged quite arbitrarily, though always with artistry and good taste. Such musical units," he wrote, "might be referred to as 'musical quanta' purposely so treated to contribute variation to the compository procedure."

217

The first movement of this symphony is marked "Pastoral." The second is a kind of scherzo, with a fugato acting as a trio section. The third is based on a somber, chorale-like tune. The animated finale starts with a folk-tune type of melody in $\frac{4}{4}$, which is followed by a gigue; and at the end the various melodic ideas are joined in an animated conclusion.

Four years separated the first two symphonies. During that period Milhaud worked on *Bolivar,* several concertos, the sonatas for viola and piano, and *La muse ménagère.* Begun in September and finished on 7 November 1944, the *Deuxième symphonie* was dedicated to the memory of Nathalie Koussevitzky and was given its first performance by Serge Koussevitzky on 20 December 1946. Virgil Thomson termed it "neo-Romantic" and described the movements in terms of their expressive content: "In this work we have Milhaud in three characteristic moods—the pastoral, the serene, and the jubilant. The second and third movements are, in addition, devoted to mystery and pain. The latter achieves an intensity of expression in the vein of dolor that is unusual to this composer and rare in all of music. The jubilant finale Alleluja is also a striking piece of discordant writing and in every way invigorating."

Between the second and third symphonies Milhaud composed the *Suite française,* the second concerto for violin, the second for cello, the third for piano, the ballet *The Bells* (inspired by Edgar Allan Poe), and several vocal and instrumental works. The *Troisième Symphonie,* subtitled "Te Deum," adds a chorus and was composed in 1946 at the request of Henri Barraud, then director of the music department of the Radiodiffusion Française. Barraud wanted a work to commemorate the victorious ending of the Second World War. The first performance took place on 30 October 1947, under the direction of Roger Desormière. The first movement is entitled "Fièrement." In the second, "Très recueilli," a wordless chorus interacts antiphonally with the orchestra. This section never fails to produce a striking effect on the audience. The "Te Deum" of the last movement is based on the text that was for a long time attributed to Saint Ambrose, bishop of Milan, but which is now thought to have originated with Nicetus, bishop of Remisianus (Nish, in Yugoslavia) around 550 A.D. As usual, critical response to this work was divided down the middle, between enthusiastic prose and invective—another illustration of the fact that Milhaud's music disturbs the listening habits of some people, while speaking directly and easily to others.

The fourth symphony followed the third by eight months. In that brief period Milhaud had completed the great *Service sacré pour le samedi* and the concerto for marimba and xylopohone. He wrote the *Quatrième symphonie* in 1947 on the ship that was taking the Milhaud family back to France for the first time since their wartime exile. It was orchestrated in Genval, near Brussels, and at Aix. Written to commemorate the Revolution of 1848, it was first performed at the Théâtre des Champs-Elysées in Paris on 20 May 1948. Milhaud himself conducted, replacing Roger Desormière, who was unable to be present. Unlike his other symphonies which portray moods, this one alludes to historical events. It embodies, as does his cantata *Mort d'un tyran,* the composer's hatred of injustice. The orchestra, which makes extensive use of wind instruments to represent the crowds in the street as well as the marching of troops, includes three flutes, three oboes, four clarinets, two saxophones, three bassoons, four each of horns, trumpets, and trombones, two tubas, and five percussionists, as well as the usual strings.

Five years later his fifth symphony made its appearance. In the interim, several important works had been produced: the fourth piano concerto, the concertinos *Eté* and *Automne,* the last five quartets, and the opera *David.* The *Cinquième symphonie* was commissioned by the Italian radio, RAI. It was written at Mills College in 1953 and was first performed in Turin in November of that year, with Milhaud as conductor. The double indications of the four movements illustrate Milhaud's most typical choice of mood designations. As usual, the slow movement is the most important of the four. Several critics have pointed to the virtuosity of the orchestral writing. The structure is based this time not on melodies, but on a collection of short motives. Alfred Frankenstein, who responded appreciatively to this work, described it in the *San Francisco Chronicle* as creating "paradoxically an impression of thickness and lightness"; while Alexander Fried, who was not attracted by it, wrote in the *San Francisco Examiner:* "In its coolly objective anti-rhetorical spirit, the music did have a kind of refreshing, almost sardonic crackle that was not without tone-texture. . . . Mainly this *Fifth* seemed made to order and even trivial." The two opinions illustrate the typical dual reaction that Milhaud's music evoked throughout his career.

Two years later, after completing *Le château de feu,* the *Concertino d'hiver,* the *Suite campagnarde,* and two concertos, Milhaud composed his *Sixième symphonie.* It was dedicated to the memory of Serge and Nathalie Koussevitzky and was performed in the year in which it was written, in October 1955, for the seventy-fifth anniversary of the Boston Symphony orchestra, Charles Munch conducting. The departure from tradition of the slow-fast-slow-fast sequence of movements added to the general dismay of the critics. Some of them liked the slow movements and disliked the fast ones. With others it was just the reverse. On the whole, though, they concurred in one opinion: the piece didn't appeal to them. In retrospect, this hostile reaction seems puzzling. However, it was much the same with Stravinsky; as each of his new works came along, it seemed to go off in a new direction from the ones preceding it, which confounded the commentators. In general, novelty of musical language, form, and content is met with something less than enthusiasm. Even Mozart, and certainly Berlioz, could bear witness to this state of affairs!

The seventh symphony followed the sixth immediately and was dedicated to the Orchestre Symphonique de la Radio Belge and its conductor Franz André. It was performed by that group in September 1955. It is a short work comprising three movements, and in general it was not well received. Commentators found it obscure, even chaotic. Swickard, however, points out certain remarkable qualities in the slow movement:

Though constructed as a fugue, the fugal procedure is not always fully recognized on first hearing, owing in part to the subject being presented by pairs of instruments passing the material alternately back and forth. The subject often seems obscured, also, by the surrounding contrapuntal activity. At times rather foreboding in its general sonority, the music reaches a great climax at the midway point; following that, the material becomes abstruse and complicated, with rather odd dissonances engendered by various combinations of heterogeneous counterpoint.

After finishing the seventh symphony, Milhaud produced his fourth quintet, the *Aspen Serenade,* and a sonatina for piano. The *Huitième symphonie* was commissioned by the University of California at Berkeley and had its first performance there in 1958 by the San Francisco Symphony Orchestra conducted by Enrique Jorda. Smetana sang of the Moldau; Milhaud celebrated his river, the Rhône. He portrayed its progress from its source in the Rhône glacier, its sojourn in Lake Geneva, its majestic journey southward, and its final passage through the Camargue before emptying into the Mediterranean. The music evokes the various aspects of the river without trying to be programmatic, except for the subtitles: "Avec mystère et violence," "Avec sérénité et nonchalance," "Avec emportement," and "Rapide et majestueux." One suspects that these reflect the composer's moods as well as those of the river. The title page of the eighth symphony designates it as being in the key of D, and the polytonal writing all seems to refer to this tonal center and to be an extension of it. Of all the symphonies, this is the one most frequently performed. Audiences find it more accessible than the others, perhaps because of its programmatic allusion.

Two and a half years later Milhaud wrote in rapid succession and within a six-month period his ninth, tenth, and eleventh symphonies. Meanwhile, he had composed *Fiesta,* the third violin concerto, a concerto for oboe, a *Symphonie concertante,* and his *Sextuor à cordes.* It seems that his creative drive increased as he grew older. All three of the above-mentioned works were composed in Paris in 1959–1960. The performance of the *Neuvième symphonie,* commissioned by the orchestra of Fort Lauderdale, Florida, was an unqualified disaster, in large part because the orchestra was not up to it. The *Dixième symphonie* was commissioned to celebrate the centennial of the founding of the State of Oregon and was first performed in Portland on 4 April 1960 with Piero Bellugi conducting. The clearly perceivable structure of this work has earned it a number of performances in London, Paris, Brussels, and Prague, as well as in the United States. It became a favorite of Josef Krips, who played it first in San Francisco. Later, when it was performed at Lincoln Center in New York, the critic Richard Freed wrote in the *New York Times:*

The sunny exuberance of the *Suite provençale* danced through the first movement. The two succeeding ones, aptly marked "Expressif" and "Fantasque," were alive with a freshness and inventiveness. The virtuosic use of winds and percussion in those movements was particularly imaginative. If the finale was the weakest part of the symphony, it was nevertheless an adequate end for a diverting work that should take its place in the repertory so far denied to its nine predecessors.

Critical response was similarly enthusiastic in Prague and Paris.

The dedication of the *Onzième symphonie* (1960) reads as follows: "Commande de la Dallas Public Library et du Dallas Symphonic Orchestra." Paul Kletzky directed the first performance in Dallas on 12 December 1960. Specially designated "en Do," this work, as others written in later years, stressed the essentially tonal quality of Milhaud's conception and served to distance him further from the atonality which had become so fashionable that even Schoenberg tried to shed the label. On the whole, the eleventh symphony has been well received in the United States, as well as in Paris and Brussels. The passionate nature of its first and third movements justify its subtitle "romantique."

One year later Milhaud terminated his series of symphonies with the composition (in June and July 1961) of his *Douzième symphonie.* That year also saw completion of *Aubade,* the sonorous *Funerailles de Phocion,* a violent *Cantate sur des poèmes de Chaucer,* the *Cantate de l'initiation,* and a *Concerto de chambre pour onze instruments.*

The "Rurale" symphony, commissioned by the University of California at Davis and performed under the direction of Enrique Jorda, recognizes by its title the great contribution made by that campus to the development of agriculture. One can imagine the chord that this concept struck in the heart of a native of Aix, who so loved the countryside and all growing things. Also in Milhaud's mind was the epigram by La Rochefoucauld: "The temperate life of a happy person results from the calm disposition with which he is fortunate enough to be endowed."

Milhaud's publisher decided that twelve symphonies was a sufficient number to carry in his catalogue. However, commissions kept coming from Europe and America, and the long period of symphonic preoccupation had opened vistas that were not easily disregarded. To avoid confusion, Milhaud decided to name his subsequent symphonic works after the locality that gave him the commission. They were also brought out by a different publisher. Composed between 1965 and 1972, some of these "Musiques pour . . ." were for full orchestra, others for chamber orchestra. Among those for full orchestra are the "Musiques" for Prague, Indiana, New Orleans, and San Francisco. More quintessential, compact, and often more audacious than the symphonies, these works have not been frequently enough performed (or recorded) to make it possible to form an idea of their place in Milhaud's total body of works.

Concertos

Throughout his career, Milhaud enjoyed writing works for solo and orchestra, and he responded with pleasure to the requests of virtuosi. Between 1920 and 1969 he wrote five piano concertos; two concertos, a suite, and a concertino for two pianos; three concertos and a concertino for violin; two concertos and a concertino for viola; two concertos for cello; and a series of concertos for various instruments, including clarinet, oboe, harp, clavecin, percussion, marimba and vibraphone, and harmonica, as well as one for flute and violin, a concertino for trombone, and a *Symphonie concertante* for the instruments that had not been used in individual concertos—that is, for trumpet, horn, bassoon, and contrabass. There were also numerous pieces for solo instruments and orchestra including such works as *Le carnaval d'Aix* (piano), the *Cinéma-fantaisie* (violin), and the *Suite cisalpine* (cello).

Soloists appreciated Milhaud's knowledge of the capabilities of various instruments, and as a result he received many commissions. Most of the resulting works were intended as showpieces for the performers and are therefore quite difficult. In purely expressive terms, the best are the first piano concerto, the second violin concerto, the second for two pianos, the percussion concerto, and the one for flute and violin. Most frequently performed are the violin and the percussion concertos and the four concertinos that constitute a cycle of the seasons: Spring (violin), Summer (viola), Autumn (two pianos), and Winter (trombone).

Modern concertos do not receive the frequent performances that many of them deserve. That is not the fault of the performers, as witness the number of works that have been recorded, but rather of a public that is more interested in hearing star performers than in coming to terms with the challenges of a new composition. Most audiences think of music in terms of execution, rather than content, and for this reason concert managers, who must keep an eye on box office receipts, almost always require soloists to repeat the tried and true repertory, so that the public can engage in its favorite pastime of comparing performers. Sometimes, to the concertos of Liszt, Brahms, Tchaikovsky, and Beethoven, and more rarely Schumann and Mozart, are added works by Bartók and Berg. Very rarely does one hear Hindemith or Milhaud.

Let us quickly review Milhaud's concerto output. Among those for piano, the *Premier concerto* (1933) is pleasant and uncomplicated. The orchestral parts are very expressive, especially the part for three clarinets that starts off the first movement. Milhaud composed the *Deuxième concerto* in 1941 for himself to perform and therefore did not make it technically difficult. The music is sensitive and eloquent. The *Troisième concerto* (1946) is likewise an easily accessible work. In the *Quatrième concerto* (1949) the avalanches of unremitting sixteenth notes and the somber mood of the second movement, with its slow trombone theme, make a generally austere impression. The *Cinquième concerto* (1955) is the most brilliant.

Among Milhaud's other compositions for solo piano and orchestra, the *Cinq études* (1920) are especially deserving of a brief analysis. The piano has the principal role, but all the instruments of the ensemble are treated soloistically, and the strings are reduced; for example, there are only four stands of first violins. The first étude is agitated. In the piano part, fourths and fifths in triplet motion trace arabesques against a background of broader melodic lines, mostly carried by the orchestra. The second étude is delicately shaded. A tranquil trombone melody rocks gently back and forth against a shimmering background of winds. Then comes a third étude in which four different fugal subjects are simultaneously exposed: a four-voice one in A major in the woodwinds; a three-voice one in D-flat major in the brasses; a four-voice F major one in the strings; and, after sixteen measures, a three-voice polytonal one in the piano. All this is discreetly punctuated by the basses. The music glows, crackles, and ends with a magnificent dynamic climax (Ex. 8–18).

Ex. 8–18.

The fourth étude is also full of intensity. It starts pianissimo and gradually increases in volume. When it reaches its dynamic peak, the thematic material reverses itself and returns, crab fashion, to its point of departure, coming to rest on a high-pitched chord in the piano, which is reinforced by a single stroke on the triangle—the only one in the piece! In general the percussion instruments are used sparingly in this movement. The "Romantique" finale is a chromatic romp, sometimes suave and restrained, at other times punctuated by trumpet calls, and is propelled to a forceful conclusion by the addition of the gong's insistent beating.

Having fled Europe under the threat of war and finding himself on the edge of the American continent once again facing disaster as war clouds gathered over the Pacific Basin, Milhaud was in a somber mood in 1941. His first concerto for two pianos, like the fourth for solo piano, reflects this state of mind. It is a tumultuous work, beginning in a sort of frenzy, which subsides, grumblingly, into a funereal mood and finally ends on a note of transcendence. The high degree of tension makes severe demands on the performers. The rigorous tempo never relaxes; cascades of notes are unrelieved. Pianistic prowess is put to test by the forceful dynamics of the first movement, and the intensity of the keyboard writing also requires the orchestra to make use of its most brilliant effects. Special demands are placed on the brasses in the first movement, and in the slow movement, "Funèbre," winds and strings must play out above the brassy sonorities. The melodic material is completely carried by the orchestra, while the pianos envelop these themes with innumerable runs and ornaments. The combination of such contrasting elements endows this concerto with a very special color and intense expressiveness.

The *Deuxième concerto* for two pianos was written twenty years later (1965). The entire orchestra consists of four percussionists. One of the composer's first concerns was to put as much distance as possible between his work and Bartók's sonata for the same combination of instruments. The pianistic style has remarkable finesse. The arabesques of the two keyboard instruments weave a kind of tonal lacework, which the percussion instruments penetrate sometimes vigorously, sometimes subtly and poetically. The concerto starts off in sunny good humor, then tends more toward tenderness and solemnity, and finally ends with a free, lively rondo. The percussion instruments play an important role in the third movement, but appear only twice in the second, the first time as an exclamation point and then (as Jean Roy put it) "mysteriously, like steps that fade away into the sunset."

The *Concertino d'automne* (1953) for two pianos and eight instruments (flute, oboe, three horns, two violas, and cello) as Jean Damon has written,

starts in the low register of the horns which diffuse a long melody through successive entrances of the other instruments. Then oboe, flute, strings, and pianos join, and the musical material expands into an opulent, vehement affirmation of the earth laden with promise. It seems as though wagons full of grapes, modeled in high relief, surge out of some antique frieze celebrating the solemn harvest of the vine. Then, as if to rejoice in the orgiastic birth of the young wine, flute, strings, and pianos join in a sparkling, heady divertissement. After the melodic and rhythmic intoxication subsides, calm returns, tinged with an aura of melancholy. It is winter that slips into the unkempt bed of Autumn.

The *Suite opus 300* for two pianos and orchestra dates from 1950, that fruitful period which produced the last quartets, the last two concertinos, and the *Cantate de proverbes*. It consists of a freely associated collection of five lively, entertaining pieces in the tradition of eighteenth-century dance suites; only here the classic dance forms have been replaced by the rhythms of the tango, samba, shimmy, and java. In the third movement, the java, the fugal subject moves from G to D, C, G, b minor, and f-sharp minor. At measure 103, the orchestra enters and repeats the same theme in retrograde. The fourth movement is a scherzo, the first an overture, and the finale a gigue, whereas the nocturne is reminiscent of a forlane.

Of the three violin concertos, the first and third are virtuosic displays pure and simple. The *Premier concerto* (1927) is not a remarkable work. It is full of difficult double stops and in general gives the impression of being a technical exercise. The third concerto, or *Concert royal* (1958), was commissioned by Queen Elisabeth of Belgium as a contestant's piece in the competition that bears her name, hence the Couperin-like title. Difficult as it is, the passage work is not merely scholastic, and the abstemious orchestral texture allows the soloist to shine.

The *Deuxième concerto* (1946) is by far the most successful. Musical values take precedence over mere virtuosity. Its breadth of ideas and expressive fervor place it among Milhaud's finest compositions. The first movement starts with an emotionally expansive introduction, which leads to a stirring march. The slow movement evolves gradually, unfolding its melodic material and alternating between passionate utterance and moments of the most exquisite tenderness. It is in all respects the center of gravity of the work. The finale, overflowing with rhythmic vitality, cheerfully concludes this particularly felicitous composition.

The delightful *Concertino de printemps* (1934) relates well to its title. Fascinating and brilliant, it is in constant motion up and down, back and forth, like a butterfly among flowers that finally disappears in a ray of sunlight.

The *Premier concerto* for viola (1929) was commissioned by Paul Hindemith, who first performed it under the direction of Pierre Monteux and later in Vienna with Anton Webern conducting. There are two versions; one, with full orchestra and the other, better one, with chamber ensemble. In the *Concertino d'été* (1950) the music basks in the heat of a midsummer afternoon, but, writes Jean Damon:

It is not oppressive, torrid heat but rather the inviting warmth of a sunny beach bordered by lush vegetation and turgescent flowers. In fact, the work opens in an idyllic, lyric mood, the flowing viola line suggesting the swaying back and forth of a hammock. The brilliant intrusions of wind instruments that punctuate this reverie are like flashes of sunlight through the leaves as the breeze rises and subsides. Soon, the mood changes to burning intensity, and the music breaks into a dance dominated by the masculine sound of the brasses. But gradually red changes to orange, where the horizon meets a turquoise sky. Little by little, infusions of mauve and deep blue usher in nightfall.

A *Deuxième concerto* (1954), more ambitious than the first, concludes this series for viola.

Of the two cello concertos, the first, written in 1934, is the shortest, with two typically good-natured fast movements separated by a slow one, which starts bitonally in a low range and rises slowly to the transparent upper registers, where it floats serenely. The *Deuxième concerto* (1945) has greater scope than the first, but again, the gaiety of the first movement is counterbalanced by the liveliness of the last, and the middle movement is all tenderness.

An oboe concerto presents the soloist in a quiet, delicate dialogue with orchestra, whereas one for clarinet, in four movements, evokes in certain places the spirit of the *Suite provençale*.

The famous percussion concerto was written in 1929. It is in a direct line with *L'homme et son désir*, the *Choéphores*, and *La création du monde*, works in which Milhaud assigned not only a rhythmic but also an expressive role to percussion instruments. In this remarkable composition one performer is called upon to exploit the entire range of possibilities of sixteen instruments.

The *Concertino d'hiver* (1953) is a piece for solo trombone with string orchestra; and to complete the list, one should not overlook the *Symphonie concertante* (1959), the light and dreamy concerto for marimba and vibraphone, dating from 1947, the harp concerto of 1953, and the diaphanous concerto for violin and flute written between 1938 and 1939. Most of these works for solo and orchestra are still to be discovered by today's performers, as are, indeed, the quartets and symphonies.

Epilogue

How can this study be brought to a close? So many works are left unanalyzed; there is so much more to be said even about those mentioned in detail. The worth of a great artist has no beginning and no end. Milhaud is part of that mighty stream of musical creation that stretches from the dawn of history into the unforeseeable future. For the one who creates it, music is a form of communication. For the listener, it is a form of knowledge: knowledge of the world, certainly, and also the illumination of a historical period as perceived by a creative individual. Music, thus, speaks for humanity. A few people are aware of its mission, but for most listeners, music is only a pleasurable pastime. For still others, it is a noisy waste of time.

Thoughtful persons throughout all ages and in all parts of the world have recognized the importance of music. A phrase by Se-Ma-Tsien aptly summarizes their attitude: "Music should never be without thought." Furthermore, music is prophetic. In a recent work (*Bruits,* 1977), Jacques Attali has written: "In theory and in practice, music is in advance of the rest of society, because it explores, within a certain code, the entire field of possibilities, moving more quickly than material reality permits. It projects the sound of a new world which only slowly becomes visible, conditions it, and gives it order; it not only reflects a state of being, but anticipates the future."

The masterful architectural complexity of Bach's fugues was not fully appreciated until around 1830, when the Industrial Revolution had begun to emphasize mechanical perfection. The so-called *musique d'ameublement* of Erik Satie did not begin to come into its own until fifty years after the composer's death, when radio and television began to bring entertainment more and more into the home. In *Le sacre du printemps* Stravinsky anticipated the destruction and sacrifice of 1914.

Milhaud's music is also prophetic. The polytonal style that he developed stemmed from a deeply felt need to convey the idea of simultaneous events. True, he received the inspiration for this stylistic concept initially from nature. But remember also that at that time—that is, around 1915—one could stand on Flemish soil and almost hear the droning of Moroccan troops patrolling their sandy shores at sunset, the epic poems being intoned by the Maoris of New Zealand, Scottish bagpipes, and the chants of the Senegalese natives, all combined into a vast human symphony. The world had become telescoped, and Milhaud's sensitivity to this fact was apparent in *Le retour de l'enfant prodigue,* the chamber symphonies, and the *Cinq études* for piano and orchestra. All these works are quite attuned to the state of mind of the traveler who leaves Europe and finds himself a few hours later in Bangkok or New York. The rapidity of communication gives one the feeling that everything is happening at once. The television screen creates a similar impression; turning from one channel to another, the eye records images of tropical forests, catastrophic accidents, industrial strikes, and idyllic alpine scenery, which become amalgamated into one huge collage.

All sorts of new horizons of expressiveness have been opened up by Milhaud's musical language. At first it attracted attention because of its novelty. But novelty per se quickly wears thin, and only after a certain amount of time has passed can one appraise the true significance of innovation. Gradually, the composer of *Les malheurs d'Orphée,* the *Orestie,* and the string quartets has begun to be considered one of the most complete of modern musicians. True, his output is unequal in quality, but what does it matter that some works are less successful when so many are of outstanding quality?

In the generation following Debussy and Ravel, Milhaud certainly occupies a position of prime eminence. It is he who contributed the most works to contemporary lyric theater; his quartets, cantatas, many of his symphonic compositions, and some songs are major additions to the literature. He succeeded in synthesizing to the most felicitous extent the mood of his own time and place with a timeless, nobler vision.

His music flowed forth day after day, unceasingly, from the deepest recesses of his heart. He sang the poetry of the sea, the grandeur of love, the gracefulness of flowers, the power of destiny, and the glory of God. And he expressed everything with conviction because it was all deeply felt. For Milhaud was not only a great musician; above all, he was a remarkable human being for whom the spirit of mankind and the magnificence of the natural world existed in close communion.

Self-portrait as bust from "his fellow citizens and his friends."

CATALOGUE OF COMPOSITIONS

COMPILED BY MADELEINE MILHAUD
FROM THE COMPOSER'S NOTEBOOKS
AND REVISED BY JANE HOHFELD GALANTE

The translator owes a debt of gratitude to Mme. Milhaud for the many hours of assistance, helpful counsel, and gracious hospitality she contributed to the revision of this catalogue. Very special appreciation is also due to R. Wood Massi for his extensive work in verifying and re-ordering data pertaining to the music, to Jean-François Denis for his excellently detailed preparation of the final copy, and to Dr. Katharine M. Warne for her constructive perusal of the proofs and her many invaluable suggestions. I should like to thank the Mills College Department of Music for providing research funds and the Mills College Library for giving me unlimited access to the Milhaud collection. I am especially grateful to Eva Konrad Kreshka for her unstinting encouragement and enthusiasm.

The careful reader will note some discrepancies between this catalogue, which is based on Milhaud's notebooks, and the printed scores, mostly in regard to exact dates, places of composition, and timing. In the majority of instances, the notebook entry is the one used except where information given on the score adds something of special interest.

J. H. G.

CATALOGUE OF COMPOSITIONS
ARRANGED CHRONOLOGICALLY BY CATEGORIES

Entry format ⎯⎯⎯⎯⎯⎯⎯⎯⎯⎯⎯⎯⎯⎯⎯⎯⎯⎯⎯⎯⎯⎯⎯⎯

Title opus number (Recording available)
(general comments)
[Text author]
Section titles
Cross references
Place, date (day, month, year) of composition
Orchestration
Publisher: (former publisher) present publisher
Dedication and/or commission
First performance: Date (day, month, year). Place. Artist
Duration: min   s

Explanation of terms _____

The designation (R) means that the work has been recorded.

In orchestral works the instrumentation is divided into three groups, two of which are designated numerically.

Thus: 2.2.2.2. — 4.3.3.1. — T.P.H.S. means 2 flutes, 2 oboes, 2 clarinets, 2 bassoons, 4 horns, 3 trumpets, 3 trombones, 1 tuba, timpani, percussion, harp, strings.

No distinction is made for piccolo, contrabassoon, etc.; therefore, 3.3.3.3. would probably mean: 1 piccolo and 2 flutes, 2 oboes and 1 English horn, 2 B-flat clarinets and 1 bass clarinet, 2 bassoons and 1 contrabassoon.

Any other instruments, such as saxophone and guitar, are separately indicated.

In smaller instrumental ensembles the individual instruments are indicated in abbreviated spelling, as follows:

piccolo	picc	marimba	mba
flute	fl	xylophone	xyl
oboe	ob	glockenspiel	glock
English horn	eng hn	vibraphone	vib
Flügelhorn	flg hn	celesta	cel
clarinet	cl	drum	drum
bass clarinet	bs cl	handclap	handclap
bassoon	bn		
contrabassoon	contrabn	piano	piano
		harpsichord	hprd
horn	hn	organ	organ
trumpet	tpt	ondes Martenot	ond Mart
trombone	tbn		
tuba	tu	guitar	gtr
euphonium	euph	string bass	stb
saxophone	sax	accordion	acc
saxhorn	saxhn	harmonica	harm
cornet	cnt	harmonium	hrm
timpani	timp	T.	narrator	narr
percussion	perc	P.	voice	voice
harp	harp	H.	soprano	sop
strings	strings	S.	mezzo soprano	mezz
violin	vln		contralto	con
viola	va		tenor	ten
violoncello	vc		countertenor	counterten
contrabass	cb		baritone	bar
			bass	bass

232

Contents

Instrumental Music

Dramatic Works

Unpublished Works

Reductions, Arrangements, & Transcriptions

INSTRUMENTAL MUSIC

Piano
☐

Piano: solo _____

Suite op. 8
Lent — Vif et clair — Lourd et rythmé — Lent et grave — Modéré-animé
Aix-Paris, 1913
Publisher: Durand
Dedication and/or commission: Jean Wiéner (Lent), Henri Cliquet (Vif et clair),
    Roger de Fontenay (Lourd et rythmé), Céline Lagouarde (Lent et grave),
    Georgette Guller (Modéré-animé)
First performance: 23 March 1914. "La Libre Esthétique," Brussels. G. Guller
Duration: 25 min 10 s

Printemps (vol. I) op. 25 (R)
Modéré — Souple — Doucement
Paris-Rio de Janeiro-La Guadeloupe, 1915–1919
Publisher: (Sirène) Eschig
Dedication and/or commission: Jeanne Herscher-Clément (Modéré), Nininha Velloso
    Guerra (Souple — Doucement)
First performance: 1920. Matinée Dada, Paris. M. Meyer
Duration: 6 min 10 s

Sonate op. 33
Decidé — Pastorale — Rythmé
Paris, 1916
Publisher: (Mathot) Salabert
Dedication and/or commission: Henri Cliquet
First performance: 1920. Salon d'Automne, Paris. M. Dron
Duration: 18 min

Tango des Fratellini op. 58c (R)
See Ballets (Le boeuf sur le toit); Transcriptions
Paris, 1919
Publisher: (Sirène) Eschig
Duration: 1 min 45 s

Printemps (vol. II) op. 66 (R)
Doucement — Vivement — Calme
Berne-Aix-Nice, 1919–1920
Publisher: (Sirène) Eschig
Dedication and/or commission: Youra Guller (Doucement), Nininha Velloso Guerra
  (Vivement), Céline Lagouarde-Bugnion (Calme)
First performance: 21 November 1920. Concert des Six, Gal. Montaigne, Paris. N.
  Velloso Guerra
Duration: 5 min 20 s

Saudades do Brazil op. 67 (R)
Sorocaba — Botofago — Leme — Copacabana — Ipanema — Gavea — Corcovado —
  Tijuca — Sumare — Paineras — Larenjeiras — Paysandu
See Large orchestra, symphonic suites; Transcriptions
Copenhagen-Aix, 1920
Publisher: (Demets) Eschig
Dedication and/or commission: Mme Régis de Oliveira (Sorocaba), Oswalda Guerra
  (Botofago), Nininha Velloso Guerra (Leme), Godofredo Leao Velloso
  (Copacabana), Arthur Rubinstein (Ipanema), Mme Henrique Oswald (Gavea),
  Mme Henri Hoppenot (Corcovado), Ricardo Vinès (Tijuca), Henri Hoppenot
  (Sumare), La Baronne Frachon (Paineras), Audrey Parr (Larenjeiras), Paul
  Claudel (Paysandu)
First performance: 21 November 1920. Concert des Six, Gal. Montaigne, Paris. N.
  Velloso Guerra
Duration: 19 min 50 s

Caramel mou (Shimmy) op. 68 (R)
See Chamber ensembles, misc.; Solo voice, with chamber ensemble
Aix, 1920
Publisher: (Sirène) Eschig
Dedication and/or commission: Georges Auric
Duration: 3 min 14 s

Trois rag caprices op. 78 (R)
See Chamber ensembles, misc.
Aix, 1922
Publisher: U.E.
Dedication and/or commission: Jean Wiéner
First performance: 23 November 1922. Conc. Wiéner, Paris. J. Wiéner
Duration: 6 min 2 s

L'automne op. 115 (R)
Septembre — Alfama — Adieu
Villeflix-Paris, 1932
Publisher: (Deiss) Salabert
Dedication and/or commission: Marcelle Meyer
First performance: June 1932. Conc. Marcelle Meyer, Paris. M. Meyer
Duration: 7 min

L'album de Madame Bovary op. 128b (R)
Emma — Pastorale — Tristesse — Chanson — Rêverie — Le Tilbury — Romance —
    Jeu — Autographe — La Saint-Hubert — Soupir — Dans les bois — Promenade —
    Pensée — Chagrin — Barcarolle — Dernier feuillet
See Music for films (Madame Bovary)
Paris, 1933
Publisher: Enoch
Dedication and/or commission: Sabine et Robert Aron
First performance: 1934. Conc. élèves Marguerite Long, Paris
Duration: 13 min 30 s

Trois valses op. 128c
See Music for films (Madame Bovary)
Paris, 1933
Publisher: Enoch
Dedication and/or commission: Jean Renoir
Duration 3 min 23

Quatre romances sans paroles op. 129 (R)
Paris, 1933
Publisher: (Deiss) Salabert
Dedication and/or commission: Raymond Deiss
First performance: 5 March 1935. Radio Luxembourg. D. Milhaud
Duration: 4 min

Four Sketches (Esquisses) op. 227
Eglogue — Madrigal — Sobre la loma — Alameda
See Duos, clarinet & piano (Eglogue, Madrigal); Quintets, wind (Eglogue, Madrigal);
    Chamber ensembles, misc.; Transcriptions (Sobre la loma)
Mills, 20 May/10 August/15 September/2 October 1941
Publisher: Mercury-Presser
Dedication and/or commission: Monique et Jean Leduc
Duration: 10 min 15 s

La muse ménagère op. 245 (R)
La mienne (dédicace) — Le réveil — Les soins du ménage — La poésie — La cuisine
    — Les fleurs dans la maison — La lessive — Musique ensemble — Le fils peintre —
    Le chat — Cartomancie — Les soins au malade — La douceur des soirées —
    Lectures nocturnes — Reconnaisance à la muse
See Chamber ensembles, misc.
Mills, 5–11 July 1944
Publisher: Elkan Vogel-Presser
Dedication and/or commission: M.M.M.M. (Madeleine Milhaud Muse Ménagère)!
First performance: 30 May 1945. Radio-Bruxelles. P. Collaer
Duration: 24 min 30 s

Deuxième sonate op. 293
Alerte — Léger — Doucement — Rapide
Mills-Carpinteria, 14 February–21 August 1949
Publisher: Heugel
Dedication and/or commission: Monique Haas
First performance: 4 March 1950. BBC, London. M. Haas
Duration: 15 min 45 s

Le candélabre à sept branches op. 315 (R)
Le premier jour de l'an — Jour de pénitence — Fête des cabanes — La résistance des
    Macchabées — Fête de la reine Esther — Fête de la Pâques — Fête de la Pentecôte
Paris, 20–28 December 1951
Publisher: I.M.P.
Dedication and/or commission: M.M.
First performance: 10 April 1952. Fest. d'Ein-gev, Israel. F. Pellag
Duration: 10 min

Hymne de glorification op. 331 (R)
Paris, 20 December 1953–5 January 1954
Publisher: Eschig
Dedication and/or commission: Nadia Boulanger
First performance: December 1954. Detroit Museum. Z. Skolowsky
Duration: 7 min

Sonatine op. 354
Decidé — Modéré — Alerte
Paris, 9–30 April 1956
Publisher: Edit. Trans.
Dedication and/or commission: Harriet Cohen
First performance: 22 March 1959. Pacific Mus. Soc., San Francisco. Josepha Heifetz
Duration: 5 min 30 s

Le globe trotter op. 358
France — Portugal — Italie — Etats-Unis — Mexique — Brésil
See Chamber ensembles, misc.; Transcriptions
Sion-Paris-Mills, 12 December 1956–16 January 1957
Publisher: Mills Mus.-Bel. M.
Duration: 16 min 40 s

Les charmes de la vie op. 360
'Hommage à Watteau'
Pastorale — L'indifférent — Plaisirs champêtres — Sérénade — Musette —
    Mascarade
See Chamber ensembles, misc.
Mills, 8–19 February 1957
Publisher: Mills Mus.-Bel. M.
Duration: 17 min 35 s

Six danses en trois mouvements op. 433
See Piano, two pianos
Aix, December 1969–5 March 1970
Publisher: Eschig
Duration: 12 m 14 s

Piano: solo pieces included in collections ⸻⸻⸻⸻⸻⸻

Mazurka
(Incl. in 'Album des Six')
1914
Publisher: Eschig
Duration: 1 min 15 s

Polka op. 95
(Incl. in 'L'Eventail de Jeanne')
See Ballets
Vienna, 1927
Publishers: Heugel

Le tour de l'Exposition op. 162
(Incl. in 'A l'Exposition')
Paris, June 1933, revised in 1937
Publisher: (Deiss) Salabert
Dedication and/or commission: Marguerite Long
First performance: June 1937. Inaug. Pavillon de la Femme et de l'Enfant, Exposition 1937, Paris. J. M. Damase Kahn (9 year-old)

Choral
(Incl. in 'Hommage à Paderewski')
Paris, 1941
Publisher: B.&H.
Duration: 2 min 10 s

La couronne de Marguerite: Valse en forme de rondo op. 353
(Incl. in 'Variations sur le nom de M. Long')
See Large orchestra, misc.
Paris, 16–21 May 1956
Publisher: Salabert

Black Keys (Touches noires)
White Keys (Touches blanches) op. 222 (R)
Mills, 11 January 1941
Publisher: Fischer

Une journée op. 269
L'aube — La matinée — Midi — L'après-midi — Le crépuscule
Mills, 18 July 1946
Publisher: Elkan Vogel-Presser
Dedication and/or commission: comm. Juilliard School of Music
First performance: October 1946. Carnegie Hall, New York. A. Foldes
Duration: 6 min 30 s

L'enfant aime op. 289
Les fleurs — Les bonbons — Les jouets — Sa mère — La vie
Mills, 30–31 November 1948
Publisher: (Leeds, M.C.A.) Bel. M.
Dedication and/or commission: Nicole Leduc (Les fleurs), Edmée Wilson (Les bonbons), Dominique Bailey (Les jouets), Niccolo Daniele Rieti (Sa mère), Catherine Valley (La vie)
Dedication and/or commission: comm. Leeds
First performance: 1 July 1949. University of Wyoming, Laramie. D. Milhaud
Duration: 9 min 15 s

Accueil amical op. 326
(fingered by Katharine M. Warne)
Pyjama rouge — Bonjour Violaine — Pyjama Bleu — Bonjour Dominique — Elma joue — Marie dort — La nouvelle dent — Mademoiselle no. 5 — Bonjour Philippine! — Pierre écrit des commentaires — Marion peint — La récréation — La douce hospitalité, les chers amis — Colin Maillard! — Petit Pierre est arrivé un beau jour d'été—Les dragées du baptême, 15 août 1948—Lettres de château
See Transcriptions
United States, 1944–1947
Publisher: Heugel

Jeu op. 302
(Incl. in the album 'Les contemporains,' premier recueil)
Paris, February 1950
Publisher: (P. Noël) Billaudot
Duration: 1 min 36 s

Enfantines (4 hands)
(based on 'Trois poèmes de Jean Cocteau,' fingered by Mme M. Long)
See Solo voice, with piano
Publisher: Eschig

Scaramouche op. 165b (R)
Vif — Modéré — Brazileira
See Solo & orchestra, clarinet/saxophone; incidental music (Le médecin volant);
  Reductions; Transcriptions (Brazileira & Scaramouche)
Paris, 1937
Publisher: (Deiss) Salabert
First performance: 1 July 1937. Exposition 1937, Paris. M. Meyer, I. Jankelevitch
Duration: 8 min

La libertadora op. 236b
(suite of 5 dances)
See Unpublished works
Mills, July 1943
Publisher: A.&S.
Dedication and/or commission: Morley et Gearhart
Duration: 6 min
This is taken from music originally conceived as a ballet in the opera "Bolivar," but
  never used in that context.

Les songes op. 237 (R)
Scherzo — Valse — Polka
See Ballets
Mills, October 1943
Publisher: (Deiss) Salabert
Dedication and/or commission: Virginia et Livingstone
First performance: 7 May 1945. Wyoming University, Laramie. A. Wilman, D.
  Milhaud
Duration: 6 min 12 s

La bal martiniquais op. 249 (R)
Chanson créole — Béguine
See Large orchestra, misc.
Mills, December 1944
Publisher: (Leeds, MCA) Bel. M.
First performance: April 1945. Radio-Bruxelles
Durationi: 7 min 15 s

Carnaval à la Nouvelle-Orléans op. 275 (R)
Mardi Gras! Chic à la paille — Domino noir de Cajun — On danse chez Monsieur
  Degas — Les mille cents coups
Mills, 7 March–6 April 1947
Publisher: (Leeds, MCA) Bel. M.
Dedication and/or commission: Gold et Fizdale
First performance: 8 July 1947. Michigan State College. A. Gold, R. Fizdale
Duration: 11 min 20 s

Kentuckiana op. 287
(Divertissement on twenty Kentucky folk songs)
See Large orchestra, misc.
Santa Barbara, 6–19 September 1948
Publisher: Elkan Vogel-Presser
First performance: December 1949. Radio-France. J. Février, J. Weill
Duration: 10 min 20 s

Six danses en trois mouvements op. 433 (R)
Tarentelle-Bourrée — Sarabande-Pavane — Rumba-Gigue
See Piano, solo
Aix, December 1969–5 March 1970
Publisher: Eschig
Dedication and/or commission: Pour les 25 ans de Geneviève Joy et de Jacqueline
    Robin
First performance: 17 December 1970. Paris. G. Joy, J. Robin
Duration: 6 min 7 s

Piano: four pianos ───

Paris op. 284 (R)
Montmartre — L'Ile Saint-Louis — Montparnasse — Bateaux-mouches —
    Longchamps — La Tour Eiffel
See Large orchestra, symphonic suites
Paris, 18 May 1948
Publisher: Eschig
Dedication and/or commission: Jean Marietti, comm. First Piano Quartet
Duration: 10 min

*For a more complete list of compositions available for 2 pianos, 3 pianos, and piano four
hands, see Reductions.*

Other solo instruments

┌─────────────────────────────┐
└─────────────────────────────┘

Other solo instruments: harp ──────────────────────────────

Sonate op. 437 (R)
(en trois mouvements)
Geneva, 6 October–6 November 1971
Publisher: Eschig
Dedication and/or commission: Anne Adams (comm.)
First performance: 19 May 1973. Conservatoire Rocquencourt. F. Pierre
Duration: 12 min 30 s

Other solo instruments: guitar ────────────────────────────

Segoviana op. 366
Paris, 26 November 1957
Publisher: Heugel
Dedication and/or commission: Andrès Segovia (comm.)
First performance: November 1969. Strasbourg
Duration: 2 min 30 s

Other solo instruments: organ ────────────────────────────

Sonate op. 112 (R)
Etude — Rêverie — Final
Paris, 1931
Publisher: (Gray) Bel. M.
Dedication and/or commission: Francesco et Anna Malipiero
First performance: 1932. SIMC, Berlin
Duration: 19 min 43 s

Pastorale op. 229 (R)
Mills, November 1941
Publisher: (Gray) Bel. M.
First performance: 1942. Cathedral, Washington, D.C. Strickland
Duration: 3 min 29 s

Neuf préludes op. 231b (R)
See Incidental music (L'annonce faite à Marie, 2nd version)
Mills, 16 March 1942
Publisher: Heugel
Dedication and/or commission: M.D.M.
First performance: 1 June 1948. Conc. La Chantrerie, Paris. M. L. Girod
Duration: 13 min 5 s

Petite suite op. 348 (R)
Entrée — Prière — Cortège
Paris, November 1955
Publisher: Eschig
Dedication and/or commission: Nicole et Daniel pour leur mariage
First performance: 9 December 1955. Synagogue Buffault, Paris. J. Bonfils
Duration: 6 min 9 s

Other solo instruments: violin ────────────────────────────

Sonatine pastorale op. 383
Entrée — Romance — Gigue
Paris, 11 March 1960
Publisher: Adès
Duration: 3 min 20 s

Duos

Duos: violin & harpsichord _____

Sonate op. 257
Nerveux — Calme — Clair et vif
Mills, 27 July–8 August 1945
Publisher: Elkan Vogel-Presser
Dedication and/or commission: Alexandre Schneider et Ralph Kirkpatrick (comm.)
First performance: 30 November 1946. Town Hall, New York. vln: A. Schneider, hprd: R. Kirkpatrick
Duration: 9 min 40 s

Duos: violin & piano _____

Première sonate op. 3 (R)
Lent et robuste, animé — Très lent — Très rythmé, joyeux
Aix, 1911
Publisher: Durand
First performance: 3 May 1913. SMI, Paris. vln: Y. Giraud, piano: G. Guller
Duration: 30 min

Le printemps op. 18 (R)
Aix, Easter 1914
Publisher: Durand
Dedication and/or commission: Yvonne Giraud
First performance: April 1919. Th. Vieux Colombier, Paris. vln: Y. Giraud, piano: D. Milhaud
Duration: 2 min 25 s

Deuxième sonate op. 40 (R)
Pastoral — Vif — Très lent — Très vif
Rio de Janeiro, May 1917
Publisher: Durand
Dedication and/or commission: André Gide
First performance: 1917. Lycée Français, Rio de Janeiro, vln: D. Milhaud, piano: N. Velloso Guerra
Duration: 16 min

Cinéma-fantaisie op. 58b (R)
See Ballets (Le boeuf sur le toit); Solo & orchestra, violin
Aix, 1919
Publisher: (Sirène) Eschig
Dedication and/or commission: René Benedetti
First performance: May 1921. Paris. vln: R. Benedetti, piano: J. Wiéner
Duration: 19 min

Trois caprices de Paganini op. 97
(Traités en duos concertants)
New York, 1927
Publisher: Heugel
Dedication and/or commission: Marquise de Casa Fuerte (#22), Paul Kochanski
 (#10), Josef Szigeti (#13)
First performance: 15 April 1928. Conc. Pro Arte, Brussels. vln: Y. de Casa Fuerte,
 piano: P. Collaer
Duration: 9 min 15 s

Dixième sonate de Baptiste Anet (1729) op. 144
(free adaptation)
1935
Publisher: Gallo
First performance: 25 November 1935. Chaux de Fonds. vln: Y. Astruc, piano:
 D. Milhaud

Sailor Song
(Concert version and simplified version, from 'Suite anglaise')
See Solo & orchestra, violin; Solo & orchestra, harmonica;
Reductions; Transcriptions
March 1944
Publisher: B.&H.
Duration: 2 min 55 s

Danses de Jacaremirim op. 256 (R)
Sambinha — Tanguinho — Chorinho
Mills, 23–25 July 1945
Publisher: (Delkas, Leeds, MCA) Bel. M.
Dedication and/or commission: Alexander Murray (comm.)
First performance: 28 April 1946. Hollywood. vln: A. Murray
Duration: 4 m 45 s

Farandoleurs op. 262
Mills, 29 January 1946
Publisher: Salabert
Dedication and/or commission: Claude Delvincourt
First performance: 1946. Concours Conser. Paris
Duration: 2 min 20 s

Duos: viola & piano —————————————————————————————————

Quatre visages op. 238 (R)
La Californienne — The Wisconsonian — La Bruxelloise — La Parisienne
Mills, 16 November 1942–1 March 1943
Publisher: Heugel
Dedication and/or commission: Germain Prévost (comm.)
First performance: January 1944. Wisconsin University. va: G. Prévost, piano: G.
  Johansen
Duration: 14 min

Première sonate op. 240 (R)
(Sur des thèmes anonymes et inédits du XVIIIe siècle)
Entrée — Française — Air — Final
See Unpublished works (Air)
Mills, February 1944
Publisher: Heugel
Dedication and/or commission: Germain Prévost (comm.)
First performance: April 1944. Wisconsin University. va: G. Prévost, piano:
  G. Johansen
Duration: 13 min 5 s

Deuxième sonate op. 244 (R)
Champêtre — Dramatique — Rude
Mills, 27 June–2 July 1944
Publisher: Heugel
Dedication and/or commission: A la mémoire d'Alphonse Onnou, comm. G. Prévost
  College, Madison. va: G. Prévost, piano: N. Boulanger
Duration: 11 min 35 s

Duos: violoncello & piano ——————————————————————————

Elégie op. 251 (R)
Mills, 21 January 1945
Publisher: B.&H.
Dedication and/or commission: Edmond Kurtz (comm.)
First performance: 16 November 1945. Town Hall, New York. vc: E. Kurtz
Duration: 4 min 35 s

Sonate op. 377 (R)
Animé et gai — Lent et grave — Vif et joyeux
Pacific Palisades-Mills, 16 March–18 April 1959
Publisher: Salabert
Dedication and/or commission: Ernst Friedlander, comm. Vancouver Festival
First performance: 18 July 1959. Vancouver Festival. vc: E. Friedlander, piano: Mrs.
  Friedlander
Duration: 13 min 35 s

Duos: flute & piano _____

Sonatine op. 76 (R)
Tendre — Souple — Clair
Aix, 1922
Publisher: Durand
Dedication and/or commission: Louis Fleury et Jean Wiéner
First performance: January 1923. Conc. Wiéner, Paris. fl: L. Fleury, piano: J. Wiéner
Duration: 7 min 50 s

Duos: pipeau & piano _____

Exercice musical op. 134 (R)
Aix, 1934
Publisher: Ois. Lyre
Dedication and/or commission: Mrs. Dyer
First performance: December 1948. Festival de Musique Française, Juilliard School,
   New York

Duos: Oboe & piano _____

Sonatine op. 337 (R)
Avec charme et vivacité — Souple et clair — Avec entrain et gaîeté
Aspen, 7–19 August 1954
Publisher: Durand
Dedication and/or commission: Lois Wann
First performance: 29 November 1954. Town Hall, New York. ob: L. Wann
Duration: 11 min

Duos: clarinet & piano _____

Sonatine op. 100 (R)
Très rude — Lent — Très rude
Aix, 1927
Publisher: Durand
Dedication and/or commission: Louis Cahuzac
First performance: 1929. S.M.I., Paris. cl: L. Cahuzac, piano: M. F. Gaillard
Duration: 8 min 55 s

Eglogue—Madrigal op. 227b
(From 'Four Sketches')
See Piano, solo; Quintets, wind; Chamber ensemble, misc.
Mills, 15 September 1941
Publisher: Elkan Vogel-Presser

Caprice op. 335
(Incl. in the collection 'La clarinette,' vol. II, ed. by F. Oubradous)
Paris, 1 May 1954
Publisher: (P. Noël) Billaudot

Duo concertant op. 351 (R)
Paris, 19–21 January 1956
Publisher: Heugel
Dedication and/or commission: Ulysse Delécluze
First performance: 1956. Concours Conserv. Paris
Duration: 7 min 15 s

Duos: saxophone & piano ⎯⎯⎯⎯⎯⎯⎯⎯⎯⎯⎯⎯⎯⎯⎯⎯⎯⎯⎯

Danse op. 335b (R)
(Incl. in the collection 'Le saxophone,' vol. II, ed. by F. Oubradous)
Paris, 2 May 1954
Publisher: (P. Noël) Billaudot

Duos: ondes Martenot & piano ⎯⎯⎯⎯⎯⎯⎯⎯⎯⎯⎯⎯⎯⎯⎯⎯

Suite op. 120c (R)
Choral — Sérénade — Impromptu — Etude — Elégie
See Accompanied vocal ensemble, vocal quartet & chamber ensemble (Adages);
    Incidental music (Le château des papes); Transcriptions (Suite)
Aix, 1932
Publisher: (Cerda) E.F.M.
Dedication and/or commission: Maurice Martenot
First performance: December 1933. Conc. Sérénade, Paris. M. Martenot
Duration: 10 min

Duos: two violins ⎯⎯⎯⎯⎯⎯⎯⎯⎯⎯⎯⎯⎯⎯⎯⎯⎯⎯⎯⎯⎯⎯⎯

Sonatine op. 221 (R)
Vif — Barcarolle — Rondo
Train Chicago-Oakland, October 1940
Publisher: (Music Press) Mercury-Presser
Dedication and/or commission: Mes élèves de Mills College
First performance: 7 December 1940. Composers' Forum, San Francisco
Duration: 3 min 20 s

Duo op. 258 (R)
Gai — Romance — Gigue
Alma-Los Gatos, 17–19 August 1945
Publisher: (Music Press) Mercury-Presser
Dedication and/or commission: Yehudi Menuhin et Roman Totenberg
First performance: 'Gai' and 'Romance' 18 August 1945. Private performance at Menuhin home, Alma. 'Gigue' 27 August 1945. Private performance at Milhaud home, Mills College
Duration: 4 min 26 s

Duos: violin & viola _____

Sonatine op. 226
Décidé — Lent — Vif (Fugue)
Mills, 6–8 May 1941
Publisher: (Music Press) Mercury-Presser
Dedication and/or commission: Laurent Halleux et Germain Prévost
Duration: 9 min

Duos: violin & violoncello _____

Sonatine op. 324
Animé — Modéré — Vif
Santa Barbara, 10–12 June 1953
Publisher: Heugel
Dedication and/or commission: Ralph et Norine, comm. Ralph Swickard
First performance: 8 July 1954. Film 'A Visit to Darius Milhaud,' Music Academy of the West, Santa Barbara. vln: E. Shapiro, vc: V. Gottlieb
Duration: 7 min 20 s

Duos: viola & violoncello _____

Sonatine op. 378
Vif — Modéré — Gai
Mills, 15–24 April 1959
Publisher: Heugel
Dedication and/or commission: Murrey Adaskin et Jim Bolle, comm. Saskatchewan University
First performance: 9 June 1959. Saskatoon, Canada
Duration: 7 min 50 s

Trios

Trios, piano & two violins

Sonate op. 15 (R)
Animé — Modéré — Très vif
Paris-Brussels, 1914
Publisher: Durand
Dedication and/or commission: Armand Lunel
First performance: 27 May 1915. Conc. Foyer Franco-Belge, Paris. vlns: Y. Astruc,
   D. Milhaud, piano: J. Herscher
Duration: 15 min 35 s

Trios, piano, violin & violoncello

Trio op. 428
Modéré — Animé — Calme — Violent
Aspen-Mills, 22 July–30 October 1968
Publisher: Heugel
Dedication and/or commission: Pour la Chamber Music Society of Lincoln Center
   (comm.)
First performance: 11 October 1969. Lincoln Center, New York
Durations: 14 min 5 s

Trios, piano, violin & clarinet

Suite op. 157b (R)
Ouverture — Divertissement — Jeu — Introduction et final
See Incidental music (Le voyageur sans bagages)
Paris, November 1936
Publisher: Salabert
Dedication and/or commission: M.D.M.
First performance: 19 January 1937. Concert Sérénade, Paris. vln: Y. Astruc, piano:
   J. Février
Duration: 11 min 50 s

Trios, violin, viola & violoncello _____

Sonatine à trois op. 221b
Très modéré — Contrepoint — Animé
Train Chicago-Oakland, 19–20 October 1940
Publisher: (Music Press) Mercury-Presser
Dedication and/or commission: Mady et Daniel
First performance: 7 December 1940. Composers' Forum, San Francisco
Duration: 8 min 20 s

Trio à cordes op. 274 (R)
Vif — Modéré — Sérénade — Canons — Jeu fugué
Mills, 20 February–1 March 1947
Publisher: Heugel
Dedication and/or commission: Carlos et Cécile Priéto, comm. Carlos Priéto
First performance: December 1947. Trio Pasquier, Paris
Duration: 13 min 30 s

Trios, oboe, clarinet, & bassoon _____

Pastorale op. 147 (R)
Brussels, 30 December 1935
Publisher: (E.S.I.) Ch. du M.
Dedication and/or commission: Trio d'anches de Paris
First performance: 5 November 1936. Bourges. Trio d'anches de Paris
Duration: 3 min 50 s

Suite d'après Corrette op. 161b (R)
Entrée et Rondeau — Tambourin — Musette — Sérénade — Fanfare — Rondeau —
    Menuets — Le Coucou
See Incidental music (Roméo et Juliette)
Paris, April 1937
Publisher: Ois. Lyre
Dedication and/or commission: Paul Collaer
First performance: November 1938. Conc. Sérénade, Paris. Trio d'anches de Paris
Duration: 8 min 30 s

Trios, two trumpets & trombone _____

Fanfare op. 400
Mills, 22 October 1962
Publisher: Heugel
Dedication and/or commission: Cent cinquante mesures pour les 150 ans de la Maison
    Heugel
First performance: 13 December 1962. Chez Heugel, Paris

Quartets

Quartets: string

Premier quatuor op. 5 (R)
Rythmique — Intime, contenu — Grave, soutenu* — Vif, très rythmé
Aix, 1912 (revised 1950)
Publisher: Durand
Dedication and/or commission: A la mémoire de Paul Cézanne
First performance: 3 May 1913. S.M.I., Paris. vln: D. Milhaud, Larbey, va: R. Siohan, vc: F. Delgrange
Duration: 13 min 25 s
*This movement was eliminated by D. Milhaud; it is included in the early edition only.

Deuxième quatuor op. 16 (R)
Modérément animé/très animé — Très lent — Très vif — Souple et sans hâte/assez animé et gracieux — Très rythmé
Aix-Paris, 1914–1915
Publisher: Durand
Dedication and/or commission: Leó Latil
First performance: 15 May 1915. Conc. Delgrange, Paris. vln: Y. Astruc, D. Milhaud, va: Jurgensen, vc: F. Delgrange
Duration: 23 min 25 s

Troisième quatuor op. 32 (with soprano) (R)
[Extrait du 'Journal intime' de Léo Latil]
Très lent — Très lent
Paris-Aix, 1916
Publisher: Durand
Dedication and/or commission: En souvenir du printemps de 1914
First performance: 1956. ORTF, Paris. Quatuor Loewenguth
Duration: 20 min 5 s

Quatrième quatuor op. 46 (R)
Vif — Funèbre — Très animé
See Transcriptions
Rio de Janeiro, 1918
Publisher: (Sénart) Salabert
Dedication and/or commission: Félix Delgrange
First performance: 5 April 1919. Conc. Delgrange, Paris. Quatuor Capelle
Duration: 9 min 45 s

Cinquième quatuor op. 64 (R)
Chantant — Vif et leger — Lent — Très animé
See Transcriptions
Aix, 1920
Publisher: (Sénart) Salabert
Dedication and/or commission: Arnold Schoenberg
First performance: 6 April 1922. S.M.I., Paris. Quatuor Carembat
Duration: 20 min 40 s

Sixième quatuor op. 77 (R)
Souple et animé — Très lent — Très vif et rythmé
Aix, April–June 1922
Publisher: U.E.
Dedication and/or commission: Francis Poulenc
First performance: February 1923. Brussels. Quatuor Pro Arte
Duration: 8 min 45 s

Septième quatuor op. 87 (R)
Modérément animé — Doux et sans hâte — Lent — Vif et gai
See Transcriptions
Balsorano-Aix, 1925
Publisher: U.E.
Dedication and/or commission: Quatuor Pro Arte
First performance: 10 November 1925. Brussels, Quatuor Pro Arte
Duration: 12 min 40 s

Huitième quatuor op. 121 (R)
Vif et souple — Lent et grave — Très animé
Cauterets-Paris, 1932
Publisher: Ch. du M.
Dedication and/or commission: Mrs. E. Sprague Coolidge (comm.)
First performance: 13 May 1933. Concert Coolidge, Asolo. Quatuor Pro Arte
Duration: 12 min 45 s

Neuvième quatuor op. 140 (R)
Modéré — Animé — Très lent — Décidé
Paris, 1935
Publisher: Ch. du M.
Dedication and/or commission: Mrs. E. Sprague Coolidge (comm.)
First performance: 21 May 1935. Concert Coolidge, Paris. Quatuor Pro Arte
Duration: 18 min 10 s

Dixième quatuor (Birthday Quartet) op. 218 (R)
Modérément animé — Vif — Lent — Très animé
Atlantic Ocean-New York, July–August 1940
Publisher: Salabert
Dedication and/or commission: Mrs. E. Sprague Coolidge, (comm.)
First performance: 30 October 1940. Library of Congress, Washington, D.C. Coolidge
   Quartet
Duration: 15 min 15 s

Onzième quatuor op. 232 (R)
Modérément animé — Vif et leger — Bien modéré — Animé
Mills, May–June 1942
Publisher: Salabert
Dedication and/or commission: Quatuor de Budapest. Ecrit à l'occasion du 20e anniversaire du League of Composers
First performance: 9 December 1942. League of Composers, New York. Budapest Quartet
Duration: 15 min 45 s

Douzième quatuor op. 252 (R)
Modéré animé, modéré — Lent — Avec entrain
Mills, 5–15 February 1945
Publisher: Salabert
Dedication and/or commission: A la mémoire de Gabriel Fauré à l'occasion du centenaire de sa naissance
First performance: 22 April 1945. National Gallery of Arts, Washington, D.C.
Budapest Quartet
Duration: 14 min 5 s

Treizième quatuor op. 268 (R)
Très décidé — Barcarolle — Mexicana
Mexico-Mills, June–October 1946
Publisher: Salabert
Dedication and/or commission: M.D.M.
First performance: 22 April 1947. Library of Congress,
Washington, D.C. Budapest Quartet
Duration 10 min 40 s

Quatorzième quatuor op. 291 (R)
Animé — Modéré — Vif
See Larger string ensembles (Octuor à cordes)
Mills, 23 November 1948–17 January 1949
Publisher: Heugel
Dedication and/or commission: Paul Collaer, avec trente ans d'amitié
First performance: 10 August 1949. Mills College. Budapest Quartet
Duration: 15 min 45 s

Quinzième quatuor op. 291 (R)
Animé — Modéré — Vif
See Larger string ensembles (Octuor à cordes)
Mills, 23 November 1948–17 January 1949
Publisher: Heugel
Dedication and/or commission: Paul Collaer, avec trente ans d'amitié
First performance: 10 August 1949. Mills College. Paganini Quartet
Duration: 15 min 45 s

Seizième quatuor op. 303 (R)
Tendre — Vif — Doux et calme — Animé
Paris, 5–25 April 1950
Publisher: Heugel
Dedication and/or commission: A Madeleine pour le 25e anniversaire de notre mariage
First performance: 2 August 1950. Music Academy of the West, Santa Barbara. Music Academy of the West Quartet
Duration: 16 min 40 s

Dix-septième quatuor op. 307 (R)
Rude — Tendre — Léger et cinglant — Robuste
Mills-Pasadena-Twentynine Palms, 4–23 December 1950
Publisher: Heugel
Dedication and/or commission: A Daniel pour ses 21 ans
First performance: April 1951. Library of Congress, Washington, D.C. Budapest Quartet
Duration: 20 min 40 s

Dix-huitième quatuor op. 308 (R)
Lent et doux — Premier hymne — Deuxième hymne — Lent et doux
Rancho Mirage-Pasadena-Mills, 29 December 1950–11 January 1951
Publisher: Heugel
Dedication and/or commission: A la douce mémoire de mes parents
First performance: 22 August 1951. Aspen Festival. Paganini Quartet
Duration: 25 min 30 s

Hommage à Igor Stravinsky op. 435
Geneva, July 1971
Publisher: B.&H.

Etudes op. 442
(Sur des thèmes liturgiques du Comtat Venaissin)
Modéré — Animé — Modéré
Geneva, 22 April 1973
Publisher: Eschig
Dedication and/or commission: comm. Braemer Foundation
First performance: 1975. New York. Adath Jeshurun String Quartet
Durations: 10 min 50 s

Quartets: piano & other instruments _____

Sonate op. 47 (R)
Tranquille — Joyeux — Emporté — Douloureux
Rio de Janeiro-Therezopolis, 1918
Piano, fl, ob, cl.
Publisher: Durand
Dedication and/or commission: N.V.G.
First performance: 12 February 1921. Exposition Wiesbaden. Soc. d'Instr. à vent,
    piano: D. Milhaud
Duration: 10 min

Quatuor op. 417
Modérément animé — Lent — Vif
Paris, 10–23 January 1966
Piano, vln, va, vc.
Publisher: Durand
Dedication and/or commission: comm. Mme. Wickett pour les 10 ans de sa fille Hélène
First performance: June 1967. Cleveland Institute of Music
Duration: 15 min

Quintets

```
┌─────────┐
│         │
└─────────┘
```

Quintets: string (with or without piano) _____

La création du monde op. 81b (R)
(Suite de concert)
Prélude — Fugue — Romance — Scherzo — Final
See Ballets; Reductions
Paris, 1926
2 vln, va, vc, piano.
Publisher: Eschig
First performance: 1927. Festival Baden-Baden. Kolisch Quartet
Duration: 15 min

Premier quintette op. 312 (R)
Avec vivacité — Avec mystère — Avec douceur — Avec emportement
Mills-Aix, 14 July–27 September 1951
2 vln, va, vc, piano.
Publisher: Heugel
Dedication and/or commission: Pour le 100e anniversaire de Mills College
First performance: 17 May 1952. Mills College Centennial Festival. Hungarian
    Quartet, piano: E. Petri
Duration: 14 min 5 s

Deuxième quintette op. 316 (R)
Modérément animé — Vif — Lent — Final
Paris, 9–24 January 1952
2 vln, va, vc, cb.
Publisher: Heugel
Dedication and/or commission: Stanley Quartet, comm. l'Université de Michigan
First performance: 8 July 1952. University of Michigan, Ann Arbor. Stanley Quartet
Duration: 16 min 40 s

Troisième quintette op. 325
Animé — Lent — Vif
Mills-Aspen, July–August 1953
2 vln, 2 va, vc.
Publisher: Heugel
Dedication and/or commission: comm. Griller Quartet
First performance: 15 November 1953. University of California, Berkeley. Griller
    Quartet, va: F. Molnar
Duration: 15 min 20 s

Quatrième quintette op. 350
Très modéré (Déploration sur la mort d'un ami) — Animé (Souvenirs de jeunesse) —
    Assez lent (La douceur d'une longue amitié) — Animé (Hymne de louanges)
Paris, 8 February 1956
2 vln, va, 2 vc.
Publisher: Heugel
Dedication and/or commission: A la mémoire d'Arthur Honegger
First performance: 29 February 1956. INR, Brussels INR string orchestra. Conductor:
    F. André
Duration: 20 min 5 s

Quintets: wind _____

La cheminée du roi René op. 205 (R)
Cortège — Aubade — Jongleurs — La Maoussinglade — Joutes sur l'Arc — Chasse à
    Valabre — Madrigal nocturne
See Music for films (Cavalcade d'amour)
Mayens de Sion, 25 June 1939
Publisher: South. Mus.
First performance: 5 March 1941. Mills College. South Wind Quintet
Duration: 11 min 13 s

Madrigal—Pastoral (originally 'Eglogue') op. 227b (R)
(from 'Four Sketches')
See Piano, solo; Duos, clarinet & piano; Chamber ensemble, misc.
Mills, 1941
Publisher: Mercury-Presser
Dedication and/or commission: Mrs. Aurelia Reinhardt

Divertissement op. 299b (R)
Balancé — Dramatique — Joyeux
See Music for films (Gauguin); Transcriptions
Paris, April 1958
Publisher: Heugel
Dedication and/or commission: David Mind
Duration: 11 min 30 s

Quintette à vent op. 443
Gai — Lent — Allègre
Geneva, 13 September 1973
Publisher: Eschig
Dedication and/or commission: comm. de l'Etat, dédié à Madeleine avec cinquante
    ans de bonheur
First performance: 1975. Avignon. Quintette à vent d'Avignon
Duration: 17 min

Quintets: miscellaneous _____

Les rêves de Jacob op. 294 (R)
L'oreiller de Jacob — Premier rêve (L'échelle de Jacob) — Prophétie — Deuxième
    rêve (Lutte avec l'ange et Bénédiction) — Israël (Hymne)
Mills, 14–29 April 1949
Ob, vln, va, vc, cb.
Publisher: Heugel
Dedication and/or commission: Mrs. E. Sprague Coolidge, comm. Coolidge
    Foundation
First performance: 19 October 1949. Jacob's Pillow Dance Festival, July 1959. Festival
    SIMC, Brussels
Duration: 16 min 30 s

Larger string ensembles

┌─────────────────────────┐
│   │
└─────────────────────────┘

Octuor à cordes op. 291 (R)
Animé — Modéré — Vif
Mills, 23 November 1948–17 January 1949
4 vln, 2 va, 2 vc
Publisher: Heugel
Dedication and/or commission: Paul Collaer — avec trente ans d'amitié
First performance: 10 August 1949. Mills College. Budapest Quartet, Paganini
    Quartet
Duration: 15 min 45 s
This octet consists of the 14th and 15th string quartets, which may be played
    separately.

Sextuor à cordes op. 368 (R)
Lent — Modéré et expressif — Animé
Paris, 18–26 January 1958
2 vln, 2 va, 2 vc.
Publisher: Heugel
Dedication and/or commission: A la mémoire de Luther Marchant, comm. Agnes
    Albert
First performance: 1958. Mills College
Duration: 13 min 30 s

Septuor à cordes op. 408 (R)
Modérément animé — Etude de hasard dirigé — Modéré et expressif — Alerte
    Paris, 26 March–1 April 1964
2 vln, 2 va, 2 vc. 5-string cb.
Publisher: Heugel
Dedication and/or commission: A la mémoire de Mrs. Elizabeth Sprague Coolidge,
    comm. Library of Congress
First performance: 3 October 1964. Library of Congress, Washington, D.C. Kroll
    Quartet, va: Trampler, vc: B. Heifetz, cb: D. Walter
Duration: 15 min 20 s

Chamber ensembles

Chamber ensembles: chamber symphonies ⸻⸻⸻⸻⸻⸻⸻⸻⸻⸻

Première symphonie op. 43 (R)
'Le printemps'
Allant — Chantant — Et vif!
Rio de Janeiro, 1917
Picc, fl, ob, cl, harp, 2 vln, va, vc.
Publisher: U.E.
Dedication and/or commission: Roger de Fontenay
First performance: 11 August 1918. Conc. Symph. Rio. Conductor: Braga
Duration: 4 min

Deuxième symphonie op. 49 (R)
"Pastorale'
Joyeux — Calme — Joyeux
South Atlantic Ocean-Rio de Janeiro, 1918
Fl, eng hn, bn, vln, va, vc, cb.
Publisher: U.E.
Dedication and/or commission: Roseau et Pipeau
First performance: 9 March 1919. Conc. Delgrange, Paris. Conductor: F. Delgrange
Duration: 4 min

Troisième symphonie op. 71 (R)
'Sérénade'
Vivement — Calme — Rondement
Paris, July 1921
Fl, cl, bn, vln, va, vc, cb.
Publisher: U.E.
Dedication and/or commission: Yvonne et Illan de Casa Fuerte
First performance: 10 December 1921. Soc. Mus. de Ch., Paris
Duration: 3 min

Quatrième symphonie op. 74 (R)
Ouverture — Choral — Etude
Paris, 1921
4 vln, 2 va, 2 vc, 2 cb.
Publisher: U.E.
Dedication and/or commission: Madeleine Milhaud
First performance: 3 May 1921. Concert Art et Action, Paris. Conductor: L. Sir
Duration: 6 min

Cinquième symphonie op. 75 (R)
Rude — Lent — Violent
Vienna-Warsaw, 1922
Picc, fl, ob, eng hn, cl, bs cl, 2 bn, 2 hn.
Publisher: U.E.
Dedication and/or commission: Marya Freund
First performance: May 1923. Soc. Instr. à Vent, Paris
Duration: 5 min

Sixième symphonie op. 79 (R)
Calme et doux — Souple et vif — Lent et très expressif
New York, 1923
Vocal quartet, ob, vc.
Publisher: U.E.
Dedication and/or commission: Germaine Schmitz
First performance: 1924. Conc. Wiéner, Paris. Conductor: D. Milhaud
Duration: 6 min

Chamber ensembles: miscellaneous ensembles _____

Caramel mou op. 68
See Piano, solo; Solo voice, with chamber ensemble
Aix, 1920
Cl, trp, tbn, piano, sax.
Publisher: Eschig
Dedication and/or commission: Georges Auric
Duration: 3 min 14 s

Trois rag caprices op. 78
See Piano, solo
Aix, 1922
1.1.1.1.–2.1.1.0.–P.S.
Publisher: U.E.
Dedication and/or commission: Jean Wiéner
Duration: 8 min

Le carnaval de Londres op. 172 (R)
Bal-Ouverture — Polly — Peachum-Mrs. Peachum — Filch-Danses de Filch —
Mazurka — Lucy — Masques — Mackie-Chelsea-Sur la Tamise —
Gigue-Romance-Danse des Gueux — Rosy-Amoureux — Jeanette-Pat'en
l'air-Cabaret-2e Gigue-Valse — Arrêt du cortège-Petite marche — La Tour de
Londres — Final
See Incidental Music (Chansons de l'opera du Gueux)
Aix, September 1937
1.1.1.1.–0.1.1.0.–sax, P.H.S.
Publisher: Salabert
First performance: 1939. Conc. Revue Musicale, Paris. Conductor: M. Rosenthal
Duration: 30 min

Opus Americanum no. 2 op. 219b
Ouverture — Modéré — Animé — Souple et animé — Animé, rude — Très lent —
Marche — Introduction et baccanale — Modéré
See Large orchestra, misc.; Ballets (Moïse)
Oakland, 25 August–September 1940
1.1.2.1.–1.2.2.0.–P.B.S.
Publisher: Elkan Vogel-Presser
Dedication and/or commission: Pierre Monteux, comm. Ballet Theater
Duration: 31 min 25 s

Four Sketches (Esquisses) op. 227
Eglogue — Madrigal — Sobre la loma — Alameda
See Piano, solo; Duos, clarinet & piano (Eglogue, Madrigal); Quintets, wind
(Eglogue, Madrigal); Transcriptions (Sobre la loma)
Mills, May 1941
1.1.1.1.–1.1.1.0.–P.H.S.
Publisher: Mercury
Dedication and/or commission: Aaron Copland
First performance: January 1943. CBS, New York
Duration: 9 min

Jeux de printemps op. 243
Alerte — Gai — Tranquille — Robuste — Nonchalent — Joyeux
See Large orchestra, misc.
Mills, 5 June 1944
Fl, cl, bn, trp, 2 vln, va, vc, cb.
Publisher: Salabert
Dedication and/or commission: Mrs. E. Sprague Coolidge, comm. Library of
    Congress
First performance: 30 October 1944. Library of Congress, Washington, D.C. Martha
    Graham Ballets
Duration: 20 min

La muse ménagère op. 245 (R)
See Piano, solo
Mills, 1944
Fl, ob, cl, bn, hn, 2 1st vln, 2 2nd vln, va, vc, cb.
Publisher: Elkan Vogel-Presser
First performance: 26 July 1945. Oakland. Conductor: H. Brubeck. Ballet entitled
    'The Ivory Tower,'

L'apothéose de Molière op. 286
(Based on music by Baptiste Anet)
Tumulte dans l'Olympe précédant l'arrivée de Molière — Molière reçu par les muses
    — Hommage de Lully et des violons du roy — Molière accueilli par ses
    personnages: Précieuses ridicules et Femmes savantes, l'Avare, le Misanthrope, les
    Fâcheux — Allégresse générale
Tanglewood, 7 August 1948
1.1.1.1., hpd, S.
Publisher: Ois. Lyre
Dedication and/or commission: comm. Radio Italienne
First performance: 15 September 1948. Festival Capri
Duration: 10 min

Le globe trotter op. 358 (R)
France — Portugal — Italie — Etas-Unis — Mexique — Brésil
See Piano, solo; Transcriptions
Sion-Paris-Mills, 12 December 1956–27 March 1957
2.1.1.1.–0.2.2.0.–sax–P.H.S (3 vln, 2 va, 2 vc, cb)
Publisher: Mills Mus.–Bel. M.
First performance: 11 September 1957. Radio Lausanne. Conductor: D. Milhaud
Duration: 16 min 40 s

Les charmes de la vie op. 360b (R)
'Hommage à Watteau'
Pastorale — L'indifférent — Plaisirs champêtres — Sérénade — Musette — Mascarade
See Piano, solo
Mills, 8–14 February 1957
1.1.1.1.–0.1.0.0.–vln, va, vc, cb.
Publisher: Mills Mus.–Bel. M.
First performance: 11 September 1957. Radio Lausanne. Conductor: D. Milhaud
Duration: 17 min 35 s

Aspen Serenade op. 361
Animé (Astir) — Souple et printanier (Springlike) — Paisible (Peaceful) — Energique (Energetic) — Nerveux et coloré (Nimble and colorful)
Mills, 28 March–9 April 1957
1.1.1.1.–0.1.0.0.–vln, va, vc, cb.
Publisher: Heugel
Dedication and/or commission: Charles Jones
First performance: 19 August 1957. Aspen Festival
Duration: 16 min 5 s

Concert de chambre op. 389
Modéré — Animé — Lent
Mills, 9 January–28 April 1961
Piano, string quintet, wind quintet
Publisher: Eschig
Dedication and/or commission: comm. Mario et Antony di Bonaventura, comm. M. di Bonaventura.
First performance: 16 November 1962. Dartmouth College, New Hampshire. Conductor: M. di Bonaventura
Duration: 14 min

Musique pour Lisbonne op. 420
Modéré, tendre — Vif et gai — Modéré, avec charme — Léger, fantasque — Vif et allègre
Paris-Aspen, 25 April–31 July 1966
2 ob, 2 hn, strings (incl. 5-string cb)
Publisher: Eschig
Dedication and/or commission: comm. Fondation Calouste Gulbenkian
First performance: 28 June 1968. Festival Gulbenkian, Lisbon. Conductor: La Rosa Parodi
Duration: 21 min

Musique pour Graz op. 429 (R)
Gracieux — Rêveur — Animé — Zélé
Mills, 20 November 1968–24 February 1969
1.1.1.1.–0.1.0.0.–vln, va, vc, cb.
Publisher: U.E.
Dedication and/or commission: comm. Radio Autrichienne
First performance: 4 November 1970. Radio Graz, Coll. Mus. Instr. der Kunst um
   Graz. Conductor: M. Heider
Duration: 14 min 15 s

Musique pour Ars Nova op. 432
Animé — Vif — Lent — Rondeau
Aix-Nice-Paris, 6 October–29 November 1969
For 13 players using a different aleatory group for each section
Fl, cl, bs cl, bn, hn, trp, trb, 2 perc, harp, piano, vln, vc.
Publisher: Eschig
Dedication and/or commission: Marius Constant, comm. ORTF for Ars Nova
First performance: 1970. Montpellier. Ars Nova. Conductor: M. Constant
Duration: 12 min

String orchestra

[   ]

Symphoniette op. 363
Animé et vigoureux — Vif et léger — Décidé et joyeux
Aspen, 9 July–7 August 1957
Publisher: Heugel
Dedication and/or commission: comm. ORTF
First performance: 1957. ORTF. Conductor: A. Girard
Duration: 10 m

Large orchestra

[   ]

Large orchestra: symphonies —————————————————————

Première symphonie op. 210 (R)
Pastoral — Très vif — Très modéré — Final
Aix, 1939
3.3.3.3.–4.3.3.1.–T.P.H.S.
Publisher: Heugel
Dedication and/or commission: comm. Chicago Symph. Orch. pour son 50e
   anniversaire
First performance: 17 October 1940. Chicago Symphony. Conductor: D. Milhaud
Duration: 27 min 8 s

Deuxième symphonie op. 247 (R)
Paisible — Mystérieux — Douloureux — Avec sérénité — Allelouia
Mills, 18 September–28 October 1944
3.3.3.3.–4.3.3.1.–T.P.H.S.
Publisher: Heugel
Dedication and/or commission: A la mémoire de Mme. Nathalie Koussevitzky, comm. Koussevitzky Foundation
First performance: 20 December 1946. Boston Symphony. Conductor: D. Milhaud
Duration: 27 min

Troisième symphonie 'Te Deum' op. 271 (R)
Fièrement — Très recueilli — Pastorale — Te Deum (Hymnus Ambrosianus)
Mills-Hollywood-Boston, 22 October–December 1946
Mixed Chorus, 3.3.4.3.–4.3.3.1.–T.P.H.S.
Publisher: Heugel
Dedication and/or commission: comm. Radio Française
First performance: Orchestre National & chorus. Conductor: R. Desormière
Duration: 31 min 25 s

Quatrième symphonie '1848' op. 281 (R)
L'insurrection — Aux morts de la république — Les joies paisibles de la liberté retrouvée — Commémoration 1948
Atlantic Ocean-Pacific Ocean-Genval-Aix, August–December 1947
3.3.4.3.–4.4.4.2.–2 sax–T.P.S.
Publisher: Salabert
Dedication and/or commission: Roger Desormière, comm. par l'Etat pour le centenaire de la révolution de 1848
First performance: Concert pour le centenaire de la révolution de 1848. Orchestre National. Conductor: D. Milhaud
Duration: 28 min 6 s

Cinquième symphonie op. 322
Vif et cinglant — Lent et tendre — Clair et léger — Alerte et rude
Mills, 15 March–May 1953
3.2.2.2.–4.3.3.1.–T.P.S.
Publisher: Heugel
Dedication and/or commission: comm. Radio Italienne
First performance: 16 November 1953. RAI, Turin. Conductor: D. Milhaud
Duration: 25 min 16 s

Sixième symphonie op. 343 (R)
Calme et tendre — Tumultueux — Lent et doux — Joyeux et robuste
Mills, 3 February–30 March 1955
3.3.3.3.–4.3.3.1.–T.P.H.S.
Publisher: Heugel
Dedication and/or commission: To the memory of Serge and Nathalie Koussevitzky, comm. for the 75th anniversary of the Boston Symphony, C. Munch, Director.
First performance: 7 October 1955. Boston Symphony. Conductor: C. Munch
Duration: 27 min 15 s

Septième symphonie op. 344
Animé — Grave — Vif
Mills, 2 March–15 May 1955
3.3.3.3.–4.3.3.1.–T.P.H.S.
Publisher: Heugel
Dedication and/or commission: A l'orchestre INR et à son chef Franz André, comm. Radio Belge
First performance: 13 September 1955. Venice Festival. Conductor: F. André
Duration: 15 min

Huitième symphonie 'Rhodanienne' op. 362 (R)
Avec mystère et violence — Avec sérénité et nonchalance — Avec emportement — Rapide et majestueux
Mills, 11–26 April 1957
3.3.3.3.–4.3.3.1.–T.P.H.S.
Publisher: Heugel
Dedication and/or commission: comm. Univ. California (Berkeley)
First performance: 22 April 1958. University of California, Berkeley. San Francisco Symphony. Conductor: E. Jorda
Duration: 21 min 15 s

Neuvième symphonie op. 380
Modérément animé (Pastoral) — Lent et sombre — Alerte et vigoureux
Paris, 10 November–14 December 1959
2.3.2.2.–2.2.2.1.–T.P.H.S.
Publisher: Heugel
Dedication and/or commission: comm. Mario di Bonaventura, pour l'orchestre symphonique de Fort Lauderdale
First performance: 29 March 1960. Fort Lauderdale, Fla. Fort Lauderdale Symphony. Conductor: M. di Bonaventura
Duration: 16 min 40 s

Dixième symphonie op. 382
Décidé — Expressif — Fantasque — Emporté
Paris, 20 November 1959–29 February 1960
3.3.3.3.–4.3.3.1.–T.P.H.S.
Publisher: Heugel
Dedication and/or commission: comm. pour le centenaire de l'Oregon
First performance: 4 April 1961. Portland Symphony. Conductor: P. Bellugi
Duration: 22 min 5 s

Onzième symphonie 'Romantique' op. 384
Intense — Méditatif — Emporté
Paris, 13 March–14 April 1960
3.3.3.3.–4.3.3.1.–T.P.H.S.
Publisher: Heugel
Dedication and/or commission: comm. Dallas Public Library et Dallas Symphony Orchestra
First performance: 12 December 1960. Dallas Symphony. Conductor: P. Kletzki
Duration: 17 min 25 s

Douzième symphonie 'Rurale' op. 390
Pastoral — Vif et gai — Paisible — Lumineux
Aspen, 26 June–26 July 1961
2.2.3.2.–2.2.3.1.–T.P.H.S.
Publisher: Heugel
Dedication and/or commission: comm. Univ. California (Davis)
First performance: 16 February 1962. University of California, Davis. San Francisco
  Symphony. Conductor: E. Jorda
Duration: 16 min 40 s

Large orchestra: symphonic suites

Première suite symphonique op. 12
Vif — Lent — Très animé
(from 'La brebis égarée')
See Operas; Reductions
Paris, 1913–1914
3.3.3.4.–4.3.3.1.–T.P.H.S.
Publisher: Eschig
Dedication and/or commission: Léo Latil
First performance: 26 May 1914. Conc. Schmitz, Paris. Conductor: R. Schmitz
Duration: 18 min

Deuxième suite symphonique op. 57 (R)
(from 'Protée')
Ouverture — Prélude et fugue — Pastorale — Nocturne — Final
See Incidental music (Protée, first version); Reductions
Aix, 1919
3.3.3.4.–4.3.3.1.–T.P.H.S.
Publisher: Durand
Dedication and/or commission: A la mémoire d'Albéric Magnard
First performance: 26 October 1920. Conc. Colonne, Paris. Conductor: G. Pierné
Duration: 19 min 40 s

Sérénade op. 62 (R)
Vif — Tranquille — Vif
See Reductions
Aix-Paris, 1920–1921
2.2.2.2.–2.2.0.0.–T.P.S.
Publisher: U.E.
Dedication and/or commission: Lucien Daudet
First performance: 14 December 1920. Conc. Symph. Winterthur. Conductor:
  A. Honegger
Duration: 11 min 50 s

Saudades do Brazil op. 67b (R)
Ouverture — Douze danses
See Piano, solo; Transcriptions
Copenhagen-Aix, 1920–1921
2.2.2.2.–2.2.2.0.–T.P.S.
Publisher: Eschig
First performance: 1921. Spectacle Loïe Fuller, Paris. Conductor: V. Golschmann
Duration: 22 min

Suite de Maximilien op. 110b (R)
See Operas (Maximilien)
Aix, 1930
3.3.4.3.–4.4.3.1.–T.P.H.S.
Publisher: U.E.
Duration: 20 min

Suite provençale op. 152c (R)
Animé — Très modéré — Modéré — Vif — Modéré — Vif — Lent — Vif
See Ballets; Incidental music (Bertran de Born)
Paris, May–June 1936
2.3.2.2.–4.3.3.1.–T.P.S.
Publisher: (Deiss) Salabert
Dedication and/or commission: M.D.M.
First performance: 12 September 1937. Festival Biennale Venise. Conductor:
   D. Milhaud
Duration: 16 min

Suite française op. 248 (R)
Normandie — Bretagne — Ile de France — Alsace-Lorraine — Provence
See Band; Reductions
Mills, 13 November 1944
2.2.2.2.–2.2.2.0–T.P.S.
Publisher: (Leeds, MCA) Bel. M.
Dedication and/or commission: M.D.M., comm. Leeds
First performance: 28 June 1945. New York Stadium. Conductor: M. Abravanel
Duration: 16 min

Les cloches op. 259b
[from 'The Bells' by Edgar Allan Poe]
Overture (Ouverture) — Silver Bells (Cloches d'argent) — Golden Bells (Cloches
   d'or) — Brazen Bells (Cloches de cuivre) — Iron Bells (Cloches de fer) —
   Bacchanale (Bacchanale)
See Ballets
Mills, January 1946
3.1.2.1.–2.2.1.0.–P.S. piano.
Publisher: Eschig
Dedicated to: M.D.M., comm. Ruth Page
Duration: 23 min 10 s

Suite campagnarde op. 329
Paysage — Nocturne — Pastorale — Danse rustique
Paris-Turin-Paris, 9 October–2 November 1953
2.2.2.2.–2.2.2.0.–T.P.S.
Publisher: Heugel
Dedication and/or commission: comm. Wilmington College
First performance: International Folk Festival, Wilmington, Ohio. Wilmington
College Orchestra. Conductor: C. Monteux
Duration: 9 min 55 s

Paris op. 284b
Montmartre — L'lle Saint-Louis — Bateaux-mouches — Longchamps — La tour
Eiffel
See Piano, four pianos
Aspen-Paris, 21 June–17 December 1959
2.2.2.2.–4.3.3.1.–T.P.H.S.
Publisher: Eschig
First performance: 10 May 1960. INR, Brussels
Duration: 10 min

Musique pour Prague op. 415
Animé — Lent — Vif
Paris, 24 October–17 November 1965
2.2.2.3.–2.3.3.1.–T.P.H.S.
Publisher: Eschig
Dedication and/or commission: comm. Festival de Printemps, Prague
First performance: 20 June 1966. Festival de Printemps, Prague. Conductor:
D. Milhaud
Duration: 14 min 10 s

Musique pour l'Indiana op. 418
Robuste — Vif — Expressif — Violent et lyrique
Paris, 30 January–30 March 1966
2.2.3.3.–2.3.3.1.–T.P.H.S.
Publisher: Eschig
Dedication and/or commission: comm. Mr. et Mrs. H. C. Krammert pour le 150e
anniversaire de l'Indiana
First performance: 1967. Indiana Symphony. Conductor J. Salomon
Duration: 19 min 15 s

Musique pour la Nouvelle-Orléans op. 422
Large — Très lent et tendre — Vigoureux
Mills, 18 October–8 December 1966
3.2.3.3.–4.3.3.1.–T.P.H.S.
Publisher: Eschig
Dedication and/or commission: comm. New Orleans Symph. Orch. pour le 250e
anniversaire de New Orleans
First performance: 1968. New Orleans Symphony
Duration: 25 min 15 s

Promenade Concert op. 424
Animé — Modéré et subtil — Vif — Rondement
Aspen, July 1967
2.2.2.2.–4.3.3.1.–T.P.H.S.
Publisher: Eschig
Dedication and/or commission: comm. New York Philharmonic Orchestra
First performance: 11 August 1968. Aspen Festival. Conductor: D. Milhaud
Duration: 13 min

Symphonie pour l'univers Claudelien op. 427b
(in six parts)
See Music for films (Paul Claudel)
Nice-Paris, 19 March–3 April 1968
2.2.3.3.–4.3.3.1.–T.P.H.S.
Publisher: Eschig
Dedication and/or commission: Hommage à Paul Claudel
First performance: 30 July 1968. Festival Aix-en-Provence. Conductor: P. Dervaux
Duration: 25 min

Suite en sol op. 431
Nonchalent ct rêveur — Alerte et léger — Très expressif — Animé
Mills, 28 April–May 1969
2.2.2.2.–4.3.3.1.–T.P.H.S.
Publisher: Eschig
Dedication and/or commission: comm. Marin County Symph. Orch.
First performance: 25 September 1971.
Marin County, California. Marin County Symphony. Conductor: S. Salgo.
Duration: 18 min

Musique pour San Francisco op. 436
Souple et animé — Calme — Vif
Geneva, 26 August–7 September 1971
2.2.2.2.–2.2.2.0.–P.S. (with audience participation)
Publisher: Eschig
Dedication and/or commission: comm. San Francisco Symph. Orch.
First performance: 3 September 1972. San Francisco Symphony. Conductor: N. Wyss
Duration: 10 min 40 s

Large orchestra: miscellaneous _____

L'homme et son désir op. 48
See Ballets; Reductions
Rio de Janeiro, 1918
2.2.2.1.–1.2.0.0.–P.H.S.
Publisher: U.E.
Duration: 20 min

Deux hymnes op. 88b
Hymne de Sion — Israël est vivant
See Solo voice, with piano
Aix, 1925
3.3.3.3.–4.3.3.1.–T.P.H.S.
Publisher: U.E.
First performance: 1927. Conc. Straram, Paris. Conductor: W. Straram
Duration: 3 min

Introduction et marche funèbre op. 153b (R)
See Band; Incidental music (Quatorze juillet)
Paris, June 1936
2.2.2.2.–2.2.2.0.–T.P.S.
Publisher: (E.S.I.) Ch. du M.
First performance: 26 November 1936. Conc. Phil., Paris. Conductor C. Munch
Duration: 6 min 30 s

Cortège funèbre op. 202b (R)
See Music for films (Espoir)
Aix, May 1939
2.1.2.(cl/sax).1.–0.2.2.1.–P.H.S.
Publisher: A.M.P.
Dedication and/or commission: Serge Koussevitzky
First performance: 4 August 1940. CBS, New York. Conductor: D. Milhaud
Duration: 14 min

Opus Americanum no. 2 op. 219b (R)
Ouverture — Modéré — Animé — Souple et animé — Animé, rude — Très lent —
    Marche — Introduction et bacchanale — Modéré
See Chamber ensemble, misc.; Ballets (Moïse)
Oakland, 17 July 1940
2.2.2.2.–2.2.2.0.–T.P.H.S.
Publisher: Elkan Vogel-Presser
Duration: 31 min 25 s

Introduction et allegro op. 220 (R)
(Orchestration of 2 excerpts from 'La Sultane' by Couperin)
Oakland, 9–11 October 1940
3.3.3.2.–3.3.3.1.–T.P.H.S.
Publisher: Elkan Vogel-Presser
Dedication and/or commission: comm. St. Louis Symph. Orch.
First performance: 1941. St. Louis Symphony. Conductor: V. Golschmann
Duration: 6 min 45 s

Jeux de printemps op. 243
Alerte — Gai — Tranquille — Robuste — Nonchalent — Joyeux
See Chamber ensemble, misc.
Mills, 1944
3.3.3.2.–4.3.3.1.–T.P.H.S.
Publisher: Salabert
Dedication and/or commission: Mrs. E. Sprague Coolidge, comm. Library of Congress
First performance: 11 December 1945. Radio Bruxelles. Conductor R. Desormière
Duration: 20 min

Le bal martiniquais op. 249
Chanson créole — Béguine
See Piano, two pianos
Mills, September 1945
2.2.2.2.–2.2.2.0.–T.P.H.S.
Publisher: Bel. M.
First performance: 6 December 1945. New York Philharmonic Orchestra. Conductor: D. Milhaud
Duration: 7 min 15 s

Deux marches op. 260 (R)
In Memoriam — Gloria Victoribus
See Band
Mills, 23–30 September 1945
2.2.2.2.–4.3.3.1.–T.P.S.
Publisher: Schirmer
Dedication and/or commission: comm. Schirmer
First performance: 12 December 1945. CBS, New York. Conductor: D. Milhaud
Duration: 6 min 5 s

Kentuckiana op. 287 (R)
(Divertissement on 20 Kentucky folk songs)
See Piano, two pianos
Santa Barbara, June–13 September 1948
2.2.2.2.–2.2.2.0.–T.P.S.
Publisher: Elkan Vogel-Presser
Dedication and/or commission: Robert Whitney, comm. Louisville Phil. Orch.
First performance: 22 May 1954. Louisville Philharmonic Orchestra. Conductor: Robert Whitney
Duration: 10 min 20 s

Ouverture méditerranéenne op. 330 (R)
Paris, 25 November–11 December 1953
2.2.2.2.–4.2.2.0.–T.P.S.
Publisher: Heugel
Dedication and/or commission: Robert Whitney, comm. Louisville Phil. Orch.
First performance: 22 May 1954. Louisville Philharmonic Orchestra. Conductor: Robert Whitney
Duration: 6 min 20 s

Valse en forme de rondo (La couronne de Marguerite) op. 353b
(Incl. in 'Variations sur le nom de M. Long')
See Piano, solo pieces included in collections
Paris, 16–21 March 1956
2.2.2.2.–2.2.0.0.–T.P.H.S.
Publisher: Salabert
Dedication and/or commission: Marguerite Long
First performance: 4 June 1956. Sorbonne, Jubilé Marguerite Long. Orchestre
    Nationale. Conductor: C. Munch

Les funérailles de Phocion op. 385
(Hommage à Nicolas Poussin)
Paris, 20 April–30 May 1960
3.2.3.3.–4.3.3.1.–T.P.S.
Publisher: Heugel
Dedication and/or commission: comm. ORTF
First performance: 18 May 1962. Radio Belge. Conductor: D. Milhaud
Duration: 7 min

Aubade op. 387
Vif — Nonchalent — Vif
Mills, 5–10 October 1960
2.2.2.2.–2.2.2.0.–T.P.H.S.
Publisher: Heugel
Dedication and/or commission: comm. Oakland Symph. Orch.
First performance: 14 March 1961. Oakland Symphony. Conductor: G. Samuel
Duration: 10 min 30 s

Ouverture philharmonique op. 397
Paris, 13 March–29 April 1962
3.3.3.3.–4.3.3.1.–T.P.H.S.
Publisher: Edit. Trans.
Dedication and/or commission: comm. New York Philharmonic Orchestra
First performance: 12 November 1962. Lincoln Center, New York. New York
    Philharmonic Orchestra. Conductor: Sir J. Barbirolli
Duration: 9 min

A Frenchman in New York op. 399 (R)
New York with fog on the Hudson River — The Cloisters — Horse and carriage in
    Central Park — Times Square — Garden on the roof — Baseball in Yankee Stadium
Mills, 25 September–18 October 1962
3.3.3.3.–4.3.3.1.–T.P.H.S.
Publisher: Salabert
Dedication and/or commission: comm. RCA Victor
First performance: 1963. Boston Pops. Conductor: A. Fiedler
Durations: 21 min

Meurtre d'un grand chef d'état op. 405
Paris, 25 November 1963
2.2.2.2.–4.3.3.1.–T.S.
Publisher: Eschig
Dedication and/or commission: A la mémoire de John Kennedy
First performance: 2 December 1963. Oakland Symphony. Conductor: G. Samuel
Duration: 3 min

Ode pour les morts des guerres op. 406
Déploration sur les populations civiles massacrées — Prière pour les morts en captivité
    et en déportation — Hymne funèbre pour les morts au champ d'honneur
Paris, March–24 December 1963
3.3.3.3.–4.3.3.1.–T.P.S.
Publisher: Eschig
Dedication and/or commission: comm. Etat
First performance: 28 June 1966. ORTF. Conductor: D. Milhaud
Duration: 15 min

Ode pour Jérusalem op. 440
Fier et violent — Mouvement recueilli — Mouvement triomphant
Geneva, 11 June–10 August 1972
2.2.2.2.–2.2.3.1.–T.P.S.
Publisher: Eschig
Dedication and/or commission: comm. Etat d'Israël
First performance: 16 July 1973. Israel Philharmonic Orchestra. Conductor:
    D. Barenboim
Duration: 13 min 5 s

Band

Introduction et marche funèbre op. 153b (R)
See Large orchestra, misc.; Incidental music (Quatorze juillet)
Paris, June 1936
4.3.5.3.–6.4.4.1.–5 sax–T.P.2 cb (chorus ad lib).
Publisher: (E.S.I.) Ch. du M.
Duration: 6 min 30 s

Suite française op. 248 (R)
Normandie — Bretagne — Ile de France — Alsace-Lorraine — Provence
See Large orchestra, symphonic suites; Reductions
Mills, 13 November 1944
3.2.5.2.–4.2.3.2.–3 cnt, 5 sax, 1 saxhn–1 cb–T.P.
Publisher: (Leeds, MCA) Bel. M.
Dedication and/or commission: M.D.M., comm. Leeds
First performance: 13 June 1945. Central Park Conc., New York. Goldman Band.
    Conductor: E. F. Goldman
Duration: 16 min

Deux marches op. 260 (R)
See Large orchestra, misc.
New York-Mills, 1945
3.1.4.1.–4.2.3.2.–2 alto sax, cnt, 3 bflat cnt–T.P.cb.
Publisher: Schirmer
Dedication and/or commission: comm. Schirmer
First performance: 1946. Central Park Conc., New York. Goldman Band. Conductor:
  E. F. Goldman
Duration: 6 min

West Point suite op. 313 (R)
Introduction — Récitatif — Fanfare
Paris, October 1951
2 bar–4.2.7.2.–8.4.3.6.–4 sax, 4 cnt, 2 flg hn–T.P.2 cb
Publisher: A.M.P.
Dedication and/or commission: comm. U.S. Military Academy, pour le 150e
  anniversaire de West Point
First performance: 5 January 1952. Carnegie Hall, New York. West Point Band.
  Conductor: Captain Resta
Duration: 7 min 50 s

Musique de théâtre op. 334b (R)
Prélude et fugue — Triomphe — Interlude — Funèbre et choral
See Incidental music (Saül)
Paris, 1970
3.3.3.2.–4.4.4.1.–P. cel, 3 cb.
Publisher: Eschig
First performance: 28 October 1972. Drancy. Orchestre Gardiens de la Paix.
  Conductor: D. Dondeyne
Duration: 10 min 30 s

Solo & orchestras (or chamber ensemble)

For piano arrangements of most of the works included in this section, see Reductions

Solo & orchestra (or chamber ensemble): harpsichord

Concerto op. 407
Alerte — Vif — Lent — Rondement
Paris, 14 January–9 March 1964
1.1.1.1.–0.1.0.0.–T.P.H.S.
Publisher: Salabert
Dedication and/or commission: Sylvia Marlowe (comm.)
First performance: 1969. ORTF, Paris. Conductor: D. Milhaud, hprd: R. Veyron
  Lacroix
Duration: 13 min 25 s

Solo & orchestra (or chamber ensemble): piano ⸻

Ballade op. 61
Aix, 1920–1923
3.2.2.2.–4.2.2.0.–T.P.H.S.
Publisher: U.E.
Dedication and/or commission: Albert Roussel
First performance: 1923. New York City Symphony. Conductor D. Foch, piano: D. Milhaud
Duration: 12 min

Cinq études op. 63
Vif — Doucement — Fugues — Sombre — Romantique
Copenhagen-Aix, 1920
1.1.1.1.–1.1.1.0.–T.P.S.
Publisher: U.E.
Dedication and/or commission: Robert Schmitz (Vif), Marcelle Meyer (Doucement), Andrée Vaurabourg (Fugues), à la mémoire de Juliette Meerovitch (Sombre), N.V.G. (Romantique)
First performance: May 1921. Conc. Golschmann, Paris. Conductor: V. Golschmann, piano: M. Meyer
Duration: 10 min

Le carnaval d'Aix op. 83b (R)
Le Corso — Tartaglia — Isabelle — Rosetta — Le bon et le mauvais tuteur — Coviello — Le capitaine Cartuccia — Polichinelle — Polka — Cinzio — Souvenir de Rio (Tango) —Final
See Ballets (Salade)
Paris, June 1926
2.1.2.1.–2.2.1.1.–T.P.S.
Publisher: Heugel
First performance: December 1926. New York Philharmonic Orchestra. Conductor: W. Mengelberg, piano: D. Milhaud
Duration: 15 min 30 s

Premier concerto op. 127 (R)
Très vif — Mouvement de barcarolle — Final
Cauterets-Aix, 1933
2.2.3.2.–2.3.2.1.–T.P.H.S.
Publisher: (Deiss) Salabert
Dedication and/or commission: Marguerite Long
First performance: 23 November 1934. Conc. Pasdeloup, Paris. Conductor: A. Wolff, piano: M. Long
Duration: 12 min

Fantaisie pastorale op. 188 (R)
Paris, March–April 1938
1.1.1.1.–1.1.1.1.–P.H.S.
Publisher: (Deiss) Salabert
First performance: February 1939. O.S.P., Paris. Conductor: D. Milhaud, piano: S. Andersen
Duration: 10 min

Deuxième concerto op. 225
Animé — Romance — Final
Mills, April 1941
2.2.2.2.–2.2.2.1.–T.P.S.
Publisher: Heugel
Dedication and/or commission: M.D.M.
First performance: 19 December 1941. Chicago Symphony. Conductor: Lange, piano: D. Milhaud
Duration: 14 min

Troisième concerto op. 270
Alerte et avec élégance — Lent — Avec esprit et vivacité
Mills, August–September 1946
2.2.2.2.–2.2.2.1.–T.P.S.
Publisher: A.M.P.
Dedication and/or commission: Emile Baume (comm.)
First performance: 26 May 1948. Festival de Printemps, Prague. Piano: E. Baume
Duration: 19 min

Quatrième concerto op. 295 (R)
Animé — Très lent — Joyeux
Mills-Laramie, May–June 1949
2.2.2.2.–2.2.2.0.–T.P.2H.S.
Publisher: Heugel
Dedication and/or commission: Zadel Skolowsky (comm.)
First performance: 3 March 1950. Boston Symphony. Conductor: C. Munch, piano: Z. Skolowsky
Duration: 18 min 45 s

Suite concertante op. 278b
Animé — Lent — Vif
See Solo & orchestra (or chamber ensemble), marimba & vibraphone (Concerto)
Paris, February 1952
2.2.2.2.–2.2.2.1.–T.P.H.S.
Publisher: Enoch
First performance: 1 June 1953. Radio France. Orchestre National. Conductor: C. Munch, piano: N. Henriot
Duration: 18 min 5 s

Cinquième concerto op. 346
Alerte — Nonchalant — Joyeux
Mills, 22 May–14 July 1955
2.2.2.2.–2.2.2.1.–T.P.H.S.
Publisher: Eschig
Dedication and/or commission: Stell Andersen, comm. Mrs. Guggenheim
First performance: 16 May 1956. New York Stadium. Conductor: P. Monteux, piano:
  S. Andersen
Duration: 18 min 40 s

Solo & orchestra (or chamber ensemble): two pianos ─────────────

Premier concerto op. 228 (R)
Animé — Funèbre — Vif et précis
Mills, June–November 1941
2.2.2.2.–2.2.2.1.–T.P.S.
Publisher: Elkan Vogel-Presser
Dedication and/or commission: Vronsky et Babin (comm.)
First performance: 13 November 1942. Pittsburgh Symphony. Conductor: F. Reiner,
  piano: V. Vronsky, V. Babin
Duration: 18 min 15 s

Suite opus 300 op. 300
Entrée — Nocturne — Java fuguée — Mouvement perpétuel — Final
Paris, January–April 1950
2.2.2.2.–2.2.3.0.–T.P.S.
Publisher: Heugel
Dedication and/or commission: Gold et Fizdale (comm.)
First performance: 14 September 1950. Vienna Festival. Conductor: H. Scherchen,
  piano: A. Gold, R. Fizdale
Duration: 18 min 15 s

Concertino d'automne op. 309 (R)
Mills, 19–29 March 1951
Fl, ob, 3 hn, 2 va, vc
Publisher: Heugel
Dedication and/or commission: Gold et Fizdale (comm.)
First performance: 19 December 1951. Town Hall, New York. Piano: A. Gold, R.
  Fizdale
Duration: 11 min

Deuxième concerto op. 394 (R)
Alerte — Tendre et ardent — Allègre
Paris, 20 November–25 December 1961
Perc, timp, cel, glock, xyl
Publisher: Eschig
Dedication and/or commission: comm. Juilliard School of Music
First performance: August 1963. Juilliard School of Music, New York. Piano: R.
  Segal, N. Segal
Duration: 21 min

Cinéma-fantaisie op. 58b (R)
See Duos, violin & piano; Ballets (Le boeuf sur le toit)
Aix, 1919
2.1.2.1.–2.2.1.0.–P.S.
Publisher: (Sirène) Eschig
Dedication and/or commission: René Benedetti
First performance: 1921, Paris. vln: R. Benedetti
Duration: 19 min

Premier concerto op. 93 (R)
Prélude — Romance — Final
Portland-Minneapolis, 1927
2.2.2.2.–2.2.2.1.–T.P.H.S.
Publisher: Heugel
Dedication and/or commission: Mme Sutter Sapin, (comm.)
First performance: 1928. Conc. Poulet, Paris. Conductor: G. Poulet, vln: Mme Sutter
 Sapin
Duration: 9 min

Concertino de printemps op. 135 (R)
Aix, 1934
1.1.1.1.–1.1.0.0.–T.P.S.
Publisher: (Deiss) Salabert
Dedication and/or commission: Y. Astruc
First performance: 21 March 1935. Paris. Conductor: D. Milhaud, vln: Yvonne Astruc
Duration: 9 min

Suite anglaise op. 234 (R)
Gigue — Sailor Song — Hornpipe
See Duos, violin & piano (Sailor Song); Solo & orchestra, harmonica; Reductions;
 Transcriptions
Mills, September 1942
2.2.2.2.–2.2.2.1.–T.P.S.
Publisher: B.&H.
First performance: 16 November 1945. Philadelphia Orchestra. Conductor: E.
 Ormandy, vln: Z. Francescatti
Duration: 15 min

Deuxième concerto op. 263 (R)
Dramatique — Lent et sombre — Emporté
Mills, 6–16 February 1946
2.3.3.2.–2.2.2.1.–T.P.S.
Publisher: A.M.P.
Dedication and/or commission: comm. Arthur Le Blanc
First performance: 7 November 1948. Concert du Conservatoire, Paris. Conductor:
 A. Cluytens, vln: A. Le Blanc
Duration: 23 min

Concert royal op. 373
(Troisième concerto)
Vif — Lent — Animé
Mills, 23 October–14 December 1958
2.2.2.2.–2.2.2.1.–T.P.H.S.
Publisher: Eschig
Dedication and/or commission: Sa Majesté la Reine Elizabeth de Belgique, comm.
  Concours International de la Reine de Belgique
First performance: 1959. Concert Royal, Brussels. Conductor: F. André, vln: J.
  Laredo
Duration: 20 min

Music for Boston op. 414
Animé — Lent — Cadence et final: Vif
Paris, 20 October 1965
Fl, cl, bn, strings.
Publisher: Elkan Vogel-Presser
Dedication and/or commission: comm. Cultural Foundation of Boston pour Roman
  Totenberg
First performance: 25 February 1966. Boston Winter Festival. vln: Roman Totenberg
Duration: 13 min

Solo & orchestra (or chamber ensemble): viola _____

Premier concerto op. 108 (R)
Animé — Lent — Souple et animé — Vif
Aix, 1929
1st version, 2.2.3.2.–2.2.1.1.–P.H.S.
2nd version, 2.1.2.1.–1.1.1.0.–P.S.
Publisher: U.E.
Dedication and/or commission: Paul Hindemith
First performance: 5 December 1929. Concertgebouw, Amsterdam. Conductor: P.
  Monteux, va: Paul Hindemith
Duration: 15 min

Concertino d'été op. 311 (R)
Mills, 1951
1.1.1.1.–1.1.0.0.–2 vc, cb.
Publisher: Heugel
Dedication and/or commission: pour le 10e anniversaire de Charleston Chamber
  Music Players
First performance: 19 November 1951. Charleston, S.C. va: R. Courte
Duration: 10 min

Deuxième concerto op. 340
Avec entrain — Avec charme — Avec esprit — Avec gaîté
Mills-Milan-Mills, 2 December 1954–30 January 1955
2.2.2.2.–2.2.2.1.–T.P.H.S.
Publisher: Heugel
Dedication and/or commission: William Primrose (comm.)
First performance: 27 November 1958. Westdeutscher Rundfunk, Cologne.
   Conductor: H. Rosbaud, va: W. Primrose
Duration: 20 min

Solo & orchestra (or chamber ensemble): violoncello _____

Premier concerto op. 136 (R)
Nonchalent — Grave — Joyeux
Aix, 1934
2.2.2.2.–2.2.2.1.–T.P.H.S.
Publisher: (Deiss) Salabert
Dedication and/or commission: Maurice Maréchal
First performance: 28 June 1935. Conc. Sérénade, Paris. Conductor: D. Inghelbrecht,
   vc: M. Maréchal
Duration: 15 min

Deuxième concerto op. 255 (R)
Gai — Tendre — Alerte
Mills, 28 June–18 July 1945
2.2.2.2.–2.2.2.1.–T.P.H.S.
Publisher: A.M.P.
Dedication and/or commission: Edmond Kurtz (comm.)
First performance: 28 November 1946. New York Philharmonic Orchestra.
   Conductor: A. Rodzinsky, vc: E. Kurtz
Duration: 18 min

Suite cisalpine op. 332 (R)
(sur des airs populaires piémontais)
Vif — Modéré — Très animé
Paris, 11–19 January 1954
2.2.2.2.–2.2.2.0.–T.P.H.S.
Publisher: Eschig
Dedication and/or commission: Grégor Piatigorsky, comm. pour le Prix Piatigorsky
First performance: 7 November 1954. Conc. Pasdeloup, Paris. Conductor: A. Wolff,
   vc: R. Flachot
Duration: 12 min 30 s

Solo & orchestra (or chamber ensemble): oboe _____

Concerto op. 365 (R)
Animé — Avec sérénité — Animé
Paris, 15 October–24 November 1957
2.0.3.0.–2.2.2.0.–2 sax–T.P.H.S.
Publisher: Heugel
Dedication and/or commission: comm. ORTF
First performance: 1958. ORTF, Paris. ob: L. Pierlot
Duration: 18 min 30 s

Stanford Serenade op. 430
Gaiement — Très lent et paisible — Vivement
Mills, 9–25 April 1969
Fl, cl, bn, tpt, perc, harp, 2 vln, va, vc, cb.
Publisher: Eschig
Dedication and/or commission: comm. Donald Leake pour Sandor Salgo et le
  Stanford Symph. Orch.
First performance: 24 May 1970. Stanford Symphony. Conductor: Sandor Salgo, ob:
  D. Leake
Duration: 12 min 5 s

Solo & orchestra (or chamber ensemble): clarinet _____

Scaramouche op. 165d
Vif — Modéré — Brazileira
See Piano, two pianos; Solo & orchestra, saxophone;
Incidental music (Le médecin volant);
Transcriptions (Brazileira)
Mills, November 1941
2.2.2.2.–2.2.2.0.–P.S.
Publisher: Salabert
Duration: 8 min

Concerto op. 230 (R)
Animé—Très décidé—Lent—Final: Animé
Mills, 22 November 1941
2.2.2.2.–2.2.2.1.–T.P.H.S.
Publisher: Elkan Vogel-Presser
Dedication and/or commission: Benny Goodman (comm.)
First performance: 3 January 1946. Marine Barracks, Washington, D.C.
Duration: 22 min 10 s

Solo & orchestra (or chamber ensemble): saxophone —————————————

Scaramouche op. 165c (R)
Vif — Modéré — Brazileira
See Piano, two pianos; Solo & orchestra, clarinet;
Incidental music (Le médecin volant);
Transcriptions (Brazileira)
Paris-Mayens de Sion, June–July 1939
2.2.2.2.–2.2.2.0.–P.S.
Publisher: Salabert
First performance: June 1940. Radio Paris. Conductor: R. Bastide, sax: A. Muhle
Duration: 8 min

Solo & orchestra (or chamber ensemble): trombone —————————————

Concertino d'hiver op. 327 (R)
Atlantic Ocean-Paris, 10–14 September/1–4 October 1953
2 vln, va, vc, cb.
Publisher: A.M.P.
Dedication and/or commission: comm. Hunterton County Art Center pour Davis
 Shuman
First performance: 1954. Brooklyn Community Symphony. tmb: D. Shuman
Duration: 12 min 15 s

Solo & orchestra (or chamber ensemble): percussion —————————————

Concerto op. 109 (R)
(one player)
See Arrangements
Paris, 1929–1930
2.0.2.0.–0.1.1.0.–S.(3.3.2.2.1.)
Publisher: U.E.
Dedication and/or commission: Paul Collaer
First performance: 1930. Conc. Pro Arte, Brussels. Conductor: D. Milhaud, perc:
 Coutelier
Duration: 7 min

Solo & orchestra (or chamber ensemble): harp —————————————

Concerto op. 323
Souple et modéré — Vif et clair — Lent — Animé
Santa Barbara-Mills, 4 June–15 July 1953
2.2.2.2.–2.2.2.0.–sax–T.P.S.
Publisher: Eschig
Dedication and/or commission: comm. Nicanor Zabaleta
First performance: September 1954. Biennale Venise. harp: N. Zabaleta
Duration: 22 min

Solo & orchestra (or chamber ensemble): marimba & vibraphone ──────────

Concerto op. 278 (R)
(One player)
Animé — Lent — Vif
See Solo & orchestra, piano (Suite concertante)
Mills, 10–16 May 1947
2.2.2.2.–2.2.2.1.–T.P.H.S.
Publisher: Enoch
Dedication and/or commission: comm. Jack Conner
First performance: 12 February 1949. St Louis Symphony. Conductor: V. Golschmann, mmb & vib: J. Conner
Duration: 18 min 50 s

Solo & orchestra (or chamber ensemble): harmonica ──────────

Suite anglaise op. 234 (R)
Gigues —Sailor Song — Hornpipe
See Duos, violin & piano (Sailor Song); Solo & orchestra, violin; Transcriptions
Mills, September 1942
2.2.2.2.–2.2.2.1.–T.P.S.
Publisher: B.&H.
Dedication and/or commission: Larry Adler (comm.)
First performance: 28 May 1947. Orch. Colonne, Paris. Conductor: G. Poulet, harm: L. Adler
Duration: 15 min

Several instruments & orchestra

Several instruments & orchestra: flute & violin ──────────

Concerto op. 197
Rondement — Très modéré — Animé
See Reductions
Paris, 1938–March 1939
2.2.2.2.–2.2.2.1.–T.P.H.S.
Publisher: (Deiss) Salabert
Dedication and/or commission: Marcel Moyse et Blanche Honegger
First performance: May 1940. Radio Suisse Romande. Conductor: E. Ansermet, vln: B. Honegger, fl: M. Moyse
Duration: 18 min

Several instruments & orchestra: trumpet, horn, bassoon, & contrabass _____

Symphonie concertante op. 376
Animé — Lent et dramatique — Clair et vif
Mills, 1959
1.1.1.1.–1.1.1.0.–T.P.S.
Publisher: Heugel
Dedication and/or commission: comm. University of California Extension (San Francisco)
First performance: 1959. San Francisco. Conductor: D. Milhaud
Duration: 11 min

VOCAL MUSIC

Solo voice
┌──────┐
└──────┘

Solo voice: unaccompanied _____

Vocalise op. 105
Paris, 1928
Publisher: Leduc
Dedication and/or commission: A. L. Hettich
Duration: 1 min 50 s

Solo voice: with piano _____

Sept poèmes de la connaissance de l'est op. 7
[Paul Claudel]
La nuit à la véranda — Décembre — Dissolution — Ardeur — Tristesse de l'eau — La descente — Le point
Aix-Paris, 1912–1913
Publisher: (Mathot) Salabert
Dedication and/or commission: Armand Lunel (La nuit à la véranda — Décembre — Tristesse de l'eau — Le point), Francis Jammes (Dissolution), Madame Ch. Lacoste (La descente)
First performance: 1913. Salon d'Automne, Paris. voice: J. Lacoste (Dissolution — Ardeur — La descente); 1917. Conc. Mathot, Paris. voice: J. Lacoste (La nuit à la véranda — Décembre — Tristesse de l'eau — Le point)
Duration: 24 min 35 s

Alissa op. 9 (R)
[From 'La porte étroite' by André Gide]
Aix-Paris, 1913
Dedication and/or commission: Céline Lagouarde
First performance: February 1920. Sorbonne, Paris. voice: J. Bathori, piano: D. Milhaud
Duration: 32 min 28 s
New version:
Aix-les-Bains, 1931
Publisher: Heugel

Trois poèmes en prose de Lucile de Chateaubriand op. 10
L'aurore (R) — A la lune — L'innocence
Hellerau-Berlin-Prague, 1913
Publisher: (Mathot) Salabert
Dedication and/or commission: Léo Latil (L'aurore), Madame Ch. Lacoste (A la lune), Armand Lunel (L'innocence)
First performance: 10 February 1916. Conc. Rouge, Paris. voice: A. Stephenson

Quatre poèmes de Léo Latil op. 20 (R)
L'abandon — Ma douleur et sa compagne — Le rossignol — La tourterelle
Aix, 1914
Publisher: Durand
Dedication and/or commission: A la memoire de Maurice de Guérin
First performance: 22 May 1915. Conc. Foyer Franco-Belge, Paris. voice: J. Bathori, piano: D. Milhaud
Duration: 13 min

Poème du Gitanjali op. 22
[Rabindranath Tagore, adapted by André Gide] 1914
Publisher: Fr. de Mus., 25 de luxe copies
Dedication and/or commission: Léo Latil
First performance: Concerts du Feu, Marseille. Voice: J. Bathori

Quatre poèmes de Paul Claudel pour baryton op. 26
Chanson d'automne — Ténèbres — Le sombre mai — Obsession
Paris-Rio de Janeiro, 1915–1917
Publisher: Durand
Dedication and/or commission: Madame Sainte-Marie Perrin (Chanson d'automne), Georges G. (Ténèbres), Léo Velloso (Sombre mai), L. (Obsession)
First performance: 10 January 1922. Conc. Hubbard, Paris. voice: Hubbard (Chanson d'automne); May 1921. Conc. Olénine d'Alheim, Paris. voice: Olénine d'Alheim (Ténèbres — Le sombre mai — Obsession)
Duration: 13 min

D'un cahier inédit du journal d'Eugénie de Guérin op. 27
Cette promenade avec toi — Nous voilà donc exilés — A mesure qu'on avance
Paris, 1915
Publisher: (Roudanez, Philippo) Combre
Dedication and/or commission: Léo Latil
First performance: May 1921. Paris. voice: Madame Vié
Duration: 8 min 40 s

Deux poèmes d'amour op. 30
[Rabindranath Tagore, translated by E. Sainte-Marie Perrin]
Amour, mon coeur languit — Paix, mon coeur
Givry-Hostel, 1915
Publisher: Schirmer
Dedication and/or commission: Madame Ch. Koechlin (Amour, mon coeur languit),
    Madame J. Herscher (Paix, mon coeur)
First performance: 1917. Lycée Français, Rio de Janeiro. voice: Valente
Duration: 5 min 55 s

Deux poèmes de Coventry Patmore op. 31
[Translated by Paul Claudel]
Le départ — L'azalée
Aix, 1915
Publisher: (deluxe edition: Stols) Heugel
Dedication and/or commission: Jane Bathori
First performance: 1922. Conc. Hubbard, Paris. voice: Hubbard
Duration: 8 min 35 s

Poèmes juifs op. 34 (R)
[Author unknown]
Chant de nourrice — Chant de Sion — Chant de laboureur — Chant de la pitié —
    Chant de résignation — Chant d'amour — Chant de forgeron — Lamentation
Paris, 1916
Publisher: (Demets) Eschig
Dedication and/or commission: G. Guller (Chant de nourrice), à la mémoire de
    Georges Levy (Chant de Sion), Ernest Bloch (Chant de laboureur), Madame B.
    Klotz (Chant de la pitié), Mademoiselle D. Sternberg (Chant de résignation),
    Marcelle Milhaud (Chant d'amour), Arthur Rubinstein (Chant de forgeron), à la
    mémoire de P.M. (Lamentation)
First performance: 10 January 1920. Société Nationale, Paris. voice: J. Bathori, piano:
    D. Milhaud
Duration: 16 min 10 s

Child Poems op. 36 (R)
[Rabindranath Tagore]
When and Why? — Defamation — Paper Boats — Sympathy — The Gift
Paris, 1916
Publisher: (Composers' Music Corporation) Fischer
Dedication and/or commission: Madeleine Koechlin
First performance: 1919. SMI, Paris. voice: J. Bathori
Duration: 13 min

Chansons bas op. 44
[Mallarmé]
Le savetier — La marchande d'herbes aromatiques — Le cantonnier — Le marchand
    d'ail et d'oignons — La femme de l'ouvrier — Le vitrier — Le crieur d'imprimés —
    La marchande d'habits
See Unpublished works (Verso Carioca)
Rio de Janeiro, 1917
Publisher: (Sirène) Eschig
Dedication and/or commission: Mrs. Audrey Parr
First performance: 30 March 1919. Théâtre Vieux Colombier, Paris. voice: J. Bathori,
    piano: D. Milhaud
Duration: 4 min 15 s

Deux petits airs op. 51
[Mallarmé]
Indomptablement a dû — Quelconque une solitude
Rio de Janeiro, 1918
Publisher: Eschig
Dedication and/or commission: Vera Janacopoulos
First performance: 7 December 1921. Conc. Heure Musicale, Paris
Duration: 2 min 5 s

Les soirées de Petrograde op. 55 (R)
[René Chalupt]
I. L'ancien régime: L'orgueilleuse — La révoltée — La martiale — L'infidèle — La
    perverse — L'irresolue
II. La révolution: La grand'mère de la révolution — Les journées d'août — Monsieur
    Protopopoff — Le convive — La limousine — Le Colonel Romanoff
Paris, 1919
Publisher: Durand
Dedication and/or commission: Valentine Gross
First performance: 24 June 1919. Gala Avant Garde, Galerie Barbazange
Duration: 10 min

Trois poèmes de Jean Cocteau op. 59 (R)
Fumée — Fête de Bordeaux — Fête de Montmartre
See Piano, easy pieces (Enfantines)
Paris, 1920
Publisher: (Sirène) Eschig
Dedication and/or commission: Erik Satie
First performance: December 1922. Galerie Montaigne, Paris. voice: P. Bertin
Duration: 2 min 30 s

Catalogue de fleurs op. 60 (R)
[Lucien Daudet]
La violette — Le bégonia — Les fritillaires — Les jacinthes — Les crocus — Le
  brachycome — L'eremurus
See Solo voice, with chamber ensemble
Aix, April 1920
Publisher: Durand
Dedication and/or commission: A la mémoire de Fauconnet
First performance: 1922. Conservatoire de Paris. voice: M. Martine
Duration: 5 min 20 s

Poème op. 73
[From the diary of Léo Latil]
Paris, 1921
Publisher: Eschig
Dedication and/or commission: Madame Olénine d'Alheim
First performance: 1922. Paris. voice: O. d'Alheim
Duration: 4 min 30 s

Six chants populaires hébraïques op. 86 (R)
[Popular texts]
La séparation — Le chant du veilleur — Chant de délivrance — Berceuse — Gloire à
  Dieu — Chant hassidique
See Solo voice, with orchestra
Paris, 1925
Publisher: Heugel
Dedication and/or commission: Madeleine Grey (La séparation), André de Groote
  (Le chant du veilleur), Marya Freund (Chant de délivrance), S. (Berceuse), Arthur
  Honegger (Gloire à Dieu), Jane Bathori (Chant hassidique)
First performance: 19 March 1925. Paris. voice: M. Grey
Duration: 10 min 50 s

Deux hymnes op. 88
[Albert Cohen]
Hymne de Sion — Israël est vivant
See Large orchestra, misc.
Paris, 1925
Publisher: U.E.
Dedication and/or commission: Chaïm Weizmann (Hymne de Sion), Victor Jacobson
  (Israël est vivant)
First performance: 1926. Paris. voice: J. Bathori
Duration: 3 min

Prières journalières à l'usage des juifs du Comtat Venaissin op. 96
[liturgical texts]
Prière du matin — Prière de l'après-midi — Prière du soir
Aix-Paris, 1927
Publisher: Heugel
Dedication and/or commission: Jane Bathori (Prière du matin), Armand Lunel
    (Prière de l'après-midi), Madame Fernand Halphen (Prière du soir)
First performance: 3 March 1928. Paris. voice: J. Bathori, piano: D. Milhaud
Duration: 7 min 36 s

Liturgie comtadine op. 125
(Cinq chants de Rosch Haschana)
[Liturgical texts]
See Solo voice, with orchestra
Paris-Aix, 1933
Publisher: Heugel
First performance: June 1934. Ecole Normale, Paris. Conductor: R. Desormière,
    voice: F. Holley
Duration: 6 min

Deux chansons op. 128d
[Gustave Flaubert]
Chanson de l'avengle — Chanson du printemps
See Music for films (Madame Bovary)
Paris, 1933
Publisher: Enoch
Dedication and/or commission: Roger Desormière
Duration: 2 min 35 s

Trois chansons de négresse op. 148b
[Jules Supervielle]
Mon histoire — Abandonnée — Sans feu ni lieu
See Incidental music (Bolivar); Solo voice, with orchestra
Malines, 1935–1936
Publisher: (Deiss) Salabert
Dedication and/or commission: M.D.M.
First performance: 17 June 1937. Paris. voice: M. Grey
Duration: 6 min

Six chansons de théâtre op. 151b (R)
See Incidental music (I, II: 'Tu ne m'échapperas jamais'; III, IV: 'La première famille';
    V, VI: 'La folle du ciel')
Paris, 1936
Publisher: Heugel

Trois chansons de troubadour op. 152b
[Valmy-Baisse]
See Incidental music (Bertran de Born)
Paris, May 1936
Publisher: Salabert
Dedication and/or commission: Pierre Bernac
Duration: 5 min 45 s

Cinq chansons op. 167 (R)
[Charles Vildrac]
Les quatre petits lions — Poupette et Patata — La pomme et l'escargot — Le malpropre — Le jardinier impatient
See Solo voice, with orchestra
Paris, 1936–1937
Publisher: (Deiss) Salabert
Dedication and/or commission: D.D.M.
First performance: 1938. Radio d'Etat, Paris. voice: M. Grey
Duration: 12 min

Chansons du carnaval de Londres op. 171b
[Based on 'The Beggar's Opera,' by John Gay, translated by H. Fluchère]
See Solo voice, with orchestra; Incidental music (Chansons de l'opera du gueux)
Paris, 1937
Publisher: Salabert

Chanson du capitaine;
La java de la femme op. 173b
[Jean-Richard Bloch]
See Incidental music (Naissance d'une cité)
Aix, 1937
Publisher: (Deiss) Salabert
Dedication and/or commission: Gilles et Julien (Chanson du capitaine), M.D.M. (La java de la femme)
Duration: 7 min 10 s

Holem tsaudi—Gam hayom op. 179
(Harmonization of a popular Palestinian tune)
Aix, 1937
Publisher: Masada-Nigun

Le voyage d'été op. 216 (R)
[Camille Paliard]
Modestes vacances — Les deux hôtels — Le boulanger — La maison inachevée — Monsieur le curé — Les trois peupliers — Paresse — Les conscrits — Le château — L'horizon — Le pêcheur — Le ruisseau — La petite bergère — Les champignons — Le retour
Aix, 16–20 April 1940
Publisher: Heugel
First performance: 27 December 1940. League of Composers, New York, voice: M. Denya, piano: D. Milhaud
Duration: 16 min 41 s

Quatre chansons de Ronsard op. 223
A une fontaine — A cupidon — Tais-toi, babillarde! — Dieu vous garde
See Solo voice, with orchestra
Mills, 24–29 January 1940–18 October 1941
Publisher: B.&H.
Dedication and/or commission: Lily Pons
Duration: 8 min 40 s

Rêves op. 233
[Anonymous 20th century texts]
Les marronniers — Toi — Confidence — Le mistral — 'Long Distance' — Jeunesse
Mills, 1942
Publisher: Heugel
Dedication and/or commission: Jane Bathori
First performance: 1945. Radio Belge, Brussels. voice: Hudsyn, piano: P. Collaer
Duration: 6 min 14 s

La libération des Antilles op. 246
[Two songs on Creole texts adapted by Alice Joyau-Dormoy]
Bonjour, messieurs les libérateurs! — Trois ans de souffrance
Mills, 21–23 July 1944
Publisher: (Leeds, M.C.A.) Bel. M.
Dedication and/or commission: Henri et Hélène Hoppenot
Duration: 8 min 16 s

Chants de misère op. 265
[Camille Paliard]
Cet hiver — Cette douleur — Silence du fond de l'allée — Tant de vagabonds
Mills, 19–20 March 1946
Publisher: Heugel
Dedication and/or commission: M.D.M. pour sa fête
First performance: November 1946. Radio-France. voice M. Dax
Duration: 7 min 50 s

Trois poèmes op. 276
[Jules Supervielle]
Ce peu . . . — Compagnons du silence — Ce bruit de la mer
Mills, 30–31 March 1947
Publisher: Heugel
Dedication and/or commission: Madeleine Grey
First performance: 3 November 1947. Paris. voice: M. Grey
Duration: 7 min 5 s

Ballade nocturne op. 296 (R)
(Incl. in a collection commemorating the Chopin centennial)
[Louise de Vilmorin]
Mills, July 1949
Publisher: Heugel
Dedication and/or commission: Doda Conrad
First performance: October 1949. Town Hall, New York. voice: D. Conrad
Duration: 2 min 10 s

Petites légendes op. 319 (R)
[Maurice Carême, English translation by Rollo Myers]
Premier recueil: Sortilèges — Les feuilles — L'amoureux — La prière — La dormeuse
— La peine
Deuxième recueil: La chance — Le lièvre et le blé — La bise — Destinée — Le beau
navire — Le charme
Aspen, 4–11 August 1952
Publisher: Heugel
Dedication and/or commission: François Heugel (Premier recueil), Philippe (Heugel)
et Gigi (Deuxième recueil)
First performance: 25 September 1952. Aspen Institute. voice: A. Bollinger, piano: V.
Babin
Duration: Premier recueil 9 min 8 s; Deuxième recueil 7 min 2 s

Fontaines et sources op. 352 (R)
[Francis Jammes]
La fontaine de Lestapis — Fontaine sainte — La source qui filtre — La grande cascade
de Gavarnie — Source au pied de Maubec — Source
See Solo voice, with orchestra
Paris, 11–14 February 1956
Publisher: P. Marconi
Dedication and/or commission: J. Micheau
Duration: 7 min 50 s

Tristesses op. 355
[Francis Jammes, English translation by Rollo Myers]
Prélude — Je la désire . . . — Elle etait déscendue — Dans le chemin toujours trempé
— Elle est gravement gaie — Parfois je suis triste — Un poète disait . . . — Son
souvenir emplit l'air — Elle avait emporté — Si tout ceci . . . — Je ne désire point —
Ô mon coeur — Nous nous aimerons tant — Faisait-il beau — Je garde une médaille
— J'ai quelqu'un dans le coeur — Vous m'avez regardé — Je songe à ce jour-là —
Les lilas qui avaient fleuri — Deux ancolies se balançaient — Parce que j'ai souffert
— Venez sous la tonnelle — Venez, ma bien-aimée — Demain fera un an
Paris, 20 May–9 June 1956
Publisher: Heugel
Dedication and/or commission: Madeleine
First performance: 1956, Aspen Festival. voice: M. Harrell, piano; V. Babin
Duration: 40 min

L'amour chante op. 409
Le vrai amour [J. du Bellay] — J'aime [A. de Musset] — Sonnet [L. Labbé] — De sa
peine et des beautés de sa dame [J. du Bellay] — Moins je la vois [M. Scève] —
Nevermore [P. Verlaine] — Veillées [A. Rimbaud] — Plusieurs de leurs corps
dénués [P. de Ronsard] — Le lai du chèvrefeuille [Marie de France]
Aspen, 20–29 July 1964
Publisher: Presser
Dedication and/or commission: Alice Esty (comm.)
First performance: 22 April 1965. Lincoln Center, New York. voice: A. Esty
Duration: 13 min 35 s

Solo voice: pieces for children _____

Récréation op. 195
[J. Kriéger]
Pas bien grand — Haut comme trois pommes — La tortue naine — Il faut obéir
Paris, 22 October 1938
Publisher: Heugel
Dedication and/or commission: Daniel
Duration: 1 min 55 s

Solo voice: with organ (or piano) _____

Cinq prières op. 231c (R)
[Latin liturgical texts adopted by Paul Claudel]
See Incidental music (L'annonce faite à Marie — 2nd version)
Mills, 10–16 March 1942
Publisher: Heugel
Dedication and/or commission: M.D.M.
Duration: 8 min 55 s

Solo voice: with chamber ensemble _____

See also Quartets, string (Troisième quatuor)

Machines agricoles op. 56
Pastorales pour chant
[Words taken from a catalogue]
La moissonneuse Espigadora — La faucheuse — La lieuse — La déchaumeuse-
   semeuse-enfouisseuse — La fouilleuse-draineuse — La faneuse
Aix, 1919
Fl, cl, bn, vln, va, vc, cb.
Publisher: U.E.
Dedication and/or commission: J. Cocteau (La moissonneuse Espigadora), L. Durey
   (La faucheuse), F. Poulenc (La lieuse), A. Honegger (La déchaumeuse-semeuse-
   enfouisseuse), G. Auric (La fouilleuse-draineuse), G. Tailleferre (La faneuse)
First performance: 11 March 1920. Conc. Sect. d'Or, Paris. Conductor: F. Delgrange,
   voice: Madame Vié
Duration: 12 min

Catalogue de fleurs op. 60 (R)
La violette — Le begonia — Les fritillaires — Les jacinthes — Les crocus — Le brachycome — L'eremurus
[Lucien Daudet]
See Solo voice, with piano
Aix, 1920
Fl, cl, bn, vln, va, vc, cb.
Publisher: Durand
Dedication and/or commission: à la mémoire de Fauconnet
First performance: 1932. Paris. Conductor: R. Desormière, voice: M. Martine
Duration: 5 min 20 s

Caramel mou (Shimmy) op. 68
[Jean Coteau]
See Piano, solo; Chamber ensembles, misc.
Aix, 1920
Cl, tpt, tbn, piano
Publisher: Eschig
Dedication and/or commission: Georges Auric
First performance: May 1921. Spec. Th. Bouffe, Paris. Conductor: V. Golschmann (danced by Gratton)
Duration: 3 min 14 s

Cocktail op. 69
[Larsen]
Paris, 1920
3 cl.
Publisher: (Almanach de Cocagne: Sirène)
First performance: 1920. Galerie Barbazange, Paris. voice: P. Bertin

Quatre poemes de Catulle op. 80
La femme que j'aime — Voilà où mon âme en est venue — Ma chère, aimons-nous — Ma chérie en presence de son mari
Aix, 1923
Vln.
Publisher: Heugel
Dedication: Heugel
Dedication and/or commission: S.
First performance: October 1923. Paris. voice: V. Janacopoulos, vln: Y. Astruc
Duration: 3 min 5 s

Couronne de gloire op. 211
[Hebrew text by Rabbi Salomon, son of Gabirol, translated by Mardochée Venture &
  Armand Lunel]
Couronne de gloire — Prière pour les âmes des persecutés — Couronne de gloire —
  Prière pour le Pape — Couronne de gloire — Prière pour le jour de réclusion —
  Couronne de gloire — Prière pour la paix et pour la France
Aix, January–March 1940
Fl, tpt, 2 vln, va, vc.
Publisher: Edit. Trans.
Dedication and/or commission: Pour le centenaire de la Synagogue d'Aix en Provence
First performance: 28 June 1954. INR, Brussels. Orchestre INR. Conductor: D.
  Milhaud, voice: Van der Weyden
Duration: 23 min

Adieu op. 410
[Excerpt from 'Une saison en enfer' by Arthur Rimbaud]
Aspen, 16–26 August 1964
Fl, va, harp.
Publisher: Elkan Vogel-Presser
Dedication and/or commission: Cathy Berberian
First performance: 1964. Palermo. voice: C. Berberian
Duration: 9 min

Solo voice: with orchestra _____

Psaume 129 op. 53b
[Translated by P. Claudel]
See Solo voice, with orchestra (Cantate de psaumes);
Transcriptions (De profundis)
New York, 1919
2.1.2.1.–0.1.0.0.–P.H.S.
Publisher: U.E.

Six chants populaires hébraïques op. 86
See Solo voice, with piano
Paris, 1925
2.2.2.2.–2.2.2.0.–T.P.S.
Publisher: Heugel
Duration: 10 min 50 s

Liturgie comtadine op. 125 (R)
(Cinq chants de Rosch Haschana)
[Liturgical texts]
See Solo voice, with piano
Paris-Aix, 1933
2.1.2.1.–0.1.0.0.–P.H.S.
Publisher: Heugel
First performance: 1934. Paris. Conductor: R. Desormière, voice: F. Hollay
Duration: 6 min

Trois chansons de négresse op. 148c
[Jules Supervielle]
Mon histoire — Abandonnée — Sans feu ni lieu
See Solo voice, with piano; Incidental music (Bolivar)
Malines-Paris, 1936–1937
1.0.1.0.–0.2.1.1.–sax–P.H.S.
Publisher: Salabert
Dedication and/or commission: M.D.M.
Duration: 6 min

Cinq chansons op. 167
[Charles Vildrac]
Les quatre petits lions — Poupette et Patata — La pomme et l'escargot — Le
    malpropre — Le jardinier impatient
Paris, 1937
See Solo voice, with piano
1.1.2.1.–0.2.1.0.–sax–P.H.S.
Publisher: Salabert
Dedication and/or commission: D.D.M.
Duration: 6 min

Cantate nuptiale op. 168
[Based on 'The Song of Songs']
Modéré — Animé — Lent — Vif
Paris, 31 August 1937
2.2.2.2.–2.2.2.0.–T.P.H.S.
Publisher: (Deiss) Salabert
Dedication and/or commission: A mes parents pour leurs noces d'or
First performance: 3 August 1937. Radio Marseille. Conductor: D. Milhaud, voice: E.
    Fels-Noth
Duration: 10 min

Chansons du carnaval de Londres op. 171b
[Based on 'The Beggar's Opera,' by John Gay, translated by H. Fluchère]
See Solo voice, with piano; Incidental music (Chansons de l'opera du gueux)
Paris, 1937
1.1.1.1.–0.1.1.0.–sax–P.H.S.
Publisher: Salabert
First performance: 28 September 1964. Radio Marseille. Conductor: D. Milhaud

Quatre chansons de Ronsard op. 223 (R)
A une fontaine — A cupidon — Tais-toi, babillarde! — Dieu vous garde
See Solo voice, with piano
Mills, 18 October 1941
2.2.2.2.–2.2.2.0.–P.S.
Publisher: B.&H.
Dedication and/or commission: L. Pons
First performance: December 1941. Waldorf Astoria, New York. Conductor: A.
    Kostelanetz, voice: Lily Pons
Duration: 8 min 30 s

Les quatre elements op. 189b (R)
L'eau — La terre — Le feu — L'air
(New version: solo soprano)
[Robert Desnos]
See Two voices, with orchestra
Paris, 1956
2.2.2.2.–2.2.2.0.–T.P.H.S.
Publisher: P. Marconi
Dedication and/or commission: Janine Micheau
Duration: 5 min 30 s

Fontaines et sources op. 352 (R)
[Francis Jammes]
La fontaine Lestapis — Fontaine sainte — La source qui filtre — La grande cascade de
   Gavarnie — Source au pied de Maubec — Source
See Solo voice, with piano
Paris, 11–14 February 1956
2.2.2.2.–2.2.2.0.–P.H.S.
Publisher: P. Marconi
Dedication and/or commission: Janine Micheau
Duration: 7 min 50 s

Cantate de psaumes op. 425
[Psalms 129, 145, 147, 136, 128, 127 translated by Paul Claudel]
See Solo voice, with orchestra (Psaume 129); Accompanied vocal ensemble, soloists,
   mixed chorus & orchestra (Psaume 136)
Aspen-Paris, 10 August–28 September 1967
2.1.2.1.–0.1.0.0.–P.H.S.
Publisher: U.E.
Dedication and/or commission: Pour le centenaire de Paul Claudel
First performance: 1968. Radio France. Conductor: D. Chabrun, voice: R. Steffner
(Includes op. 53)

Spoken voice, with chamber ensemble

Cantate de l'enfant et de la mère op. 185 (R)
[Maurice Carême]
Trelex-Paris, January 1938
1st version: piano, 2 vln, va, vc.
2nd version: piano, fl, cl, vln, vc.
Publisher: Heugel
Dedication and/or commission: P. Collaer et Quatuor Pro Arte
First performance: 18 May 1938. Palais des Beaux Arts, Brussels. Pro Arte Quartet,
   piano: P. Collaer, narr: M. Milhaud (1st version); 1941. Juilliard School of Music,
   New York. narr: M. Milhaud (2nd version)
Duration: 9 min 35 s

Suite de quatrains op. 398 (R)

[Francis Jammes]

Première partie: Le citron — Sur une capucine — Belle-de-jour — La paternité du chêne — La bergeronnette — La rose de Jericho

Deuxième partie: L'automne — Pénitente — Le don — Dialogue — Frappées — Une enfant

Troisième partie: Partie liée — La leçon de calcul — Le dieu muet — La joueuse — Anciennes grandes vacances — Le retardataire

Aspen, 24 July–6 August 1962

Fl, bs cl, sax, harp, vln, vc, cb.

Publisher: Salabert

First performance: June 1963. Festival Mills. Conductor: D. Milhaud, narr: M. Milhaud

Duration: 12 min

For other works using the spoken voice see also Accompanied vocal ensemble, vocal quartet & chamber ensemble (Cantate pour l'inauguration du Musée de l'Homme); Accompanied vocal ensemble, soloists, mixed chorus, & organ (Borechou, Schema Israël; Kaddish; Service sacré); Accompanied vocal ensemble, mixed chorus, orchestra (Miracles de la foi; La sagesse; Service sacré; Le mariage de la feuille et du cliché; Ani maamin); Unpublished works (Caïn et Abel; L'choh dodi).

Two voices

Two voices: with strings ———————————————————————

Trois élégies op. 199

Dis-moi, dis-moi — Sur le sable des allées — Mon amour, disais-tu

[Francis Jammes]

Paris, 1939

Sop, ten, S(5.5.4.3.2.)

Publisher: B.&H.

Dedication and/or commission: Clovis, Steele (comm.)

First performance: 7 December 1980. Festival d'Orleans, Nouv. Orch. Philh. de Radio France. Conductor: S. Cambreling, sop: J. Chamonin, ten: J.-P. Chevalier

Two voices: with orchestra ———————————————————————

Prends cette rose op. 183

[Ronsard]

Paris, 1937

Sop, ten, 2.2.2.2.–2.2.2.0.–T.P.H.S.

Publisher: B.&H.

Dedication and/or commission: Clovis, Steele (comm.)

First performance: April 1937. OSP, Paris. Conductor: J. Morel, voice: Clovis, Steele

Duration: 4 min

Les quatre elements op. 189
[Robert Desnos]
L'eau — La terre — Le feu — L'air
See Solo voice, with orchestra
Aix, Easter 1938
Publisher: P. Marconi-Billaudot
Dedication and/or commission: duo Clovis-Steele
First performance: February 1939. Paris. Conductor: D. Milhaud, vo: Clovis-Steele
Duration: 7 min 50 s
This version is no longer in existence.

Hommage à Comenius op. 421
[Comenius]
Le soleil — L'instruction universelle
Aspen, 5–28 August 1966
Sop, bar, 2.2.2.2.–2.2.2.1.–T.P.H.S.
Publisher: Eschig
Dedication and/or commission: pour le 20e anniversaire de l'UNESCO., comm. Etat
First performance: 15 November 1966. ORTF, Paris. Conductor: M. Rosenthal
Duration: 17 min

A cappella ensemble

A cappella ensemble: women's quartet (or chorus) ————————————————

Deux élégies romaines op. 114
[Goethe, translated by J.-P. Samson]
Eclaire donc, gamin—Pourquoi donc?
Paris, 4 February 1932
Publisher: (Deiss) Salabert
Dedication and/or commission: Suzanne Peignot
First performance: April 1933. Conc. Sérénade, Paris. vocal quartet: S. Peignot
Duration: 2 min 50 s

Devant sa main nue op. 122
[Marcel Raval]
Paris, 1933
Publisher: (Deiss) Salabert
Dedication and/or commission: M.D.M.
First performance: 4 February 1933. Conc. Sérénade, Paris. vocal quartet: S. Peignot
Duration: 4 min 15 s

A cappella ensemble: mixed quartet (or chorus) _____

Deux poèmes op. 39 (R)
Eloge [Saint Léger Léger] — Le brick [René Chalupt]
Paris, 1916 (Eloge), 1919 (Le brick)
Publisher: Durand
Dedication and/or commission: Marquise de Casa-Fuerte
First performance: May 1921. Paris. vocal quartet Vié
Duration: 4 min 22 s

Deux poèmes de Cendrars op. 113 (R)
La danse des animaux — Le chant de la mort
Paris, 1932
Publisher: (Deiss) Salabert
Dedication and/or commission: Pour la League of Composers
First performance: April 1933. League of Composers, New York
Duration: 3 min 25 s

Cantique du Rhône op. 155 (R)
[Paul Claudel, English translation by M. Farquhar]
Qu'il est beau . . . — Ah! qu'il la prenne déracinée . . . Et le bonheur . . . Il faut bien
   des montagnes . . .
Aix, September 1936
Publisher: Elkan Vogel-Presser
Dedication and/or commission: M.D.M., pour les Chanteurs de Lyon
First performance: 2 January 1937. Conc. Sérénade, Paris. Les Chanteurs de Lyon
Duration: 9 min

Six sonnets composés au secret op. 266 (R)
[Jean Cassou]
La barque funéraire — Mort à toute fortune — A peine si le coeur — Bois cette tasse
   de ténèbres — C'était une chanson — Quel est ton nom?
Mills, 8–14 April 1946
Publisher: Heugel
Dedication and/or commission: comm. du groupe de Bâle de la SIMC
First performance: 9 February 1947. Internat. Gesellschaft für Neue Musik, Bâle.
   Conductor W. Aeschbachen, Salvatti Quartet
Duration: 12 min 30 s

Deux poèmes op. 347
[Louise de Vilmorin]
Fado (fantaisie) — L'alphabet des aveux
Aspen, 1955
Publisher: Heugel
Duration: 4 min 20 s

A cappella ensemble: men's chorus _____

Psaume 126* op. 72 (R)
[Translated by Paul Claudel]
Paris, 1921
Publisher: U.E.
Dedication and/or commission: Harvard Glee Club
First performance: 1922. Harvard Glee Club, New York. Conductor: Davison
Duration: 4 min 50 s
*The printed score designates this work as 'Psaume 121.'

Incantations op. 201
[Aztec poems, adapted by Alejo Carpentier]
Invocation du pêcheur à son filet — Invocation pour conjurer la fureur des abeilles —
    Invocation pour vaincre les ennemis
Paris-Versailles, 27 April–1 June 1939
Publisher: Eschig
Dedication and/or commission: The Hague Singers
First performance: 5 June 1945. Orpheus Soc., Oakland. Conductor: M. Jones
Duration: 7 min 30 s

A cappella ensemble: mixed chorus _____

Cantate de la paix op. 166 (R)
[Paul Claudel, English translation by H. Torrey]
Paris, May 1937
Men's and children's chorus
Publisher: Schirmer
Dedication and/or commission: pour le 100e anniversaire de Briand, à la
    Manécanterie des Petits Chanteurs à la Croix de Bois
First performance: June 1937. La Sorbonne, Paris. Les Petits Chanteurs à la Croix de
    Bois. Conductor: Abbé Maillet
Duration: 9 min 40 s

Main tendue à tous op. 169 (R)
[Charles Vildrac]
Mayens de Sion, July 1937
Publisher: (E.S.I.) Ch. du M.
First performance: 12 July 1937. Congres L.I.C.A., Paris. Féd. de mus. populaire
Duration: 4 min

Les deux cités op. 170 (R)
[Paul Claudel, English translation by H. Torrey]
Aix, August 1937
Publisher: Schirmer
Dedication and/or commission: L'Abbé Maillet et les Petits Chanteurs à la Croix de Bois
First performance: Holy Week 1938. Conc. Sérénade, Saint-Etienne du Mont, Paris. Les Petits Chanteurs à la Croix de Bois. Conductor: Abbé Maillet
Duration: 13 min 5 s

Quatrains valaisans op. 206 (R)
[Rainer Maria Rilke]
Pays arrêté à mi-chemin — Rose de lumière — L'année tourne — Chemins — Beau papillon
Mayens de Sion, 20–21 July 1939
Publisher: Heugel
Dedication and/or commission: Georges Haenni et 'La Chanson Valaisanne'
First performance: 1948. Maison pensée française, Paris. Choeur Populaire de Paris. Conductor: F. Lamy
Duration: 3 min 30 s

Cantate de la guerre op. 213 (R)
[Paul Claudel, English translation by H. Torrey]
Choeur du peuple criminel — Vox domini — Choeur des martyrs — L'heure de Dieu
Aix, February 1940
Publisher: Schirmer
Dedication and/or commission: Abbé Maillet
First performance: 16 May 1947. Oregon University, Eugene. University a cappella Choir. Conductor: D. W. Allton
Duration: 10 min 45 s

Naissance de Vénus op. 292 (R)
(Cantata)
[Jules Supervielle, English translation by R. Myers]
Les heures — Venus — Le vent — Les heures
Mills, 1949
Publisher: Heugel
Dedication and/or commission: Marcel Couraud et son ensemble
First performance: 30 November 1949. Radio France. Ensemble Marcel Couraud. Conductor: M. Couraud
Duration: 5 min

Trois psaumes de David op. 339 (R)
(Alternating Gregorian Chant and four-part polyphony)
Psaume 51 (Vulgate 50) — Psaume 150 — Psaume 114 et 115 (Vulgate 113)
Mills, 17–21 October 1954
Publisher: Eschig
Dedication and/or commission: Au Révérand Père David Nicholson O.S.B., aux
    moines bénédictins de Mount Angel (Oregon) et à mon très cher ami le Révérand
    Père Clément Jacob O.S.B.
First performance: 1 May 1955. Stanford University. University Chorus. Conductor:
    H. Schmidt
Duration: 15 min 45 s

Huit poèmes de Jorge Guillen op. 371
[Translated by M. Pomes]
Elevacion de la claridad (Elévation de la clarté) — Presencia del aire (Présence de
    l'air) — Primavera delgada (Printemps délié) — Las doce en el reloj (Midi) —
    Advenimiento (Evènement) — Viento saltado (Dans le vent) — Muchachas
    (Jeunes filles) — La persona (La personne)
Aspen, 25 July–21 August 1958
Publisher: Heugel
Dedication and/or commission: comm. choeur de RIAS
First performance: 5 November 1958. Conc. Xe anniversaire choeur RIAS, Berlin.
    Chorus: RIAS.
Duration: 14 min 40 s

Traversée op. 393
[Paul Verlaine]
Paris, 10–12 November 1961
Publisher: Salabert
Dedication and/or commission: comm. Festival Cork
First performance: 17 May 1962. Cork, Ireland. Madrigal RTF. Conductor: Y.
    Gouverné
Duration: 6 min 15 s

Promesse de Dieu op. 438
Isaïe 54 — Isaïe 65 — Isaïe 62 — Ezechiel 36
Paris, 26 December 1971–25 January 1972
Publisher: Eschig
Dedication and/or commission: comm. Dickinson College pour son 200e anniversaire
First performance: 19 May 1973. Dickinson College, Carlisle, Pennsylvania
Duration: 10 min 15 s

Les momies d'Egypte op. 439
(Choral Comedy)
[Régnard]
Geneva, 18 February–12 March 1972
Publisher: U.E.
Dedication and/or commission: comm. Radio Graz
First performance: 26 October 1972. Radio Graz
Duration: 20 min

Accompanied vocal ensemble

Accompanied vocal ensemble: vocal quartet & chamber ensemble

L'annonce faite à Marie op. 117
[Paul Claudel]
See Incidental music (opus 117 and opus 231)
Aix, 1932
2 fl, ob, 2 sax, 2 ond Mart, vib, T.P.S. organ, piano 4 hands.
Publisher: (Deiss) Salabert
Dedication and/or commission: M.D.M.
First performance: 23 November 1933. Concert Doucet. Conductor: M. Abravanel
Duration: 19 min

Adages op. 120b
[André de Richaud]
See Duos, ondes Martenot & piano (Suite); Incidental music (Le château des papes)
Aix, 1932
Fl, cl, bn, hn, vln, va, vc, cb.
Publisher: (Deiss) Salabert
First performance: January 1934. Cité Universitaire, Pavillon Hellén., Paris. Bathori Vocal Quartet
Duration: 13 min 45 s

Pan et la Syrinx op. 130
(Cantata)
Nocturne I — Pan et Syrinx [de Piis] — Nocturne II — L'invention de la gamme [Paul Claudel] — Nocturne III — La danse de Pan [Paul Claudel]
Paris-Malines-Aix, 1934
Sop, bar, vocal quartet, fl, ob/eng hn, sax, bn, piano.
Publisher: (Deiss) Salabert
First performance: November 1934. Conc. Pro Arte, Brussels. Conductor: F. André
Duration: 15 min

Les amours de Ronsard op. 132 (R)
La rose — La tourterelle — L'aubépin — Le rossignol
See Accompanied vocal ensemble, mixed chorus & orchestra
Aix, 1934
Fl, cl, bs, hn, vln, va, vc, cb, piano.
Publisher: (Deiss) Salabert
Dedication and/or commission: A la mémoire de Claude Debussy
First performance: 4 July 1935. His Majesty's Theater, London (danced by Alanova)
Duration: 11 min 7 s

Cantate pour l'inauguration du Musée de l'Homme op. 164
[Robert Desnos]
Paris, June 1937
Spoken voice, fl, ob, sax, bn, perc, piano
Publisher: Salabert
Dedication and/or commission: Vicomte et Vicomtesse Charles de Noailles (comm.)
First performance: 11 October 1937. Radio Paris. Conductor, M. Rosenthal
Duration: 20 min

Suite de sonnets op. 401
(Cantate sur des vers du XVIe siecle)
Prélude I — Jeux rustiques d'un vanneur de blé [Joachim du Bellay] — Prélude II —
    J'aime le vert laurier [Etienne Jodelle] — Prélude III — Bienheureux est celui
    [Olivier de Magny] — Prélude IV — A Venus pour la paix [Amadis Jamyn]
Mills, 27 February–13 March 1963
Sop, high contraten, ten, bas, fl, ob, bn, tmb, va, hpd.
Publisher: Eschig
Dedication and/or commission: A la chère mémoire de Francis Poulenc, comm.
    ORTF
First performance: 25 July 1963. Festival Dieppe. Ensemble Ravier
Duration: 17 min

Accompanied vocal ensemble: five voices & orchestra _____

Le retour de l'enfant prodigue op. 42 (R)
(Cantata)
[André Gide]
See Reductions
Rio de Janeiro, 1917
Mez, ten, 3 bar, 2.2.2.1.–1.1.1.0.–T.H.S. (2.2.2.2.1.)
Publisher: U.E.
Dedication and/or commission: Paul Claudel
First performance: 23 November 1922. Conc. Wiéner. Conductor: D. Milhaud
Duration: 42 min

Accompanied vocal ensemble: three-part women's chorus & chamber ensemble _____

Cantata from Proverbs op. 310 (R)
[Biblical text]
Who crieth: 'Woe' ? (L'ivrognerie et ses suites, Proverbs XXIII: 29–35) — The
   Woman Folly (Banquet de la folie, Proverbs IX: 13–18) — The Woman of Valour
   (La femme forte, Proverbs XXXI: 10–31)
Mills, 1951
Harp, ob, vc.
Publisher: Mercury-Presser
Dedication and/or commission: The United Temple Chorus. Ernest Bloch Award
   (comm.)
First performance: 18 May 1951. Lawrence High School, New York. United Temple
   Choir. Conductor: Freed
Duration: 9 min 50 s

Accompanied vocal ensemble: women's chorus & orchestra _____

Invocation à l'ange Raphaël op. 395
[Paul Claudel]
Quel est-ce paysage désolé? — Dieu connait ses brebis — Douleur, douleur à l'orient
   — Et quels sont ces tourbillons de noire fumée?
Paris, January–February 1962
2.2.3.3.–2.2.2.0.–T.P.S.
Publisher: Eschig
Dedication and/or commission: comm. ORTF. Pour 'La Maîtrise'
First performance: 31 May 1962. Paris. Orchestre Radio Française. Conductor: P.
   Dervaux, chorus: La Maîtrise
Duration: 14 min

Accompanied vocal ensemble: mixed chorus & orchestra (or chamber ensemble) ____

See also Large orchestra, symphonies [Troisième symphonie (Te Deum)]

Cantate pour louer le Seigneur op. 103
(Psalms 117, 121, 123, 150)
Aix, 1928
Mixed chorus and children's chorus 1.1.1.1.–1.1.1.0.–T.P.S.–organ
Publisher: U.E.
Dedication and/or commission: Louis de Vocht
First performance: June 1929. Cloître Aix-en-Provence. Conductor: Chanoine Cellier
Duration: 10 min

La mort d'un tyran op. 116 (R)
[Lampride, Diderot]
Paris, 1932
Picc, cl, tu, 6 perc.
Publisher: (E.S.I.) Ch. du M.
First performance: 25 May 1933. Conc. Sérénade, Paris. Conductor: R. Desormière
    (danced by Alanova)
Duration: 6 min 10 s

Les amours de Ronsard op. 132
La rose — La tourterelle — L'aubépin — Le rossignol
See Accompanied vocal ensemble, vocal quartet, & chamber ensemble
Aix, 1934
Fl, cl, bs, hn, vln, va, vc, cb
Publisher: (Deiss) Salabert
Dedication and/or commission: A la mémoire de Claude Debussy
Duration: 11 min 7 s

Magali op. 194 (R)
(Provençal folk song)
Paris, 1938
1.1.1.1.–1.2.1.0.–T.S.
Publisher: (E.S.I.) Ch. du M.
First performance: June 1938. Conc. E.S.I., Paris. Conductor: R. Desormière
Duration: 1 min 40 s

Barba Garibo op. 298
(Divertissement on Menton folk tunes)
[Armand Lunel]
Berceuse — Barba Garibo — Saint-Jean, Saint-Jean — Rassemblons-nous clocher —
    Le petit corbillon au bras — Le romarin fleuri — Le pâtre — Gian Braghetta — Un,
    deux, trois (final) — Salut au public et retraite
See Ballets (La cueillette des citrons)
Paris, 4 December 1949–13 January 1950
2.2.2.2.–2.2.2.0.–T.P.S.
Publisher: Heugel
Dedication and/or commission: Daniel, comm. Radio France
First performance: 19 February 1950. 'La Fête du citron,' Menton. Orch. Radio
    Symph. and 'La chanson mentonnaise' chorus. Conductor: E. Bigot
Duration: 20 min 40 s

Le château de feu op. 338 (R)
[Jean Cassou]
Mills, 1–17 October 1954
3.3.3.3.–0.2.2.0.–T.P.–va, vc. cb.
Publisher: Eschig
Dedication and/or commission: Dédié à la mémoire de mon neveu
   Jean Milhaud et à celle d'Eric et d'Hélène Allatini, deportés pendant la guerre
   1939–1945 et assassinés par les allemands. Ecrit à la demande du Réseau du
   Souvenir.
First performance: 30 November 1955. Palais Chaillot, Paris. Orch. Colonne.
   Conductor: D. Milhaud, chorus: Y. Gouverné
Duration: 12 min 30 s

La tragédie humaine op. 369
[From 'Les Tragiques' by Agrippa d'Aubigné]
Misère — La chambre dorée — Les feux — Vengeance — Jugement
Paris, 1958
2.2.3.3.–2.3.3.1.–T.P.S.
Publisher: Salabert
Dedication and/or commission: comm. de l'Etat
First performance: 1958. Brussels Exposition
Duration: 27 min 5 s

Cantate sur des poèmes de Chaucer op. 386
(French adaptation by Darius Milhaud)
Prelude I — Captivity — Prelude II — Escape — Prelude III — Rejection
   Aspen-Mills, 17 August–19 September 1960
2.2.2.2.–2.2.2.0.–T.P.S.
Publisher: Heugel
Dedication and/or commission: comm. University of Iowa
First performance: 10 May 1961. University of Iowa. Conductor: Olefsky
Duration: 15 min

Cantate de l'initiation (Bar mitzvah Israël 1948–1961) op. 388
[Liturgical texts]
Hymne — L'appel (Aliyah) — Lecture de la Thorah (Extrait de Ki Tabo) —
   Benédiction après la Thorah—Bénédiction précédant la Haphtarah—Lecture de
   la Haphtarah
Mills, 26 October–20 November 1960
2.2.0.2.–2.2.0.0.–P.S.
Publisher: Heugel
Dedication and/or commission: comm. Etat d'Israël
First performance: 28 August 1962. Jerusalem. Conductor: Bertini
Duration: 14 min 13 s

Caroles op. 402
[Charles d'Orléans, English and French texts]
Mills-Aspen, 4 May–4 July 1963
1st group: picc, fl, ob, eng hn, cl, tpt, vln.
2nd group: timp, xyl, cel.
3rd group: contra bn, tu, harp, cb.
4th group: mixed chorus
5th group: tmb, hn, bn, bs cl, vc.
Publisher: Eschig
Dedication and/or commission: comm. de l'Etat
First performance: 3 June 1964. Radio France, Paris. Conductor: M. Constant
Duration: 12 min

Accompanied vocal ensemble: soloist, mixed chorus, & organ ⸻⸻⸻

Borechu
Schema Israël op. 239
[liturgical texts]
Mills, January 1944
Cantor, mixed chorus, organ.
Publisher: Schirmer
First performance: March 1944. Temple Park Avenue, New York. Cantor: Putterman
Duration: 2 min 55 s

Kaddish op. 250
Prière pour les morts
Mills, 9 January 1945
Cantor, mixed chorus ad lib., organ.
Publisher: Schirmer
Dedication and/or commission: To the memory of my parents
First performance: 11 May 1945. Temple Park Avenue, New York. Cantor:
    Putterman
Duration: 4 min 10 s

Service sacré op. 279 (4 parts) (R)
[Liturgical texts with additional prayers for Friday evening]
See Accompanied vocal ensemble, soloist, mixed chorus & orchestra
Mills, 10–16 May 1947
Bar, narr, mixed chorus, organ
Publisher: Salabert
Dedication and/or commission: Mrs. E. S. Heller (comm.)
First performance: Friday evening, 17 August 1949. Temple Emanu-El, San
    Francisco. University of California Chorus (Berkeley). Conductor: E. Lawton,
    cantor: R. Rinder, voice: E. Jones
Duration: 60 min

Cantata from Job op. 413
[Biblical texts]
At this also my heart trembleth — Then the Lord answered Job
Aspen-Paris, 10–13 August 1965/16 April 1966
Bar, mixed chorus, organ.
Publisher: Presser
Dedication and/or commission: comm. Synagogue de Buffalo pour le consécration du
Temple Beth Zion
First performance: 24 April 1967. Beth Zion Temple, Buffalo
Duration: 16 min 55 s

Accompanied vocal ensemble: soloist, mixed chorus, & orchestra ─────────────

Psaume 136 op. 53
[Translated by Paul Claudel]
See Solo voice, with orchestra (Cantate de psaumes)
1918
Solo voices, men's chorus, 2.1.2.1.–0.1.0.0.–P.H.S.
Publisher: U.E.
First performance: 1928. Berlin
Duration: 8 min

La sagesse op. 141
[Paul Claudel]
Paris-Aix, 1935
4 voices, narr, mixed chorus, 4.3.4.3.–2.3.3.1.–2 sax–T.P.H.S.
Publisher: Heugel
Dedication and/or commission: Mme Ida Rubinstein (comm.)
First performance: 8 November, 1945. Orch. de la Radio Belge Conductor: P. Collaer;
first staged, February 1950. Opera Rome. Conductor: Previtali
Duration: 60 min

Service sacré op. 279 (4 parts) (R)
[Liturgical texts with additional prayers for Friday evening]
See Accompanied vocal ensemble, soloist, mixed chorus & organ
Mills, June 1947
Bar, narr, mixed chorus, 2.2.2.2.–2.2.2.0.–T.P.H.S.
Publisher: Salabert
Dedication and/or commission: Mrs. E. S. Heller (comm.)
First performance: 18 May 1949. Temple Emanu-El, San Francisco. San Francisco
Symphony, University of California Chorus. Conductor: D. Milhaud, cantor: R.
Rinder, voice: E. Jones
Duration: 60 min

Miracles de la foi op. 314
[Biblical text]
Introduction — Daniel et Nebuchadnezzar — Daniel et Belshazzar — Daniel et
   Darius
Paris, 27 October–4 December 1951
Ten, narr, mixed chorus, 1.1.2.2.–1.1.1.0.–P.S.
Publisher: Schirmer
Dedication and/or commission: comm. pour le 100e anniversaire de Coe College
First performance: 18 May 1952. Coe College, Cedar Rapids, Iowa. Coe College
   Chorus and Orchestra
Duration: 19 min 45 s

Le mariage de la feuille et du cliché op. 357 (R)
(Fantaisie)
[Max Gerard]
Mills-Sion, 9 November–11 December 1956
Spoken voice, vocal quartet, mixed chorus, 1.1.1.1.–1.1.1.0.–sax–T.P.S. with
   'musique concrète' by Pierre Henry
Publisher: Heugel
Dedication and/or commission: comm. Charles Draeger
Duration: 29 min

Cantate de la croix de charité op. 381
[Loys Masson]
Le ciel (Modéré) — La terre (Animé) — La charité (Modéré)
Paris-Florence-Paris, 26 December 1959–13 January 1960
Sop, ten, bas, mixed chorus, children's chorus, 2.3.3.2.–2.2.2.0.–T.P.S.
Publisher: Heugel
Dedication and/or commission: comm. ORTF pour l'émission internationale de la
   Croix-Rouge
First performance: 8 May 1960 (broadcast in 65 countries). Orch. Philh and ORTF
   chorus. Conductor: D. Milhaud, voice: J. Brumaire, M. Caron
Duration: 22 min 15 s

Pacem in terris op. 404 (R)
(Choral symphony)
[Excerpt from the Papal Encyclical of Pope John XXIII, 11 April 1963]
Aspen, 23 July–6 August 1963
Con, bar, mixed chorus, 2.2.3.3.–2.2.3.1.–T.P.S.
Publisher: Salabert
Dedication and/or commission: En mémoire de Jean XXIII aux hommes de bonne
   volonté. Comm. de la Radiodiffusion Télévision Française
First performance: 20 December 1963. ORTF. Paris. Orch. Philh. and ORTF chorus.
   Conductor: C. Munch, voice: J. Peters, L. Quilico
Duration: 46 min

Ani maamin, un chant perdu et retrouvé op. 441
[Elie Wiesel, translated by Marion Wiesel in 'Ani maamin 'A song lost and found,'
  New York: Random House, 1973]
Geneva-Paris, 3 September–10 October 1972
Sop, 4 narr, mixed chorus, 2.2.2.2.–0.2.3.1.–T.P.H.S.
Publisher: Eschig
Dedication and/or commission: comm. Union for American Hebrew Congregations
First performance: 11 November 1973. Carnegie Hall, New York. Conductor: L. Foss
Duration: 70 min

Accompanied vocal ensemble: children's chorus & organ

Service pour la veille du Sabbat op. 345
(Liturgy in Hebrew, French, and English)
Mills, 30 May 1955
Publisher: Heugel
First performance: 4 November 1957. Congrès de musique juive, Temple de la
  Victoire, Paris.
Duration: 5 min 30 s

For children's voices, see also Accompanied vocal ensemble, soloists, mixed chorus, &
orchestra (Cantate de la croix de charité); Accompanied vocal ensemble, women's
chorus, & orchestra (Invocation à l'ange Raphaël)

Accompanied vocal ensemble: easy pieces (with piano or a small ensemble of violins and violoncellos)

A propos de bottes op. 118
[René Chalupt]
Chanson du savetier et de la pie — Chanson de Babolin, le livreur — Chanson d'Alfred
  — Chanson d'Alfred et de la pie — Chanson du fantôme — Chanson des
  anthropophages — Chanson du chinois — Chanson du cinéaste, Chanson d'Alfred
  et de la Star, Chanson de l'ogre, Chanson finale
Cauterets, August 1932
Publisher: Durand
Dedication and/or commission: Alice Pelliot
First performance: May 1933. Th. Marioniettes, Paris
Duration: 16 min

Un petit peu de musique op. 119
[Armand Lunel]
Le petit examen — Pour sauter à la corde — La lecture enfantine — Pour tirer au sort — Mademoiselle Lunette — Mea culpa — Le maître pion Jujube — Un éloge mérité — La dispute — L'orchestre des bons élèves — L'orchestre des mauvais élèves — Choeur final en l'honneur de la radio
Aix-les-Bains—Lausanne, October 1932
Publisher: Durand
Dedication and/or commission: Mrs. E. Sprague Coolidge
First performance: February 1933. Conc. Triton, Paris. Enfants de l'Ecole Primaire. Conductor: D. Milhaud
Duration: 13 min 20 s

Un petit peu d'exercice op. 133
[Armand Lunel]
Chant du départ — Repos hebdomadaire — Tohu-bohu des sportifs (Farniente des débonnaires) — La culture physique — Le sportif paisible — Natation — Le vélo — La raquette — Le jeune homme studieux — Le chant du skieur — Jeunes filles d'autrefois — Choeur final de réconciliation
Paris, 1934
Publisher: Durand
First performance: 1934. Expos. Arts Ménagers, Paris. Conductor: D. Milhaud, voice: L. Daniels
Duration: 17 minm 40 s

DRAMATIC WORKS

'Opéras-minute'

Les
==============

L'enlèvement d'Europe op. 94 (R)
[Henri Hoppenot]
Vienna-Budapest, 1927
4 solo voices, vocal sextet, 1.1.1.1.–0.1.0.0.–T.P.S. (1.0.1.1.1.).
Publisher: U.E.
Dedication and/or commission: M.D.M.
First performance: July 1927. Festival Baden-Baden. Conductor: Moëlich
Duration: 9 min

L'abandon d'Ariane op. 98 (R)
[Henri Hoppenot]
Aix, 1927
4 solo voices, vocal sextet, 2.1.2.1.–1.2.0.0.–T.P.S. (1.1.1.1.0.).
Publisher: U.E.
Dedication and/or commission: H.H.H.
First performance: April 1928. Th. Wiesbaden. Conductor: J. Rosenstock
Duration: 10 min

La délivrance de Thésée op. 99 (R)
[Henri Hoppenot]
Aix, 1927
5 solo voices, vocal quartet, 1.1.1.1.–1.1.0.0.–T.P.S. (1.1.1.1.1.).
Publisher: U.E.
Dedication and/or commission: E. H.
First performance: April 1928. Th. Wiesbaden. Conductor: J. Rosenstock
Duration: 8 min

Operas

[   ]

The works for which no duration is indicated are intended to provide a full evening's entertainment.

La brebis égarée op. 4
(3 acts)
[Francis Jammes]
See Large orchestra, symphonic suites (Première suite symphonique)
Paris-Aix, 1910–1914
Solo voices, 3.3.3.4.–4.3.3.1.–T.P.H.S.
Publisher: Eschig
Dedication and/or commission: Léo Latil
First performance: December 1923. Opéra Comique, Paris. Conductor: A. Wolff

L'Orestie
(3-part cycle)
[Adapted from Aeschylus by Paul Claudel]
I. **Agamemnon** op. 14
Hellerau, 1913
Sop, men's chorus, 3.3.3.2.–4.3.3.1.–T.P.H.S.
Publisher: Heugel
Dedication and/or commission: Jacques Benoist-Méchin
First performance: April 1927. Conc. Straram, Paris. Conductor: W. Straram, voice: M. Bunlet; first staged, April 1963. Berlin Opera. Conductor: H. Hollreiser
Duration: 10 min
II. **Les choéphores** op. 24 (R)
Paris-Lyon-Aix, 1915–1916
Sop, bar, narr, mixed chorus, 3.3.3.4.–4.3.3.1.–T.15P.H.S.
Publisher: Heugel
Dedication and/or commission: Charles Koechlin
First performance: 15 June 1919. Conc. Delgrange, Paris. Conductor F. Delgrange, voice: J. Bathori; first staged, 27 March 1935. Th. de la Monnaie, Brussels. Conductor: C. de Thoran
Duration: 30 min

III. **Les euménides** op. 41 (R)
(3 acts)
Rio de Janeiro-Fort de France-Aix, 1917–1922
Solo voice, mixed chorus, 3.3.3.4.–4.4.3.1.–4 sax, 4 saxh–T.15P.H.S.
Publisher: Heugel
Dedication and/or commission: Jacques Heugel
First performance: 27 November 1927. Nouv. Conc. Anvers. Conductor: L. de Vocht
  (Le Final); Conc. Monteux, Paris. Conductor: P. Monteux (Ouverture); 1949.
  I.N.R., Brussels. Conductor: F. André (complete version); first staged, April 1963,
  Berlin Opera. Conductor: H. Hollreiser
Duration: 90 min

Les malheurs d'Orphée op. 85 (R)
(3 acts)
[Armand Lunel]
Aix-Malines, 22 September–2 November 1924
Bar, sop, 10 solo voices, 1.1.2.1.–0.1.0.0.–T.P.H.S. (1.0.1.1. 5-string cb)
Publisher: Heugel
Dedication and/or commission: Princesse Edmond de Polignac (comm.)
First performance: 7 May 1926. Th. de la Monnaie, Brussels. Conductor: C. de Thoran
Duration: 35 min

Esther de Carpentras op. 89
(Comic opera in 2 acts)
[Armand Lunel]
Aix-Malines, 1925–1927
Solo voices, 3.3.3.2.–4.3.3.1.–T.P.H.S.
Publisher: Heugel
Dedication and/or commission: M.D.M.
First performance: May 1937. Radio Rennes. Conductor: M. Rosenthal; first staged,
  1 February 1938. Opéra Comique, Paris. Conductor: R. Desormière
Duration: 65 min

Le pauvre matelot op. 92 (R)
'Complainte' (3 acts)
[Jean Cocteau]
Aix, 1926
1st version: sop, ten, bar, bas, 2.2.3.3.–2.3.1.0.–T.P.H.S.
2nd version: sop, ten, bar, bas, 1.1.1.1.–1.1.1.0.–P.S. (1.1.1.1.1.)
Publisher: Heugel
Dedication and/or commission: Henri Sauguet
First performance: December 1927. Opéra Comique, Paris. Conductor: Lauweryns
Duration: 30 min

Christophe Colomb op. 102
(2 acts, 27 tableaux)
[Paul Claudel]
Paris-Aix, 1928
Solo voices, mixed chorus, 3.3.4.3.–4.3.3.1.–cel, hrm–T.P.H.S.
Publisher: U.E.
Dedication and/or commission: Manuel de Falla
First performance: 5 May 1930. Berlin Opera. Conductor: E. Kleiber; new version
  (2 acts reversed) 27 June 1968. Graz Opera. Conductor: Klobicar
Duration: 150 min

Maximilien op. 110
(3 acts, 9 tableaux)
(Libretto by R. S. Hoffman on a play by F. Werfel, translated by A. Lunel]
See Large orchestra, symphonic suites (Suite de Maximilien)
Aix, 1930
Solo voices, mixed chorus, 3.3.4.3.–4.4.3.1.–T.P.H.S.
Publisher: U.E.
Dedication and/or commission: M.D.M.
First performance: 5 January 1932. Paris Opera. Conductor: F. Ruhlman

Médée Op. 191
(1 act)
[Madeleine Milhaud]
Aix, Summer 1938
2 sop, cont, ten, bar, mixed chorus, 2.2.2.3.–2.3.3.1.–P.S.
Publisher: Heugel
Dedication and/or commission: comm. Etat 1938
First performance: 7 October 1939. Opéra Flamand, Anvers. Conductor: M. J.
  Sterkens.
Duration: 70 min

Bolivar op. 236
(3 acts)
[Jules Supervielle, Madeleine Milhaud]
See Piano, two pianos (La libertadora)
Mills, 31 January–3 June 1943
Solo voices, mixed chorus, 2.2.2.2.–4.3.2.1.–T.P.H.S.
Publisher: Salabert
Dedication and/or commission: Swanee
First performance: 12 May 1950. Paris Opera. Conductor: A. Cluytens

David op. 320
(5 acts)
[Armand Lunel]
Aspen-Mills, 5 August 1952–17 February 1953
Solo voices, mixed chorus, 2.2.2.2.–4.3.3.1.–T.P.H.S.
Publisher: I.M.P.
Dedication and/or commission: Ecrit à la mémoire de Nathalie et de Serge
    Koussevitzky. Dedié au peuple d'Israël. Comm. Koussevitzky Found. pour le 3000e
    anniversaire du roi David et de la fondation de Jerusalem
First performance: 1 June 1954. Jerusalem. Conductor: G. Singer; first staged, 2
    February 1955. La Scala, Milan. Conductor: N. Sanzogno
Duration: 170 min

Fiesta op. 370
(1 act)
[Boris Vian]
Paris, 27 April–6 May 1958
10 solo voices, fl, ob, cl, bs cl, bn, sax, tpt, tbn, perc, harp, 3 vln, 2 vc, cb.
Publisher: Heugel
Dedication and/or commission: Hermann Scherchen, comm. Berliner Festwochen
First performance: 3 October 1958. Städtische Oper, Berlin. Conductor: H. Scherchen
Duration: 22 min 30 s

La mère coupable op. 412
[Adapted from Beaumarchais by Madeleine Milhaud]
Mills, 23 September 1964–26 March 1965
2 sop, mez, ten, 3 bar, bas, 2.2.3.3.–2.2.2.1.–T.P.H.S.
Publisher: Ricordi
First performance: 13 June 1965. Grand Théâtre, Geneva. Conductor: S. Baudo
Duration: 105 min

Saint-Louis, Roi de France op. 434
(Opera-oratorio in 2 parts)
[Poem by Paul Claudel, libretto by Henri Doublier]
Paris-Geneva, 19 November 1970–4 January 1971
2 sop, ten, bas, 2 narrators, 2 choruses: one on stage, one in the pit, pit orchestra:
    1.1.2.1.–2.2.2.1.–T.P.S., stage orchestra: 1.1.1.1.–0.1.1.0.–P.H.S. (1.1.1.1.1.).
Publisher: Eschig
Dedication and/or commission: comm. Etat
First performance: 18 March 1972. RAI, Rome. Conductor: La Rosa Parodi; first
    staged, 14 April 1972. Th. Rio de Janeiro
Durations: 90 min

Recitatives

Récitatifs pour **Une éducation manquée** (Chabrier) op. 82
Paris, 1923
Publisher: Enoch
First performance: January 1924. Monte Carlo Opera. Ballets Russes Diaghilev.
    Conductor: V. Scotto

Ballets

L'homme et son désir op. 48 (R)
['Poème plastique' by Paul Claudel]
See Large orchestra, misc.; Reductions
Rio de Janeiro, 1918
Vocal quartet, 2.1.2.0.–0.1.0.0.–P.H.S. (solo cb)
Publisher: U.E.
First performance: 6 June 1921. Th. Champs Elysées, Paris. Ballets Suèdois de Rolf de
    Maré. Conductor: D. Inghelbrecht
Duration: 20 min

Le boeuf sur le toit op. 58 (R)
[Jean Cocteau]
See Piano, solo (Tango des Fratellini); Duos, violin & piano (Cinéma-fantaisie); Solo
    & orchestra (or chamber ensemble), violin (Cinéma-fantaisie); Reductions;
    Transcriptions (Tango des Fratellini)
Paris, 1919
2.1.2.1.–2.2.1.0.–P.S.
Publisher: Eschig
Dedication and/or commission: Jean Cocteau
First performance: 21 February 1920. Com. des Champs Elysées. Conductor: V.
    Golschmann
Duration: 18 min

Les mariés de la Tour Eiffel (R) op. 70
[Jean Cocteau]
Marche nuptiale
Sortie de la noce
2.2.2.2.–2.2.2.1.–T.P.S.
Fugue du massacre op. 70b*
2.2.2.2.–4.3.3.1.–T.P.S.
Paris, 1921
Publisher: Salabert
First performance: 18 June 1921. Th. Champs Elysées, Paris. Ballets Suèdois de Rolf
  de Maré.
Duration: 6 min 10 s
*The original was lost; a second version was written in Geneva, 1971.

La création du monde op. 81 (R)
[Blaise Cendrars]
See Quintets, string; Reductions
Paris, 1923
2.1.2.1.–1.2.1.0.–sax–T.P.S. (1.1.0.1.1.) piano.
Publisher: Eschig
Dedication and/or commission: Paul Collaer et Roger Desormière
First performance: 25 October 1923. Paris. Ballets Suèdois de Rolf de Maré.
  Conductor: V. Golschmann. Costume & set design: F. Leger. Choreography: J.
  Börlin
Duration: 15 min

Salade op. 83 (R)
('Ballet chanté' in 2 acts)
[Albert Flament]
See Solo & orchestra, piano (Le carnaval d'Aix)
Paris-Valmont, 5–20 February 1924
Solo voices, men's chorus, 2.1.2.1.–2.2.1.1.–T.P.S. piano.
Publisher: Heugel
Dedication and/or commission: Comtesse Etienne de Beaumont
First performance: 17 May 1924. Soirées de Paris. Conductor: R. Desormière.
  Costume & set design: G. Braque. Choreography: L. Massine
Duration: 40 min

Le train bleu op. 84 (R)
(In 10 sections)
[Jean Cocteau]
See Reductions; Transcriptions
Paris-Valmont, 12 February–5 March 1924
3.3.3.2.–4.3.3.1.–T.P.S.
Publisher: Heugel
Dedication and/or commission: Serge Diaghilev
First performance: 20 June 1924. Th. des Champs Elysées, Paris. Ballets Russes
  Diaghilev. Conductor: A. Messager. Costume design: G. Chanel. Choreography:
  Mme Nijinska
Duration: 22 min 15 s

Polka (L'éventail de Jeanne) op. 95
('Spectacle collectif')
See Piano, solo pieces included in collections
Vienna, 1927
2.2.2.2.–2.2.0.0.–P.S.
Publisher: Heugel
Dedication and/or commission: Jeanne Dubost
First performance: 1928. Paris Opera. Conductor: J. Szyfer

La bien-aimée op. 101
(Adapted from Schubert-Liszt)
Paris, 1928
Mechanical piano, 3.3.3.3.–4.3.3.1.–T.P.H.S.
New orchestration: opus 101b, 1941
Publisher: U.E.
Dedication and/or commission: Comm. Ida Rubenstein
First performance: 22 November 1928. Paris Opera. Spectacle Ida Rubinstein.
    Conductor: W. Straram

Les songes op. 124 (R)
[André Derain]
See Piano, two pianos; Reductions
Paris, 1933
1.1.1.1.–1.1.1.0.–P.S. piano.
Publisher: (Deiss) Salabert
Dedication and/or commission: M.D.M.
First performance: June 1933. Ballets 1933, Th. des Champs Elysées, Paris.
    Conductor: M. Abravanel. Costume & set design: A. Derain. Choreography: G.
    Balanchine
Duration: 30 min

Suite provençale op. 152d (R)
Guardians — Cueillette des amandes — Joueurs de boules — Chasseurs —
    Vendangeurs — Berger — Farandole
See Large orchestra, symphonic suites; Incidental music (Bertran de Born)
Paris, June–July 1936
2.3.2.2.–4.3.3.1.–T.P.S.
Publisher: (Deiss) Salabert
Dedication and/or commission: M.D.M.
First performance: 1 February 1938. Ballets Opéra Comique, Paris. Conductor: R.
    Desormière
Duration: 16 min

Moïse op. 219 (R)
Ouverture — Moïse découvert parmi les joncs — La cour de Pharaon — Les miracles
de Moïse devant le Pharaon — Moïse tue un contremaître — Moïse dans le
désert-Promesse de Dieu — La traversée de la Mer Rouge — Introduction et
bacchanale — Le veau d'or-Moïse brise les tablettes — Moïse aperçoit la terre
promise de Piagah
See Large orchestra, misc.; Chamber ensemble, misc. (Opus Americanun no. 2)
Oakland, 25 August–7 September 1940
1.1.2.1.–1.2.2.0.–T.P.S. or 2.2.2.2.–2.2.2.0.–T.P.H.S.
Publisher: Elkan Vogel-Presser
Dedication and/or commission: comm. Ballet Theater, New York
First performance: 1950. Rome Opera
Duration: 31 min 25 s

Introduction
Marche
Fête de la victoire op. 254
(Addition to the ballet arrangement of the 'Suite française')
Mills, 4 April 1945
2.2.2.2.–2.2.2.0.–T.P.S.
Publisher: (Leeds, MCA) Bel. M.

Les cloches op. 259
[From 'The Bells' by Edgar Allan Poe]
Overture (Ouverture) — Silver Bells (Cloches d'argent) — Golden Bells (Cloches
d'or) — Brazen Bells (Cloches de cuivre) — Iron Bells (Cloches de fer) —
Bacchanale (Bacchanale)
See Large orchestra, symphonic suites
Mills, 20 March–30 August 1945
3.1.2.1.–2.2.1.0.–T.P.S. piano.
Publisher: Eschig
Dedication and/or commission: M.D.M., comm. Ruth Page
First performance: 26 April 1946. Chicago University Ballet
Duration: 23 min 10 s

'Adame miroir op. 283
[Jean Genet]
Paris, March–April 1948
1.1.1.1.–1.1.1.0.–T.P.H.S.
Publisher: Heugel
Dedication and/or commission: comm. Roland Petit
First performance: 31 May 1948. Th. Marigny, Paris. Ballets Roland Petit
Duration: 18 min

La cueillette des citrons op. 298b
(Intermède provençale)
[Armand Lunel]
See Accompanied vocal ensemble, mixed chorus & orchestra
Paris, 4 December 1949–13 January 1950
2.2.2.2.–2.2.2.0.–T.P.S.
Publisher: Heugel
Duration: 20 min

Vendanges op. 317
[Philippe de Rothschild]
See Transcriptions (Divertissements)
Paris-Mills, 2–25 July 1952
2.2.2.2.–2.3.3.1.–T.P.H.S.
Publisher: Eschig
First performance: 1970. Opéra Nice
Duration: 50 min

La rose des vents op. 367
(In 10 sections)
[Albert Vidalie, Roland Petit]
12–20 December 1957
2.1.2.1.–2.2.1.0.–P.H.S. piano.
Publisher: Salabert
Dediction and/or commission: comm. Roland Petit
First performance: 13 February 1958. Paris. Ballets Roland Petit. Conductor: M.
  Constant
Duration: 22 min

La branche des oiseaux op. 374
[André Chamson]
L'antiquité — Le moyen-age — La poésie d'aujourd'hui
Mills, 16 December 1958–27 March 1959
3.3.3.–4.3.3.0.–T.P.H.S.
Publisher: Heugel
Dedication and/or commission: comm. pour le centenaire de 'Mireille'
First performance: 18 May 1962, Brussels, RTB. Staged: 1 April 1965. Cimiez
Duration: 30 min

Incidental music

Much of the music written for films, radio, television, and as incidental music for theatrical productions is unpublished. However, in order to show Milhaud's total output in these various categories, all compositions whether published or unpublished have been listed together under the appropriate headings.

L'ours et la lune*
[Paul Claudel]
1918
3 spoken voices, drum.
Publisher: Gallimard
*Mme Milhaud found this work among D. Milhaud's papers after his death. He had never listed it in his catalogues nor assigned an opus number to it.

Protée op. 17
(First version)
[Paul Claudel]
See Large orchestra, symphonic suites (Deuxième suite symphonique); Reductions
See also second version Incidental Music, op. 341
Combault-Paris, 1913/Aix, 1919
Mixed chorus, 3.3.3.4.–4.3.3.1.–T.P.H.S.
Publisher: Durand
Dedication and/or commission: A la mémoire d'Alberic Magnard
First performance: June 1929. Groningen Theatre. Groningen University Orchestra
This 'first version' is actually the last of three different versions composed during 1913–1919. The two earlier versions, never performed, were superseded by this final one.

L'annonce faite à Marie op. 117
(First version)
[Paul Claudel]
See Accompanied vocal ensemble, vocal quartet & chamber ensemble
See also second version Incidental Music, op. 231
Aix, 1932
Vocal quartet, 2 fl, ob, 2 sax, 2 ond Mart, vib, piano 4-hand, organ, T.P.S.
Publisher: Salabert
Dedication and/or commission: M.D.M.
First performance: 21 January 1934. Palais des Beaux Arts, Brussels. Conductor: A. Prevost
Duration: 19 min

Le château des papes op. 120
[André de Richaud]
See Duos, ondes Martenot & piano (Suite); Accompanied vocal ensemble, vocal
    quartet & chamber ensemble (Adages)
Aix, 1932
Vocal quartet, 2 piano, ond Mart, tpt.
First performance: 1932. Théâtre Atelier, Paris. Stage director: C. Dullin

Se plaire sur la même fleur op. 131
[Moreno, translated by Casa Fuerte]
Ritournelle, 6 chansons
Aix, 1934

Le cycle de la création op. 139
[Dom Luigi Sturzo]
Aix, 1934
Sop, mixed chorus, 2.1.2.2.–1.2.1.1.–ond Mart–T.P.H.S.
First performance: 21 May 1986. Quirinal Palace, Rome. RAI orchestra and chorus.
    Conductor: M. Atzman, voice: C. Gaedia

Le faiseur op. 145
[Balzac]
Paris, 1935
Fl, cl, sax, perc.
First performance: 30 November 1935. Th. Atelier, Paris. Stage director: C. Dullin

Bolivar op. 148
[Jules Supervielle]
See Solo voice, with piano (Trois chansons de négresse); Solo voice, with orchestra
    (Trois chansons de négresse)
Malines-Paris, 1935–1936
Solo voices, mixed chorus, 1.0.1.0.–0.2.1.1.–sax–H.S. ond Mart.
Dedication and/or commission: M.D.M.
First performance: 28 February 1936. Com. Française, Paris. Conductor: R.
    Charpentier

La folle du ciel op. 149
[R. Lenormand]
See Solo voice, with piano (Six chansons de théâtre)
Paris, 1936
Voice, ond Mart, harp.
First performance: 17 February 1936. Th. Mathurins, Paris. Stage director: G. Pitoeff

Tu ne m'échapperas jamais op. 151
[M. Kennedy]
See Solo voice, with piano (Six chansons de théâtre)
Paris, April 1936
Voice, piano.
Dedication and/or commission: Ludmilla Pitoeff
First performance: April 1936. Th. Galeries, Brussels. Stage director: G. Pitoeff

Bertran de Born op. 152
[Valmy Baisse]
See Large orchestra, symphonic suites (Suite provençale); Solo voice, with piano
   (Trois chansons de troubadours); Ballets (Suite provençale)
Paris, May–June 1936
Solo voices, mixed chorus, 2.3.2.2.–4.3.3.1.–T.P.S.
First performance: 2 August 1936. Th. Antique, Orange. Conductor: P. Paray, voice:
   M. Herrand

Le quatorze juillet op. 153
('Spectacle collectif')
[Romain Rolland]
Final du premier acte.
See Large orchestra, misc. (Introduction et Marche funèbre); Band
(Introduction et Marche funèbre)
Paris, June 1936
First performance: 13 July 1936. Th. Alhambra, Paris. Conductor: R. Desormière

Le conquérant op. 154
[Jean Mistler]
See Unpublished works (Fragments dramatiques)
Aix, August 1936
1.1.1.1.–1.1.1.0.–P.S.
First performance: 13 November 1936. Th. Odéon, Paris.

Amal, ou La lettre du roi op. 156
[Rabindranath Tagore adapted by André Gide]
Paris, October 1936
Piano, vln, cl.
First performance: 1936. Th. Mathurins, Paris. Stage director: G. Pitoeff

Le voyageur sans bagages op. 157
[Jean Anouilh]
See Trios, piano, violin & clarient (Suite)
Paris, October–November 1936
Piano, vln, cl.
First performance: 1936. Th. Mathurins, Paris. Stage director: G. Pitoeff

Jules César op. 158
[Shakespeare adapted by S. Jollivet]
Paris, December 1936
Fl, cl or sax, tpt, tu, perc.
First performance: 4 January 1937. Th. Atelier, Paris. Stage director: C. Dullin

Le trompeur de Seville op. 152e
[A. Obey]
Paris, January 1937
3 tpt, 3 tbn, tu, perc.
First performance: 25 January 1937. Th. Porte Saint-Martin, Paris. Conductor: R. Desormière

La duchesse d'Amalfi op. 160
[Webster adapted by Fluchère]
Paris, April 1937
Ob, cl, bn.
First performance: 1937. Th. Rideau Gris, Marseille. Stage director: L. Ducreux

Liberté op. 163
('Spectacle collectif')
Ouverture — Interlude
Paris, March 1937
1.1.1.1.–1.1.1.1.–P.S.
First performance: 1937. Th. Champs Elysées, Paris. Conductor: M. Jaubert

Roméo et Juliette op. 161
[Shakespeare adapted by A. Jouve]
See Trios, oboe, clarinet & bassoon (Suite d'après Corrette)
Paris, April 1937
Ob, cl, bn
First performance: 7 June 1937. Th. Mathurins, Paris. Stage director: G. Pitoeff

Le médecin volant op. 165
[Molière adapted by Vildrac]
See Piano, two pianos (Scaramouche); Solo & orchestra, clarinet (Scaramouche); Solo & orchestra, saxophone (Scaramouche); Reductions; Transcriptions (Brazileira); Transcriptions (Scaramouche)
Paris, May 1937
Piano, cl or sax.
First performance: 23 March 1937. Th. Scaramouche, Com. Champs Elysées, Paris. Stage director: H. Pascar

Chansons de l'opéra du gueux op. 171
[John Gay adapted by H. Fluchère]
See Chamber ensemble, misc. (Le carnaval de Londres); Solo voice, with piano (Chansons du carnaval de Londres); Solo voice, with orchestra (Chansons du carnaval de Londres)
Aix, September 1937
1.1.1.1.–0.1.1.0.–sax–P.H.S.
Publisher: (Deiss) Salabert
First performance: 1937. Th. Rideau Gris, Marseille. Stage director: L. Ducreux

Naissance d'une cité op. 173
('Spectacle collectif')
[Jean Richard Bloch]
Chanson du captaine — La java de la femme
See Solo voice, with piano
Paris, June–October 1937
Voice, piano.
Publisher: (Deiss) Salabert
First performance: 16 October 1937. Palais des Sports, Paris

Hecube op. 177
[Euripides adapted by A. de Richaud]
Aix, August 1937
Fl, cl, bn, tpt, perc.
First performance: 6 September 1937. Com. Champs Elysées, Paris. Stage director:
    M. Herrand

Macbeth op. 175
[Shakespeare]
Paris, November 1937
Fl, cl, bn, tpt, perc, vln, cb.
Dedication and/or commission: Margotine
First performance: 23 November 1937. Old Vic, London. Stage director: M. Saint
    Denis

Plutus op. 186
[Aristophanes, S. Jollivet]
Paris-Nyon, 1938
Fl, cl (ou sax), tpt, perc, piano.
First performance: 1 February 1938. Th. Atelier, Paris. Stage director: C. Dullin

Tricolore op. 190
[Lestringuez]
Aix, Summer 1938
2.1.2.1.–0.2.2.1.–sax–T.P.S.
First performance: 14 October 1938. Com. Française, Paris. Conductor: R.
    Charpentier

Le bal des voleurs op. 192
[Jean Anouilh]
Allegro — Modéré — Allegro
See Transcriptions (Petit concert)
Aix, August 1938
Cl.
Publisher: Billaudot
First performance: 1938. Th. des Arts, Paris. Stage director: A. Barsacq

La première famille op. 193
[Jules Supervielle]
See Solo voice, with piano (Six chansons de théâtre)
Aix, September 1938
Voice, piano.
First performance: 1938. Th. Mathurins, Paris. Stage director: G. Pitoeff

Hamlet op. 200
[Jules Laforgue]
Paris, April 1939
Tpt, bn, ond Mart, perc, piano.
First performance: April 1939. Th. Atelier, Paris. Stage director: J. L. Barrault

Un petit ange de rien du tout op. 215
[C. A. Puget]
Aix, April 1940
Fl, cl, sax, bn, tpt, vln, perc, ond Mart.
First performance: 29 April 1940. Th. Michel, Paris. Conductor: R. Charpentier

L'annonce faite à Marie op. 231
(Second version)
[Paul Claudel]
See Other solo instruments, organ (Neuf Préludes); Solo voice, with organ (or piano)
    (Cinq Prières)
See also first version Incidental Music, op. 117
Mills, 18 March 1942
2.1.1.1.–0.3.1.0.–T.P.S.
First performance: 13 October 1942. Christmas Play, Mills College

Lidoire op. 264
[G. Courteline]
Prélude — Postlude
Mills, 4 March 1946
Cl, bn, tpt, tbn, acc, T.P.S.
First performance: April 1946. Spect. Courteline, Paris. Stage director: J. Mercure

La maison de Bernarda Alba op. 280
[García Lorca]
Mills, July 1947
Fl, ob, bn, perc.
First performance: September 1947. Coronet Theater, Los Angeles. Stage director: V.
    Sokoloff

Sheherazade op. 285
[Jules Supervielle]
Paris, June 1948
Cl, sax, vln, va, vc, cb.
First performance: July 1948. Festival Avignon. Stage director: J. Vilar, Conductor:
    G. Delerue

Le jeu de Robin et Marion op. 288
(Adapted from Adam de la Halle)
[English translation by R. Maren]
Mills, 1948
7 voices, fl, cl, sax, vln, vc.
Publisher: Marks
Dedication and/or commission: comm. Juilliard School of Music, New York
First performance: 28 October 1951. Hessiches Staats-Theater Wiesbaden.
   Conductor: E. Helm

Le conte d'hiver op. 306
[Shakespeare adapted by C. A. Puget]
Prélude — Chansons — Danses
Mills-Carpinteria, August 1950
2.1.2.1.–1.2.2.0.–P.
First performance: November 1950. Com. Française, Paris. Conductor: A. Jolivet

Christophe Colomb op. 318
[Paul Claudel]
Paris, February–March 1952
Mixed chorus, 1.0.1.1.–0.1.0.0.–P.H. vln, va, vc, cb.
Publisher: U.E.
First performance: May 1953. Fest. Bordeaux. Stage director: J.-L. Barrault

Saül op. 334
[André Gide]
See Band (Musique de théâtre)
Paris, March-April 1954
3.3.3.2.–4.4.4.1.–P. cel, 3 cb.
First performance: 2 July 1954. Spect. Douking, Citadelle de Toulon. Mus. de la Flotte

Protée op. 341
(second version)
[Paul Claudel]
See also first version Incidental Music, op. 17
Mills, January 1955
Voice, fl, bn, vln, vc.
Publisher: Durand
First performance: 1965. Com. Champs Elysées, Paris. Conductor: J. Bondon

Juanito op. 349
[P. Humblot]
Paris, 16–30 December 1955
Fl. cl, sax, bn, tpt, vln, va, vc, cb.
First performance: 1961. Th. des Capucines, Paris. Stage director: L. Ducreux

Mother Courage op. 379
[B. Brecht, English translation R. Bentley]
Aspen-Atlantic Ocean-Florence-Mills, April-October 1959
Voice, 1.1.1.1.–0.1.1.0.–T.P. 3 vln, 2 vc, cb.

Judith op. 392
[J. Giraudoux]
Paris, 18–26 October 1961
Chamber ensemble; fl, cl, bn, tpt, perc, vln, vc, vocal quartet.
With tape: ob, eng hn, bs cl, hn, tpt, tbn, ond Mart, perc, vln, va, vc, cb.
First performance: 17 November 1961. Th. de France, Paris. Stage director: J.-L.
    Barrault, Conductor: A. Girard

Jerusalem à Carpentras op. 419
[Armand Lunel]
Paris, 13–18 April 1966
Fl, cl, vln, va, vc, perc.
First performance: 25 May 1966. Th. Carpentras

L'histoire de Tobie et Sara op. 426
[Paul Claudel]
7 November 1967
1e version: 2.1.2.2.–2.0.1.0.–T.P.S. cb.
2e version: chorus, 2.0.0.1.–0.0.1.0.–T.P. cb.
First performance: 1st version, 18 April 1968. Th. du Rideau, Brussels. Stage director:
    P. Laroche

Music for films

Actualités op. 104 (R)
A l'exposition de la presse — Aviateurs reçus officiellement — Kangourou boxeur —
    Application industrielle de l'eau — Un attentat sur la voie ferrée — Le Derby
Baden-Baden, 1928
2 cl, 2 tpt, tbn, perc, 2 vln, 2 va, 2 vc, cb.
Publisher: U.E.
Dedication and/or commission: Paul et Gertrude Hindemith
First performance: 14 July 1928. Fest. Baden-Baden. Conductor: Dressel
Duration: 7 min

La p'tite Lilie op. 107 (R)
[A. Cavalcanti]
Chanson
Paris, 1929
1.1.1.1.–1.1.1.1.–T.P.S. piano.
Publisher: U.E.
Dedication and/or commission: M.D.M.
First performance: 1929. Fest. Baden-Baden
Duration: 15 min

Hallo Everybody op. 126
[H. Richter]
Paris, 1933
1.1.1.1.–1.1.1.1.–2 sax–P.H. piano.
Recording conducted by: D. Milhaud, 1933. Eindhoven, Holland.

Madame Bovary op. 128
[Flaubert adapted by Jean Renoir]
See Piano, solo (L'album de Madame Bovary & Trois valses); Solo voice, with piano
    (Deux chansons); Transcriptions
Paris, 1933
1.1.1.1.–1.1.1.1.–sax–P.H. piano, 2 vln, vc.
Publisher: Enoch
Recording conducted by: R. Desormière
First screening: 12 January 1934. Ciné Opéra, Paris

L'hippocampe op. 137
[Jean Painlevé]
Paris, 1934
1.1.1.1.–0.1.1.0.–P.S. piano
Recording conducted by: M. Jaubert.
First screening: 10 May 1935. Ciné Opéra, Paris

Tartarin de Tarascon op. 138
[A. Daudet adapted by R. Bernard]
Paris, 1934
Recording conducted by: M. Jaubert
First screening: 1935. Ciné Marivaux, Paris

Voix d'enfants op. 146
[Reynaud et la Manécanterie]
Paris, 1935
Fl, cl, bn, sax, tbn, perc, 2 vln, vc.
Recording conducted by: M. Jaubert
First screening: 1935. Ciné Marivaux, Paris

The Beloved Vagabond op. 150
[K. Bernhard]
London-Paris, 1936
1.1.2.1.–0.2.2.1.–sax–T.H.S. piano.
Recording conducted by: Roger Desormière
First screening: 7 May 1936. Ciné Marignan, Paris

Mollenard op. 174
[Gilbert adapted by Siodmak]
Paris, October 1937
Recording conducted by: M. Rosenthal
First screening: 28 January 1938. Ciné Normandie, Paris

La citadelle du silence op. 176
[M. L'Herbier in collaboration with A. Honegger]
Mayens de Sion, July 1937
Cl, sax, bn, piano, 2 vc, perc.
Recording conducted by: M. Rosenthal

Grands feux op. 182
[Alexeieff]
(Cartoon for 'Four Martin')
Paris, 30 November 1937
2.0.1.1.–2.2.2.1.–sax–T.P. piano.
Recording conducted by: D. Milhaud

La conquête du ciel op. 184
[H. Richter]
Paris, December 1937
1.0.1.1.–0.1.1.1.–sax, perc, piano, 2 vln, vc.
Recording conducted by: R. Blum, Zurich

La tragédie impériale, Raspoutine op. 187
[M. L'Herbier]
Paris, 1938
Orchestration: R. Desormière
Recording conducted by: R. Desormière
First screening: 1938. Ciné Marignan, Paris

Les otages op. 196
[R. Bernard]
Paris, December 1938
Orchestration: R. Desormière
Recording conducted by: R. Desormière
First screening: 1939. Ciné Marivaux, Paris

Islands op. 198
[A. Cavalcanti]
Paris, March 1939
Recording conducted by: M. Jaubert
First screening: 1939. New York World's Fair

Espoir op. 202
[A. Malraux]
See Large orchestra, misc. (Cortège funèbre)
Aix, May 1939
Recording conducted by: M. Rosenthal
First screening: 1939. New York World's Fair

Cavalcade d'amour op. 204
[R. Bernard in collaboration with A. Honegger]
See quintets, wind (La cheminée du roi René)
Paris, June 1939
Orchestration: R. Desormière
Recording conducted by: R. Desormière
First screening: January 1940. Ciné Marivaux, Paris

Gulf Stream op. 208
[Alexeieff]
Aix, 9 August 1939
Fl, cl, sax, 2 tpt, tbn, perc, cb, piano.

The Private Affairs of Bel-Ami op. 272
[Maupassant adapted by A. Lewin]
Hollywood, November 1946
Recording conducted by: D. Milhaud, March 1947, Cleveland

Dreams that Money Can Buy op. 273
[H. Richter]
'Man Ray' sequence
Mills, 5–6 February 1947
Fl, ob, sax, bn, perc, piano.
First screening: 1947. Festival International du Film, Brussels

Gauguin op. 299
[A. Resnais]
See Quintets, wind (Divertissement)
Paris, 1950
1.1.1.1.–0.2.2.1.–sax–P.S. piano.
Recording conducted by: M. Rosenthal
First screening: September 1950. Festival de Venise

La vie commence demain op. 304
[N. Vedrès]
Paris, June 1950
Orchestration: M. Rosenthal
Recording conducted by: M. Rosenthal
First screening: September 1950. Festival de Venise

Ils étaient tous des volontaires op. 336
(Documentary film for the 10th anniversary of the Liberation)
Rome-Paris, 11–14 May 1954
2.1.2.1.–0.2.1.1.–sax–P.H.S.
Recording conducted by: J. Metehen
First screening: 10 June 1954. France

Celle qui n'était plus op. 364
(Histoire d'une folle)
[Colpi]
Sion-Paris, September–October 1957
Fl, ob, sax, bn, tpt, perc, vln, va, vc, cb.

Paul Claudel op. 427
[A. Gillet]
See Large orchestra, symphonic suites (Symphonie pour l'univers Claudelien)
Paris, 1968
2.2.3.3.–4.3.3.1.–T.P.H.S.
Publisher: Eschig
Dedication and/or commission: Hommage à Paul Claudel

Music for radio

[   ]

Agamemmon
[Aeschylus]
Paris, 1938
First performance: 1938. Radio France, Paris. Producer: C. Dullin

Voyage au pays du rêve op. 203
[Ravenne]
Paris, May 1939
Dedication and/or commission: comm. Radio France
First performance: 15 June 1939. Radio France, Paris. Conductor: D. Milhaud

Le grand testament op. 282
[N. Franck]
Paris, February 1948
1.1.1.1.–0.2.2.0.–sax–P.H. 3 vln, 2 va, 2 vc, cb.
First performance: April 1948. Radio France, Paris. Conductor: R. Desormière

La fin du monde op. 297
[B. Cendrars]
Paris, November 1949
2.1.2.1.–0.2.2.1.–sax–P.H.S.
Dedication and/or commission: comm. Radio France
First performance: 31 December 1949. Radio France, Paris. Conductor: D. Milhaud.
  Producer: M. Milhaud

Le repos du septième jour op. 301
[Paul Claudel]
Paris-Menton, February 1950
2.0.2.1.–0.2.2.1.–2 P.H. vln, va, vc, cb.
Dedication and/or commission: comm. Radio France
First performance: 14 March 1950. Radio France, Paris. Conductor: D. Milhaud

Samaël op. 321
[A. Spire]
Mills, March 1953
2.1.1.1.–0.1.1.0.–sax–P.H.S. (1.1.1.1.1.).
Dedication and/or commission: comm. Radio France
First performance: 5 December 1953. Radio France, Paris

Le Dibbouk op. 328
[Anski]
Paris, 6 October 1953
Men's chorus, 0.1.1.1.–0.1.0.0.–P.H. vln, vc.
Dedication and/or commission: comm. Radio France
First performance: 5 December 1953. Radio France, Paris

Etude poétique op. 333
(Musical pastiche)
[Claude Roy]
Paris, March 1954
First performance: 1954. Emission 'Recherches,' Radio France, Paris. Conductor: D.
   Milhaud, editing: J. E. Marie

Music for television

Péron et Evita op. 372
(Documentary)
Mills, September 1958
2.1.2.1.–2.3.2.1.–P. 2 vln, 2 va, 2 vc, cb.
Dedication and/or commission: comm. CBS-TV
First performance: 20 November 1958. 20th Club CBS-TV, New York

Burma Road op. 375
(Documentary)
Mills, 13–26 January 1959
2.1.2.1.–2.3.2.1.–P.S.
Dedication and/or commission: comm. CBS-TV
First performance: 15 March 1959. 20th Club CBS-TV, New York

Manuscripts that have disappeared are marked by an asterisk (*)

Poèmes de Francis Jammes
Premier recueil, op. 1
Avec ton parapluie — J'ai vu revenir les choses — Au bord de l'eau verte — La procession des campagnes — Au beau soleil — C'était affreux — J'aime l'âne — Je crève de pitié — Pourquoi les boeufs

Deuxième recueil, op. 1
Prière pour être simple — Prière pour aller au paradis avec les ânes* — Prière pour qu'un enfant ne meure pas* — Prière pour demander une étoile — Tristesse — Si tu pouvais — Ne me console pas*
Aix-Paris, 1910–1912
Voice, piano
Dedication and/or commission: Léo Latil (Avec ton parapluie — J'ai vu revenir les choses — La procession des campagnes — J'aime l'âne — Prière pour qu'un enfant ne meure pas — Prière pour demander une étoile — Tristesse — Si tu pouvais); Mme. Berthelier (Au bord de l'eau verte); Tipia (Au beau soleil); Céline Lagouarde (C'était affreux — Je crève de pitié — Pourquoi les boeufs — Prière pour être simple — Prière pour aller au paradis avec les ânes — Ne me console pas)

Troisième recueil, op. 6
Clara d'Ellebeuse — Almaïde d'Etremont — Pomme d'anis — Bernadette*
Paris, 1912–1913
Voice, piano
Dedication and/or commission: Léo Latil (Clara d'Ellebeuse — Almaïde d'Etremont — Bernadette); Mme F. Jammes (Pomme d'anis)

Quatrième recueil, op. 50
La gomme coule — Viens je te mettrai . . .* — Je le trouvai . . .*
Rio de Janeiro, 1918
Voice, piano
Dedication and/or commission: Céline Lagouarde (La gomme coule); Jeanne Latil (Viens je te mettrai . . . — Je le trouvai . . .)
First performance: 30 March 1919. Vieux Colombier, Paris. Voice: J. Bathori, piano: D. Milhaud

Trois poèmes de Léo Latil* op. 2
Prière à mon poète et à la petite Bernadette, sa fille — Clair de lune — Il pleut doucement
Aix, 1910–1916
Voice, piano
First performance: 30 March 1919. Vieux Colombier, Paris. Voice: J. Bathori, piano: D. Milhaud

Trois poèmes romantiques op. 11
1e série
Les siècles ont creusé . . .* [M. de Guérin] — L'isolement [A. de Lamartine] —
Sonnet [H. de la Morvonnais]
Paris-Aix, 1913–1914
Voice, piano
Dedication and/or commission: Raymond Bonheur (Les siècles ont creusé . . .);
André Gide (L'isolement); Francis Jammes (Sonnet)
First performance: 21 December 1913. Assoc. Mus. Aix-en-Provence. Voice: J.
Lacoste

Poème sur un cantique de Camargue* op. 13
Aix-Paris, 1913
Piano, orchestra
Dedication and/or commission: Léo Latil
First performance: 5 December 1915. Conc. Colonne, Paris. Conductor: G. Pierné,
piano: L. Lévy

Trois poèmes romantiques op. 19
2e série
Plainte [A. Tastu] — Elégie [Mme Dufrénoy] — Lassitude [L. Collet]
Marseille, 1914
Voice, piano
Dedication and/or commission: Léo Latil (Plainte — Elégie); Georgette Guller
(Lassitude)

Le château op. 21
[Armand Lunel]
Les enfants — Le sifflet — Les châtelaines — Le cavalier — Les libellules —
L'agriculteur — L'octobre — L'adieu
Aix, 29 July 1914
Voice, piano

Variations sur un thème de Cliquet* op. 23
Paris, 1915
Piano
Dedication and/or commission: André Gédalge

L'arbre exotique op. 28
(Allusion aux malheurs d'un exilé)
[Chevalier Gosse]
Paris, 10 May 1915
Voice, piano
Dedication and/or commission: M. Veillet-Lavallée

Notre Dame de Sarrance op. 29
(Hymne)
[Francis Jammes]
Paris, 1915
Voice

Deux poèmes du Gardener* op. 35
[Rabindranath Tagore translated by E. Ste. Marie Perrin]
Ne gardez pas — Ayez pitié de votre serviteur
Atlantic Ocean, 1916–1917
2 voices, piano
Dedication and/or commission: M. et Mme. Engel

Trois poèmes op. 37
[Alice Maynell, Christina Rosetti]
Paris, 1916
Voice, piano/chamber ensemble
Dedication and/or commission: A la mémoire de G. L.
First performance: 18 July 1916. Salle d'Antin, Paris. Voice: A. Stephenson

No 34 de l'église habillée de feuilles op. 38
[Francis Jammes]
Paris, 1916
Vocal quartet, piano 6 hands

Verso Carioca op. 44b
(To follow 'Chansons bas')
[Paul Claudel]
Le rémouleur — Le marchand de sorbets
Rio de Janeiro, 21 March 1917
Voice, piano

Deux poèmes de Rimbaud op. 45
Marine — Aube
Rio de Janeiro, 1917
Voice, piano
Dedication and/or commission: Paul Claudel

Deux poèmes tupis* op. 52
(Indian texts)
Caïné—Catiti
Rio de Janeiro, 1918
4 women's voices, handclap
Dedication and/or commission: Jacaremirim
First performance: 15 May 1919. Vieux Colombier, Paris. Groupe Bathori

Poèmes de Francis Thompson* op. 54
[Translated by Paul Claudel]
Atlantic Ocean, 1919
Voice, piano
Dedication and/or commission: Gabrielle Gills
First performance: Paris. Voice: Hubbard

Feuilles de température op. 65
[Paul Morand]
Don Juan — Révérence — Etrennes
Paris, 1920
Voice, piano
Dedication and/or commission: Marie Laurencin (Don Juan); Irène Lagut (Révérence)
First performance: June 1933. Coll. de France, Paris. Voice: J. Bathori

Pièce de circonstance op. 90
[Jean Cocteau]
Malines, 1926
Voice, piano
Publisher: musical supplement of the magazine 'Créer'; 10 gift copies
Dedication and/or commission: Jane Bathori
First performance: 6 December 1926. Paris. Voice: J. Bathori

Impromptu* op. 91
Paris, 1926
Vln, piano
Dedication and/or commission: Denyse Bertrand

Quatrain op. 106
[Francis Jammes]
Paris, 8 February 1929
Voice, piano
Publisher: (Rev. Mus., 100 gift copies)
Dedication and/or commission: Hommage à Albert Roussel
First performance: Festival Roussel. Voice: J. Bathori

Choral op. 111
Paris, 1930
Piano
Dedication and/or commission: A la mémoire de Raymonde Linossier

A Flower Given to My Child
[James Joyce]
Paris, summer 1930
Voice, piano

Le funeste retour* op. 123
[Sailor's song, 17th century Canadian text]
Paris, 1933
Dedication and/or commission: Marianne Oswald
First performance: 'Le Boeuf sur le Toit.' voice: M. Oswald

Le cygne I et II* op. 142
[Paul Claudel]
1935
Voice, piano

Quatrain op. 143
[A. Flament]
Paris, 1935
Voice, piano
Publisher: (Programme du Bal des Petits Lits Blancs)

Fragments dramatiques op. 154b
See Incidental music (Le conquérant)
Aix, August 1936
1.1.1.1.–1.1.1.0.–P.H.S.
First performance: 9 December 1936. Conc. Revue Mus.,
Paris. Conductor: P. Monteux

La fête de la lumière op. 159
(Ballet céleste)
[Paul Claudel]
Paris, December 1936–January 1937
Solo voice, 1.1.1.1.–1.1.1.1.–3 sax–P.H. piano, 3 vln, va, vc.
First performance: 1937. Fêtes de lumière et d'eau, Esposition 1937, Paris. Conductor:
    D. Milhaud, voice: E. Fels Noth, light. effects: Beaudoin, Lodz

Rondeau op. 178
[P. de Corneille]
Paris, 1937
Voice, piano

Quatrain op. 180
[Mallarmé]
Paris, 28 October 1937
Voice, piano
Dedication and/or commission: Marie-Laure de Noailles

L'oiseau* op. 181
Paris, November 1937
2.1.2.1.–1.2.1.1.–T.P.H.S.
First performance: 30 January 1938. O.S.P., Paris. Conductor: D. Milhaud

La reine de Saba* op. 207
(Harmonization for string quartet of a Palestinian tune)
Aix, 8 August 1939
First performance: 1939. Radio Jerusalem

Fanfare op. 209
Aix, 14–16 August 1939
3.3.3.3.–4.3.3.1.–T.P.H.S.
Dedication and/or commission: St. Louis Symph. Orch. pour son 60e anniversaire
  (comm.)
First performance: St. Louis Symphony. Conductor: V. Golschmann

Indicatif et marche pour les bons d'armement op. 212
Aix, 1940
3 tpt, 2 tbn, tu, perc.
Dedication and/or commission: comm. Ministère des Finances
First performance: 1940. Radio d'Etat. Conductor: R. Desormière

Sornettes op. 214
[Popular Provençal texts, translated by Frédéric Mistral]
Aix, 12 March 1940
2 children's voices
Dedication and/or commission: Daniel

Cours de solfège; Papillon, papillonette op. 217
[Henri Fluchère]
Aix, 16–20 April 1940
Children's voices, piano
First performance: February 1950. Emission mélodies inédites de Jane Bathori:
  Maîtrise de la radio, Radio France. Conductor: M. Couraud

Mills Fanfare op. 224
Oakland, February 1941
String ensemble
First performance: 16 April 1941. Mills Orchestra. Conductor: W. Herbert

Fanfare de la liberté op. 235
Mills, 4 November 1942
3.3.3.3.–4.3.2.1.–T.P. cb.
Dedication and/or commission: Cincinnati Symph. Orch.
First performance: Spring Concert, Washington, D.C. Navy School Band

La libertadora op. 236b
See Piano, two pianos
Mills, November 1943
Piano

Cain et Abel op. 241
[Biblical text]
Mills, 1944
Spoken voice, 2.2.3.2.–2.2.2.0.–P.S.
Dedication and/or commission: comm. Shilkret
First performance: 21 October 1945. Hollywood. Janssen Symph. Orch.

Air op. 242
See Duos, viola & piano (Première sonate)
Mills, March 1944
Va, orchestra.
First performance: April 1944. University of Wisconsin. Va: G. Prévost

Printemps lointain op. 253
[Francis Jammes]
Mills, 2 April 1945
Voice, piano.
Dedication and/or commission: P. Monteux pour ses 70 ans.

Pledge to Mills op. 261
(Student song)
[George Hedley]
Mills, 28 January 1946
First performance: February 1946. Mills College Assembly. Conductor: H. Brubeck

Sept danses sur des airs palestiniens op. 267
Mills, 17–18 May 1946 (7th dance: 7 August 1947)
First six danses: ob, cl, bn, tpt, perc, harp, vln, vc.
7th danse: fl, ob, 2 cl, bn, 2 tpt, tbn, 2 perc, strings
Dedication and/or commission: comm. Corinne Chochem

Méditation op. 277
Mills, 30 April 1947
Piano
Dedication and/or commission: Elsa Baraine
First performance: 27 April 1980. San Francisco Women Musicians Club. Piano: J.
    Galante

L'choh dodi op. 290
[Liturgical text]
Mills, 18–19 November 1948
Cantor, mixed chorus, organ.
Dedication and/or commission: Reverend Robert* Rinder
First performance: 10 December 1948. Temple Emanu-El, San Francisco. Cantor: R.
    Rinder
Duration: 2 min 30 s
The work is listed in Milhaud's notebooks as having been published by Schirmer.
    Apparently this publication was never released.
*This is an error. The Cantor at Temple Emanu-El was Reuben Rinder

Les temps faciles op. 305
[Marsan]
Paris, 14 June 1950
Voice, piano
Dedication and/or commission: La 100e repr. des 'Temps difficiles' d'Edouard
    Bourdet
First performance: Chez 'Carrière'

Eglogue op. 335c
Paris, June 1954
Fl, piano

Pensée amicale op. 342
Mills, 8 February 1955
String ensemble
Dedication and/or commission: pour les 80 ans (4.4) de Pierre Monteux
First performance: 4 April 1955. Boston Symphony. Conductor: C. Munch

Le chat op. 356
[Jean Cocteau]
Paris, 1956
Voice, piano
Dedication and/or commission: Marya Freund pour ses 80 ans

Ecoutez mes enfants op. 359
Mills, 7 February 1957
Voice, organ

Neige sur le fleuve op. 391
(Deux cadences)
[Tsang Yuang, 773–819]
Florence, 8 October 1961
Fl, cl, bn, tpt, perc, vln, vc, cb.
Dedication and/or commission: pour les 60 ans du Dr. Schlee

Fanfare op. 396
Paris, 12 November 1962
4 cl, 3 tmp, 3 tbn, tu.
Dedication and/or commission: Ft. Lauderdale band

Préparatif à la mort en allégorie martime op. 403
[Agrippa d'Aubigné]
Mills, 9 June 1963
Voice, piano.
Dedication and/or commission: A la mémoire de Francis Poulenc
First performance: 13 January 1964. Carnegie Hall, New York. Voice A. Esty

Adam op. 411
[Jean Cocteau]
1964
Sop, 2 ten, 2 bar.
Dedication and/or commission: A la demande de la Revue Adam; aux chères
    mémoires de Jean et de Francis

Elégie pour Pierre op. 416
Paris, 1965
Va, perc.
Dedication and/or commission: Pierre Monteux

Vezelay 'La colline éternelle' op. 423
[Maurice Druon]
Mills, 11 January–14 March 1967
Voice, 2.2.2.2.–4.3.3.1.–H.S.
Dedication and/or commission: comm. Préfecture de l'Yonne
First performance: 1967. 'Son et Lumière,' Vezelay. Conductor: D. Milhaud, voice:
  E. Pierre

The following two works, in the Bibliothèque Nationale, have opus numbers that must have corresponded to a numbering of youthful manuscripts lost during the war.

Désespoir 'op. 33'
[Armand Lunel]
1909
Voice, piano.
Publisher: V. Morlot
Dedication and/or commission: José de Bérys

A la Toussaint 'op. 47'
[Baronne de Grand Maison]
1911

REDUCTIONS, ARRANGEMENTS, & TRANSCRIPTIONS

Reducitons

Reductions: for piano (two hands) ────────────────

Les songes
Publisher: Salabert

Le train bleu
Publisher: Heugel

Reductions: for piano (four hands) ────────────────

Le boeuf sur le toit
Publisher: Eschig

La création du monde
Publisher: Eschig

L'homme et son désir
Publisher: U.E.

Sérénade
Publisher: U.E.

Suite française
Publisher: Bel. M.

Première suite symphonique
Publisher: Eschig

Deuxième suite symphonique
Publisher: Durand

Reductions: for two pianos ————————————————————————

Ballade
Publisher: U.E.

Le carnaval d'Aix
Publisher: Heugel

Premier concerto de piano
Publisher: Salabert

Deuxième concerto de piano
Publisher: Heugel

Troisième concerto de piano
Publisher: A.M.P.

Quatrième concerto de piano
Publisher: Heugel

Cinquième concerto de piano
Publisher: Eschig

Fantaisie pastorale
Publisher: Salabert

Le retour de l'enfant prodigue
Publisher: U.E.

Reductions: for three pianos ─────────────────────────────

Premier concerto pour deux pianos
Publisher: Elkan Vogel-Presser

Reductions: for solo instruments & piano ─────────────────

Concertino d'été (va)
Publisher: Heugel

Concertino d'hiver (tbn)
Publisher: A.M.P.

Concertino de printemps (vln)
Publisher: Salabert

Premier concerto d'alto
Publisher: U.E.

Deuxième concerto d'alto
Publisher: Heugel

Concerto de batterie (perc)
Publisher: U.E.

Concerto de clavecin
Publisher: Salabert

Concerto de harpe
Publisher: Eschig

Concerto de marimba et vibraphone
Publisher: Enoch

Deuxième concerto de violon
Publisher: A.M.P.

Premier concerto de violoncelle
Publisher: Salabert

Deuxième concerto de violoncelle
Publisher: A.M.P.

Concerto pour flûte et violon
Publisher: Salabert

Concerto pour hautbois
Publisher: Heugel

Concert royal (vln)
Publisher: Eschig

Music for Boston (vln)
Publisher: Elkan Vogel

Scaramouche (cl)
Publisher: Salabert

Scaramouche (sax)
Publisher: Salabert

Stanford Serenade (ob)
Publisher: Eschig

Suite anglaise (vln)
Publisher: B.&H.

Suite anglaise (harm)
Publisher: B.&H.

Suite cisalpine (vc)
Publisher: Eschig

Most of the operas as well as compositions for voice with instrumental ensemble are available as piano scores.

Arrangements by Darius Milhaud

[   ]

Adieu New York, Georges Auric
Piano 4 hands.
Publisher: Eschig

Cinq grimaces, Erik Satie
Piano.
Publisher: U.E.

Entr'acte, Erik Satie
Piano 4 hands.
Publisher: Salabert

Gymnopédie, Erik Satie
Piano 4 hands.
Publisher: Salabert

Jack in the Box, Erik Satie
Orchestra.
Publisher: U.E.

Overture and Allegro
(From 'La sultane suite,' François Couperin)
3.3.3.2.–3.3.3.1.–T.P.H.C.
Publisher: Elkan Vogel

Ouverture
(Finale of the 'Sonate de piano 4 mains,' Francis Poulenc)
Orchestra.
Publisher: Chester

Suite
(From 'Morceaux en forme de poire,' Erik Satie)
Vln, piano.
Publisher: U.E.

Transcriptions of Milhaud's works by other composers

Accueil amical
Orchestrated by J. Veyrier
Publisher: Heugel

Brazileira
(From 'Scaramouche')
Arrangement for violin & piano, by Jascha Heifetz
Publisher: Salabert

Brazileira
(From 'Scaramouche')
Arrangement for band
Publisher: Salabert

Concerto for percussion
Arrangement by Jerry Neil Smith
Publisher: Presser

Corcocovado, Sorocaba
(From 'Saudades do Brazil')
Arrangement for violoncello & piano, by M. Maréchal
Publisher: Eschig

De profundis
[Psalm 129]
Arrangement for voice & organ, by Helmut Bornefeld
Publisher: U.E.

Divertissements
(From 'Vendanges')
Arrangement for 2 pianos, by Victor Babin
Publisher: Eschig

Le globe trotter
Arrangement for band, by Maxim Koch
Publisher: Bel. M.

Madame Bovary
Arrangement for orchestra from the film score, by Chapelier
Publisher: Enoch

Petit concert
(From 'Le bal des voleurs')
Arrangement for b-flat clarinet and piano by R. Calmel
Publisher: Billaudot

Quatrième quatuor
Arrangement for piano 4 hands, by Nininha Velloso Guerra
Publisher: (Senart) Salabert

Cinquième quatuor
Arrangement for piano 4 hands, by Nininha Velloso Guerra
Publisher: (Senart) Salabert

Saudades do Brazil
Arrangement for violin & piano, by Claude Lévy
Publisher: Eschig

Scaramouche
Arrangement for alto saxophone & wind quintet, by D. Stewart
Publisher: Salabert

Scaramouche
Arrangement for 12 saxophones, by J. M. Londeix
Publisher: Salabert

Sobre la loma
(From 'Four Sketches')
Arrangement for dance orchestra
Publisher: Mercury

Suite
Arrangement of 'Septième quatuor' for string orchestra, by A. Willner
Publisher: U.E.

Suite
Arrangement for ondes Martenot & chamber orchestra, by R. Calmel
Publisher: Cerda

Suite anglaise
Arrangement for accordion & orchestra, by M. Ellegaard
Publisher: B.&H.

Sumare
(From 'Saudades do Brazil')
Arrangement for violoncello & piano, by Maurice Gendron
Publisher: Eschig

Tango des Fratellini
(From 'Le boeuf sur le toit')
Orchestrated by H. Mouton
Publisher: Eschig

Le train bleu
6 excerpts orchestrated by H. Mouton
Publisher: Heugel

CATALOGUE OF COMPOSITIONS
ARRANGED BY OPUS NUMBERS

Opus	Year	Title and Category
1	1910–12	Poèmes de Francis Jammes (1er et 2e recueil): Unpublished works
2	1910–16	Trois poèmes de Léo Latil: Unpublished works
3	1911	Première sonate: Duos, violin & piano
4	1910–14	La brebis égarée: Operas
5	1912	Premier quatuor: Quartets, string
6	1912–13	Poèmes de Francis Jammes (3e recueil): Unpublished works
7	1912–13	Sept poèmes de la connaissance de l'est: Solo voice, with piano
8	1913	Suite: Piano, solo
9	1913, 31	Alissa: Solo voice, with piano
10	1913	Trois poèmes en prose de Lucile de Chateaubriand: Solo voice, with piano
11	1913–14	Trois poèmes romantiques: Unpublished works
12	1913–14	Première suite symphonique: Large orchestra, symphonic suites: Reductions
13	1913	Poème sur un cantique de Camargue: Unpublished works
14	1913	Agamemnon: Operas
15	1914	Sonate: Trios, piano & two violins
16	1914–15	Deuxième quatuor: Quartets, string
17	1913–19	Protée: Incidental music
18	1914	Le printemps: Duos, violin & piano
19	1914	Trois poèmes romantiques: Unpublished works
20	1914	Quatre poèmes de Léo Latil: Solo voice, with piano
21	1914	Le château: Unpublished works
22	1914	Poème du Gitanjali: Solo voice, with piano
23	1915	Variations sur un thème de Cliquet: Unpublished works
24	1915–16	Les choéphores: Operas
25	1915–19	Printemps (vol. I): Piano, solo
26	1915–17	Quatre poèmes de Paul Claudel pour baryton: Solo voice, with piano
27	1915	D'un cahier inédit du journal d'Eugénie de Guérin: Solo voice, with piano
28	1915	L'arbre exotique: Unpublished works
29	1915	Notre Dame de Sarrance: Unpublished works
30	1915	Deux poèmes d'amour: Solo voice, with piano
31	1915	Deux poèmes de Coventry Patmore: Solo voice, with piano
32	1916	Troisième quatuor: Quartets, string
33	1916	Sonate: Piano, solo
34	1916	Poèmes juifs: Solo voice, with piano

Opus	Year	Title and Category
35	1916–17	Deux poèmes du Gardener: Unpublished works
36	1916	Child Poems: Solo voice, with piano
37	1916	Trois poèmes [Meynell, Rosetti]: Unpublished works
38	1916	No. 34 de l'église habillée de feuilles: Unpublished works
39	1916–19	Deux poèmes [St. Léger Léger, Chalupt]: A cappella ensemble, mixed quartet (or chorus)
40	1917	Deuxième sonate: Duos, violin & piano
41	1917–22	Les euménides: Operas
42	1917	Le retour de l'enfant prodigue: Accompanied vocal ensemble, five voices & orchestra; Reductions
43	1917	Première symphonie: Chamber ensembles, chamber symphonies
44	1917	Chansons bas: Solo voice, with piano
44b	1917	Verso Carioca: Unpublished works
45	1917	Deux poèmes de Rimbaud: Unpublished works
46	1918	Quatrième quatuor: Quartets, string; Transcriptions
47	1918	Sonate: Quartets, piano & other instruments
48	1918	L'homme et son désir: Large orchestra, miscellaneous; Ballets; Reductions
49	1918	Deuxième symphonie: Chamber ensembles, chamber symphonies
50	1918	Poèmes de Francis Jammes (4e recueil): Unpublished works
51	1918	Deux petits airs: Solo voice, with piano
52	1918	Deux poèmes Tupis: Unpublished works
53	1918	Psaume 136: Accompanied vocal ensemble, soloist, mixed chorus & orchestra
53b	1919	Psaume 129: Solo voice with orchestra; Transcriptions
54	1919	Poèmes de Francis Thompson: Unpublished works
55	1919	Les soirées de Petrograde: Solo voice, with piano
56	1919	Machines agricoles: Solo voice, with chamber ensemble
57	1919	Deuxième suite symphonique (Protée): Large orchestra, symphonic suites; Reductions
58	1919	Le boeuf sur le toit: Ballets; Reductions
58b	1919	Cinéma-fantaisie: Duos, violin & piano; Solo & orchestra (or chamber ensemble), violin
58c	1919	Tango des Fratellini: Piano, solo; Transcriptions
59	1920	Trois poèmes de Jean Cocteau: Solo voice, with piano
60	1920	Catalogue de fleurs: Solo voice, with piano; Solo voice, with chamber ensemble
61	1920–23	Ballade: Solo & orchestra (or chamber ensemble), piano; Reductions
62	1920–21	Sérénade: Large orchestra, symphonic suites; Reductions
63	1920	Cinq études: Solo & orchestra (or chamber ensemble), piano
64	1920	Cinquième quatuor: Quartets, string; Transcriptions
65	1920	Feuilles de température: Unpublished works
66	1919–20	Printemps (vol. II): Piano, solo
67	1920	Saudades do Brazil: Piano, solo
67b	1920–21	Saudades do Brazil: Large orchestra, symphonic suites; Transcriptions

Opus	Year	Title and Category
68	1920	Caramel mou: Piano, solo; Chamber ensembles, miscellaneous ensembles; Solo voice, with chamber ensemble
69	1920	Cocktail: Solo voice, with chamber ensemble
70	1921	Les mariés de la Tour Eiffel: Ballets
70b	1971	Fugue du massacre: Ballets (Les mariés de la Tour Eiffel)
71	1921	Troisième symphonie: Chamber ensembles, chamber symphonies
72	1921	Psaume 126 ('Psaume 121'): A cappella ensemble, men's chorus
73	1921	Poème [Latil]: Solo voice, with piano
74	1921	Quatrième symphonie: Chamber ensembles, chamber symphonies
75	1922	Cinquième symphonie: Chamber ensembles, chamber symphonies
76	1922	Sonatine: Duos, flute & piano
77	1922	Sixième quatuor: Quartets, string
78	1922	Trois rag caprices: Piano, solo; Chamber ensembles, miscellaneous ensembles
79	1923	Sixième symphonie: Chamber ensembles, chamber symphonies
80	1923	Quatre poèmes de Catulle: Solo voice, with chamber ensemble
81	1923	La création du monde: Ballets
81b	1926	La création du monde: Quintets, string; Reductions
82	1923	Une education manquée: Recitatives
83	1924	Salade: Ballets
83b	1926	Le carnaval d'Aix: Solo & orchestra (or chamber ensemble), piano; Reductions
84	1924	Le train bleu: Ballets; Reductions; Transcriptions
85	1924	Les malheurs d'Orphée: Operas
86	1925	Six chants populaires hébraïques: Solo voice, with piano; Solo voice, with orchestra
87	1925	Septième quatuor: Quartets, string; Transcriptions
88	1925	Deux hymnes: Solo voice, with piano
88b	1925	Deux hymnes: Large orchestra, miscellaneous
89	1925–27	Esther de Carpentras: Operas
90	1926	Pièce de circonstance: Unpublished works
91	1926	Impromptu: Unpublished works
92	1926	Le pauvre matelot: Operas
93	1927	Premier concerto: Solo & orchestra (or chamber ensemble), violin
94	1927	L'enlèvement d'Europe: "Opéras-minute"
95	1927	Polka: Piano, solo pieces included in collections; Ballets
96	1927	Prières journalières à l'usage des juifs du Comtat Venaissin: Solo voice, with piano
97	1927	Trois caprices de Paganini: Duos, violin & piano
98	1927	L'abandon d'Ariane: "Opéras-minute"
99	1927	La délivrance de Thesée: "Opéras-minute"
100	1927	Sonatine: Duos, clarinet & piano
101	1928	La bien-aimée: Ballets
101b	1941	La bien-aimée (new orchestration): Ballets
102	1928	Christophe Colomb: Operas

Opus	Year	Title and Category
103	1929	Cantate pour louer le Seigneur: Accompanied vocal ensemble, mixed chorus & orchestra
104	1928	Actualités: Music for films
105	1928	Vocalise: Solo voice, unaccompanied
106	1929	Quatrain [Jammes]: Unpublished works
107	1929	La p'tite Lilie: Music for films
108	1929	Premier concerto: Solo & orchestra (or chamber ensemble), viola; Reductions
109	1929–30	Concerto: Solo & orchestra (or chamber ensemble), percussion; Reductions
110	1930	Maximilien: Operas
110b	1930	Suite de Maximilien: Large orchestra, symphonic suites
111	1930	Choral: Unpublished works
112	1931	Sonate: Other solo instruments, organ
113	1932	Deux poèmes de Cendrars: A cappella ensemble, mixed quartet (or chorus)
114	1932	Deux élégies romaines: A cappella ensemble, women's quartet (or chorus)
115	1932	L'automne: Piano, solo
116	1932	La mort d'un tyran: Accompanied vocal ensemble, mixed chorus & orchestra
117	1932	L'annonce faite à Marie: Accompanied vocal ensemble, vocal quartet & chamber ensemble; Incidental music see also opus 231
118	1932	A propos de bottes: Accompanied vocal ensemble, easy pieces
119	1932	Un petit peu de musique: Accompanied vocal ensemble, easy pieces
120	1932	Le château des papes: Incidental music
120b	1932	Adages: Accompanied vocal ensemble, vocal quartet & chamber ensemble
120c	1932	Suite: Duos, ondes Martenot & piano; Transcriptions
121	1932	Huitième quatuor: Quartets, string
122	1933	Devant sa main nue: A cappella ensemble, women's quartet (or chorus)
123	1933	Le funeste retour: Unpublished works
124	1933	Les songes: Ballets; Reductions
125	1933	Liturgie comtadine: Solo voice, with piano; Solo voice, with orchestra
126	1933	Hallo Everybody: Music for films
127	1933	Premier concerto: Solo & orchestra (or chamber ensemble), piano; Reductions
128	1933	Madame Bovary: Music for films; Transcriptions
128b	1933	L'album de Madame Bovary: Piano, solo
128c	1933	Trois valses: Piano, solo
128d	1933	Deux chansons: Solo voice, with piano
129	1933	Quatre romances sans paroles: Piano, solo
130	1934	Pan et la Syrinx: Accompanied vocal ensemble, vocal quartet & chamber ensemble
131	1934	Se plaire sur la même fleur: Incidental music

Opus	Year	Title and Category
132	1934	Les amours de Ronsard: Accompanied vocal ensemble, vocal quartet & chamber ensemble; Accompanied vocal ensemble, mixed chorus & orchestra
133	1934	Un petit peu d'exercice: Accompanied vocal ensemble, easy pieces
134	1934	Exercice musical: Duos, pipeau & piano
135	1934	Concertino de printemps: Solo & orchestra (or chamber ensemble), violin; Reductions
136	1934	Premier concerto: Solo & orchestra (or chamber ensemble), violoncello; Reductions
137	1934	L'hippocampe: Music for films
138	1934	Tartarin de Tarascon: Music for films
139	1934	Le cycle de la création: Incidental music
140	1935	Neuvième quatuor: Quartets, string
141	1935	La sagesse: Accompanied vocal ensemble, soloist, mixed chorus & orchestra
142	1935	Le cygne I et II: Unpublished works
143	1935	Quatrain [Flament]: Unpublished works
144	1935	Dixième sonate de Baptiste Anet (1729): Duos, violin & piano
145	1935	Le faiseur: Incidental music
146	1935	Voix d'enfants: Music for films
147	1935	Pastorale: Trios, oboe, clarinet & bassoon
148	1935–36	Bolivar: Incidental music
148b	1935–36	Trois chansons de négresse: Solo voice, with piano
148c	1936–37	Trois chansons de négresse: Solo voice, with orchestra
149	1936	La folle du ciel: Incidental music
150	1936	The Beloved Vagabond: Music for films
151	1936	Tu ne m'échapperas jamais: Incidental music
151b	1936	Six chansons de théâtre: Solo voice, with piano
152	1936	Bertran de Born: Incidental music
152b	1936	Trois chansons de troubadour: Solo voice, with piano
152c	1936	Suite provençale: Large orchestra, symphonic suites
152d	1936	Suite provençale: Ballets
152e	1937	Le trompeur de Seville: Incidental music
153	1936	Le quatorze juillet: Incidental music
153b	1936	Introduction et marche funèbre: Large orchestra, miscellaneous; Band
154	1936	Le conquérant: Incidental music
154b	1936	Fragments dramatiques: Unpublished works
155	1936	Cantique du Rhone: A cappella ensemble, mixed quartet (or chorus)
156	1936	Amal, ou La lettre du roi: Incidental music
157	1936	Le voyageur sans bagages: Incidental music
157b	1936	Suite: Trios, piano, violin & clarinet
158	1936	Jules César: Incidental music
159	1936–37	La fête de la lumière: Unpublished works
160	1937	La duchesse d'Amalfi: Incidental music
161	1937	Romeo et Juliette: Incidental music
161b	1937	Suite d'après Corrette: Trios, oboe, clarinet & bassoon

Opus	Year	Title and Category
162	1933, 37	Le tour de l'Exposition: Piano, solo pieces included in collections
163	1937	Liberté: Incidental music
164	1937	Cantate pour l'inauguration du Musée de l'Homme: Accompanied vocal ensemble, vocal quartet & chamber ensemble
165	1937	Le médecin volant: Incidental music
165b	1937	Scaramouche: Piano, two pianos
165c	1939	Scaramouche: Solo & orchestra (or chamber ensemble), saxophone
165d	1941	Scaramouche: Solo & orchestra (or chamber ensemble), clarinet; Reductions; Transcriptions
166	1937	Cantate de la paix: A cappella ensemble, mixed chorus
167	1936–37	Cinq chansons: Solo voice, with piano; Solo voice, with orchestra
168	1937	Cantate nuptiale: Solo voice, with orchestra
169	1937	Main tendue à tous: A cappella ensemble, mixed chorus
170	1937	Les deux cités: A cappella ensemble, mixed chorus
171	1937	Chansons de l'opéra du gueux: Incidental music
171b	1937	Chansons du carnaval de Londres: Solo voice, with piano; Solo voice, with orchestra
172	1937	Le carnaval de Londres: Chamber ensembles, miscellaneous ensembles
173	1937	Naissance d'une cité: Incidental music
173b	1937	Chanson du capitaine; Java de la femme: Solo voice, with piano
174	1937	Mollenard: Music for films
175	1937	Macbeth: Incidental music
176	1937	La citadelle du silence: Music for films
177	1937	Hécube: Incidental music
178	1937	Rondeau: Unpublished works
179	1937	Holem tsaudi—Gam hayom: Solo voice, with piano
180	1937	Quatrain [Mallarmé]: Unpublished works
181	1937	L'oiseau: Unpublished works
182	1937	Grands feux: Music for films
183	1937	Prends cette rose: Two voices, with orchestra
184	1937	La conquête du ciel: Music for films
185	1938	Cantate de l'enfant et de la mère: Spoken voice, with chamber ensemble
186	1938	Plutus: Incidental music
187	1938	La tragédie impériale, Raspoutine: Music for films
188	1938	Fantaisie pastorale: Solo & orchestra (or chamber ensemble), piano; Reductions
189	1938	Les quatre elements: Two voices, with orchestra
189b	1956	Les quatre elements: Solo voice, with orchestra
190	1938	Tricolore: Incidental music
191	1938	Médée: Operas
192	1938	Le bal des voleurs: Incidental music; Transcriptions
193	1938	La première famille: Incidental music
194	1938	Magali: Accompanied vocal ensemble, mixed chorus & orchestra

Opus	Year	Title and Category
195	1938	Récréation: Solo voice, pieces for children
196	1938	Les otages: Music for films
197	1938–39	Concerto: Several instruments & orchestra, flute & violin; Reductions
198	1939	Islands: Music for films
199	1939	Trois élégies: Two voices, with strings
200	1939	Hamlet: Incidental music
201	1939	Incantations: A cappella ensemble, men's chorus
202	1939	Espoir: Music for films
202b	1939	Cortège funèbre: Large orchestra, miscellaneous
203	1939	Voyage au pays du rêve: Music for radio
204	1939	Cavalcade d'amour: Music for films
205	1939	La cheminée du roi René: Quintets, wind
206	1939	Quatrains valaisans: A cappella ensemble, mixed chorus
207	1939	La reine de Saba: Unpublished works
208	1939	Gulf Stream: Music for films
209	1939	Fanfare: Unpublished works
210	1939	Première symphonie: Large orchestra, symphonies
211	1940	Couronne de gloire: Solo voice, with chamber ensemble
212	1940	Indicatif et marche pour les bons d'armement: Unpublished works
213	1940	Cantate de la guerre: A cappella ensemble, mixed chorus
214	1940	Sornettes: Unpublished works
215	1940	Un petit ange de rien du tout: Incidental music
216	1940	Le voyage d'été: Solo voice, with piano
217	1940	Cours de solfège; Papillon, papillonette: Unpublished works
218	1940	Dixième quatuor: Quartets, string
219	1940	Moïse: Ballets
219b	1940	Opus Americanum no 2: Chamber ensembles, miscellaneous ensembles; Large orchestra, miscellaneous
220	1940	Introduction et allegro: Large orchestra, miscellaneous
221	1940	Sonatine: Duos, two violins
221b	1940	Sonatine à trois: Trios, violin, viola & violoncello
222	1941	Black Keys (Touches noires): White Keys (Touches blanches): Piano, easy pieces
223	1940–41	Quatre chansons de Ronsard: Solo voice, with piano; Solo voice, with orchestra
224	1941	Mills fanfare: Unpublished works
225	1941	Deuxième concerto: Solo & orchestra (or chamber ensemble), piano; Reductions
226	1941	Sonatine: Duos, violin & viola
227	1941	Four Sketches (Esquisses): Piano, solo; Chamber ensembles, miscellaneous ensembles; Transcriptions
227b	1941	Madrigal; Pastoral (originally 'Eglogue'): Duos, clarinet & piano; Quintets, wind
228	1941	Premier concerto: Solo & orchestra (or chamber ensemble), two pianos; Reductions
229	1941	Pastorale: Other solo instruments, organ
230	1941	Concerto: Solo & orchestra (or chamber ensemble), clarinet

Opus	Year	Title and Category
231	1942	L'annonce faite à Marie: (2nd version) Incidental music
231b	1942	Neuf préludes: Other solo instruments, organ
231c	1942	Cinq prières: Solo voice, with organ (or piano)
232	1942	Onzième quatuor: Quartets, string
233	1942	Rêves: Solo voice, with piano
234	1942	Suite anglaise: Solo & orchestra (or chamber ensemble), violin; Solo & orchestra (or chamber ensemble), harmonica; Transcriptions
235	1942	Fanfare de la liberté: Unpublished works
236	1943	Bolivar: Operas
236b	1943	La libertadora: Piano, two pianos; Unpublished works
237	1943	Les songes: Piano, two pianos
238	1942–43	Quatre visages: Duos, viola & piano
239	1944	Borechou; Schema Israël: Accompanied vocal ensemble, soloist, mixed chorus, & organ
240	1944	Première sonate: Duos, viola & piano
241	1944	Caïn et Abel: Unpublished works
242	1944	Air: Unpublished works
243	1944	Jeux de printemps: Chamber ensembles, miscellaneous ensembles; Large orchestra, miscellaneous
244	1944	Deuxième sonate: Duos, viola & piano
245	1944	La muse ménagère: Piano, solo; Chamber ensembles, miscellaneous ensembles
246	1944	La libération des Antilles: Solo voice, with piano
247	1944	Deuxième symphonie: Large orchestra, symphonies
248	1944	Suite française: Large orchestra, symphonic suites; Band; Reductions
249	1945	Le bal martiniquais: Piano, two pianos; Large orchestra, miscellaneous
250	1945	Kaddisch: Accompanied vocal ensemble, soloist, mixed chorus & organ
251	1945	Elégie: Duos, violoncello & piano
252	1945	Douzième quatuor: Quartets, string
253	1945	Printemps lointain: Unpublished works
254	1945	Introduction; Marche; Fête de la victoire: Ballets
255	1945	Deuxième concerto: Solo & orchestra (or chamber ensemble), violoncello; Reductions
256	1945	Danses de Jacarémirim: Duos, violin & piano
257	1945	Sonate: Duos, violin & harpsichord
258	1945	Duo: Duos, two violins
259	1945	Les cloches: Ballets
259b	1946	Les cloches: Large orchestra, symphonic suites
260	1945	Deux marches: Large orchestra, miscellaneous; Band
261	1946	Pledge to Mills: Unpublished works
262	1946	Farandoleurs: Duos, violin & piano
263	1946	Deuxième concerto: Solo & orchestra (or chamber ensemble), violin; Reductions
264	1946	Lidoire: Incidental music
265	1946	Chants de misère: Solo voice, with piano

Opus	Year	Title and Category
266	1946	Six sonnets composés au secret: A cappella ensemble, mixed quartet (or chorus)
267	1946, 47	Sept danses sur des airs palestiniens: Unpublished works
268	1946	Treizième quatuor: Quartets, string
269	1946	Une journée: Piano, easy pieces
270	1946	Troisième concerto: Solo & orchestra (or chamber ensemble), piano: Reductions
271	1946	Troisième symphonie (Te Deum): Large orchestra, symphonies
272	1946	The Private Affairs of Bel-Ami: Music for films
273	1947	Dreams that Money Can Buy: Music for films
274	1947	Trio à cordes: Trios, violin, viola & violoncello
275	1947	Carnaval à la Nouvelle Orleans: Piano, two pianos
276	1947	Trois poèmes [Supervielle]]: Solo voice, with piano
277	1947	Méditation: Unpublished works
278	1947	Concerto: Solo & orchestra (or chamber ensemble), marimba & vibraphone: Reductions
278b	1952	Suite concertante: Solo & orchestra (or chamber ensemble), piano
279	1947	Service sacré: Accompanied vocal ensemble, soloist, mixed chorus, & organ; Accompanied vocal ensemble, soloist, mixed chorus, & orchestra
280	1947	La maison de Bernada Alba: Incidental music
281	1947	Quatrième symphonie: (1848) Large orchestra, symphonies
282	1948	Le grand testament: Music for radio
283	1948	'Adame miroir: Ballets
284	1948	Paris: Piano, four pianos
284b	1959	Paris: Large orchestra, symphonic suites
285	1948	Sheherazade: Incidental music
286	1948	L'apothéose de Molière: Chamber ensembles, miscellaneous ensembles
287	1948	Kentuckiana: Piano, two pianos; Large orchestra, miscellaneous
288	1948	Le jeu de Robin et Marion: Incidental music
289	1948	L'enfant aime: Piano, easy pieces
290	1948	L'choh dodi: Unpublished works
291	1948–49	Quatorzième quatuor: Quartets, string
		Quinzième quatuor: Quartets, string
		Octuor à cordes: Larger string ensembles
292	1949	Naissance de Vénus: A cappella ensemble, mixed chorus
293	1949	Deuxième sonate: Piano, solo
294	1949	Les rêves de Jacob: Quintets, wind
295	1949	Quatrième concerto: Solo & orchestra (or chamber ensemble), piano; Reductions
296	1949	Ballade nocturne: Solo voice, with piano
297	1949	La fin du monde: Music for radio
298	1949–50	Barba Garibo: Accompanied vocal ensemble, mixed chorus & orchestra
298b	1949–50	La cueillette des citrons: Ballets
299	1950	Gauguin: Music for films

Opus	Year	Title and Category
299b	1958	Divertissement: Quintets, wind
300	1950	Suite opus 300: Solo & orchestra (or chamber ensemble), two pianos
301	1950	Le repos du septième jour: Music for radio
302	1950	Jeu: Piano, easy pieces
303	1950	Seizième quatuor: Quartets, string
304	1950	La vie commence demain: Music for films
305	1950	Les temps faciles: Unpublished works
306	1950	Le conte d'hiver: Incidental music
307	1950	Dix-septième quatuor: Quartets, string
308	1950–51	Dix-huitième quatuor: Quartets, string
309	1951	Concertino d'automne: Solo & orchestra (or chamber ensemble), two pianos
310	1951	Cantata from Proverbs: Accompanied vocal ensemble, three-part women's chorus & chamber ensemble
311	1951	Concertino d'été: Solo & orchestra (or chamber ensemble), viola; Reductions
312	1951	Premier quintette: Quintets, string
313	1951	West Point Suite: Band
314	1951	Miracles de la foi: Accompanied vocal ensemble, soloist, mixed chorus, & orchestra
315	1951	Le candélabre à sept branches: Piano, solo
316	1952	Deuxième quintette: Quintets, string
317	1952	Vendanges: Ballets; Transcriptions
318	1952	Christophe Colomb: Incidental music
319	1952	Petites légendes: Solo voice, with piano
320	1952–53	David: Operas
321	1953	Samaël: Music for radio
322	1953	Cinquième symphonie: Large orchestra, symphonies
323	1953	Concerto: Solo & orchestra (or chamber ensemble), harp; Reductions
324	1953	Sonatine: Duos, violin & violoncello
325	1953–54	Troisième quintette: Quintets, string
326	1944–47	Accueil amical: Piano, easy pieces; Transcriptions
327	1953	Concertino d'hiver: Solo & orchestra (or chamber ensemble), trombone; Reductions
328	1953	Le Dibbouk: Music for radio
329	1953	Suite campagnarde: Large orchestra, symphonic suites
330	1953	Ouverture meditérranéenne: Large orchestra, miscellaneous
331	1953–54	Hymne de glorification: Piano, solo
332	1954	Suite cisalpine: Solo & orchestra (or chamber ensemble), violoncello; Reductions
333	1954	Etude poétique: Music for radio
334	1954	Saül: Incidental music
334b	1970	Musique de théâtre: Band
335	1954	Caprice: Duos, clarinet & piano
335b	1954	Danse: Duos, saxophone & piano
335c	1954	Eglogue: Unpublished works
336	1954	Ils étaient tous des volontaires: Music for films

Opus	Year	Title and Category
337	1954	Sonatine: Duos, oboe & piano
338	1954	Le château de feu: Accompanied vocal ensemble, mixed chorus & orchestra
339	1954	Trois psaumes de David: A cappella ensemble, mixed chorus
340	1954–55	Deuxième concerto: Solo & orchestra (or chamber ensemble), viola; Reductions
341	1955	Protée: Incidental music
342	1955	Pensée amicale: Unpublished works
343	1955	Sixième symphonie: Large orchestra, symphonies
344	1955	Septième symphonie: Large orchestra, symphonies
345	1955	Service pour la veille du Sabbat: Accompanied vocal ensemble, children's chorus & organ
346	1955	Cinquième concerto: Solo & orchestra (or chamber ensemble), piano; Reductions
347	1955	Deux poèmes [de Vilmorin]: A cappella ensemble, mixed quartet (or chorus)
348	1955	Petite suite: Other solo instruments, organ
349	1955	Juanito: Incidental music
350	1956	Quatrième quintette: Quintets, string
351	1956	Duo concertant: Duos
352	1956	Fontaines et sources: Solo voice, with piano; Solo voice, with orchestra
353	1956	La couronne de Marguerite: Valse en forme de rondo: Piano, solo pieces included in collections
353b	1956	Valse en forme de rondo: Large orchestra, miscellaneous
354	1956	Sonatine: Piano, solo
355	1956	Tristesses: Solo voice, with piano
356	1956	Le chat: Unpublished works
357	1956	Le mariage de la feuille et du cliché: Accompanied vocal ensemble, soloist, mixed chorus, & orchestra
358	1956–57	Le globe trotter: Piano, solo; Chamber ensembles, miscellaneous ensembles; Transcriptions
359	1957	Ecoutez mes enfants: Unpublished works
360	1957	Les charmes de la vie: Piano, solo; Chamber ensembles, miscellaneous ensembles
361	1957	Aspen serenade: Chamber ensembles, miscellaneous ensembles
362	1957	Huitième symphonie (Rhodanienne): Large orchestra, symphonies
363	1957	Symphoniette: String orchestra
364	1957	Celle qui n'était plus: Music for films
365	1957	Concerto: Solo & orchestra (or chamber ensemble), oboe; Reductions
366	1957	Segoviana: Other solo instruments, guitar
367	1957	La rose des vents: Ballets
368	1958	Sextuor à cordes: Larger string ensembles
369	1958	La tragédie humaine: Accompanied vocal ensemble, mixed chorus & orchestra
370	1958	Fiesta: Operas

Opus	Year	Title and Category
371	1958	Huit poèmes de Jorge Guillen: A cappella ensemble, mixed chorus
372	1958	Péron et Evita: Music for television
373	1958	Concert royal: Solo & orchestra (or chamber ensemble), violin; Reductions
374	1958–59	La branche des oiseaux: Ballets
375	1959	Burma Road: Music for television
376	1959	Symphonie concertante: Several instruments & orchestra. trumpet, horn, bassoon & contrabass
377	1959	Sonate: Duos, violoncello & piano
378	1959	Sonatine: Duos, viola & violoncello
379	1959	Mother Courage: Incidental music
380	1959	Neuvième symphonie: Large orchestra, symphonies
381	1959–60	Cantate de la croix de charité: Accompanied vocal ensemble, soloist, mixed chorus & orchestra
382	1959–60	Dixième symphonie: Large orchestra, symphonies
383	1960	Sonatine pastorale: Other solo instruments, violin
384	1960	Onzième symphonie (Romantique): Large orchestra, symphonies
385	1960	Les funérailles de Phocion: Large orchestra, miscellaneous
386	1960	Cantate sur des poèmes de Chaucer: Accompanied vocal ensemble, mixed chorus & orchestra
387	1960	Aubade: Large orchestra, miscellaneous
388	1960	Cantate de l'initiation: Accompanied vocal ensemble, mixed chorus & orchestra
389	1961	Concert de chambre: Chamber ensembles, miscellaneous ensembles
390	1961	Douzième symphonie (Rurale): Large orchestra, symphonies
391	1961	Neige sur le fleuve: Unpublished works
392	1961	Judith: Incidental music
393	1961	Traversée: A cappella ensemble, mixed chorus
394	1961	Deuxième concerto: Solo & orchestra (or chamber ensemble), two pianos
395	1962	Invocation à l'ange Raphaël: Accompanied vocal ensemble, women's chorus & orchestra
396	1962	Fanfare: Unpublished works
397	1962	Ouverture philharmonique: Large orchestra, miscellaneous
398	1962	Suite de quatrains: Spoken voice, with chamber ensemble
399	1962	A Frenchman in New York: Large orchestra, miscellaneous
400	1962	Fanfare: Trios, two trumpets & trombone
401	1963	Suite de sonnets: Accompanied vocal ensemble, vocal quartet & chamber ensemble
402	1963	Caroles: Accompanied vocal ensemble, mixed chorus & orchestra
403	1963	Préparatif à la mort en allégorie maritime: Unpublished works
404	1963	Pacem in terris: Accompanied vocal ensemble, soloist, mixed chorus & orchestra
405	1963	Meurtre d'un grand chef d'état: Large orchestra, miscellaneous
406	1963	Ode pour les morts des guerres: Large orchestra, miscellaneous

Opus	Year	Title and Category
407	1964	Concerto: Solo & orchestra (or chamber ensemble), harpsichord; Reductions
408	1964	Septuor à cordes: Larger string ensembles
409	1964	L'amour chante: Solo voice, with piano
410	1964	Adieu: Solo voice, with chamber ensemble
411	1964	Adam: Unpublished works
412	1964–65	La mère coupable: Operas
413	1965–66	Cantata from Job: Accompanied vocal ensemble, soloist, mixed chorus & organ
414	1965	Music for Boston: Solo & orchestra (or chamber ensemble), violin; Reductions
415	1965	Musique pour Prague: Large orchestra, symphonic suites
416	1965	Elégie pour Pierre: Unpublished works
417	1966	Quatuor: Quartets, piano & other instruments
418	1966	Musique pour l'Indiana: Large orchestra, symphonic suites
419	1966	Jerusalem à Carpentras: Incidental music
420	1966	Musique pour Lisbonne: Chamber ensembles, miscellaneous ensembles
421	1966	Hommage à Comenius: Two voices, with orchestra
422	1966	Musique pour la Nouvelle-Orleans: Large orchestra, symphonic suites
423	1967	Vezelay 'La colline éternelle': Unpublished works
424	1967	Promenade Concert: Large orchestra, symphonic suites
425	1967	Cantate de psaumes: Solo voice, with orchestra
426	1967	L'histoire de Tobie et Sara: Incidental music
427	1968	Paul Claudel: Music for films
427b	1968	Symphonie pour l'univers Claudelien: Large orchestra, symphonic suites
428	1968	Trio: Trios, piano, violin, & violoncello
429	1968–69	Musique pour Graz: Chamber ensembles, miscellaneous ensembles
430	1969	Stanford Serenade: Solo & orchestra (or chamber ensemble), oboe; Reductions
431	1969	Suite en sol: Large orchestra, symphonic suites
432	1969	Musique pour Ars Nova: Chamber ensembles, miscellaneous ensembles
433	1969–70	Six danses en trois mouvements: Piano, solo; two pianos
434	1970	Saint-Louis, Roi de France: Operas
435	1971	Hommage à Igor Stravinsky: Quartets, string
436	1971	Musique pour San Francisco: Large orchestra, symphonic suites
437	1971	Sonate: Other solo instruments, harp
438	1971–72	Promesse de Dieu: A cappella ensemble, mixed chorus
439	1972	Les momies d'Egypte: A cappella ensemble, mixed chorus
440	1972	Ode pour Jerusalem: Large orchestra, miscellaneous
441	1972	Ani maamin, un chant perdu et retrouvé: Accompanied vocal ensemble, soloist, mixed chorus & orchestra
442	1973	Etudes: Quartets, string
443	1973	Quintette à vent: Quintets, wind

CATALOGUE OF COMPOSITIONS

ARRANGED ALPHABETICALLY BY TITLE

A

abandon d'Ariane (L') op. 98
Accueil amical op. 326
Actualités op. 104
Adages op. 120b
Adam op. 411
'Adame Miroir op. 283
Adieu op. 410
Agamemnon op. 14
Air op. 242
album de Madame Bovary (L') op. 128b
Alissa op. 9
Amal, ou La lettre du roi op. 156
amour chante (L') op. 409
amours de Ronsard (Les) op. 132
Ani maamin, un chant perdu et retrouvé op. 441
annonce faite à Marie (L') op. 117; 231
apothéose de Molière (L') op. 286
A propos de bottes op. 118
arbre exotique (L') op. 28
Aspen Serenade op. 361
Aubade op. 387
automne (L') op. 115

B

bal des voleurs (Le) op. 192
bal martiniquais (Le) op. 249
Ballade op. 61
Ballade nocturne op. 296
Barba Garibo op. 298
Beloved Vagabond (The) op. 150
Bertran de Born op. 152
bien-aimée (La) op. 101; 101b
Black Keys (Touches noires); White Keys (Touches blanches) op. 222
boeuf sur le toit (Le) op. 58
Bolivar op. 148
Bolivar op. 236
Borechou op. 239
branche des oiseaux (La) op. 374
brebis égarée (La) op. 4
Burma Road op. 375

C

cahier inédit du journal d'Eugénie de Guérin (D'un) op. 27
Caïn et Abel op. 241

candélabre à sept branches (Le) op. 315
Cantata from Job op. 413
Cantata from Proverbs op. 310
Cantate de la croix de charité op. 381
Cantate de la guerre op. 213
Cantate de la paix op. 166
Cantate de l'enfant et de la mère op. 185
Cantate de l'initiation op. 388
Cantate de psaumes op. 425
Cantate nuptiale op. 168
Cantate pour l'inauguration du Musée de l'Homme op. 164
Cantate pour louer le Seigneur op. 103
Cantate sur des poèmes de Chaucer op. 386
Cantique du Rhône op. 155
Caprice op. 335
caprices de Paganini (Trois) op. 97
Caramel mou op. 68
Carnaval à la Nouvelle Orleans op. 275
carnaval d'Aix (Le) op. 83b
carnaval de Londres (Le) op. 172
Caroles op. 402
Catalogue de fleurs op. 60
Cavalcade d'amour op. 204
Celle qui n'était plus op. 364
Chanson du capitaine op. 173b
chansons (Cinq) op. 167
chansons (Deux) op. 128d
Chansons bas op. 44
Chansons de l'opéra du gueux op. 171
chansons de négresse (Trois) op. 148b
chansons de négresse (Trois) op. 148c
chansons de Ronsard (Quatre) op. 223
chansons de théâtre (Six) op. 151b
chansons de troubadour (Trois) op. 152b
Chansons du carnaval de Londres op. 171b
Chants de misère op. 265
chants populaires hébraïques (Six) op. 86
charmes de la vie (Les) op. 360
chat (Le) op. 356
château (Le) op. 21
château de feu (Le) op. 338
château des papes (Le) op. 120
cheminée du roi Rene (La) op. 205
Child Poems op. 36
choéphores (Les) op. 24
Choral op. 111
Christophe Colomb op. 102; 318
Cinéma-fantaisie op. 58b
citadelle du silence (La) op. 176
cloches (Les) op. 259; 259b
Cocktail op. 69

duchesse d'Amalfi (La) op. 160
Duo op. 258
Duo concertant op. 351

E
Ecoutez mes enfants op. 359
education manquée (Une) op. 82
Eglogue op. 335c
Elégie op. 251
élégies (Trois) op. 199
Elégie pour Pierre op. 416
élégies romaines (Deux) op. 114
enfant aime (L') op. 289
Enfantines (no opus) *see* op. 59
enlèvement d'Europe (L') op. 94
Espoir op. 202
esquisses (Quatre) see Sketches (Four) op. 227
Esther de Carpentras op. 89
Etude poétique op. 333
Etudes op. 442
études (Cinq) op. 63
euménides (Les) op. 41
éventail de Jeanne (L') *see* Polka
Exercice musical op. 134

F
faiseur (Le) op. 145
Fanfare op. 209; 396; 400
Fanfare de la liberté op. 235
Fantaisie pastorale op. 188
Farandoleurs op. 262
fête de la lumière (La) op. 159
Fête de la victoire op. 254
Feuilles de température op. 65
Fiesta op. 370
fin du monde (La) op. 297
Flower Given to My Child (A) no opus, *see* unpublished works
folle du ciel (La) op. 149
Fontaines et sources op. 352
Fragments dramatiques op. 154b
Frenchman in New York (A) op. 399
Fugue du massacre op. 70b
funérailles de Phocion (Les) op. 385
funeste retour (Le) op. 123

G
Gauguin op. 299
globe trotter (Le) op. 358
Grands feux op. 182
grand testament (Le) op. 282
Gulf Stream op. 208

H

Hallo Everybody op. 126
Hamlet op. 200
Hécube op. 177
hippocampe (L') op. 137
histoire de Tobie et Sara (L') op. 426
Holem tsaudi—Gam hayom op. 179
Hommage à Comenius op. 421
Hommage à Igor Stravinsky op. 435
homme et son désir (L') op. 48
Hymne de glorification op. 331
hymnes (Deux) op. 88; 88b

I

Ils étaient tous des volontaires op. 336
Impromptu op. 91
Incantations op. 201
Indicatif et marche pour les bons d'armement op. 212
Introduction et allegro op. 220
Introduction op. 254
Introduction et marche funèbre op. 153b
Invocation a l'ange Raphaël op. 395
Islands op. 198

J

java de la femme (La) op. 173b
Jerusalem à Carpentras op. 419
Jeu op. 302
jeu de Robin et Marion (Le) op. 288
Jeux de printemps op. 243
journée (Une) op. 269
Juanito op. 349
Judith op. 392
Jules César op. 158

K

Kaddisch op. 250
Kentuckiana op. 287

L

L'choh dodi op. 290
libération des Antilles (La) op. 246
libertadora (La) op. 236b
Liberté op. 163
Lidoire op. 264
Liturgie comtadine op. 125

M

Macbeth op. 175
Machines agricoles op. 56
Madame Bovary op. 128

P

Pacem in terris op. 404
Pan et la Syrinx op. 130
Papillon, papillonette op. 217
Paris op. 284; 284b
Pastoral op. 227b
Pastorale op. 147; 229
Paul Claudel op. 427
pauvre matelot (Le) op. 92
Pensée amicale op. 342
Péron et Evita op. 372
petit ange de rien du tout (Un) op. 215
petit peu d'exercise (Un) op. 133
petit peu de musique (Un) op. 119
Petites légendes op. 319
Petite suite op. 348
petits airs (Deux) op. 51
Pièce de circonstance op. 90
Pledge to Mills op. 261
Plutus op. 186
Poème [Latil] op. 73
Poème du Gitanjali op. 22
Poème sur un cantique de Camargue op. 13
poèmes (Deux) [de Vilmorin] op. 347
poèmes (Deux) [St. Leger Leger, Chalupt] op. 39
poèmes (Trois) [Meynell, Rosetti] op. 37
poèmes (Trois) [Supervielle] op. 276
poèmes d'amour (Deux) op. 30
poèmes de Catulle (Quatre) op. 80
poèmes de Cendrars (Deux) op. 113
poèmes de Coventry Patmore (Deux) op. 31
Poèmes de Francis Jammes op. 1; 6; 50
Poèmes de Francis Thompson op. 54
poèmes du Gardener (Deux) op. 35
poèmes de Jean Cocteau (Trois) op. 59
poèmes de Jorge Guillén (Huit) op. 371
poèmes de la connaissance de l'est (Sept) op. 7
poèmes de Léo Latil (Trois) op. 2
poèmes de Léo Latil (Quatre) op. 20
poèmes de Paul Claudel pour baryton (Quatre) op. 26
poèmes de Rimbaud (Deux) op. 45
poèmes en prose de Lucile de Chateaubriand (Trois) op. 10
Poèmes juifs op. 34
poèmes romantiques (Trois) op. 11; 19
poèmes Tupis (Deux) op. 52
Polka op. 95
préludes (Neuf) op. 231b
première famille (La) op. 193
Prends cette rose op. 183
Préparatif a la mort en allégorie maritime op. 403
prières (Cinq) op. 231c

Prières journalières à l'usage des juifs du Comtat Venaissin op. 96
Printemps op. 25; 66
printemps (Le) op. 18
Printemps lointain op. 253
Private Affairs of Bel-Ami (The) op. 272
Promenade Concert op. 424
Promesse de Dieu op. 438
Protée op. 17; 341
Psaume 121 *see* Psaume 126
Psaume 126 op. 72
Psaume 129 op. 53b
Psaume 136 op. 53
psaumes de David (Trois) op. 339
p'tite Lilie (La) op. 107

Q
quatorze juillet (Le) op. 153
Quatrain [Flament] op. 143
Quatrain [Jammes] op. 106
Quatrain [Mallarmé] op. 180
Quatrains valaisans op. 206
quatre éléments (Les) op. 189; 189b
Quatre visages op. 238
Quatuors (string) op. 5; 16; 32; 46; 64; 77; 87; 121; 140; 218; 232; 252; 268; 291; 303; 307; 308
Quatuor op. 417
Quintette op. 312; 316; 325; 350
Quintette à vent op. 443

R
rag caprices (Trois) op. 78
Récréation op. 195
reine de Saba (La) op. 207
repos du septième jour (Le) op. 301
retour de l'enfant prodigue (Le) op. 42
Rêves op. 233
rêves de Jacob (Les) op. 294
romances sans paroles (Quatre) op. 129
Roméo et Juliette op. 161
Rondeau op. 178
rose des vents (La) op. 367

S
sagesse (La) op. 141
Sailor Song *see* Suite anglaise
Saint-Louis, Roi de France op. 434
Salade op. 83
Samaël op. 321
Saudades do Brazil op. 67; 67b
Saül op. 334
Scaramouche op. 165b; 165c; 165d

Schema Israël op. 239
Segoviana op. 366
Se plaire sur la même fleur op. 131
Septuor à cordes op. 408
Sérénade op. 62
Service sacré op. 279
Service pour la veille du Sabbat op. 345
Sextuor à cordes op. 368
Sheherazade op. 285
Shimmy *see* Caramel mou
Sketches (Four) op. 227
soirées de Petrograde (Les) op. 55
Sonate: harp op. 437
Sonate: organ op. 112
Sonate: piano op. 33
sonate (Deuxième): piano op. 293
Sonate: piano, fl, ob, cl. op. 47
Sonate: piano, 2 vln. op. 15
Sonate: vln, hprd. op. 257
sonate (Première): va, piano. op. 240
sonate (Deuxième): va, piano. op. 244
sonate (Première): vln, piano. op. 3
sonate (Deuxième): vln, piano. op. 40
Sonate: vc, piano. op. 377
Sonate de Baptiste Anet 1729 op. 144
Sonatine: cl, piano. op. 100
Sonatine: fl, piano. op. 76
Sonatine: ob, piano. op. 337
Sonatine: piano op. 354
Sonatine: vln, va. op. 226
Sonatine: vln, vc. op. 324
Sonatine: va, vc. op. 378
Sonatine: 2 vln op. 221
Sonatine à trois op. 221b
Sonatine pastorale op. 383
songes (Les) op. 124; 237
sonnets composés au secret (Six) op. 266
Sornettes op. 214
Stanford Serenade op. 430
Suite: ond Mart, piano. op. 120c
Suite: piano op. 8
Suite: piano, vln, cl op. 157b
Suite anglaise op. 234
Suite campagnarde op. 329
Suite cisalpine op. 332
Suite concertante op. 278b
Suite d'après Corrette op. 161b
Suite de Maximilien op. 110b
Suite de quatrains op. 398
Suite de sonnets op. 401
Suite en sol op. 431

Suite française op. 248
Suite opus 300 op. 300
Suite provençale op. 152c;
Suite provençale op 152d
suite symphonique (Première) op. 12
suite symphonique (Deuxième) op. 57
Symphonie: chamber ensemble op. 43; 49; 71; 74; 75; 79
Symphonie: large orchestra op. 210; 247; 271; 281; 322; 343; 344; 362; 380; 382; 384; 390
Symphonie concertante op. 376
Symphonie pour l'univers Claudelien op. 427b
Symphoniette op. 363

T

Tango des Fratellini op. 58c
Tartarin de Tarascon op. 138
temps faciles (Les) op. 305
Touches noires, touches blanches op. 222
tour de l'Exposition (Le) op. 162
Toussaint (A la) "op. 47"
tragédie humaine (La) op. 369
tragédie impériale, Raspoutine (La) op. 187
train bleu (Le) op. 84
Traversée op. 393
Tricolore op. 190
Trio op. 428
Trio à cordes op. 274
Tristesses op. 355
trompeur de Séville (Le) op. 152e
Tu ne m'échapperas jamais op. 151

V

Valse en forme de rondo op. 353b
valses (Trois) op. 128c
Variations sur un thème de Cliquet op. 23
Vendanges op. 317
Vezelay 'La colline éternelle' op. 423
Verso Carioca op. 44b
vie commence demain (La) op. 304
Vocalise op. 105
Voix d'enfants op. 146
Voyage au pays du rêve op. 203
voyage d'été (Le) op. 216
voyageur sans bagages (Le) op. 157

W

West Point Suite op. 313

DISCOGRAPHY

The present edition does not contain a discography as did its French counterpart. The decision to omit it was made because the Bibliothèque Nationale of Paris, through its Département de la Phonothèque et de l'Audiovisuel (2 rue de Louvois, F-75002 Paris) has just compiled a complete list of recordings of Milhaud's works edited by Françine Bloch.

At best, any discography becomes obsolete on the day of its publication because of the continuing release of new recordings, but the list compiled by the Bibliothèque Nationale is far more complete and up to date than anything that could be included here. For historical reasons, however, we list recordings that feature Milhaud himself as performer (or as conductor). Mlle. Bloch has very graciously contributed the following information.

Abbreviations

m	monophonic record
s	stereophonic record
sc	compatible stereophonic record
t	magnetic tape
p	date of publication
r	date of recording

INA	Institut National de l'Audiovisuel
RTB	Radio Télévision Belge
RAI	Radio Télévision Italienne
ORTF	Office de Radiodiffusion-Télévision Française

Entry Format

Title opus number
Performers
Record label, record number, technical description, date

Les amours de Ronsard op. 132
La rose — La tourterelle — L'aubépin — Le rossignol
Sop: A. Bollinger, con: H. Glaz, ten: L. Chabay, bass: M. Harrell, Philharmonic Chamber ensemble, conductor: D. Milhaud
Contemporary Records NY, AP102, 33⅓ rpm, 25 cm, m, p ca 1953
Excerpts: La rose — L'aubépin — Le rossignol
Sop: R. Mahé, mezz: E. Schenneberg, ten: C. Rouquetty, Pierre Froumenty et Orchestre, conductor: D. Milhaud
V.S.M., DB4999, 78 rpm, 30 cm, p 1936
Victor, JD932, 78 rom, 30 cm

Aspen Serenade op. 361
Fl: J-P. Rampal, ob: P. Pierlot, cl: J. Lancelot, tpt: P. Thibaud, bn: P. Hongne, vln: G.
  Jarry, va: S. Collot, vc: M. Tournus, cb: J. Cazauran, conductor: D. Milhaud
Adès, 15.503, 33 rpm, 30 cm, sc, p 1966
Adès, 17.005, 33 rpm, 17 cm, sc
Everest, LPBR6176, 33 rpm, 30 cm, m, p ca 1967
Everest, SDBR3176, 33 rpm, 30 cm, s, p ca 1967

Aubade op. 387
Orchestre philharmonique de l'ORTF, conductor D. Milhaud
B202M280, r 1970
102M338, p 1 January 1971, INA

Le boeuf sur le toit op. 58
Orchestre du Théâtre des Champs-Elysées, conductor: D. Milhaud
Discophiles français, 525.125, 33 rpm. 30 cm, m, p 1959
(Grand Prix du disque de l'Académie Charles Cros 1959)
Discophiles français, 530.300, 33 rpm, 30 cm, s
Republished by: Charlin, SLC17, 33 rpm, 30 cm, p 1964
Discophiles français, DI25/32, 33 rpm, 30 cm, m
Discophiles français, DI125/132, 33 rpm, 30 cm, s, p 1966
Nonesuch, H112, 33 rpm, 30 cm, m, p 1964
Nonesuch, H71122, 33 rpm, 30 cm, s, p 1966

Bolivar op. 236
Excerpts: Air de Manuela — Berceuse
Sop: J. Micheau, Orchestre de la Société des Concerts du Conservatoire, conductor:
  D. Milhaud
Columbia, FCX556S, 33 rpm, 30 cm, m, p 1957
Angel, 35441, 33 rpm, 30 cm, m, p ca 1958
Republished by VSM, 2C051-73075, 33 rpm, 30 cm, p 1982

La branche des oiseaux op. 374
Orchestre de la RTB, conductor: D. Milhaud
Broadcast at RTB, 18 May 1962

Cantata from proverbs op. 310
Mezzo: H. Bouvier, con: J. Collard, conductor: D. Milhaud
Versailles, ARTX10.001, 33 rpm, 30 cm, m, p ca 1956

Cantate nuptiale op 168
Sop: J. Micheau, Orchestre de la Société des Concerts du Conservatoire, conductor:
  D. Milhaud
Columbia, FCX5565S, 33 rpm, 30 cm, m, p 1957
Angel, 35441, 33 rpm, 30 cm, m, p ca 1958
Republished by VSM, 2C051-73075, 30 rpm, 30 cm, p 1982

Le carnaval d'Aix op. 83
Piano: C. Seaman, Orchestre de Radio-Luxembourg, conductor: D. Milhaud
Candide, CE 31013, 33 rpm, 30 cm, sc, p 1969
CBS, S72.925, 33 rpm, 30 cm, sc, p 1971
Vox, STGBY640, 33 rpm, 30 cm, sc, p 1971

Quatre chansons de Ronsard op. 223
Sop: J. Micheau, Orchestre de la Société des Concerts du Conservatoire, conductor:
    D. Milhaud
Columbia, FCX556S, 33 rpm, 30 cm, m, p 1957
Angel, 35441, 33 rpm, 30 cm, m, p ca 1958
Republished by VSM, 2C051-73075, 33 rpm, 30 cm, p 1982

Les charmes de la vie op. 360
Los Angeles Chamber Ensemble, conductor: D. Milhaud
Decca, DL9965, 33 rpm, 30 cm, m, p 1958
Republished by Varèse Sarabande, 81051, 33 rpm, 30 cm, m, p 1979

Le château de feu op. 338
Orchestre philharmonique de Paris, conductor: D. Milhaud, Choeur de l'ORTF,
    conductor: Y. Gouverné
Chant du Monde, LDA8179, 33 rpm, 30 cm, m, p 1957
Republished by Chant du Monde, LDXA8325, 33 rpm, 30 cm, m, p 1964
Chant du Monde, LDXA48325, 33 rpm, 30 cm, s, p 1964
Chant du Monde, LDX A78325, 33 rpm, 30 cm, sc, p 1968

Child Poems op. 36
Excerpt: Paper Boats
Voice: J. Héricard, piano: D. Milhaud
Vega, C35A14, 33 rpm, 30 cm, m, p ca 1957

Les Choéphores op. 24
Narr: M. Milhaud, sop: L. Malimpietri, N. Pucci, bass: H. Rehfuss, orchestre et
    choeur de la RAI, conductor: D. Milhaud
t, RAI, November 1953

Concert de chambre op. 389
Piano: A. Bonaventura, conductor: D. Milhaud
Recorded at the first performance, 16 November 1962, Hanover, N.H., USA, private
    tape

Concert royal op. 373
Vln: D. Erlih, Orchestre symphonique de RTB, conductor: D. Milhaud
Recorded in May 1962 by RTB

Les quatre saisons:
Concertino d'automne op. 309
Concertino d'été op. 311
Concertino de printemps op. 135
Concertino d'hiver op. 327
Piano: G. Joy, J. Bonneau, va: E. Wallfisch, vln: S. Goldberg, tbn: M. Suzan,
    Ensemble de solistes des Concerts Lamoureux, conductor: D. Milhaud
Philips, 00.575L, 33 rpm, 30 cm, m
Philips, 835-499AY, 33 rpm, 30 cm, s, p ca 1959
Epic, LC3666, 33 rpm, 30 cm, m, p 1960
Epic, BC1069, 33 rpm, 30 cm, s p 1960

Republished by Philips, 839-270, 33 rpm, 30 cm, sc, p 1969
Philips, 6504-aas, 33 rpm, 30 cm, sc, p 1974
Philips, 6529-167 (collection: Excellence), 33 rpm, 30 cm, sc, p 1983

Concertino d'été op. 311
Va: R. Courte, Philharmonic Chamber Ensemble, conductor: D. Milhaud
Contemporary Records, NY-AP102, m, p ca 1953
Excerpt
Va: E. Wallfisch, Ensemble de solistes des concerts Lamoureux, Conductor: D.
  Milhaud
Heugel, 70, 33 rpm, 17 cm, sc, p 1970

Concertino de printemps op. 135
Vln: Y. Astruc, conductor: D. Milhaud
Decca, CA8025, 78 rpm, 30 cm
Polydor, 516.616, 78 rpm, 30 cm, p 1935
Polydor, 566,288, 78 rpm, 30 cm, p ca 1935
Vln: L. Kaufman, Orchestre National de l'ORTF, conductor: D. Milhaud
Capitol, 886.013, 78 rpm, 30 cm, r 1949
Republished by Capitol, CTL7005, 33 rpm, 30 cm, m
Capitol P8071, 33 rpm, 30 cm, m, p 1950
Orion, 76250E, 33 rpm, 30 cm, sc, p ca 1977

Premier concerto op. 108
Va: W. Trampler, Aspen Festival Orchestra, conductor: D. Milhaud
t, 1 October 1963
Va: W. Koch, Orchestre de Radio-Luxembourg, conductor: D. Milhaud
Candide, CE31013, 33 rpm, 30 cm, sc, p 1969
CBS, S72-925, 33 rpm, 30 cm, sc, p ca 1971
Vox, STGBY640, 33 rpm, 30 cm, sc

Concerto op. 109
Perc: F. Daniel, Orchestre de Radio-Luxembourg, conductor: D. Milhaud
Candide, CE31013, 33 rpm, 30 cm, sc, p 1969
CBS, S72-925, 33 rpm, 30 cm, sc, p 1971
Vox, STGBY640, 33 rpm, 30 cm, sc

Concerto op. 407
Hprd: R. Veyron-Lacroix, Orchestre philharmonique de l'ORTF, conductor: D.
  Milhaud
B202M280
102M338, INA, 1 January 1971

Concerto op. 228
Piano: I. Marika, G. Joy, Orchestre de la Société des Concerts du Conservatoire,
  conductor: D. Milhaud
Vega, C30A355, m, 1962
Westminster, XWN19101, m, 1966
Westminster, WST17101, s, 1966

Concerto op. 323
Harp: M. de Gray, Aspen Festival Orchestra, conductor: D. Milhaud
Aspen, 15 July 1962

Concerto (oboe) op. 365
Grand Orchestre Symphonique de la RTB, conductor: D. Milhaud
RTB, 1962

Premier concerto op. 127
Piano: M. Long, conductor: D. Milhaud
Columbia, LFX375/6, 2 78 rpm, 30 cm, 1935
Columbia, 68737/8D (album X-67), 2 78 rpm, 30 cm
Columbia, COLC319, 33 rpm, 30 cm, m, 1966
VSM, C05116.349 (collection: Références), 33 rpm, 30 cm, 1979
Piano: P. Entremont, Orchestre de la Société des Concerts du Conservatoire, conductor: D. Milhaud
CBS, S75660, 33 rpm, s, 1968

Deuxième concerto op. 225
Piano: G. Johannesen, Orchestre de Radio Luxembourg, conductor: D. Milhaud
Turnabout, TVS34496, 33 rpm, 30 cm, sc, ca 1974
Excerpt: first movement
Heugel, 74, 33 rpm, 17 cm, 1974

Quatrième concerto op. 295
Piano: Z. Skolowski, Orchestre National de l'ORTF, conductor: D. Milhaud
Columbia, LFX924/5, 2 78 rpm, 30 cm, 1950
Columbia, ML4523, 33 rpm, 30 cm, m, 1951

Deuxième concerto op. 263
Vln: L. Kaufman, Orchestre National de l'ORTF, conductor: D. Milhaud
Capitol, CTL7005, 33 rpm, 30 cm
Capitol, P8071, 33 rpm, 30 cm, 1950
Capitol, 76250E, 33 rpm, 30 cm, sc, 1977

Couronne de gloire op. 211
Voice: B. Demigny, conductor: D. Milhaud
Versailles, ARTX10.001, 33 rpm, 30 cm, m, 1956

La création du monde op. 81
19 players conducted by D. Milhaud
Columbia, LFX251/2, 2 78 rpm, 30 cm
Columbia, 68094/5D, 2 78 rpm, 30 cm, (album × 18) (???)
Columbia MX70420/1D
Festival, FLD76A, 33 rpm, 30 cm, m, 1957
Orchestre du Théâtre des Champs-Elysées, conductor: D. Milhaud
Discophiles français, 521-125, 33 rpm, 25 cm, m, 1959
Discophiles français, 530-300, 33 rpm, 25 cm, s
Charlin, SLC17, 33 rpm, 30 cm, s, 1964
Discophiles français, DI25/32, 33 rpm, 30 cm

Discophiles français, SDI125/132, 33 rpm, 30 cm, 1966
Nonesuch, H1122, 33 rpm, 30 cm, m, 1966
Nonesuch, H71122, 33 rpm, 30 cm,s

Etude poétique op. 333
Mezzo: I. Kolassi, narr: M. Milhaud, Claude Roy, conductor: D. Milhaud
Festival, FLD76A, 33 rpm, 30 cm, m, 1957

La fin du monde op. 297
Narr: A. Rignault, M. Milhaud, R. Iglesis, A. Tainsy, J. Denoel, J. Bertheau
   Orchestre Radio-Lyrique, conductor: D. Milhaud. Maison de la Radio, Paris, 21
   December 1949.
B LO 4986, INA

Fontaines et sources op. 352
Sop: J. Micheau, Orchestre de la Société des Concerts du Conservatoire, conductor:
   D. Milhaud
Columbia, FCX556S, 33 rpm, 30 cm, m, 1957
Angel, 35441, 33 rpm, 30 cm, m, 1958
VSM, 2C051-73075, 33 rpm, 30 cm, 1982
Sop: R. Serverius, Orchestre symphonique de la RTB, conductor: D. Milhaud
RTB, May 1962

Les funérailles de Phocion op. 385
Orchestre symphonique de la RTB, conductor: D. Milhaud
RTB, 18 May 1962

Le globe trotter op. 358
Los Angeles Chamber Ensemble, conductor: D. Milhaud
Decca, DL9965, 33 rpm, 30 cm, m, p 1958
Varèse Sarabande, 81051, 33 rpm, 30 cm, m, p 1979

L'homme et son désir op. 48
Ensemble vocal et instrumental de Roger Desormière, conductor: D. Milhaud
Champrosay, TC11/12, 78 rpm, 30 cm, 1948
B. a M., LD029, 33 rpm, 30 cm, m, 1957
B. a M., LD5029, 33 rpm, 30 cm, 1974
Festival, FLD76, 33 rpm, 30 cm, m, 1957
Voice: J. Doemer, M. J. Klein, V. Arend, R. Koster; Orchestre de la
   Radio-Luxembourg, conductor: D. Milhaud
Candide, CE31008, 33 rpm, 30 cm, sc, 1968
CBS, S72.803, 33 rpm, 30 cm, sc, 1970
Vox, STGBY626, 33 rpm, 30 cm, sc
Vox, 678.080, cassette

Introduction et marche funèbre op. 153b
Orchestre Philharmonique de Paris, conductor: D. Milhaud
Chant du monde, LDXM8179, 33 rpm, 30 cm, m, p ca 1957
Chant du monde, LDXA8325, 33 rpm, 30 cm, m
Chant du monde, LDXA48325, 33 rpm, 30 cm, s, p ca 1964

Liturgie comtadine op. 125
Sop: H. Bouvier, conductor: D. Milhaud
Versailles, ARTX10001, 33 rpm, 30 cm, m, p ca 1956

Les malheurs d'Orphée op. 85
Sop: J. Brumaire, C. Collart, con: J. Collard, bar: B. Demigny, solistes de l'Orchestre
   du Théâtre National de l'Opéra de Paris, conductor: D. Milhaud
Vega, C30A68, 33 rpm, 30 cm, m, p ca 1957
Westminster, OPW11031, 33 rpm, 30 cm, m, p ca 1957

Deux marches op. 260
Excerpt: In memoriam
CBS Symphony Orchestra, conductor: D. Milhaud
Columbia, 72.242D (Album MM704), 4 78 rpm, 30 cm, p ca 1948

Les mariés de la Tour Eiffel op. 70
Orchestre National de l'ORTF, Phono: P. Bertin, J. Duby, conductor: D. Milhaud
Adès, 15.501, 33 rpm, 30 cm, sc, p April 1966
Republished by Ades, 14.007, 33 rpm, 30 cm, sc, p 1980
Adès, C12003, cassette, p 1980

Meutre d'un grand chef d'état op. 405
Aspen Symphony Orchestra, Conductor: D. Milhaud
t, private recording

La muse ménagère op. 245
Piano: D. Milhaud
Columbia, ML4305, 33 rpm, 25 cm, m, p ca 1950
Republished by Odyssey, Y33790, 33 rpm, 30 cm, m, p 1976
CBS, Classics 61.130, 33 rpm, 30 cm, m, p 1981

Musique pour la Nouvelle-Orléans op. 422
Orchestre du Festival d'Aspen, conductor: D. Milhaud
t, private recording, 11 August 1968

Musique pour la l'Indiana op. 418
Orchestre philharmonique de l'ORTF, conductor: D. Milhaud
B202M280
102M338, INA, 1971

Musique pour Prague op. 415
Conductor: D. Milhaud
t, private recording during the Prague Spring Festival

Ode pour les morts des guerres op. 406
Orchestre National de l'ORTF, conductor: D. Milhaud
B101M152
201M92, INA

'Opéras-minute'
L'envlèvement d'Europe op. 94
L'abandon d'Arianne op. 98
La délivrance de Thésée op. 99
Voice: J. Bathori, Bouteron, Brega, Valencin, Hazart, Petit, Planel, conductor: D. Milhaud
Columbia, D15137/9, 3 78 rpm, 30 cm, p ca 1929

Opus Americanum no 2 op. 219b
Membres de l'Orchestre National de l'ORTF, conductor: D. Milhaud
Capitol, CTL7008, 33 rpm, 30 cm, m, p ca 1950
Capitol P8114Z, 33 rpm, 30 cm, m, p ca 1950

Le pauvre matelot op. 92
Sop: J. Brumaire, ten: J. Giraudeau, bass: X. Depraz, A. Vessières, Solistes de l'orchestre du Théâtre National de l'Opéra de Paris, conductor: D. Milhaud
Vega, C30A69, 33 rpm, 30 cm, m, p ca 1957
Westminster, OPW11030, 33 rpm, 30 cm, m, p ca 1957

Trois poèmes de Jean Cocteau op. 59
Sop: J. Bathori, piano: D. Milhaud
Columbia, D15195, 78 rpm, 30 cm, p ca 1930
Columbia, SW276, 78 rpm, 30 cm
Gramophone, GDA4894, 78 rpm, 30 cm
Republished by Columbia, FCX50030, 33 rpm, 30 cm, m, p ca 1964

Poèmes juifs op. 34
Excerpts: Chant de nourrice — Chant de résignation — Chant d'amour
Sop: J. Bathori, piano: D. Milhaud
Columbia, D15.194, 78 rpm, 30 cm, p ca 1930
Columbia, SW275, 78 rpm, 30 cm
Republished by Columbia, FCX50030, 33 rpm, 30 cm, m, p ca 1964

Printemps op. 25
Piano: D. Milhaud
Columbia, LF25, 78 rpm, 25 cm

Promenade Concert op. 424
Aspen festival Orchestra, conductor: D. Milhaud
t, private recording, 17 August 1969

Les quatre éléments op. 189b
Sop: J. Micheau, Orchestre de la Société des Concerts du Conservatoire, conductor: D. Milhaud
Columbia, FCX556S, 33 rpm, 30 cm, m, p ca 1957
Angel, 35441, 33 rpm, 30 cm, m, p ca 1958
Republished by VSM, 2C051-73075, 33 rpm, 30 cm, p 1982
Sop: R. Serverius, Orchestre Symphonique de la RTB, conductor: D. Milhaud
t, RTB, May 1962

Le retour de l'enfant prodigue op. 42
A. Vessières, M. Caron, sop: J. Collard, ten: B. Demigny, bar: G. Bacquier, Solistes de l'Orchestre du Théâtre National de l'Opéra de Paris, conductor: D. Milhaud
Vega, C30A284, 33 rpm, 30 cm, m, p ca 1960

Les rêves de Jacob op. 294
Ob: P. Pierlot, vln: R. Gendre, va: C. Leuquen, vc: M. Lepinte, cb: J. Cazauran, conductor: D. Milhaud
B. a M., LD029A, 33 rpm, 30 cm, m, p ca 1957
B. a M., LD5029, sc, p ca 1972
First movement republished by: Heugel, 72, 33 rpm, 17 cm, sc, p 1972

Salade op. 83
Excerpts: Duo — Tango
P. Froumenty, sop: R. Mahé, ten: C. Rouquetty, E. Chastenel, conductor: D. Milhaud
Gramophone, DA4886, 78 rpm, 25 cm, p 1936

Saudades do Brazil op. 67
Concert Arts Orchestra, conductor: D. Milhaud
Capitol, P8558, 33 rpm, 30 cm, m, p ca 1957
Excerpts: Sorocaba — Ipanema — Corcovado — Sumare
Reduction for piano
Piano: D. Milhaud
Columbia, LFX40, 78 rpm, 30 cm, p ca 1940

Scaramouche op. 165b
Piano: M. Meyer, D. Milhaud
VSM, DB5086, 78 rpm, 30 cm, p 1938
Republished by World Records, SH227, 33 rpm, 30 cm, m, p 1975

Service sacré op. 279
Bar: H. Rehfuss, choeur de la RTF, conductor: D. Milhaud
Vega, C30A178, 33 rpm, 30 cm, m, p ca 1958
Westminster, XWN19052, 33 rpm, 30 cm, m, p ca 1964
Westminster, WST17052, 33 rpm, 30 cm, s, p ca 1964; republished by Westminster, WGS8281, 33 rpm, 30 cm, s, p 1975
Adès, 140061 (collection: Editions recommées), 33 rpm, 30 cm, s. p 1983

Les soirées de Petrograde op. 55
Sop: J. Bathori, piano: D. Milhaud
Columbia, D15135, 78 rpm, 30 cm, p ca 1930

Les songes op. 124
Orchestre Symphonique de Paris, conductor: D. Milhaud
Columbia, LF133/4, 78 rpm, 25 cm, p ca 1934
Columbia, 17038/9D, 78 rpm, 25 cm

Suite de quatrains op. 398
Narr: M. Milhaud, fl: J-P. Rampal, sax: D. Deffayet, bas cl: L. Montaigne, harp: F.
  Pierre, vln: G. Jarry, vc: M. Tournus, cb: J. Cazauran, conductor: D. Milhaud
Adès, 15503, 33 rpm 30 cm, sc, p ca 1966
Everest, LPBR6176, 33 rpm, 30 cm, m, p ca 1967
Everest, SDBR3176, 33 rpm, 30 cm, s, p ca 1967

Suite française op. 248
New York Philharmonic Orchestra, conductor: D. Milhaud
Columbia, 12395/6D (Album MX268), 78 rpm, 30 cm, p 1949
Columbia, LFX860/1, 78 rpm, 30 cm, p ca 1949
Republished by Columbia, ML2093, 33 rpm, 30 cm, m, p ca 1950
Columbia, FC1003, 33 rpm, 25 cm, m, p ca 1952
Columbia, C1027, 33 rpm, 25 cm, m, p ca 1954
Columbia, RL6629, 33 rpm, m, p ca 1954
Philips, A01256L, 33 rpm, 30 cm, m, p ca 1958

Suite provençale op. 152c
Concert Arts Orchestra, conductor: D. Milhaud
Capitol, P8538, 33 rpm, 30 cm, m, p ca 1957

Première symphonie op. 210
CBS Symphony Orchestra, conductor: D. Milhaud
Columbia, 72242/5D (Album MM704), 4 78 rpm, 30 cm, p ca 1948
Republished by Columbia, ML2082, 33 rpm, 30 cm, m
Columbia, ML4784, 33 rpm, 30 cm, m, p ca 1954
Philips, A01.256L, 33 rpm, 30 cm, m, p ca 1958

Troisième symphonie (Te Deum) op. 271
Orchestre de la Société des Concerts du Conservatoire and Elisabeth Brasseur
  Chorus, conductor: D. Milhaud
Vega, C30A355, 33 rpm, 30 cm, m, p 1962
Westminster, WST17101, 33 rpm, 30 cm, s, p ca 1966; republished by Westminster,
  XWN19101, 33 rpm, 30 cm, m, p ca 1966
Excerpt from the Vega recording
Heugel, 67A et B, 33 rpm, 17 cm, m, p 1967 (gift copies)

Quatrième symphonie op. 281
Orchestre philharmonique de l'ORTF, conductor: D. Milhaud
Erato, STU70452, 33 rpm, 30 cm, sc, p ca 1968

Cinquième symphonie op. 322
Turin RAI orchestra conductor: D. Milhaud
t, RAI, 16 November 1953

Septième symphonie op. 344
Orchestre de l'INR, Brussels, conductor: D. Milhaud
t, RTB, 22 February 1956

Huitième symphonie (Rhodanienne) op. 362
Orchestre philharmonique de l'ORTF, conductor: D. Milhaud
Erato, STU70452, 33 rpm, 30 cm, sc, p ca 1968
Excerpt from the Erato recording
Heugel, 69-1B, 33 rpm, 17 cm, sc, p ca 1969

Dixième symphonie op. 382
RTB orchestra, conductor: D. Milhaud
t, RTB, ca 1962

Onzième symphonie (Romantique) op. 384
RTB Grand Orchestre, conductor: D. Milhaud
t, RTB, 1962

Symphonie concertante op. 376
Turin RAI orchestra, conductor: D. Milhaud
t, RAI, 8 June 1959
Tpt: L. Vailland, hn: L. Courtinat, bn: R. Plessier. cb: J. Toraille, Orchestre National
    de l'ORTF, conductor: D. Milhaud
BLM141(SR67) INA, 3 November 1959

Première symphonie 'Le printemps' op. 43
Deuxième Symphonie 'Pastorale' op. 49
Troisième symphonie 'Serenade' op. 71
Cinquième symphonie op. 75
Concert Hall Chamber Orchestra, conductor: D. Milhaud
Concert Hall Society, B11, 2 78 rpm, 30 cm
Republished by Concert Hall Society, 1076, 33 rpm, 30 cm, m, p ca 1950
Musical Masterpiece Society, 108, 33 rpm, 30 cm, m, p ca 1954
Guilde Internationale du Disque, MMS108, 33 rpm, 25 cm, m, p ca 1956, Orchestre de
    Radio-Luxembourg, conductor: D. Milhaud
CBS, S72.803, 33 rpm, 30 cm, sc, p ca 1970
Candide, CE31.008, 33 rpm, 30 cm, sc, p, 1968
Vox, STGBY626, 33 rpm, 30 cm

Quatrième symphonie op. 74
Orchestre de Radio-Luxembourg, conductor: D. Milhaud
CBS, S72.803, 33 rpm, 30 cm, sc, p ca 1970
Candide, CE31.008, 33 rpm, 30 cm, sc, p, 1968
Vox, STGBY626, 33 rpm, 30 cm

Sixième symphonie op. 79
Sop: J. Doemer, con: M-J. Klein, ten: V. Arend, bass: R. Koster, ob: N. Matern, vc:
    G. Mallach, Orchestre de Radio-Luxembourg, conductor: D. Milhaud
CBS, S72.803, 33 rpm, 30 cm, sc, p ca 1970
Candide, CE31.008, 33 rpm, 30 cm, sc, p. 1968
Vox, STGBY626, 33 rpm, 30 cm

La tragédie humaine op. 369
ORTF chorus and orchestra, chorus conductor: R. Alix, conductor: D. Milhaud
B LM141(SR67), INA, 3 November 1959

Darius Milhaud vous parle et présente son oeuvre avec des extraits de: **La cantate des deux cités, L'Orestie d'Eschyle, la Troisième symphonie de chambre, L'homme et son désir,** les 3e et 4e **Etudes** pour piano et orchestre, **La création du monde, l'Octuor** (finale) et **Etude poétique**
Voice: D. Milhaud
Festival. FLD76A, 33 rpm, 30 cm, m, p ca 1957

BIBLIOGRAPHY

Compiled by R. Wood Massi

The following is a selected bibliography of works in English. The citation of a book by Milhaud and a chronological list of articles written by him is followed by a list of books and articles by other authors. Many reviews of compositions by Milhaud have been included, but not reviews of performances. A number of reference, history, and music appreciation books make mention of Milhaud. Only a few of the more important ones have been listed, since more or less the same information is given by all.

For a list of works in other languages, see: Drake, Jeremy, ed. Notes sur la musique: Essais et chroniques. *Paris: Flammarion, 1982.*

Lists of many performance reviews are contained in The Music Index *(Detroit, 1949—). A collection of scores, recordings, program notes, and films can be found in the Milhaud Archives at Mills College in Oakland, California.*

Works by Darius Milhaud

Books

Notes without Music: An Autobiography. Edited by Rollo Myers. Translated by Donald Evans. London: Dobson, 1952. American ed., with an added final chapter edited by Herbert Weinstock and translated by Arthur Ogden. New York: Knopf, 1953. Reprint. New York: Da Capo, 1970. 355 pp. (Translation of *Notes sans musique.* Paris: René Julliard, 1949. Rev. & enl. as *Ma vie heureuse.* Paris: Belford, 1974.)

Articles

"Arthur Honegger." *The Chesterian,* n.s. 19 (December 1921): 65–69.

"The evolution of modern music in Paris and in Vienna." *North American Review* 217 (April 1923): 544–554.

"The jazz band and Negro music." *Living Age* 323 (October 1924): 169–173.

"Polytonality and atonality." *Pro Musica Quarterly* (New York) 2 (October 1924).

"The day after tomorrow." *Modern Music* 3 (November–December 1925): 22–24.

"Louis Fleury." *The Chesterian* 7 (July–August 1926): 264–265.

"Farewell to Diaghilev." *Modern Music* 7 (December–January 1929): 12–15.

"Experimenting with sound film." *Modern Music* 7 (February–March 1930): 11–14.

"Paris opera just before the occupation." *Modern Music* 18 (November–December

1940): 45–46.

"Through my California window." *Modern Music* 21 (January–February 1944): 89–95.

"To Arnold Schoenberg on his seventieth birthday: Personal recollections." *Musical Quarterly* 30 (October 1944): 379–384.

"Music and politics." *Modern Music* 22 (November–December 1944): 5–6.

"French music between two wars." *Circle* 7–8 (1946): 106–108.

Preface to *Poetics of Music,* by Igor Stravinsky. New York: Random House, 1947.

"Music for the films." *Theatre Arts* 31 (September 1947): 27–29.

" 'Modern music' is nonsense." *Etude* 67 (September 1949): 9, 58–59.

"Thirty-seven years." In *Stravinsky in the Theatre,* edited by Minna Lederman, 131–32. New York: Pellegrini & Cudaby, 1949.

"In memoriam Richard Strauss." *Books Abroad* 23 (Autumn 1949): 333–334.

"The Western Round Table on Modern Art," 1949; D. Milhaud, participant. Modern Artists in America, 1st ser., no. 1. New York: W. Schultz, 1952.

Foreword to *Composers, Conductors, and Critics,* by Claire R. Reis. New York: Oxford University Press, 1955.

"Farewell to Paul Claudel." *Books Abroad* 29 (Spring 1955): 133.

"Reminiscences of Debussy and Ravel." *The Listener* (May 29, 1958). Reprinted in *Essays on Music: An Anthology from "The Listener,"* edited by F. Aprahamian, 78–83. London: Cassell, 1967.

"Of men, music, and machines: Conversations between Darius Milhaud and Leon Kirchner." *Mills Quarterly* 41 (February 1959): 94–98.

"The composer speaks." In *The New Book of Modern Composers,* edited by David Ewen, 267–269. 3d ed., rev. & enl. New York: Knopf, 1961.

Preface to *Crowell's Handbook of World Opera,* by F. L. Moore. New York: Crowell, 1961.

" 'The Six.' " *The Listener* 67 (February 22, 1962): 336–337.

"The image: Three views: Ben Shahn, Darius Milhaud, and James Baldwin debate the real meaning of a fashionable term." *Opera News* 27 (8 December 1962): 8–12.

"My first encounter with jazz," from *Notes Without Music,* by D. Milhaud. In *Contemporary Composers on Contemporary Music,* edited by Elliot Schwartz and Barney Childs, 34–39 New York: Holt, Rinehart & Winston, 1967.

"I am always interested in what is coming." *Christian Science Monitor,* 20 May 1968, 8.

Foreword to *Treatise on the Fugue,* by André Gédalge. Translated and edited by Ferdinand Davis. Norman, Oklahoma: University of Oklahoma Press, 1965.

"Stravinsky: A composer's memorial." *Perspectives of New Music* 9 & 10 (1971): 9–10.

Works about Darius Milhaud

Abraham, Gerald. *This Modern Music.* 3d ed. London: Duckworth, 1955.

Auric, Georges. "Paris resurgent." *Modern Music* 22 (May–June 1945): 247–250.

Austin, William W. *Music in the Twentieth Century.* New York: Norton, 1966.

Barrell, E. A. "A decade of 'The Six'." *Etude* 47 (December 1929): 883 & 944.

Barzun, Jacques. Review of *Notes without Music,* by Darius Milhaud. *Notes* 10 (June 1953): 441–442.

Baskerville, David Ross. *Jazz Influence on Art Music to Mid-century*. Ph.D. diss., University of California, Los Angeles, 1965.

Bauer, Marion. "Darius Milhaud." *Musical Quarterly* 28 (April 1942): 139–159.

———. *Twentieth Century Music*. Rev. ed. New York: Putnam, 1947.

Berger, Arthur W. "Darius Milhaud, promulgator of polytonality." *American Music Lover,* February 1936, 296.

Bernstein, Leonard. *The Infinite Variety of Music*. New York: Simon & Schuster, 1962.

Blanks, F. R. "Darius Milhaud." *Canon* 12, no. 6 (January 1959): 203–204.

Bobbitt, Richard B. *The Harmonic Idiom in the Works of Les Six*. Ph.D. diss., Boston University, 1963.

Bolcom, William. "Reminiscences of Darius Milhaud." *Musical Newsletter* 7 (Summer 1977): 3–11.

Breitrose, Henry. "Conversation with Milhaud." *Music Educators Journal* 56 (March 1970): 55–56.

Broeckx, Jan L. "Current Chronicle: Brussels *(Les Eumenides)*." *Musical Quarterly* 36 (April 1950): 285–286.

Brown, Royal S. "French music since Debussy and Ravel." *High Fidelity/Musical America* 23 (September 1973): 50–65.

Calvocoressi, M. D. "Darius Milhaud." *Living Age* 350 (April 1936): 140–141.

Campbell, Alan. "San Francisco." *Musical Courier* 155 (June 1957): 26.

Campbell, Francean. *"Homage à Milhaud."* *Mills Quarterly* 53 (May 1971): 15–16.

Casella, Alfredo. "Tone problems of today." *Musical Quarterly* 10 (October 1924): 159–171.

Chanan, Michael. "Darius Milhaud." *The Listener* 82 (October 1962): 461.

Chase, Gilbert. *America's Music*. New York: McGraw-Hill, 1955.

———. "Darius Milhaud." In *Great Modern Composers,* edited by Oscar Thompson, 192–198. New York: Dodd, Mead, 1941.

Cherry, Paul W. "A cornucopia of quartets: The string quartets of Darius Milhaud." *American String Teacher* 33, no. 1 (1983): 56ff.

———. *The String Quartets of Darius Milhaud*. Ph.D. diss., University of Colorado, Boulder, 1980.

———. "Two unknown string quartets by Darius Milhaud." In *Report on the Proceedings on the Ph.D. in Music,* edited by W. Kearns. Boulder: University of Colorado, 1986.

Cocteau, Jean. *A Call to Order*. Translated by Rollo H. Myers. London: Faber & Gwyer, 1925.

———. "Cock and Harlequin." Translated by Rollo H. Myers. *Dial* 70 (January–June 1921): 55–62.

Cohn, Arthur. *Twentieth Century Music in Western Europe*. Philadelphia: Lippincott, 1965.

Collaer, Paul. *A History of Modern Music*. Translated by Sally Abeles. New York: World, 1961. Translation of *La musique moderne*. Brussels: Elsevier, 1955.

"A composer's life. Darius Milhaud talks to *Opera News*." *Opera New* 30 (4 June 1966): 8–11.

Cook, J. Douglas. "The composer tells how." *Saturday Review,* 26 June 1954, 43.

Cooper, Grosvenor. "Three Milhauds." *Modern Music* 18 (January-February 1941): 118–120.

Cooper, Martin. *French Music*. London: Oxford University Press, 1951.

————. "How it's done." *Saturday Review,* 25 April 1953, 35–36.

Copland, Aaron. "The art of Darius Milhaud." *Saturday Review of Literature,* 26 June 1948, 43.

————. *Copland on Music.* New York: Doubleday, 1960.

————. "The lyricism of Milhaud." *Modern Music* 6 (January–February 1929): 14–19.

————. "Music since 1920." *Modern Music* 5 (March–April 1928): 16–20.

————. *Our New Music.* New York: McGraw-Hill, 1941. Rev. & enl. as *The New Music.* New York: Norton, 1969.

Copp, Laura R. "Whither the trend of modern music? An interview with the famous French modernist, Darius Milhaud." *Etude* 46 (April 1928): 277–278.

Cowell, Henry. *New Musical Resources.* New York: Knopf, 1930. Reprint. New York: Something Else, 1969.

————. "New terms for new music." *Modern Music* 5 (May–June 1928): 21–27.

Craft, Robert. *Stravinsky: Chronicle of a Friendship 1948–1971.* New York: Knopf, 1972.

Crichton, Ronald. "Darius Milhaud: Obituary." *Music Time* 115 (August 1974): 684–685.

Dallin, Leon. *Techniques of Twentieth Century Composition.* Dubuque, Iowa: Wm. Brown, 1957.

Daniel, K. W. "A preliminary investigation of pitch-class set analysis in the atonal and polytonal works of Milhaud and Poulenc." *In Theory Only* 6 (September 1982): 22–48.

"Darius Milhaud, rebel composer, dies." *New York Times,* 25 June 1974, 40.

Demarquez, Suzanne. "Paris honors Milhaud and Honegger at 60." *Musical Courier* 145 (May 1952): 5.

Demuth, Norman. *French Piano Music with Notes on Its Performance.* London: Museum Press, 1959.

————. *Musical Trends in the Twentieth Century.* London: Rockliff, 1952.

DeRhen, A. "Milhaud retrospective." *High Fidelity/Musical America* 22 (July 1972): 22.

Deri, Otto. *Exploring Twentieth Century Music.* New York: Holtz, Rinehart & Winston, 1968.

Dickinson, Peter. "Milhaud." *Music and Musicians* 14 (March 1966): 22–25, 59.

Downes, Olin. "Milhaud arrives to teach." *New York Times,* July 21, 1940, sec. 10, 5.

Drew, David. "Modern French music." In *European Music in the Twentieth Century,* edited by Howard Hartog, 232–295. New York: Praeger, 1957.

Evans, Edwin. "Milhaud." In *Cobbett's Cyclopedic Survey of Chamber Music,* 140–145. London: Oxford University Press, 1929.

Ewen, David. "The Jew in modern symphonic music." *Jewish Tribune* (New York), 1 July 1927, 8–9 & 11.

————. *The World of Twentieth Century Music.* Englewood Cliffs, N.J.: Prentice-Hall, 1968.

Ewen, David, ed. *The New Book of Modern Composers,* 266–277. 3d ed., rev & enl. New York: Knopf, 1961.

Faurot, Albert. *Concert Piano Repertoire.* Metuchen, N.J.: Scarecrow, 1974.

Fels-Noth, Elena. "Excerpts from a portrait of Darius Milhaud." *Occidental* (September 1949). Reprint in *Jewish Music Notes* (April 1952).

Fine, Irving. "Milhaud at home." *New York Times,* 8 January 1950, sec. 2, 9.

Forte, Allen. "Darius Milhaud: 'Midi' from *Une Journée.*" In *Contemporary Tone Structures,* 39–47 & 154–155. New York: Columbia University, 1955.

Frankenstein, Alfred. "Current chronicle: Oakland." *Musical Quarterly* 49 (October 1963): 514–517.

————. Review of *Notes Without Music,* by Darius Milhaud. *Mills Quarterly* 35 (May 1953): 117.

Freed, Richard. "Darius Milhaud at eighty." *Stereo Review* 29 (September 1972): 94.

Freeman, John W. "Darius Milhaud, obituary." *Opera News* (September 1974): 66.

Friskin, James, and Irwin Freundlich. *Music for the Piano.* New York: Dover, 1974.

Fuller, Donald. "Forecast and review: Prokofieff and Milhaud, winter of 1944." *Modern Music* (22 January–February 1945): 103–107.

Gilbert, Richard. "Honegger, Poulenc and Milhaud." *Disques* 1, No. 5 (July 1930): 162–165.

Goetze, Wilhelm A. A. *An Analytical Study of Milhaud's Neuf preludes for Organ.* Ed.D. diss., Columbia University, 1976.

Golea, Antoine. "French music since 1945." In *Contemporary Music in Europe: A Comphrehensive Survey,* edited by Paul Henry Lang and Nathan Broder, 22–37. Translated by Lucile H. Brockway. New York: Schirmer, 1965.

Gradenwitz, Peter. "Israel's public festival-minded." *Musical Courier* 146 (August 1952): 8.

Graham, William Allen. *The Choral Works of Darius Milhaud, 1960–1974: A Stylistic Analysis.* D.M.A. final project, Stanford University, 1975.

Green, Christopher. *Léger and the Avant-garde.* New Haven: Yale University Press, 1976.

Hansen, Peter S. *An Introduction to Twentieth Century Music.* 4th ed. Boston: Allyn & Bacon, 1978.

Harding, James. *The Ox on the Roof: Scenes from Musical Life in Paris in the Twenties.* London: Macdonald, 1972.

Haughton, John Allen. "Darius Milhaud: A missionary of the *Six*" *Musical America* 37 (January 1923): 3–42.

Helm, E. "Darius Milhaud: A personal reminiscence." *Music Review* 37, no. 4 (1976): 301.

Henahan, Donald. "Milhaud: He churned out music but fulfilled the composer's role." *New York Times,* 7 July 1974, sec. D, 13.

Hendrick, Kimmis. "Chatting with Darius." *Christian Science Monitor,* 20 May 1968, 6.

Hill, Edward Burlingame. *Modern French Music.* Boston: Houghton-Mifflin, 1924.

Hodgson, Kenneth Dorsey. *An Examination of the Compositions of Darius Milhaud for Unaccompanied Mixed Voices.* D.M.A. diss., University of Illinois, Urbana-Champaign, 1979.

Honegger, Arthur. *I Am a Composer.* Translated by Wilson O. Clough. London: Farber & Farber, 1966.

Howe, W. "The percussionist's guide to Darius Milhaud's *La création du monde.*" *Percussionist* 17, no. 1 (1979): 37–48.

Hughes, Allen. "*Les Six*: A generation later their youthful spirit endures." *Musical America* 74 (February 1954): 12.

Hutcheson, Ernest. *The Literature of the Piano*. New York: Knopf, 1952.

Jacob, Arthur Review of *Notes Without Music*, by Darius Milhaud. *Music Teacher and Piano Student* 31 (October 1952): 491.

Jade, Ely. "Darius Milhaud." *Pro Musica Quarterly* (New York) 4 (May–June 1926): 36–40.

Jones, Charles, ed. "American music abroad: A symposium." *Juilliard Review* 3 (Winter 1955–56): 12.

Kaplan, A. R. *A Performance Analysis of Five Major Recital Works: Concerti for Solo Trombone and Orchestra*. Ph.D. diss., New York University, 1978.

Kay, Norman. Review of *Notes Without Music*, by Darius Milhaud. *Music and Musicians* 19 (November 1970): 72.

Kerr, Russell M. "New publications in review." *Musical Courier* 142 (September 1950): 34.

Kirby, Frank E. *A Short History of Keyboard Music*. New York: Free Press, 1966.

Knickerbocker, Paine. "Milhaud at Mills." *Mills Quarterly* 23 (November 1950): 99–100.

Koechlin, Charles. "Tradition in French music." Translated by Lester Burton. *Rice Institute Pamphlet* 6, no. 2 (April 1919): 112–117.

Kolodin, Irving. "Music to my ears." *Saturday Review,* 23 August 1952, 27.

Křenek, Ernst. *Exploring Music*. Translated by Margaret Schenfield and Geoffrey Skelton. London: Calder & Boyers, 1966.

———. "Milhaud." In *The Book of Modern Composers,* edited by David Ewen, 187–193. New York: Knopf, 1942.

Krockover, Rosalyn. Review of *Concerto for Two Pianos and Orchestra*, by Darius Milhaud. *Musical Courier* 141 (15 April 1950): 31.

Landormy, Paul. "Darius Milhaud." *Musical Times* 72 (January 1931): 28–32.

Larson, Robert M. *Stylistic Characteristics in A Cappella Composition in the United States, 1940–1953: As Indicated by the Works of Jean Berger, David Diamond, Darius Milhaud, and Miklos Rozsa*. Ph.D. diss., Northwestern University, 1953.

Laughton, John C. *A Comprehensive Performance Project in Clarinet Literature with an Essay on the Woodwind Music of Darius Milhaud*. D.M.A. diss., University of Iowa, 1980.

———. "The Brazilian Milhaud." *Art* 9, special English issue by *Revista da Escola de Música e Artes Cênicas,* Bahia, Brazil (December 1983): 91–101.

Lee, Patricia Taylor. *The Solo Piano Music of Darius Milhaud with Suggestions for Its Instructional Use*. D.M.A. diss., Temple University, 1979.

Lockspeiser, Edward. "The mixture that is Milhaud." *High Fidelity* 11 (March 1961): 42–43, 98, 100–103.

Longyear, Rey M. "Principles of neglected musical repertoire." *Journal of Research in Music Education* 18 (Summer 1970): 167–177.

Lyon, Margaret. "Music-Milhaud-Music." *Mills Magazine* 3 (November–December 1971): 2–7.

McCarthy, Peter J. *The Sonatas of Darius Milhaud*. D.M.A. diss., Catholic University of America, 1972.

McCrory, M., and B. Hieronymus. "Interviews with famous men." *South Western Musician* 18 (1951): 9.

McDonagh, Don. *Martha Graham: A Biography*. New York: Praeger, 1973.

McGuire, Thomas H. "Charles Koechlin." *American Music Teacher* 25 (January 1976): 19–22.

Machlis, Joseph. *Introduction to Contemporary Music.* New York: Norton, 1961.

Mason, Colin. "The chamber music of Milhaud." *Musical Quarterly* 43 (July 1957): 326–341.

Matson, R. and P. Tanner. "More on the Milhaud marimba/vibe concerto." *Percussion Notes* 14, no. 3 (1976): 9.

Mellers, Wilfrid. *Studies in Contemporary Music.* London: Dobson, 1947.

Meltzer, Charles H. "The polytonic *Six* of Paris." *Forum and Century* (December 1921): 530–537.

Morgan, Robert P. "Towards a more inclusive musical literacy: Notes on easy twentieth century piano music." *Musical Newsletter* 1 (April 1971): 12.

Morrill, Dexter G. *Contrapuntal Tonality in the Early Works of Darius Milhaud.* Ph.D. diss., Cornell University, 1970.

Myers, Rollo H. "Milhaud." In *the Music Masters,* edited by A. L. Bacharach; vol. 6, 208. Baltimore: Penguin, 1957.

——. *Modern French Music: From Fauré to Boulez.* New York: Praeger, 1971.

——. "A music critic in Paris in the nineteenth-twenties." *Musical Quarterly* 63 (October 1977): 524–544.

Newman, William S. Reviews of *Quatrième concerto pour piano et orchestre* and *Deuxième sonate,* by Darius Milhaud. *Notes* 8 (December 1950): 134–135.

Nin-Culmell, Joaquin. "Tribute to Milhaud." Delivered before the Society of California Pioneers, 14 January 1965. Typescript, 6 pp. Milhaud Archives, Mills College, Oakland, California.

Noble, Natoma N. *The Neoclassic Aesthetic in Two Early Song Cycles by Darius Milhaud.* D.M.A. diss., University of Texas, Austin, 1981.

Noss, Luther. Review of *Sonata for Organ,* by Darius Milhaud. *Notes* 8 (December 1950): 134.

Palmer, Christopher. "Milhaud at 80." *Musical Times* 113 (September 1972): 861–863.

——. "Milhaud, Darius." In *The New Grove Dictionary of Music and Musicians,* edited by Stanley Sadie; vol. 12, 305–310. London: Macmillan, 1980.

Pearsall, Ronald. "The sophistication of the graceful." *Music Review* 23 (1962): 205–207.

Perlis, Vivian. Interview of Darius Milhaud at Aix-en-Provence, France, 25 July 1970. Typescript, 30 pp. Milhaud Archives, Mills College, Oakland, California.

Petrella, Robert L. *The Solo and Chamber Music for Clarinet by Darius Milhaud.* D.M.A. diss., University of Maryland, 1979.

Pimentel, L. "The marimba bar." *Percussion Notes* 14, no. 2 (1976): 40.

Prunières, Henry. "Darius Milhaud." In *A Dictionary of Modern Music and Musicians,* edited by A. Eaglefield-Hull, 331–332. New York: Da Capo, 1971.

Rasin, Vera. "*Les Six* and Jean Cocteau." *Music and Letters* 38 (April 1957): 164–169.

Roberts, William B. *Darius Milhaud and His Choral Works with Biblical Texts: A Conductor's Study.* D.M.A. diss., Southern Baptist Theological Seminary, 1984.

Robinson, Forrest. "The music of Darius Milhaud for piano and orchestra." *American Music Teacher* 18 (November-December 1968): 20.

——. "The two-piano music of Darius Milhaud." *American Music Teacher* 16 (April-May 1967): 27.

——. *The Works of Darius Milhaud for Piano and Orchestra.* Ph.D. diss.,

Boston University, 1966.

Rogers, Robert M. "Jazz influence on French music." *Musical Quarterly* 21 (January 1935): 53–68.

Rosen, Jerome. "A note on Milhaud." *Perspectives of New Music* 2 (Fall-Winter 1963): 115–119.

Rosenfeld, Paul. *Discoveries of a Music Critic.* New York: Harcourt, Brace, 1936.

Rostand, Claude. *French Music Today.* Translated by Henry Marx. New York: Merlin, 1957.

———. "The operas of Darius Milhaud." Translated by Denis Stevens. *Tempo* 19 (Spring 1951): 23–28.

Rothe, Friede F. "The leader of the famous Six: A conference with Darius Milhaud." *Etude* 59 (September 1941): 589 & 640.

Rothmuller, Aaron Marko. *The Music of the Jews: An Historical Appreciation.* Rev. ed. New York: Yoseloff, 1967.

Rubsamen, Walter. "Current chronicle: Informal Milhaud festival." *Musical Quarterly* 35 (October 1949): 610–614.

Rupert, M. J. *The Piano Music of Darius Milhaud: A Survey.* Ph.D. diss., University of Indiana, 1974.

Sabin, Robert. "Second piano concerto by Darius Milhaud issued." *Musical America* 70 (November 1949): 29.

Salazar, Adolfo. *Music in Our Time.* Translated by Isabel Pope. New York: Norton, 1946.

Saleski, Gdal. *Famous Musicians of Jewish Origin.* New York: Bloch, 1949.

Salzman, Eric. *Twentieth Century Music: An Introduction.* Englewood Cliffs, N.J.: Prentice-Hall, 1967.

Schaeffer, S. G. *The Organ Works of Darius Milhaud.* D.M.A. diss., University of Cincinnati, 1977.

Schonberg, Harold. *The Lives of the Great Composers.* New York: Norton, 1970.

Schumann, Marguerite E. *A Souvenir of Milhaud, His Friends and His Works: An Oral History with Madame Madeleine Milhaud.* Reproduction of typescript. Copy deposited at Milhaud Archives of Mills College, Oakland, California, 1986.

Searle, Humphrey. *Twentieth Century Counterpoint.* London: Williams & Norgate, 1954.

Sendrey, Alfred. *Bibliography of Jewish Music.* New York: Columbia University Press, 1951.

Shapero, Harold. Reviews of *Ouverture mediterranéene, Cinqième symphonie,* and *Le carnaval d'aix,* by Darius Milhaud. *Notes* 13 (December 1955): 148–149.

Siegmeister, Elie. "Conversations with Milhaud." *Musical America* 82 (October 1962): 6, 8, & 44.

Slonimsky, Nicolas. *Baker's Biographical Dictionary of Musicians, 1971 Supplement.* New York: Schirmer, 1971.

———. *Lexicon of Musical Invective.* 2d ed. New York: Coleman-Ross, 1965.

———. *Music Since 1900.* 4th ed. New York: Scribners, 1971.

Slonimsky, Nicolas, ed. *Baker's Biographical Dictionary of Musicians.* 5th ed. New York: Schirmer, 1958.

Smith, Cecil M. "Milhaud's *Orphée* and *The Bells.*" *Modern Music* 23 (June–July 1946): 205–207.

———. "New Milhaud opera: *Simon Bolivar.*" *Musical America* 70 (June 1950): 7.

———. "A new organ sonata by Darius Milhaud," and "New publications offer sampling of French piano music." *Musical America* 70 (November 15, 1950): 30 & 31.

Strangeways, A. H. Fox. Review of *Darius Milhaud: Catalogue chronologique complet de son oeuvre,* by Georges Beck. *Music and Letters* 39 (July 1958): 307.

Stuckenschmidt, H. H. *Twentieth Century Music.* Translated by Richard Deveson. New York: McGraw-Hill, 1969.

Swickard, R. J. *The Symphonies of Darius Milhaud: An Historical Perspective and Critical Study of Their Musical Content, Style, and Form.* Ph.D. diss., University of California, Los Angeles, 1973.

Swift, Richard. Review of *Musique pour Ars Nova,* by Darius Milhaud. *Notes* 29 (December 1962): 321.

Temianka, Henri. *Facing the Music.* New York: D. McKay, 1973.

Thomson, Virgil. *American Music Since 1910.* New York: Holt-Rinehart, 1970.

———. "Current chronicle: San Francisco (*Sabbath Morning Service*)." *Musical Quarterly* 36 (January 1950): 99–105.

———. "More and more from Paris." *Modern Music* 16 (May–June 1939): 229–237.

———. *Music Reviewed 1940–1954.* New York: Random House, 1967.

Trickey, Samuel M. *Les Six.* Ph.D. diss., North Texas State College, 1955.

Vernazza, Marcelle. "Darius Milhaud: A muse for the young." *Clavier* 20 (November 1981): 15–19.

Vuillermoz, Emile. "The legend of the Six." *Modern Music* 1 (February–November 1924): 15–19.

Walker, R. "The early symphonies of Milhaud." *Music and Musicians* 25 (October 1976): 28–30ff.

Waters, Edward N. "Variations on a theme: Recent acquisitions of the Music Division." *Quarterly Journal of the Library of Congress* 27, no. 1 (1970): 62.

Wilkins, N. "Erik Satie's letters to Milhaud and others." *Musical Quarterly* 66 (July 1980): 404–428.

Willoughby, R. "The operas of Darius Milhaud: An ungathered harvest." *Opera Journal* 5, no. 3 (1972): 20–25.

Winter, Maria Hannah. "The function of music in sound film." *Musical Quarterly* 27 (April 1941): 146–164.

Wolffers, Jules. Review of *Fourth Piano Concerto,* by Darius Milhaud. *Musical Courier* 141 (1 April 1950): 8.

Zinar, Ruth. *Greek Tragedy in Theater Pieces of Stravinsky and Milhaud.* Ph.D. diss., New York University, 1968.

Publishers

In the case of two or more editions of a work, the editions are listed chronologically and those which are no longer available are in parenthesis.

Following is a list of publishers for which addresses are available:

Adès	Adès 54 rue St. Lazare, F-75009 Paris
A.&S.	Ahn & Simrock 66 Taunusstrasse, D-6200 Berlin (USA: see A.M.P.)
A.M.P.	Associated Music Publishers (see Schirmer)
Bel. M.	Belwin Mills Publishing Corporation c/o Columbia Pictures Publications 15800 Northwest 48th Avenue Miami, FL 33014 (Rental: see Presser)
Billaudot	Gérard Billaudot, Ed. 14 rue de l'Echiquier, F-75010 Paris (USA: see Presser)
B.&H.	Boosey & Hawkes 295 Regent Street, London W1R 8JH (USA: 200 Smith St., Farmingdale, NY 11735)
Cerda	Cerda (see E.F.M)
Ch. du M.	Chant du Monde (Distrib. by: Schott Frères, 35 avenue Jean Moulin, F-94300 Vincennes)
Combre	Editions M. Combre 24 Boulevard Poissonnière, F-75009 Paris
Deiss	Deiss (see Salabert)
Delkas	Delkas (see MCA)
Durand	Durand & Cie. 21 rue Vernet, F-75008 Paris (USA: see Presser)

Edit. Trans.	Editions Musicales Transatlantiques 50 rue Joseph de Maistre, F-75018 Paris (USA: see Presser)
E.F.M.	Editions Françaises de Musique (USA: see Presser)
Elkan Vogel	Elkan-Vogel, Inc. (see Presser)
Enoch	Enoch & Cie. 193 boul. Péreire, F-75017 Paris (USA: see A.M.P.)
Eschig	Editions Max Eschig 48 rue de Rome, F-75008 Paris (USA: see A.M.P.)
E.S.I.	Editions Sociales Internationales (see Ch. du M.)
Fischer	Carl Fischer, Inc. 62 Cooper Square, New York, NY 10003
Gallo	CH-1411 Donneloye, Switzerland
Gray	The H. W. Gray Co., Inc. (see Belwin Mills)
Heugel	Heugel & Cie. (see Leduc)
I.M.P.	Israeli Music Publishers, Ltd. 25 Keren, Jerusalem 91188 (USA: see Presser)
Leduc	Alphonse Leduc S.A. 175 rue St. Honoré, F-75001 Paris (USA rental: see Presser)
Leeds	Leeds Music Ltd. (see Belwin Mills)
Leonard	Hal Leonard Publications 8112 W. Blue Mound Rd., Milwaukee, WI 53213
Marks	E. B. Marks Music Corp., 1190 Broadway, New York, NY 10019 (Sales: see Leonard Rentals: see Presser)

Mathot	Mathot (see Salabert)
MCA	MCA Music Publishing (see Belwin Mills)
Mercury	Mercury Music Corp. (see Presser)
Ois. Lyre	Editions de l'Oiseau Lyre 4 rue des Remparts, Monaco
P. Marconi	Pathé Marconi 94–96 rue Lauriston, F-75016 Paris
P. Noël	Pierre Noël (see Billaudot)
Presser	Theodore Presser Co. Presser Place, Bryn Mawr, PA 19010
Ricordi	G. Ricordi & Co. 2 via Berchet, I-20121 Milan (USA: see Schirmer)
Salabert	Editions Salabert 22 rue Chauchat, F-75009 Paris (USA: see Schirmer)
Schirmer	G. Schirmer Inc. (Sales: see Leonard) (Rental: Music Sales, Inc. 24 East 22nd Street, New York, NY 10010)
Sénart	Maurice Sénart (see Salabert)
Sirène	Editions de la Sirène (see Eschig)
South. Mus.	Southern Music Publishing Co. (Peer-Southern Concert Music) (see Presser)
U.E.	Universal Edition Bösendorferstrasse 12, A-1015 Vienna (USA: European-American Music Dist. Box 850, Valley Forge, PA 19482)

DATE DUE